T0321267

BALLS OF CONFUSION

PRO BASKETBALL GOES TO WAR

(1965-1970)

BOB KUSKA

From Way Downtown Publishing

Shepherdstown, WV

Evolution, revolution, gun control, sound of soul
Shooting rockets to the moon, kids growing up too soon.
Politicians say more taxes will solve everything—
And the band played on

So, round and around and around we go
Where the world's headed, nobody knows . . .
Just a ball of confusion
Oh yeah, that's what the world is today

From The Temptations' *Ball of Confusion (That's What the World is Today)*, 1970

TABLE OF CONTENTS

ACKNOWLEDGEMENTS

So many people to thank, and I sincerely thank everyone whom I've met along the way. Some, living and many now gone, deserve an extra tip of the cap, starting most reverentially with all the great journalists who recorded the NBA-ABA years in print so that guys like me can lap it up and write books later. Here are a few of my favorites: George Kiseda, Frank Deford, Joe Jares, Leonard Lewin, Milton Gross, Jim O'Brien, Jack Kiser, Phil Musick, Al Goldstein, Dick Denny, Bob Ryan, Leigh Montville, Robert Lipsyte, Merv Harris, Bob Logan, Joe Falls, and so many more. As print journalism today struggles to survive, these true greats remind us of the human touch that's now endangered in our mad technology-driven rush to, quite frankly, who knows where.

I did countless interviews with so many sources that I've honestly lost count. Among those who "shot me straight" and have my enduring gratitude are: Archie Clark, Joe Caldwell, Neil Isaacs, Roger Noll, Lee Meade, Dick Tinkham, Earl Foreman, Al Bianchi, Jim Gardner, Don Regan, Bill Erickson, Fred Cranwell, Carl Scheer, Bob Carlson, and Michael Burns.

A special thanks goes out to basketball historian Ray Lebov for all of our conversations and his willingness to share his many insights and his library of articles over the years. Gratitude goes out to author Mark Montieth for sharing his thoughts on the pros and cons of self-publishing. Your guidance was invaluable. My sincere thanks go out to all who helped on the editorial end: Holly Kondras, Joanne Erickson, and Phil Velikan. It's been my pleasure.

My biggest thanks of all goes out to my wife, Lynn Wagner, for sharing the house with my living, growing basketball archive, nodding along with my latest ah-hah (especially during the stir-crazy pandemic), and rolling with all of my time spent hunched over the keyboard. And yes, Ramsey was the total package. But Zora, Mazy, and Marvin are totally awesome, too.

Last but not least, thanks to readers like you for purchasing this book and sharing in my labor of love. I think *Balls of Confusion* will nail down for you an era of pro basketball that was incredibly important and which has plenty yet to tell. Enjoy!

INTRODUCTION

What the Civil War is to American history, the NBA-ABA War is to the history of modern professional basketball. This bitter, nine-year battle came to a grinding halt in the mid-1970s and, though to the NBA victors went the spoils, peace brought a needed Reconstruction of the pro game. The NBA folded in the ABA's four surviving franchises and gradually worked in the loser's better ideas: marketing the game's athleticism, the three-point shot, and expanding or relocating NBA franchises to several former ABA cities already primed for pro basketball. The latter solidified the NBA's footprint in all regions of the country and boosted the league's national appeal for greater things to come.

The Reconstruction also locked in player free agency, which the NBA owners fought tooth and nail since the 1950s. Free agency ensured that the inflated salaries of the NBA-ABA war years would remain in effect and, with player agents now accepted at the negotiating table to strike a harder bargain, the dollar figures would rise. The Reconstruction also pounded the final nail into the NBA's longstanding four-year rule, which stipulated that young players could turn pro only after their college classes graduated. Though the U.S. Supreme Court already had nixed the four-year rule, the NBA had hemmed and hawed on ethical grounds to keep some revised version in place. Or, reading between the lines, the NBA wanted to preserve the mutually beneficial college farm system that developed and promoted its incoming rookies for free. The four-year wait was now gone, never to return.

Most important, the NBA owners and the players shook hands as business partners during the Reconstruction. Both sides agreed that, for the good of the game, they would balance their pro-and-often-con interests through collective bargaining. That included settling individual contract disputes in-house through arbitration. No longer would players or their union haul the NBA into open federal court, where landmark antitrust decisions restricted the league's autonomy during basketball's Civil War.

"Now we could focus on the facts," the NBA's then-lead attorney and future commissioner David Stern described the partnership to me shortly before his death. "Now the players and the league could work together to grow the game instead of beating their brains out traveling around the country litigating major class-action suits."[1]

Thankfully, several books and documentaries already have chronicled bits and pieces of pro basketball's Civil War. Hats off to the authors and producers for all their hard work. Here's my "but." The best of the bunch are the oral histories, which are long on opinion and sometimes short on fact. Take Terry Pluto's *Loose Balls*, the most-popular ABA history since its publication in 1990. It remains a fun, well-crafted verbal account of the ABA's leading figures, on and off the court. Yet, it doesn't take much follow-up research to discover that some of Pluto's sources misremembered details, left out a few things, or overstated their points. That's what happens with oral histories.

Another "but" is of more recent vintage: telling the NBA-ABA War through the eyes of the retired players who survived the madness. This approach is certainly valid—but only up to a point. NBA and ABA players were never at war with each other. For players of this era, two leagues were always better than one. Two leagues offered more jobs, more money, more negotiating leverage. The players took care of their business on the court, while the team owners and their lawyers skulked in the shadows to booby-trap the other league's latest tactical innovation.

"I've been asked on too many occasions whether the ABA would survive," wrote the dean of ABA reporters Jim O'Brien in the summer of 1976. "After a while, my stock reply was to say there really was no such entity as an ABA . . . just owners, more owners, new owners, old owners, and that as long as there were owners, there'd be ABA scores in the sports sections of newspapers. Whenever those owners, whomever they happened to be at the time, were successful in affecting a merger with the NBA, then there'd be no ABA scores to be found anywhere."[2]

The same goes for the NBA. Just owners. Just business people anxious to protect their investments against any and all comers. Sports economist Roger Noll summed up their call to arms in my very first interview for *Balls of Confusion*: "The first thing that happens in a sports war is the incumbent league tries to put the upstart out of business by vastly bidding up its salaries to more than anybody would be willing to pay, just in order to get them to go away. They also threaten broadcasters that if you broadcast those guys, we'll never deal with you.

"Roughly half the time that works. Two or three years later, the entrant goes away. Then, the other half of the time, it doesn't work because the entrant has some owners who are just as stubborn and just as rich as the incumbent league. So, you have a spending war. That was exactly what happened with the ABA. You had owners who said, 'You know if I lose several million dollars a year for even 10 years, then I end up with a $500 million franchise, I'm better off.' So, when the new leagues are organized with the appropriate time horizon and don't face a serious short-term financial constraint, they typically succeed and force a merger."[3]

Balls of Confusion is the first book to take a deep dive into the NBA-ABA War. I've taken my hundreds of interviews and subjected them to the sometimes confirming, sometimes corrective light of other relevant sources. These include an Everest of newspaper and magazine articles, stacks of legal documents and league meeting notes, personal correspondences, and even a few bank records. I've compiled so much information that, to benefit future sports historians, I'm publishing *Balls of Confusion* in two volumes to give it the needed space and documentation that is hard to negotiate these days with traditional publishers.

Pro Basketball Goes to War (1965-1970), the first installment, presents the hows and whys that prompted this interleague conflict, then weaves its way through the early fog of war to the filing in federal court of the game-changing Oscar Robertson et al. vs. NBA case. The second installment, soon to come, chronicles among other things the culmination of the war, the court cases (including Robertson v. NBA), and concludes with what's commonly called "the merger" in the summer of 1976.

Much of the credit goes to the NBA's then-new commissioner Lawrence O'Brien for bringing the warring parties to the table to find peace and ultimately prosperity. With equal parts shrewdness and pragmatism honed during his former career in politics, O'Brien built consensus among his team owners to settle the Robertson case for the good of the league. He followed up for the good of the game with the same consensus-building exercise that ultimately forced "the merger" and the Reconstruction.

Until O'Brien's arrival, the NBA's Board of Governors had been about as chaotic as a dog pound at dinnertime. There were big dogs and small-market yappers, all clamoring for attention, howling their personal grievances, and sometimes baring their teeth. Some woofed non-stop for O'Brien and especially his predecessor Walter Kennedy to modernize the league. They commissioned bold marketing studies. They demanded heftier television contracts and louder national exposure. They envisioned huge profits from spinning off all variety of NBA-approved merchandise in department stores.

For others, mainly the old-timers, conquering national television and American department stores missed the point. All basketball, like politics, was local. Keep the local turnstiles turning, that's how pro basketball worked, one nickel, one dime, one arena at a time. This fusty mindset traced back to the 1940s and the Basketball Association of America (BAA), the NBA's starter seed. The BAA begot the NBA's chaotic boardroom culture and its rigid bylaws, the ones that O'Brien and Kennedy fought to protect from ABA incursion and which is a major theme of this book. That makes the BAA the perfect place to introduce the NBA's side of our story. And that story starts decades earlier with slabs of ice.

In 1920s, the electric refrigerator was still several years away from revolutionizing the American kitchen. Perishable food was stored the old-fashioned way: in a metal icebox with a 100-pound slab of ice to freeze out mold and decay. There was, however, something different about these old-fashioned slabs. No longer were they chiseled from frozen lakes and other natural ice sources. The new slabs were mass-produced in factories employing what was then touted as the modern miracle of ice-making technology.

The factory owners, hoping to showcase their breakthrough technology for greater gain and company branding, often built large indoor rinks for public ice skating. "Stay young and active," shilled a Kentucky newspaper in 1924, "for ice skating is invigorating and healthful, both for young and old, and is much more pleasant when enjoyed indoors out of the wintry blasts. Music at all sessions."[4]

By the mid-1930s, however, the ice business began melting. Electric refrigerators, mass produced and more affordable, had arrived in American kitchens. That left factory owners with a thawing market for their slabs of ice, heavy debt on the expensive ice-making machinery, and a broken American economy in a credit crunch turned full-blown depression. Many factory owners, facing bankruptcy, unloaded their ice-skating palaces. The same went for the keepers of larger municipal auditoriums that also featured ice rinks. Snatching up these "white elephants" at fire sale prices were opportunistic promoters and real-estate vultures who asked the same wide-eyed, seat-of-the-pants question. Whaddya do with an ice rink?

Start a hockey team. And so, one nickel, one dime, one arena at a time, they assembled teams like Salvation Army bands, dressed them in scratchy uniforms, and entered them in hockey's no-money-down minor leagues. It was a tricky business selling slapshots, body checks, and occasional fisticuffs. But keeping the costs low and the local publicity high, these minor-league operations survived the Depression and skated into the mid-1940s and the end of World War II.

But the arena owners faced a scheduling problem. While their boys skated on enemy ice, their home arenas often sat empty with no backup attraction to keep the popcorn popping and the mortgage paid. That's why on June 6, 1946, gathered around a table at New York's Commodore Hotel, the arena owners organized the Basketball Association of America as their fingers-crossed side hustle and out of no abiding love for the sport. A basketball court, portable and rapidly assembled, would fit inside of an ice rink like a mat in a bathtub.[5]

Of course, the more sports-savvy arena owners browbeat their less-enlightened colleagues that pro basketball was the next great promotional frontier. It just needed a push in the right direction. Like college basketball. In the 1920s, the collegians played in the same basements and sardine-can gymnasiums as the pros. Then in 1934, newspaperman Ned Irish moved the All Americans into New York's classy Madison Square Garden, and a hot Saturday night of doubleheaders and interregional showdowns was born. Now, the nation's top collegiate teams played the Garden, like musicians played Carnegie Hall, and then bounced to Buffalo, Boston, Philadelphia, Chicago, and a whole circuit of sold-out arenas on the way home.

That's not to say others hadn't already tried giving pro basketball a push. The latest shove forward came from the National Basketball League (NBL), a Midwest-centric mishmash of company and club teams that struggled through the World War II years. Though the NBL was back to eight teams, the arena owners were dismissive of its one nickel, one dime, one arena at a time, especially the league's enduring footprint in "minor-league" cities such as Oshkosh, Sheboygan, and Fort Wayne.

As the BAA made clear at its first meeting, "The Chairman called to the attention of the members the fact that the newly organized Association was a major league in every possible meaning of the term."[6] The term "major league" meant returning pro basketball to New York, Boston, and the nation's other major metropolises. To pull it off, the BAA soon recruited the influential promoter Arthur Wirtz and his partner James Norris. Between them, they operated Chicago Stadium, Detroit Olympia, and St. Louis Arena. They also had major financial stakes in Cincinnati Gardens, Omaha Coliseum, Indianapolis Arena, and New York's Madison Square Garden.[7] Thanks to the latter interest, they sucked in college basketball's super promoter Ned Irish to run the future New York Knickerbockers.

Major league also meant the BAA would go with the flow. It would replicate the breezy, fast-paced play of the collegians. More important, they would build their teams around the greatest All Americans of yesteryear brought back for curtain calls as high-scoring pros who were even better than their college days.

Eleven arena owners founded the BAA in cities along the East Coast and a few Midwestern outposts. All vowed to keep expenses low. Franchises cost just $1,000 (about $14,000 today), and the arena owners enjoyed the luxury of playing for free in their own network of arenas, where workmen inexpertly slapped down hardwood floors over their ice rinks and hoped nobody important slipped on the seepage. The arena owners also agreed to a hard salary cap of $40,000 per team to start.[8] And no player, regardless of talent, could make more than $5,000 per season.

The BAA's highbrow aspirations ran straight into the lowbrow NBL. Contrary to Roger Noll's modern tit-for-tat corporate sports war, the incumbent NBL didn't try to put the BAA out of business. Pro basketball wasn't corporate just yet. It remained a Wild West of traveling teams, not leagues, that rolled into town like medicine shows. This wayfaring business culture, laissez-faire to the core, still animated the pro game and explains why NBL-affiliated teams continued to barnstorm on the side.

It also explains why the NBL would turn the other cheek at the BAA's incursion into its domain. As long as the newcomers stayed away from NBL cities, the two could coexist and prosper. After all, the more well-run teams and leagues there were, the merrier it would be to grow the pro game. Leaders of both leagues preemptively shook hands on using the same standard uniform player contract. They also vowed never to steal the other's players, adopted a framework for future interleague trades, and agreed to an annual joint college draft that would prevent cost-inflating bidding wars for rookies that would crash both leagues.

All good stuff, except the NBL had a 12-year head start on the BAA and a near-monopoly on the player market. That left the first-year BAA with plenty of large arenas and almost no marquee names to wow the big-city masses. Just 800,000 tickets sold that winter for the BAA's 660 total contests. That came to an average attendance of 1,212 for the clank of missed shots (on a good night, the best teams shot 30 percent from the field) and the thump of bodies banging for the rebound. Aesthetically pleasing ball it wasn't; neither was it sustainable financially. Most arena owners had no cash in reserve for their predictable first-season shortfall. In fact, most BAA teams combined possessed a fourth—or maybe a fifth—of the capital resources of, say, New York's Madison Square Garden. Three BAA teams bailed after the first season, and others persevered for the league's survival, but only under certain conditions.

The most-consequential condition came a year later from the Chicago Stags, the league's ailing flagship Midwestern franchise, led by the influential Arthur Wirtz. The Stags pinned their hard times on the BAA's dearth of Midwestern attractions. "Give us [NBL] teams like Fort Wayne and Indianapolis, and we can sell the game [in Chicago]," one reportedly pleaded. "But we cannot build up western rivalries with Atlantic sea-sprayed teams like Washington and Baltimore."[9]

In other words, plunder the NBL. In the winter of 1948, the BAA's portly president Maurice Podoloff started dropping hints to select NBL owners to come join his league. His selling point was the one thing that the BAA arena owners got right: For pro basketball to prosper, it had to return to the nation's big cities and their larger municipal venues. Big cities equaled big league equaled big publicity and big profits. It was a point that the more ambitious in the NBL crowd couldn't ignore. The NBL, sending all its stars barnstorming into too many cramped gyms in too many minor-league Midwestern towns, never would amount to a modern major-league circuit.

In May 1948, the NBL's top four franchises—Minneapolis, Fort Wayne, Indianapolis, Rochester—jumped to the bright lights and big cities of the BAA. With Minneapolis onboard, the BAA got George Mikan, the game's towering superstar who was recognized across America for his signature Clark Kent horn-rimmed glasses. Mikan, whose name alone would appear on the Madison Square Garden marquee, brought much-needed credibility to the ailing BAA.

The NBL, down to five teams and punchy for payback, declared war. The league killed the joint college draft and declared open bidding on the graduating class of 1948. "The idea that major league basketball must be played in big cities and that huge seating capacity is necessary to big-time and profitable operation is erroneous," scoffed an NBL supporter.[10]

A war of words and rookie contracts ensued that, by July 1948, dead-ended into interleague peace talks. After some back and forth, new NBL head Ike Duffy excused himself from the room. That's when Podoloff noticed that Duffy had scribbled the following draft telegram: "Members, Executive Board, National Basketball League: No possible chance agreement with BAA. Stop. Consider yourself free to operate as you see, fit and contacting and signing any of the players. Stop."[11]

The NBL built itself back up to nine teams by the fall of 1948. But by the next summer, the red ink was rising for both leagues . . . fast. More peace talks commenced. This time, the leagues dropped their weapons and merged into a 17-team jigsaw puzzle called the National Basketball Association.

The "National" was a negotiated holdover from the first word and letter in NBL and, in these days of difficult cross-country travel, a coast-to-coast league amounted to wishful thinking. The St. Louis Bombers and Denver Nuggets were the only franchises west of the Mississippi, and both tanked after just one NBA season. Joining them in bankruptcy court were four other first-season flops. At the start of its third season, the NBA had slimmed down to the survival of its 10 fittest franchises—six on the East Coast, four in the Midwest, including the mighty Minneapolis Lakers with Mikan and a roster of future Hall of Famers. The Lakers claimed three of the first four NBA championships to prompt early mumblings of a pro basketball dynasty.

"Wouldn't I be silly to think about quitting?" Mikan dispelled rumors of his retirement. "Where else can I make this kind of money?" Mikan made $20,000 per season (today about

$225,000) and counted on an assortment of endorsements to pad his income. "The Joe DiMaggio, Joe Louis, and Sid Luckman of pro basketball," a writer described his celebrity. Even Edward R. Morrow, the great journalistic inquisitor of presidents and kings, would soon sit down with Mikan for an exclusive one-on-one interview. The same exclusivity went for his championship Lakers. Reporters from all the big national magazines had popped up in the locker room with pencils in hand, prompting the head of the local chamber of commerce to quip, "There was no single project ever undertaken here prior to the Lakers which got us more favorable publicity."[12]

Or gave the fledgling NBA a more favorable flight pattern into the American mainstream. And yet, nearly all the teams, Minneapolis included, lost money in 1953. Indianapolis folded after the season, and two more (Philadelphia and Milwaukee) nearly joined them.

From the 80th floor of the Empire State Building, the Manhattan skyline and the waterways beyond seemed to stretch forever. Maurice Podoloff, the founding BAA and now NBA president (today commissioner), rarely had time to appreciate the stunning view outside his window. He had reports to write and a league to keep resuscitating in preparation for the 1953-54 season.

"Connie, would you get me . . ." Podoloff called out continuously to his trusted, young secretary Connie Maroselli, one of two full-time employees in the three-office suite 8020 that housed what then passed for a lean-mean corporate NBA machine. The other full-timer was Haskell Cohen, the league's likable publicity director and a walking, talking basketball encyclopedia who dropped the names of the East Coast's finest hoopsters like jazz aficionados celebrated saxophone players.

The names sounded like a polysyllabic collision to Podoloff, who'd attended one basketball game in his life before joining the BAA. That he now sold basketball for a living had its comical side. Podoloff stood 5-foot-2 and waddled around the office like an Emperor penguin. But this penguin, with droopy eyes and red suspenders, was a highly capable Yale Law grad, class of 1915. He was also the successful former president of the American Hockey League and an experienced arena owner in New Haven.

Though vertically challenged, Podoloff exuded a brusque, overbearing, full-steam-ahead demeanor that only a trial lawyer could love. He'd learned to leaven the overbearing with self-deprecating humor (often about his height), a clever vocabulary, and compassion for the least of his NBA brothers struggling to make payroll. The latter quality created trust around the table and ultimately job security, which was paramount. Podoloff had worked on one-year contracts since entering pro basketball.

The trust also helped the governors overlook Podoloff's glaring shortcoming: he hated basketball. Try as he may, Podoloff couldn't get excited about watching 10 tall guys toss around the "casaba," as folks liked to call a basketball, and some of the rules and strategy still gave him fits. The joke was "Poodles" or "Pumpernickel," as the players purposely butchered their chief executive's last name, couldn't tell a pick-and-roll play from a white picket fence.

Pumpernickel sat courtside at NBA games, eying the clock, critiquing, worrying, making mental fix-it notes. He'd passed on his curt, clean-up-your-act observations weekly since the BAA days. "It would seem unnecessary to have to call to your attention the elementary rule that players and referees must not expectorate on the playing court," he once noted. Pumpernickel also memorably instructed the players to "come out on the floor briskly and alertly and give the impression of being athletes rather than a bunch of old men starting in on an unpleasant job."

All to no avail. The NBA president feared that the fans were just as bored as he was with the "white picket fences" and "old men" jostling non-stop for position under the basket. With fewer arena owners left, the NBA played in some real neighborhood dives. In working-class Baltimore, for example, the 3,900-seat Coliseum featured unvarnished, crudely hewn floorboards that groaned, squeaked, and rumbled like a minor earthquake rolling through the arena whenever teams ran the floor. The makeshift court was always shrouded in a dense fog of exhaled white tobacco smoke that obscured the numbers on the scoreboard and the straggle of people standing in the foyer. Among them were the unseemly old timers in heavy overcoats near the concession stand, puffing cigars and jawing over their NBA bets for the evening like they were at Pimlico.

The NBA might have caved under the weight of its dysfunction, if not for Podoloff's micro-management and the apparent good will of Abe Saperstein, the owner/operator of the Harlem Globetrotters. His all-Black traveling team had for years thrilled millions worldwide with their impossible trick shots, razzle-dazzle passing, and vaudeville-style gags. They were hands down the most popular attraction in basketball and probably all of sports.

Saperstein, a dark-haired, middle-aged man who stood 5-foot-3 and was built like Mr. Peanut. would upon request book his "Magicians of the Court" as an added attraction before the NBA main event. His Globetrotters always packed the NBA house, helping many a financially distressed team make payroll and keep their players fed.

But the NBA governors already had bitten the hand that fed them. When the BAA and NBL merged in the summer of 1949, the governors continued to draw the color line, in part to stay in Saperstein's good graces. In March 1950, the governors abruptly integrated the league. The about face wasn't grounded in the Bible or the civil rights movement. The ringleaders of NBA integration in New York and Boston wanted to upgrade their rosters. And so, a month later, New York and Boston stole two Globetrotters in the NBA draft.

Saperstein predictably threatened to sue NBA offenders to kingdom come and vowed his Globetrotters would never play a doubleheader for any of the integrating franchises. A few days later, Saperstein swallowed hard and let bygones be bygones. He negotiated the release of his two NBA draftees, winked at Washington for signing two Black collegians, and continued booking the Globetrotters before NBA games.

Why the Mr. Nice Guy? Saperstein wanted his own NBA team. In fact, while Saperstein threatened to sue, he was in negotiations to purchase the NBA's failing Chicago franchise and would directly benefit from lifting the color line. Though he later withdrew his bid (the price wasn't right), Saperstein remained anxious to join the NBA and continued to turn on the charm and braggadocio. "Abe Saperstein called Maurice Podoloff, president of the NBA, from London the other day to report his Globetrotters were breaking all sorts of attendance records in Europe," wrote NBA scribe Haskell Cohen in June 1950.

For Podoloff, welcoming Saperstein into the NBA made sense. He was a millionaire several times over, a national celebrity of sorts, a brilliant promoter, an astute businessman, and a calling card to muckety-mucks across the globe. He was also a handful. To know the diminutive dynamo, as some called him, was to listen to him wax on about knowing better about pro basketball. He was a little NBA dictator in the making.

At Board of Governors meetings, the dysfunction continued. Podoloff recited the disappointing attendance figures, which rounded out league-wide to an average of 3,200 per game. All but two teams (New York and Syracuse) lost money, with Fort Wayne topping the loser board at a then-hefty $59,000 followed by Boston at $53,000.[13] Milwaukee, Philadelphia, and Baltimore were running low on cash, and players in Fort Wayne were living dangerously. Word leaked to Podoloff that some Fort Wayne players were fixing games and consorting with gamblers.

Podoloff hired a private eye to tap phones, tail Fort Wayne players, and report back on the details. All the while, he feared the worst. In 1951, several college players were fingered for shaving points and possibly dumping games. This full-blown scandal, featuring players in cuffs and federal prosecutors vowing justice, nearly killed college basketball. If the feds investigated the NBA for roughly the same thing, the public stigma would empty arenas and almost certainly kill pro basketball.

Thanks to his legal training and assertiveness, Podoloff seems to have convinced the feds to pass on the shenanigans in Fort Wayne. Podoloff then strategically contained the scandal by publicly scapegoating Fort Wayne's rakish rookie Jack Molinas, who unwisely admitted to Podoloff that he bet on NBA games. "A personal psychiatric aberration," Podoloff diagnosed the rookie.[14] Internally, the banishment was meant as a stern warning to several suspected dumpers to clean up their acts. Next time wouldn't be pretty.

Podoloff also got his owners to give the technological miracle of television a try. Every Sunday, the DuMont television network broadcast the NBA Game of the Week. Though DuMont paid just $3,000 per game ($39,000 per season)[15] for the broadcast rights, it was a start to tap into greater network riches. Equally important, television would provide national exposure, which would help the NBA expand out West one day and get the league on track as big-league, national entertainment.

Or so Podoloff envisioned. But the league had another glaring problem. The planned thrills and spills of the NBA's college-style game had devolved further into nightly pushing-and-shoving matches. "The area under the basket was a no-man's-land, with guards rarely daring to drive in close to the hoop," wrote one commentator. "Hot-handed shooters were often cooled off with heavy-handed policing" that sent them sprawling to the deck.[16] There were now on average 59 fouls whistled per game, which might have been far higher had some teams not routinely stalled in the final quarter to secure wins and send irate fans to the ticket booths demanding their money back. The final scores had dropped on average below the 80-point threshold, and already-sagging attendance drooped further.

This physical brand of basketball was on full display each week on DuMont and grew more brutal in the playoffs, culminating in a televised championship series beat-down that would live on in NBA infamy. "The game encompassed all the repulsive features of the grab-and-hold philosophy," journalist Leonard Koppett summed up a contest. "It lasted three hours, and the final seconds of a one-point game were finally abandoned by the [DuMont] network. The arguments with the referees were interminable and degrading. What had been happening, as a matter of course, in dozens of games for the last couple of years was shown to a national audience in unadulterated impurity."[17]

DuMont bailed on the NBA, and the governors voted to penalize teams that fouled too much as a way to clean up the rough stuff. They also agreed to experiment with a 24-second shot clock to speed up the action.

This was just the shot of adrenaline that the doctor ordered. Scoring rose, and the outlines of the modern NBA game came into popular view during the 1954-1955 season. The assertive Podoloff already had finagled the league onto NBC for more games and a little more money. But his good deed didn't go unpunished. NBC wrote into the contract that Podoloff must attend all televised contests to personally ensure two properly spaced timeouts were called per quarter to allow commercial breaks. As a sportswriter later razzed:

My name's Maurice Podoloff, Pumper-nick Podoloff . . .
No genius will I ever be
My fame will come only
When I sell baloney,
Co-sponsored by [NBC's] Tom Gallery[18]

Podoloff had more than baloney on his mind. George Mikan, the league's superstar and America's Mr. Basketball, retired. Who would shine before the NBC cameras? The top candidate was Boston's shifty six-footer Bob Cousy, who dished out nifty no-look passes to his teammates for easy scores. He called it "spreading the sugar." Would Cousy's sugar be sweet enough for NBC to keep paying $3,000 per game?

"To me, everything was threatened with death—the NBA, the TV deal, and me also," Podoloff recalled. "I was 64 years old. Where could I get a job" when the NBA folded?[19]

Death took another NBA team in 1954. The Baltimore Bullets had flatlined a few weeks into the season. With Thanksgiving approaching, the Bullets couldn't meet payroll, nor could they pay for an upcoming road trip to New York, which might have been a blessing. The Bullets had lost 32 straight games on the road. Podoloff and the governors didn't attempt to resuscitate the franchise, leaving eight NBA teams for the season, six of which were ailing.

Though Podoloff tried to hope it away, the league also had a festering labor problem: The players wanted to unionize. They wanted to become equal "partners" with the team owners in managing pro basketball's future. Partners? That's not how pro sports worked. Players played; management managed. For Podoloff and his owners, there could be no other way.

The players' union was Bob Cousy's baby. In 1953, Cousy started dishing to a few journalists about his profound frustrations with the league's second-rate conditions. By midsummer 1954, Cousy put pen to frustration and sent a form letter to a select member of each of the league's other eight teams. The recipients, like Cousy, were the so-called "untouchables," whose popularity on their teams and in their communities would seemingly protect them from any retribution if word of the letter and the union organizing leaked to management.

Cousy explained in his letter that the union wouldn't push immediately for the big stuff, higher salaries and a pension. The NBA was too fragile financially. What needed to be addressed first and foremost were basic housekeeping issues. In some venues, rims were crooked. Staff sometimes set up baskets higher than the regulation 10 feet. Several courts had phantom dead spots that swallowed up dribbles during games. Don't even mention the staggering travel schedule and overload of games. In New York, gamblers routinely sat courtside booing and cheering to cover the point spread. When the point spread tightened, especially in the last two minutes of a game, the gamblers congregated behind the basket with their shirts off, waving them like pinwheels to make a player miss a decisive free throw.

"We need class," he told a sportswriter. "We've got to stabilize so we can demand respect."

"Is that your job?"

"It's everybody's job," Cousy answered. "We can't go around apologizing because we're professional basketball players. We've got to have pride—pride in ourselves and our teams and in our league. What's good for the NBA is good for us all—and what's bad is bad for us all."[20]

That was easy for a big star like Cousy to say. For the run-of-the-mill guys—and there were plenty of them—they went along to get along. Complain too loudly about playing time or bonuses, and you were replaceable with a snap of the fingers. The league's uniform player contract left everyone, even

Cousy, subject to immediate dismissal and their salaries weren't guaranteed upon termination.

For most, that snap of the fingers would be painful. They'd been stars in college and hoped to play ball for a few more years. Plus, the pro money was decent right out of college in an era when the average home cost just over $8,000. Starting at the league minimum of $3,000 per season, they could double their salaries in a few seasons and live comfortably. Though they'd never bring home the elite $20,000 salary of Cousy, some could get further ahead in the offseason with a second job. Why bite the NBA hands that fed them. They were lucky to be numbered among the league's roughly 85 players

That number included six established African Americans. They were mostly expected to set screens, rebound the misses, and suffice with playing fifth or sixth fiddle to the white leading men on their teams. Rochester's Maurice Stokes would soon invalidate this "get-in-there-and-do-the-dirty-work" job description with his high-scoring rookie season in 1956. Stokes, Woody Sauldsberry, Bill Russell, Wilt Chamberlain, and others proved to NBA front offices that they could feature a crowd-pleasing Black player and still pack their arenas without inciting white hooliganism. But, for now, any Black player who advocated unionization did so at extreme professional risk.

And yet, virtually every player, Black or white, could agree with Cousy that that life in the NBA could get downright weird. In Anderson, Indiana during the late 1940s, the locker rooms had cockroaches that were "literally the size of humming birds" and flew in swarms from wall to wall. In Waterloo, Iowa, when the road team shot free throws, fans cranked up the hot-air blowers that heated the gym, whiffling each attempt like knuckleballs. In Fort Wayne, where the gym was known as "the Bucket of Blood," fans liked to whack visiting players with hand bags, umbrellas, newspapers, game programs. In Syracuse, there was "The Strangler," a short, barrel-chested heckler who liked to grab players by the neck as they headed for the locker room and lift them into the stands. Then there was an elderly woman in Syracuse who enjoyed jabbing Boston coach Red Auerbach with a stick pin whenever he entered the arena. Auerbach even went roaring into the stands after her once.

By August 1954, the seven NBA teams surveyed responded favorably to forming a players' union. (The members of the Fort Wayne Pistons, who answered to an anti-union owner, Fred Zollner, abstained.) Now came the hard part: convince the struggling NBA owners (Zollner included) to recognize the union as a "partner."

Cousy requested a meeting to broach the subject with "Pumpernickel." No reply. Undaunted, Cousy held the union's first organizational meeting at the 1955 All-Star game. The day-long session generated five demands of the league: Pay the season salaries of each member of the newly defunct Baltimore Bullets; limit exhibition games to 20; players get $25 for public appearances; supply arbitration for salary disputes; and abolish the "whisper fine." The latter was a $10 fine levied by referees for an infraction too serious to ignore but not worthy of a full-blown $25 technical foul. These fines brought no whistle, stoppage of play, or free throws. Just the whisper, "That'll cost you 10 bucks."

Cousy sent the demands to Podoloff for comment. No reply. Cousy crashed NBA headquarters several weeks later to speak with Podoloff. He made Cousy wait . . . and stew . . . like trying to run off a pesky salesman. Podoloff finally relented, and Cousy took a seat in the president's office staring up at the little man behind the elevated wooden desk. The height was intended to intimidate all ye who enter here.

"Everything will be taken care of," Podoloff reassured Cousy, referring to the demands.

"When?"

Podoloff deflected the question, mostly out of duty. Podoloff worked for the owners, and they would approve a players' union when pigs could fly, a point now abundantly clear to Cousy.[21]

The NBA Players Association reconvened at the 1956 all-star game. But with the continued ice-cold response from Podoloff and the Board of Governors, Cousy's rebellion stalled. Several players lost interest, but Cousy and his small circle of supporters regrouped. Cousy doubled back to canvass the players about striking for union recognition. His foil Podoloff promised to banish any player who dared and killed the strike. But in April, Cousy followed up by demanding a pro basketball "Bill of Rights" in the widely read *Sport Magazine* and repeating the five demands. Podoloff ignored him.

But for only so long. On April 18, 1957, at Podoloff's unexpected urging, the Board of Governors voted to recognize the NBA Players Association (NBAPA). The turning point had been Cousy's random threat that the NBAPA, ignored for too long by the owners, might just affiliate with the American Guild of Variety Artists (AGVA). The guild represented not only actors and actresses but circus artists and nightclub performers, including exotic dancers who pole-danced in bawdy strip clubs that were notorious for their Mob ties. In fact, those ties were rumored to have infiltrated the AGVA. For Podoloff, who hired private detectives to snoop on NBA players, the thought of Cousy manning the picket line with sword swallowers, strippers, and tough guys named Rocco was too much to bear.

By the late 1950s, Abe Saperstein had become a full-blown pest to the NBA. He'd recently bought a minority share of the Philadelphia Warriors, now owned by his old friend Eddie Gottlieb, and that gave him an excuse to surface occasionally at Board of Governors meetings and banter with the boys around the card table. Breaking out a deck of cards between sessions, lighting up a cigar, and burning through the latest gossip had become a tradition at board meetings. High-stakes poker it wasn't. Gin rummy was more the speed of these nickel-and-dime operators.[22]

Abe's presence at the card table and unsolicited business advice irked some of the NBA governors, and it fell to President Podoloff to help manage his know-it-all friend. That was easier said than done. Stuck in Saperstein's head was his simple formula for promotional success: Basketball skill plus entertainment plus showmanship equal profit. The NBA kept getting the ingredients wrong, and Abe wouldn't shut up about how he would handle things differently.

And yet, more than ever, Abe viewed these NBA screw-ups as a threat to his Globetrotter empire. An integrated NBA had first call on the best Black collegiate players. Every day, Abe opened the newspaper and read the latest NBA scores. The more America identified with the thrill of NBA victory, the more irrelevant became his just-for-laughs vaudeville show team.

Abe sensed the basketball business slipping through his uproarious brand. The NBA had almost completely cut ties with him financially, hosting their own four-team doubleheaders and moving on with pro basketball sans anything Globetrotters. He'd dominated pro basketball for too long to let these new guys cut him out of the millions to be gained on pro basketball in the 1960s, that is, if they played their cards right.

Abe's solution to his conundrum was to double down on joining the association and gaining control from within the NBA threat. Abe, world traveler that he was, bent the ear of his friend Pumpernickel about the rise of modern aviation, with its jet-propelled engines that now made coast-to-coast travel faster, cheaper, and more reliable. The NBA needed teams in California, and Abe, with his endless connections, offered to do the honors in Los Angeles under one condition: give him a franchise on the cheap as payback for all he'd done for the league. To demonstrate his commitment to his future business partners, Saperstein even loaned some of his Trotters—including seven-foot teenage national sensation Wilt Chamberlain—to help the Philadelphia Warriors fill the stands. It was just like old times.

Saperstein waited for his thank you. But when his buddy Gottlieb wouldn't return Chamberlain and Podoloff insisted on full price for an NBA franchise, Abe went on the warpath. His revenge was to form the rival American Basketball League (ABL), an idea that he'd been kicking around in case of an NBA double cross. Saperstein would use the ABL to expand the pro basketball market, especially out West, and introduce a livelier brand of the game to entertain the masses. If all went well, the NBA would yell uncle in two or three seasons, and Saperstein would be back sitting on top of the pro basketball world.

The ABL sent letters to all NBA players, welcoming them to jump to the new league for greater opportunity and slightly more money. Saperstein and his lawyers tried calling in a few favors to get the ABL on national television from the start.

To no avail. The networks took a pass at airing more pro basketball, and the ABL enticed roughly a half dozen NBA journeymen to give the new league a whirl. Because the journeymen were still technically under contract to their former NBA teams, Podoloff sued the ABL for all it was worth, asking in some cases for $1 million in damages for the loss of players with salaries under $10,000 per season. The filings were mostly for show. Podoloff eventually settled most of the cases out of court for a nominal fee. But the NBA's underlying message was real: There would be legal consequences if the ABL hooked any of the larger NBA fish.

But the league had a whopper of a problem, ironically, with Saperstein. The ABL's self-appointed president continued to focus almost full-time on the Globetrotters, his claim to fame. He spent weeks at a time on the road "spinnin' the globe" with them and cabling from Berlin and Sao Paulo with his belated two-line responses to the latest ABL business. The confusion meant players and creditors didn't get paid on time, and the league barely survived its first season, dropping $1.5 million (about $13 million today).

Saperstein wasn't ready to throw in the towel just yet, especially after the ABL's big signing. In mid-May, the ABL-champion Cleveland Pipers signed the plum of the 1962 college draft, Jerry Lucas, the most-prominent college player in years. They did it wielding a briefcase full of charts, not cash, that eased the misgivings of the uber-intellectual Lucas about a career in pro basketball. So tight was the sales pitch, the Pipers got the greatest thing since Wilt Chamberlain for $20,000 over two seasons, or $70,000 less than the NBA's unusually generous three-year offer.

The sophisticated sales pitch had been delivered by Cleveland owner George Steinbrenner, later the shipping tycoon who bankrolled the baseball New York Yankees. Steinbrenner broke into pro sports in his pre-tycoon days as the fiery, 30-year-old president of the Cleveland Basketball Club, Inc., a consortium of local businessmen. In 1960, the consortium had snapped up the Pipers, an established local semi-pro team, and jumped into the ABL to ride Saperstein's famous coattails to national glory. By the summer of 1962, with Lucas in tow and the ABL in trouble, Steinbrenner hoped to pack up his Pipers and jump to the even-greater glory of the NBA.

Steinbrenner reportedly charmed his way into a secret, just-hear-me-out meeting with Podoloff aboard the latter's small yacht on the Connecticut River. Steinbrenner brought his briefcase and charts promising advantages to the NBA, large and small. Among the former, Steinbrenner said he would combine his team with the ABL's talented Kansas City franchise. Podoloff nodded. Who said history didn't repeat itself? Just as the BAA had stolen rival teams in the 1940s to win the pro basketball war, Podoloff could eliminate two ABL franchises by adding one NBA team. That would leave four, maybe five, ABL teams and spell curtains for Saperstein.[23]

Podoloff said it would take $460,000 to close the deal. Steinbrenner promised to cover it, and Podoloff promised to line up the needed seven (of the nine NBA governors) to approve the transfer. To avoid litigation, Podoloff preemptively waved the olive branch that all ABL owners could purchase an ownership stake in the Cleveland-Kansas City franchise and join the NBA.

The plan was a little too brilliant. Steinbrenner and his two ABL business partners missed their first payments to join the NBA, and the governors quickly quashed the deal to avoid inheriting a deadbeat franchise. What's more, Pipers or no Pipers, the ABL had committed to a second season, with Saperstein reportedly ready to bankroll the enterprise mostly on his own "for the good of basketball."

The ABL crashed and burned midway through what turned out to be its wing-and-a-prayer second season. According to most, the malfunction owed to Abe Saperstein's continued absenteeism. The ABL's demise also seemingly took with it several bright ideas: the 30-second shot clock, a widened 18-foot center lane, and a three-point basket to bring the little guy back into a game dominated by giants.

When the ABL crashed, Podoloff had already announced his resignation, effective at the end of the 1962-1963 season. At age 71, the founding NBA president had seen enough.

For some, Podoloff departed as a jolly good fellow. He'd kept the NBA afloat during the rough patches in the early 1950s, and since then league attendance, though still not great at 5,383 per game, continued to trend upward, reaching 1.94 million in his last season. The NBA had relocated franchises to Los Angeles and San Francisco to gain a bicoastal look and feel. Meanwhile, nearly all of the NBA's small-market yawns had relocated to big-league Philadelphia, Cincinnati, and Detroit, and even added an expansion team in Chicago. In New

York, Madison Square Garden loved the Knicks, if they could just win a championship.

Pro basketball franchises, which Podoloff peddled for $1,000 ($14,000 today) in the BAA days, were now selling for real money. The Baltimore Bullets, for example, would soon sell for an astonishing, league-record $1.1 million.[24] Larger paydays loomed as the NBA transitioned from the mostly hand-to-mouth "arena owners" to the mostly flush "millionaire owners." They were a new breed of sports entrepreneur who lived off of several income streams and viewed their teams as potentially lucrative investments, not a one-night show to pay the rent.

For others, Podoloff was an aging little dictator whose value as president had been slipping. It wasn't just the Steinbrenner mess. It was also the NBA Game of the Week debacle. Podoloff had never ceased micromanaging the broadcast, agreeing with NBC executives to fire popular announcer Marty Glickman, considered the golden voice of basketball, because viewers might perceive the NBA's broadcast team as "too Jewish."[25] Gutsy move, predicable result. At the end of the 1961-1962 season, NBC canceled Podoloff and the NBA Game of the Week from its 170-station network, claiming rotten ratings and weak ad sales. The cancelation cost the league roughly $260,000 in revenue. Podoloff, the NBA's original television evangelist, couldn't square another TV deal, and the suddenly TV-happy governors were dismayed.

Also dismaying to the governors was Podoloff's greenlighting the NBA Players Association. The union hadn't been brought to heel, as Podoloff had promised. Instead, the rabble-rousing Bob Cousy handed the keys in 1962 to the union to his outspoken teammate Tom Heinsohn. He'd now enlisted the help of a young New York labor attorney named Larry Fleisher, who kept showing up unannounced at league events. He was becoming a real pain in the neck.

Endnotes

[1] David Stern, Interview with author, October 2018.

[2] Jim O'Brien, "O'Brien Led the Way," *The Sporting News*, July 3, 1976.

[3] Roger Noll, Interview with author, April 2009.

[4] "Ice Skating," *Kentucky Post* (Covington), January 16, 1924.

[5] The hockey story is pieced together from multiple sources. Most notably: Neil Isaacs, interview with author, April 2014; Maurice Podoloff's oral history, published in Isaacs' *Vintage NBA*, 1996; and various *Chicago Tribune* stories on Arthur Wirtz.

[6] Robert Peterson, *Cages to Jump Shots*, 1990, p. 151-152.

[7] Barney Nagler, *James Norris and the Decline of Boxing*, 1964, p. 43.

[8] *Cages to Jump Shots*, p. 152.

[9] Elliot Cushing, "Royals Reported Willing to Join BAA," *Rochester Democrat and Chronicle*, May 10, 1948.

[10] No Byline, "The Pros," *Basketball Illustrated*, 1949.

[11] *Cages to Jump Shots*, p. 164.

[12] Robert Krishef, *Thank You, America*, 1982, p. 136.

[13] David Surdam, *The Rise of the National Basketball Association*, 2012, p. 186.

[14] Leonard Koppett L, *24 Seconds to Shoot*, 1968, p. 79.

[15] *Vintage NBA*, p. 234.

[16] David Neft et al, *The Sports Encyclopedia*, Pro Basketball, 1975, p. 106.

[17] *24 Seconds to Shoot*, p. 81.

[18] Dick Young, "How Television Tampers with Sports," *Sport*, July 1961, p. 76-78.

[19] *Vintage NBA*, p. 234.

[20] Bill Reynolds, *Cousy*, 2005, p. 149.

[21] Bob Cousy, *Basketball is My Life*, 1957, p. 165.

[22] Earl Foreman, Interview with author, April 2011.

[23] Bill Livingston, *George Steinbrenner's Pipe Dream*, 2015, p. 190-191.

[24] *Washington Bullets Official Yearbook and Press Guide, 1974-75*, p. 58.

[25] Marty Glickman, *The Fastest Kid on the Block*, 1996, p. 85.

1

Boston, June 9, 1965—Shortly after noon, thunder rumbled over Boston's Back Bay, followed by the hard, rhythmic patter of raindrops. The dozen or so NBA governors, in town for the league's two-day board meeting at the Hotel Somerset, watched the wet stuff from the hotel lobby, then looked at each other. Guess they'd better stay indoors. While the mostly short, mostly middle-aged men debated their culinary options at the hotel, New York governor Ned Irish decided he wasn't hungry. He called out to NBA commissioner Walter Kennedy standing outside the conference room where the governors had spent the morning reviewing the league budget. Poor Walter. There went his lunch hour. Irish wasn't pleased about something, usually picayune, and he wanted to belabor some budgetary food for thought.

By 1:30 p.m., it was back to NBA business and finalizing next season's schedule. The discussion devolved into the usual grievances over unfair costs, followed by impatient pleas to move on to the next agenda item please. The next item would be even more unpleasant. Another visit from the players' union. Oscar Robertson, one of the league's brightest stars and the newly elected president of the NBA Players Association, waited in a snappy suit and tie outside the meeting room to make his pitch on behalf of his membership. Joining him was a short white guy in a dark, rumpled business suit. He was Larry Fleisher, general counsel for the players association and *attorney non grata* at board meetings.

Poor Walter, it was his job to shoo away Fleisher with the warning: no attorneys allowed inside the conference room.

Fleisher complied and disappeared down the hallway, while Kennedy hurried over to a reporter to justify the expulsion. "If the owners can't sit down with the players themselves and iron out any disputed items with mutual trust and respect, it would just be bad," he said.[1]

Inside the conference room, the governors sat flipping through their paperwork and taking drags off cigarettes. Robertson offered his perfunctory greeting and launched into his first request: health insurance. Medical bills were stacking up for some players and their families, and they needed help. Robertson also insisted that trainers must travel with their teams on the road. Ankles weren't getting taped properly, and players were getting needlessly injured. A few questions followed, and Robertson concluded with the current $8-per-day travel per diem (equal to $66 today) was inadequate. It should be bumped up to $10 per day.[2] The governors nodded and punted Robertson's requests to a three-man subcommittee, headed by Kennedy, where they would remain buried in the slow grind of administrative process for as long as possible. That's how the NBA governors managed their labor issues. Benign neglect. And it was working, no attorneys in the room.

The next morning, the governors were back in the Hotel Somerset to tackle "the league's general welfare."[3] The mood was more like a livestock auction. St. Louis' fiery Ben Kerner got things going by making a big cash offer to Baltimore's Arnie Heft for his seven-footer Walt Bellamy. Irish hushed the room with his higher offer. "Thanks fellas," Heft bantered, "but you can't play dollars at center."[4]

After some lesser trade offers, Boston's Red Auerbach decried the Euro menace. European pro teams were bidding on American college players, and Auerbach didn't like it one bit. He said Boston had just lost draftee, Toby Kimball, to an Italian team for $30,000 a season, tax free. (Auerbach would later order Kimball to "come home" or he'd ban him from the NBA. Kimball relented and signed with Boston for $8,500 a season.[5]) In a sign of sneaky NBA doings to come, Auerbach suggested the league consider signing the best college players while they were still in school to thwart the foreign influence.

Auerbach's pitch was pure heresy. The NBA, like a parasite, fed off of the college game's greatest graduating stars and their legendary four-year exploits. The beauty of it all was the NBA didn't pay a red cent to develop its rising young stars, like Major League Baseball did via its serpentine minor-league system.

The governors moved on, and Detroit's Fred Zollner, the old quiet one, shuffled to the podium. He came in peace, not heresy, throwing himself upon the mercy of his fellow board members. Zollner said he needed a "draft waiver." That translated to those in the room granting Detroit the exclusive rights to Cazzie Russell, the University of Michigan's All-Everything senior and the certain first pick in the NBA's upcoming college draft. Times were hard in Detroit, and Zollner needed Russell to turn around his Pistons. Tacit in Zollner's plea, his fellow governors owed him this irregularity. Since the 1950s, the super-wealthy Zollner served as the NBA's amiable Daddy Warbucks. Whenever the league fell into a financial bind, Zollner was too rich and kind-hearted to say no. That made him extremely popular among his peers in need of a few bucks. And, as everyone at the table could attest, whenever called upon, Zollner gave generously to help the lesser of his NBA brothers.

Indebtedness, however, couldn't take the next leap of faith to compensation. The NBA gossiped, and the whispers insinuated that Zollner's problems in Detroit were self-inflicted. He had fired five coaches and four general managers since moving to Detroit eight years ago, with each new hire seemingly quirkier than the last. Detroit's current player-coach was the 24-year-old Dave DeBusschere, known around the league as "the boy coach." Who in their right mind hired a boy coach?

And who in their right mind would hand off a presumed once-in-a-decade talent like Russell and help a rival franchise prosper? Sensing skepticism in the room, Zollner offered a compromise. Restore the NBA territorial draft for one more season. This was the NBA's "other" college draft, wheeled out years ago to give teams first dibs on top local college heroes and grow their fanbase. With the NBA now on more solid financial ground, the league had mothballed the territorial draft in the past year, stating geography shouldn't dictate where the next Wilt Chamberlain landed in the NBA. If the league extended the draft one more year for Zollner, several teams might be shooting themselves in foot with no All Americans in their localities to make it worth their while.

So, Zollner played the final card up his sleeve: extend the territorial draft for four more years. That would give each team plenty of extra time to target that one popular local collegian who might sell out their arenas. The proposal quickly snagged on a 7-foot-2 catch. The "next Wilt Chamberlain" would be UCLA's 7-foot-2 sophomore sensation Lew Alcindor. Helping Zollner meant handing Alcindor to Los Angeles and the arrogant, barely tolerated Lakers' owner Jack Kent Cooke. Never. Zollner, like a favorite crazy NBA uncle, regrettably would have to take his chances on Russell just like everybody else.

Detroit, Jan. 29, 1966—By the third quarter, Jerry West looked like he owned Cobo Arena. He kept dribbling to his favorite spots on the floor, always taking a final extra-hard dribble, like hammering a nail, and lifting into the air ahead of his defender as straight as an arrow. Then came a swishing sound. Nothing but net.

Those sweet swishing sounds had West's visiting Los Angeles Lakers up big and the Detroit Pistons looking out of sorts. Watching it all was the plump, pear-shaped Fred Zollner. Now in his early 60s, Zollner was once aptly described as "a friendly man with a taste for expensive striped suits and the engaging knack of making them look as if he'd worn them to bed." His dark, wavy hair also looked like it had joined in the tossing and turning, prompting another reporter to quip that his "unruly coiffure . . . suggests he is about to mount a podium and conduct Beethoven's Ninth."[6]

This Beethoven, however, spent most of his life conducting the low-rumble of the family factory in Fort Wayne. During the 1930s, that factory started rolling out a line of pistons (engineered by Zollner himself for extra durability) that cornered the automobile and aviation industries. As both industries grew like weeds over the next few decades, Zollner's bank account climbed beyond his wildest dreams.

He rarely attended Pistons games anymore, having semi-retired to his winter mansion in Miami, where he entertained himself on many days aboard his 48-foot cruiser bobbing through the turquoise waters of Biscayne Bay. Back in port, the quiet one sipped Scotch at the yacht club with the other wind-chapped millionaires. While toasting the good life, Zollner's fortune swelled. His factory in Fort Wayne had never been busier, cranking out $30 million (today, $234 million) worth of his precision pistons annually. Zollner flew north a few times per month on his plane, dubbed the Flying Z, for meetings and to tend to his responsibilities as a college trustee, philanthropist, and president of the booming Lincoln National Bank and Trust.

Or, as he'd done today, fly to Detroit to fret over his Pistons. Zollner had been egged on a decade ago by his NBA colleagues to shift his franchise from sleepy Ft. Wayne to busy Detroit and help add another big-league city to the bunch. Motown had proved profoundly disinterested in pro basketball, and Zollner had lost a small fortune. In his more realistic moments, Zollner knew that he needed to sell off the Pistons and part ways with his ungrateful NBA colleagues.

And yet, the NBA was growing in stature. League attendance was up 24 percent this season,[7] and the NBA's successful franchises were now selling in the millions. In the old days, Zollner opened his checkbook and bought his way to basketball success. But the league's greater stature brought more rules and accountability, which prevented him from snagging Cazzie Russell and asking for forgiveness later. Two days earlier, Zollner had made one final heartfelt plea for Russell at the latest Board of Governors' gathering. No go. Zollner's only shot at Snazzy Cazzie, as he was known, was failure. The Pistons had to finish dead last in the NBA's Western Division, entitling the team to take part in a coin flip with the Eastern Division's worst failure, probably New York, to decide who gets Russell.

Zollner sat in his reserved box seat in Section A-5 separated from the masses by 14 empty seats in each direction, and soaked up the ambiance. The salty smell of popcorn and the choke of tobacco smoke. The static white noise of the sparse crowds. The Black hipsters in the bleacher seats featuring the flashy Motown look. The engine-like thrusts of the Lakers to exert their collective will upon the Pistons. And West's nothing but nets.

Zollner suddenly sensed two men breaching his 14-seat bubble. He recognized the older one with the glasses. He was with the *Detroit News* newspaper. It was the tall, young Black man in his wake whom he couldn't quite place.

"Mr. Zollner, I have somebody I'd like you to meet."

"Who's that?"

"This is Cazzie Russell."

Zollner, his eyes sparkling, extended his right hand to finally meet the Michigan Wolverine of his dreams.[8] Now, if he could win that blasted coin flip that fate seemed to be forcing on him, Snazzy Cazzie could make his franchise sparkle for him, the fans, and a potential million-dollar buyer.

Ann Arbor, Mich., April 27, 1966—Cazzie Russell glanced at the black rotary telephone mounted on his kitchen wall. It was time to dial into the NBA coin flip. In a matter of minutes, Russell would finally know whether he would be a New York Knickerbocker or a Detroit Piston. Russell, in his more candid moments, hoped for the latter. Michigan had been very good to him.

Forty miles down the interstate, the Knicks contingent had arrived by cab at Detroit's stately Sheraton-Cadillac Hotel, where the Pistons rented office space. Proceeding up the escalator to the hotel lobby were Ned Irish, looking sporty in a navy-blue business suit; Dick McGuire, nicknamed "Mumbles," the taciturn coach of the Knickerbockers; and Commissioner Walter Kennedy, the designated coin flipper.

The trio rode the elevator up to Suite 1618 and the warm welcome of Fred Zollner, looking a little loud in his cream-colored suit. Beside him was the more conservatively dressed Dave DeBusschere, the boy coach, who, at 6-foot-6, towered over the old timers. Irish small-talked in his flat, assertive New York accent. Speaking to him was like trying to chat up a bank inspector. In the strange alchemy of the NBA, Irish and the soft-spoken Zollner were on good terms However, Irish wasn't about to cut him any breaks. Business was business. Irish had voted against Zollner's draft waiver, mainly because he believed the Knicks, as the league's flagship franchise was informally called, needed Russell more.

A gaggle of local reporters, photographers, and cameramen had already positioned themselves in the next room around a conference table decked with a green velvet covering. Most weren't particularly interested in the Pistons. Russell was the story. Detroit had just lost its bid to host the 1972 Olympic Summer Games. Winning the popular Russell might prove some small consolation.

After the usual technical difficulties with cameras and microphones, Kennedy stepped forward to explain the ground rules. He would flip a coin, and, as pre-agreed, Detroit would call it in the air. Any questions? The reporters jotted it all down like a secret code that they'd need to swallow or burn afterwards. Standing behind Kennedy, as stiff as a Marine at attention, was DeBusschere. Zollner had asked his boy coach to make the fateful head-or-tails call for him.

The eccentric millionaire then handed Kennedy a St. Gaudens $20 gold piece, minted in 1907. It was from Zollner's personal coin collection and had been presumably the object of many a recent incantation to fall for the Pistons. Zollner retreated beside DeBusschere, then promptly hid behind a vacant stare crowned by his unruly coiffure.

Kennedy twirled the shiny coin into the air, and DeBusschere hurried to call out "TAILS." In that split second, a camera flashed and freeze-framed Zollner's momentary deer-in-the-headlights "oh no" for time and all eternity. DeBusschere glanced down a millisecond later, winced, and strode out of the room.

"It's heads," Kennedy announced. "New York will receive the first draft choice."

Forty miles up the interstate, Russell's head visibly sank in disappointment. "I kind of feel sorry for Detroit," Russell confessed.

What Russell did next was extraordinary for the times. He consulted Arthur Morse, his lawyer. In the mid-1960s, rising rookies didn't hire lawyers. Doing so signaled to management that they were too smart for their britches and would be trouble in the locker room. But Russell, a straightlaced kid who'd grown up poor in Chicago, wanted to be smart with his pro money. He hired Morse, at least initially, to help him sort out his taxes, not buck the system.

Nevertheless, he had bucked the system. If Russell succeeded in getting Morse into the room, he would set the precedent for future top picks to have the right to equal representation. But as for the rest of the first-round class of 1966, they'd better not push it. Just ask Jim Barnett.[9]

Eugene, Ore., May 11, 1966—It was finals week at the University of Oregon when Jim Barnett got the news. The Boston Celtics had selected him in the first round of the NBA draft, the eighth choice overall. That was seven picks after the Knicks made it official and grabbed their franchise player, Cazzie Russell.

Barnett, studying for a final exam in Introductory Geology, was rocked by the news. He'd never ventured further east than Chicago, and now the 6-foot-4 West Coaster would be eating lobster and shoveling snow in a few months as a member the world-champion Boston Celtics. The phone rang, and Red Auerbach, the team's famous coach-turned-general manager, wanted Barnett to fly to Boston at the team's expense as soon as finals were over. They needed to "take care" of his contract.

Barnett called his father in Southern California with the big news. In between "Celtics" and "Boston Garden's parquet floor," the idea of hiring a lawyer to negotiate the contract never crossed Barnett's mind. Neither did his college coach offer any sage advice. In these days when "amateur" was a closely guarded designation, college and pro basketball generally didn't mix. Barnett and the other first rounders (Cazzie Russell excluded) were on their own to enter the next stage in their sports careers.

A few days later, Barnett stepped into the Celtics' front office suite at bustling North Station. The home of the NBA champions looked like an oversized living room, adorned with bright green Celtics memorabilia. Barnett locked onto a woman with a gigantic beehive hairdo seated like an all-seeing sentry at a front desk. Her name was Mary.

Barnett introduced himself as the team's top draft choice, and Mary showed him into Auerbach's cramped office, measuring maybe 10 feet-by-10 feet, and a quirky collection of letter openers displayed like daggers on a wall. The boss had just demolished lunch (a fried salami sandwich) and was considering a cigar. He rose to his feet, sizing up his top pick for the first time. He wasn't impressed, or at least wasn't willing to show it.

"Have a seat," Auerbach ordered in his slow Brooklyn staccato.

Barnett angled in his long, lanky frame at the end of a small table across from Auerbach. An unctuous gloom filled the air. Auerbach had likely never seen Barnett in action. Frank Ramsey, the team's player-turned-scout, had recommended Barnett as a possible replacement for stalwart guard K.C. Jones, who was contemplating retirement. Ramsey liked Barnett's ability to run the floor, a trait that Auerbach also appreciated.

Auerbach flashed his crooked, tough-guy grin and segued into his mostly perfunctory sales pitch. Auerbach said he could pull a few strings to get Barnett into the Massachusetts National Guard, which had an exceedingly long waiting list. That meant Barnett could bypass the military draft and a mandatory two-year stint in the Army just as the Vietnam War escalated. That was an incredible perk, Barnett thought. As a member of the National Guard, he could focus on the NBA, then take part in offseason training maneuvers.

"Let's talk about your contract," Auerbach transitioned abruptly.

"Sure."

"Before I do, I want to read you something," Auerbach's tone stiffening.

He extracted a certified letter sent by Chicago attorney Arthur Morse who was representing Leon Clark, Boston's second-round draft choice. Auerbach read each ominous word as though he were reciting *The Communist Manifesto*. Morse "looked forward" to meeting with Auerbach and specified that his client hoped to negotiate a two-year guaranteed contract at $20,000 per annum. The dollar figure was ambitious for a rookie. The average NBA salary was $17,500 per season. What made the letter so radical were the words "attorney" (attorneys weren't welcome in his office), negotiate (players didn't negotiate), and "guaranteed" (money wasn't guaranteed in the NBA).

"You know what I'm going to do with this letter?"

"No sir."

Auerbach ripped it in two, balled the paper into the trashcan, and picked up their conversation in a less combative tone. "What we had in mind for you is . . ."

"That's fine, I'll take it," Barnett heard himself blurt out to avoid any conflict and get on with his pro career.

Auerbach reached for a standard NBA player contract. The salary had already been neatly typed in at $11,000 for one season, plus a $500 signing bonus. Barnett reached for a pen. The "negotiation" had taken less than five minutes.

What about Leon Clark? He reluctantly signed Auerbach's stingy offer near the $7,500 league minimum. The dollar figure was meant to teach a lesson to Clark and his fancy Chicago lawyer, Morse. Except a few months later, Clark bailed on Auerbach. Morse got him a better offer tax-free in Europe.

New York, Sept. 12, 1966—It took Boston's Red Auerbach less than five minutes to sign Jim Barnett. It took 139 days for New York's Ned Irish and his minions to ink Cazzie Russell.

The announcement came during a 1:00 p.m. press conference at Mama Leone's Ristorante, a popular spot in 1960s Manhattan. Between the pasta and the spumoni, Irish dished from the podium about Russell's record three-year, $200,000 rookie contract (worth roughly $66,000 annually). The money wasn't guaranteed. But still. The number $200,000 rolled off the tongue like banker's pay, and New York's working-class boroughs buzzed in a mix of envy and incredulity. "For $800,000 more, they could have gotten [actor] Richard Burton," wisecracked the *New York Daily News*.[10]

Afterwards, the crowd reassembled outside Madison Square Garden for Irish and Russell, dapper in a dark suit, to pose for photographs to memorialize this joyous occasion. As cameras clicked, Russell extended his right hand, stock still like a bronze statue, palming a basketball. Yankee Stadium had Mickey Mantle, Shea Stadium had "Broadway" Joe Namath ("the $600,000 man"), and Madison Square Garden now had the highest-paid, must-see rookie in NBA history, an athlete so remarkable that his college coach raved, "Cazzie makes my day just by showing up. For practice."

A way from the cameras, the members of the Knicks front office were more circumspect. Enriching a 22-year-old kid for some cheap publicity had never been their intention. Things just got out of control.

Eddie Donovan, the Knicks' often-dour basketball-obsessed general manager, remembered the turning point. It came right after the coin flip. Donovan had dutifully arranged a meeting with Russell, in 1960s NBA parlance, to "take care" of his contract. That meant, like Auerbach's strong-arming of Barnett, a five-minute, "sign-here, welcome-to-the-Knicks" encounter. He got an Abbott & Costello comedy skit instead.

"My lawyer," Russell gestured toward Arthur Morse.

"My client," smirked Morse.

"My pocketbook," Donovan quipped.

"Exactly," said Morse.[11]

Donovan could have "pulled an Auerbach" and told Morse to scram. The Knicks, like all NBA teams, didn't negotiate player contracts with lawyers present. But Donovan lacked that luxury. The Knicks were a perennial NBA doormat; Auerbach's Celtics were the league's dynasty. Auerbach could live without

Barnett or Leon Clark, but Donovan needed Russell to jump-start the sputtering Knicks.

And so, Donovan played along with Morse, an impish, hyperactive man in a dark suit with horn-rimmed glasses and a creative comb-over of his nearly bald middle-aged pate. Donovan flapped open his briefcase and proceeded in a calm monotone with NBA business as usual. He said the Knicks had an unusual two-year contract (most were one-year) ready for Russell to sign at $28,000 per season, with a $5,000 signing bonus. By NBA standards, Donovan was dangling a salary befitting a top draft choice who stood 7 feet, not 6-foot-5. Donovan paused to let the dollar figures sink in. He expected Morse, the earlier "pocketbook" quip notwithstanding, to advise his client to take the deal on the table. Fast.

To Donovan's surprise, Morse shook his head no. He leaned forward, the thick lenses of his eyeglasses magnifying his bug-like eyes, and harrumphed that his client already had an offer worth twice that from the Harlem Globetrotters. He was also awaiting other lucrative offers from, you guessed it, Europe.

Morse's strategy was simple, but revolutionary, in this less-evolved NBA era: Don't let New York dictate the financial terms of the contract. He would dictate them based on his own credibility. Morse had longstanding ties to Chicago Stadium, where he had started promoting college basketball doubleheaders in the 1930s, or shortly after he quit driving a cab at night to put himself through law school. A decade later, Morse joined the BAA (now NBA) as a part owner of the founding Chicago Stags. The Stags flopped, but Morse remained on collegial terms with several NBA higher-ups, including Walter Kennedy. Morse knew the business.

Morse already had concocted a counteroffer to slide across the table. His financial formula? "I base my figures on a formula figured out by accountants I deal with," Morse explained cryptically. "The formula is a combination of logic and arithmetic. I analyze every club and where the boy fits into the club's picture. I am well-supplied with the information on how much each club can afford."[12]

Much of Morse's "analysis" almost certainly came from conversations with the opinionated Arthur Wirtz, who owned and operated Chicago Stadium. Until the courts intervened in the 1950s, Wirtz also ran Madison Square Garden and reportedly resented Irish for taking too big a cut of the profits for himself. As Morse had heard for years, Irish had money to burn working for the Garden.

No documents remain showing how much of the Garden's money Morse proposed to burn. But it clearly had an extra zero on the end, and talking in six figures unnerved Donovan. Those extraordinary numbers were reserved for future Hall of Famers, not rookies. Donovan clasped his briefcase. There was nothing more to discuss. "I never had to deal with an agent before," Donovan confessed afterwards. "Wives yes, agents no."[13]

Russell might have feared his pro career was over, except Morse already had prepped him for this moment.[14] Let Donovan walk, Morse said, it was part of the negotiation. Morse waxed on shrewdly about his past successes for several National Football League players, including two contracts in the $300,000s, minus his 10 percent cut. He said Russell, a devout Christian, needed to believe that Donovan would return, unclasp his briefcase, and offer a whole lot more money.

Score one for Morse. The briefcase reopened a few weeks later. The Knicks already had opened training camp, and Irish finally intervened. The new Madison Square Garden was set to open in another year, and Irish badly needed a marquee attraction. For now, Snazzy Cazzie Russell was it. Lots of money in Gotham equals lots of publicity, and Irish went for broke. The Garden could afford it.

Around the NBA, from Auerbach to Zollner, the sentiment was the blankety-blank Irish had yet again placed his in-house interests above theirs and had sabotaged the NBA. Not only would future top draft picks cost more, lawyers could now insist on a seat at the bargaining table and lobby for more— higher salaries, bigger bonuses, longer contracts, guaranteed payouts, and special privileges galore. Give it 10 years, and the inmates and their crafty lawyers would be running the asylum.

But it wouldn't take that long. While Russell posed in front of Madison Square Garden, a group of young men huddled in a four-story townhouse at 124 E. 38th Street in Manhattan's Murray Hill neighborhood. From these huddles would emerge a rival red, white, and blue pro league eventually called the American Basketball Association. The ABA would set in motion a tangled chain of events that would soon make Russell's big payday seem like chump change.

Endnotes

[1] Jack Barry, "NBA Owners Bar Players' Attorney," *Boston Globe*, June 11, 1965.

[2] Ibid.

[3] No Byline, "NBA to Hold Meeting Here," *Boston Globe*, June 1, 1965.

[4] Jack Barry, "Bullets Veto $250,000 Offer for Bellamy," *Boston Globe*, June 10, 1965.

[5] Toby Kimball, Interview with author, November 2010.

[6] Rodger Nelson, *The Zollner Piston Story*, 1995, p.9.

[7] Phil Elderkin, "Rimming the NBA," *Sporting News*, March 26, 1966.

[8] Jerry Green, *The Detroit Pistons*, 1991, p. 65.

[9] Jim Barnett, Interview with author, July 2021.

[10] Robert Sylvester, "Dream Street," *New York Daily News*, September 17, 1966.

[11] Sandy Padwe, "Yes, Cazzie Had an Agent," *Cincinnati Post*, September 14, 1966.

[12] Sandy Padwe, "Morse Code Key to Leroy Keyes," *Philadelphia Inquirer*, May 31, 1969.

[13] Padwe, *Cincinnati Post*, September 14, 1966.

[14] Cazzie Russell, Interview with author, June 2010.

2

Wilt Chamberlain dunked hundreds of times during his NBA career. Some were polite putbacks, others were vicious, get-outta-here backboard shakers topped off with a passing glare and maybe a clipped verbal warning to an especially irritating defender. But no matter how ornery the dunk or glare, Chamberlain never pumped his fist to the crowd or broke into dance. Neither did Jerry West, Bill Russell, or Pogo Joe Caldwell.

In the early 1960s, NBA players were expected to act like professionals and not incite the crowd. It wouldn't look good. In training camp, all were told the cold-hard facts of NBA life, authored by the arena owners in the leaner 1940s. Pro basketball is a tough, nickel-and-dime business. Without bold ownership willing to take considerable capital risks to operate an inherently unprofitable business, most players would be back home in Scranton or Sioux Falls scuffling on a factory floor. They should be grateful, not greedy, about playing pro ball.

Players were advised to comport themselves as respectable ambassadors of the game. When called upon by their team's publicity director, players were expected to drop everything to sign autographs, mug for photos, and help sell the thrills of bounce passes and hook shots. None were reimbursed for their time and trouble. Their in-event thanks for coming, handed to them as tokens of appreciation "in lieu of cash," were mainly felt hats, shaving kits, wristwatches, and other dime-store wares. Players tossed them into drawers. Who needed 20 wristwatches?

All of the above prompted players to gripe privately about these freebie appearances. In 1954, one of the NBA Players Association's first demands was "payments of $25 expenses for public appearances other than radio, television, or certain charitable functions." The NBA Board of Governors scoffed.

But change was in the air, starting with baseball. A former New York Yankees front office staffer named Frank Scott launched a groundbreaking business in Manhattan's Biltmore Hotel to help baseball stars arrange their own *paid* public appearances to supplement their incomes. Scott's stated mission: "to make the term 'in lieu of cash' obsolete."

Others followed in Scott's footsteps. In 1966, two recent law school grads Steve Arnold and Marty Blackman founded one of the country's first sports marketing agencies, Pro Sports, Inc. The agency opened on a shoestring budget in the Manhattan apartment of Arnold's parents. Whenever the phone rang, the family poodles barked incessantly in the background. "We'd have to tell people," Blackman later laughed, "that one of our clients just walked into our office with a dog."[1]

Through the barks and the blather, both believed in the inherent good of player management, based on their earlier stints in advertising. "Players were such easy marks because they lacked representation," said Arnold. "I remember negotiating with a prominent NFL star to do a commercial for Mennen [shaving cream]. I asked him what he charged, and he bluffed $500 an hour. I said, 'Fine, the filming will take two hours.' He replied, 'Okay, I'll do it for $750.'

"After about four or five of these lowball deals, I said this is crazy," he continued. "I started talking to the players and said, 'Look, don't you want some help? We're in New York and can get you commercials.'"

Within two years, Arnold and Blackman had moved into a canine-free, third-floor office on Madison Avenue and counted approximately 75 clients, mainly pro football players but a few New York Knicks. They charged the players nothing for their services but took a 10-percent cut of each contract. "That wasn't a problem because we usually doubled or tripled their previous contracts," said Arnold. "Our clients always came out way ahead."[2]

By the early- to-mid-1960s, news of the player management industry arrived in the NBA boardroom with a thud. The Old Guard viewed these managers—these marketeers—as leeches living off their product and cutting them out of the profits. Jack Kent Cooke, the new millionaire owner of the Los Angeles Lakers, implored the Old Guard to get in front of change, co-opt the sports marketeers and use their entrepreneurial energy to boost the league's popularity. The Old Guard again grumbled that Cooke had it wrong. Pro basketball, at its core, is a gate-receipt business. This was true in the 1940s, and in their view, always would be. The expansion fees and television contracts helped greatly. But both were short-acting and unpredictable shots in the arm. Like politics, all NBA franchises were local. Teams had to focus their limited resources on connecting with their communities, not Madison Avenue.

But the genie was out of the bottle. The managers had granted the financial wishes of the reigning superstars. To the owners: Good luck trying to stuff these genies back into the bottle. The managers—soon called, agents—were here to stay.

Riding this initial sports-marketing wave was Professional Sports Management Company, Inc. (PSM) in Manhattan's Murray Hill neighborhood. The small firm was led by a peppy, 40-year-old Yale grad named Constantine Seredin. "Connie," as everyone called him, had penetrating, deep-set eyes, loved words and Broadway shows, and had formerly worked as a TV scriptwriter. Seredin aimed high—"divine" was his favorite exclamation—hoping to expand sports marketing into new, uncharted realms.

Among his uncharted realms was "Girl Watch," PSM's groundbreaking (and admirable) attempt for female athletes to gain equal marketing opportunities as men. Another was the Professional Pocket Billiard Players Association. In the 1930s, America's top billiards players organized into an ill-fated pro circuit of the same name to sanction members-only tournaments and world championships. In 1964, Seredin revived the idea, reportedly talking billiards legend Willie Mosconi into serving as a special advisor to attract the top hustlers with the promise of guaranteed base salaries and other workplace lucre.

Seredin's best ideas, however, typically bore a divine ulterior motive. For placing a bunch of guys nicknamed Fats and Sticks on firmer financial ground, Seredin required that the pool sharks contract their publicity and merchandising exclusively with PSM. In other words, the messenger became the sports boss.

But the messenger quickly boxed himself in behind the eight ball. Seredin couldn't find investors to pay for it all, and that sent him—along with his PSM partners—back to the drawing board to divine the next new realm in sports marketing. "We were sitting around one rainy day and said, 'Let's start another league,'" recalled Barry Murtha, one of Seredin's partners. "The conversation drifted to this, that, and the other. Finally, we knocked it down to there was already a rival American Football League, and pro hockey had expanded. There wasn't too much else except for basketball."[3]

They settled on launching a minor-league basketball circuit. Murtha remembers calling potential financial backers and getting nowhere. The moneymen explained that if they were going to invest in basketball, it had to be a big-league operation, recent history be damned. In 1960, the late Abe Saperstein, the wealthy, well-connected father of the Harlem Globetrotters, had gone head-to-head with the NBA. His American Basketball League (ABL), featuring the first long-range three-point basket, went bust in less than two seasons. But a more meticulous postmortem identified the cause of death as suicide, brought on by Saperstein's neglect and the league's administrative difficulties.

This second postmortem convinced Seredin that history didn't have to repeat itself. He cold-called George Mikan, America's beloved former Mr. Basketball, to ask him, as he'd done with billiards legend Mosconi, to serve as an advisor. Mikan gee-whizzed, then explained that his basketball days were over. He'd recently invested in a Minneapolis travel agency and had thoughts of chasing a legal or political career. Seredin thanked Mikan and left his phone number just in case.

Days passed, and Seredin was surprised to get a phone call from somebody named Dennis Murphy. Never heard of him. With good reason. The 39-year-old Murphy was a regular, clock-punching employee of a Southern California engineering firm. He worked in the marketing department. Off the clock, Murphy was politically active, serving on the city council and as mayor of his Orange County suburb. While in office, Murphy had locked onto pro sports as a local revenue generator and, now out of office, he hoped to start a pro basketball league of his own and make some money.

Murphy said he'd recently spoken with George Mikan, who'd passed along Seredin's phone number with a chuckle that great minds and entrepreneurs think alike. Murphy suggested working together. East meets West. Seredin dropped a few well-placed divines, and these two dreamers met in L.A., where Murphy unveiled his Western basketball league like a new brand of soup.

Murphy, a short, cheerful man, cut to the chase. Selling hoops wasn't his first choice. His dream had been securing an expansion team for Anaheim in the upstart American Football League (AFL). Midway through his successful application process, the AFL abruptly halted all future expansion to focus on merging its existing teams with the rival NFL. Though Murphy was out of luck, he wasn't out of ideas. He'd filed one away a few years ago: the Western pro basketball league.[4] The idea was more timely than brilliant. The NBA, having relocated recently to Los Angeles and now San Francisco, was eager to blanket the West. Murphy reasoned that if he jumped in first with a league that claimed the remaining major Western cities, the NBA would have to merge to claim the West. In that case, franchises in Murphy's league, purchased for $10,000, would be worth more than $1 million.

Seredin had never considered merging his pro basketball enterprise with the NBA. A merger would destroy his brand, though Seredin was open to this "money concept." The two agreed on a follow-up meeting in New York, where Seredin would roll out the fat-cat investors behind his basketball venture.

Murphy and three associates flew east ready to be wowed by the investors and their dollar figures. Instead, they were shuffled off to a room for a spin through PSM's business prospectus. Murphy smelled a hustle. He asked to meet the investors. Seredin demurred, and around they went remaining civil, though struggling to communicate.

Murphy flew home considering the trip "a complete fiasco" and Seredin to be "a carney."[5] It was par for Murphy's basketball course. Last year, he'd wooed former NBA great Bill Sharman, an organizational whiz, to head his Western league. Sharman seemed interested—but dropped out in March for an NBA coaching job. In October, Murphy thought he'd hooked millionaires Gene Klein and Sam Schulman to help him get the league off the ground.[6] But both had backed out a few weeks ago. They had another offer for an NBA franchise. And now, after months of slogging away, Murphy still had no teams, no league, no wealthy investors, and now an East Coast partner who seemingly had nothing to bring to the table.

That might have been the end of this tale of two basketball coasts had it not been for John McShane, a Murphy acquaintance who'd also traveled to New York to meet

Seredin. He was a former late-night radio host ("listen to McShane from 12 o'clock till dawn") who now ran the public relations firm McShane Associates. Seredin's heavy-on-the-marketing prospectus had been music to his ears. McShane also realized that Seredin wasn't bluffing. He had potential investors, some wealthy and some not, in New York, Pittsburgh, Cleveland, and Indianapolis. Over the next weeks, McShane bonded with Seredin and served as the go-between for Murphy to forge ahead with a formal organizational meeting at the Beverly Hills Hilton for this melding of east and west called initially the United Basketball League.[7]

Being PR guys, McShane and Seredin leaked the upcoming meeting to the press. McShane, in particular, also told some real whoppers, starting with how Laker stars Jerry West and possibly Elgin Baylor had secretly committed to joining the proposed eight-city United Basketball League.[8] West hadn't even heard of the league. Neither were investors "setting aside more than $1 million" to cover the league's start-up costs. There were no investors. Neither did those investors include: Wilt Chamberlain, George Mikan, and former Los Angeles Lakers owner Bob Short. Though all had been contacted in passing, all had been standoffish, with the exception of Chamberlain. He was thinking about it.

In the wake of these lies, damned lies, and pure desperation, a new pro basketball league would defy the odds and somehow get off the ground. Its takeoff has been retold many times over the past 60 years, though incompletely as oral history from the West Coast group, sans McShane, who died young. Here's a more complete retelling. It's pulled from multiple sources, including the actual minutes of the ABA organizational meetings, compliments of former league secretary Joe Geary.

In Joe Geary's ABA file sits a three-page synopsis of the inaugural public meeting of the now-renamed American Basketball Association. The first page records the date as

Tuesday, December 20, 1966. The location: the Royal Suite at the fashionable Beverly Hills Hilton (the self-described "most sumptuous hotel in the world"). No explanation is given for the league's new name, like a coat of paint, though it's very likely that the marketing-mad Connie Seredin and John McShane had been bouncing around concepts. Like an "American" basketball league is catchier than a "united" one. God Bless America . . . and the ABA.

Geary didn't attend the inaugural meeting, but the designated ABA notetaker captured the moment, line by painstaking line: "Meeting was called to order at 10:25 a.m. by John McShane acting as temporary chairman. A brief explanation of the history of the American Basketball Association was given by John McShane."

Staring back were maybe two dozen prospective investors from around the country, many appearing jet-lagged. Mixed in among the long faces were several fresh ones. Mum was the word, but they were Murphy's "gofers," a bunch of mostly young guys who ran errands for him. The former mayor, dusting off an old political trick to pad attendance at his campaign rallies, asked his gofers to pose as moneymen. Their instructions: Sit up straight, look alive, and dash out of the room at the end of each session pretending to call their business associates.[9] Murphy hoped the flurry of phone calls would create the impression that ABA franchises were in high demand, and the legitimate investors had better grab them while they still could.

McShane, in on the ruse, wrapped up his introductory comments and handed the microphone to his friend Seredin, dressed like a Madison Avenue executive and sounding like the streets of New York personified. The meeting notes report that Seredin launched into a "brief summary of the program proposal of Professional Sports Management (PSM) . . . This included a discussion of business and marketing techniques." Seredin dropped the bomb that each ABA team must pay PSM a monthly fee of $1,500 (annually $18,000, then a hefty ask) for league promotion, with 10 percent going toward obtaining television, radio, and other media contracts. PSM also wanted an exclusive 10-year agreement to handle "league merchandising, endorsements, promotions, publicity, and public relations."

Several investors had heard enough. "He may know his business," one later grumbled, "but when he gets into areas of finance and other business aspects, he would scare you to death. Some of his statements made me wince."[10]

Murphy's runners dashed to the phones, while some legitimate investors let their minds dash to the departure times of their return flights. This basketball league was a bust. Then, in walked the ABA's seven-foot saving grace. Wilt Chamberlain, who was in town with the NBA's Philadelphia 76ers, had agreed to join the organizing meeting. Though the meeting notes don't go into detail, Chamberlain was coaxed to the Beverly Hills Hilton by Mark Binstein, a smooth-talking Jersey City stockbroker and former basketball star at West Point. Binstein, a Seredin recruit who'd emptied his modest bank account to fly to Los Angeles and place dibs on the New York franchise, stated "unequivocally" that the seven-footer had agreed to join his team as a player and part owner.

The meeting notes read: "Mr. Mark Binstein, representative of the New York group, and Mr. Wilt Chamberlain briefly explained their plan of becoming a public stock issue, and also, a brief summary of player recruitment." The latter referred to the many reportedly disgruntled players waiting to flee the NBA for greener pastures. Chamberlain, with his strong NBA connections, would steer them to the new league and marketplace. Chamberlain vanished minutes later, never to steer, play, own, or organize the ABA into existence. Binstein had unequivocally fibbed about Chamberlain's involvement.

After lunch, McShane had big news. He'd received the requisite $1,000-per-franchise down payments[11] on five ABA teams: New York, Anaheim, Kansas City, Phoenix, and Seattle. The first three landed in relatively good hands, though Murphy, as a sign of his limited influence, got shafted on Anaheim, the location that he coveted. McShane secretly gave Anaheim to the league's lone wealthy investor, Jim Ackerman, and his sidekick and basketball guru, Art Kim.[12] Murphy quickly staked out Kansas City, though not with his own limited funds. He'd sweet-talked the head of his engineering firm, James Trindle, to give pro basketball a whirl. That made three legitimate investors. As for the Phoenix and Seattle franchises, they existed on paper only. In fact, Seattle belonged to two of Murphy's gofers.

No matter, the ABA now had a pulse. That afternoon, the five founding groups signed certificates of incorporation, agreed on the league's address (1811 West Katella Avenue, Anaheim, Calif.), prepared to open an ABA bank account, formed the first league committees, and named Binstein acting president. His top priority: Find more investors, field more teams.

Before departing for the airport, Seredin insisted on rolling out their league ASAP. He chaired the press conference committee and, crossing off the next two weeks for Christmas and the winter holidays, Seredin calculated that they had roughly a month to finish organizing the league and adding teams. Come February, the NBA would have a "divine" competitor.

Detroit, Jan. 16, 1967—But first, the NBA would have another labor dispute to hash out. At issue: The owners alone determined where players earned their paychecks, for how much, and for how long. Player input wasn't welcome.

The dispute involved the Los Angeles Lakers, off to a rotten start this season. Everyone in Laker-land was on edge over the losing, and, making matters worse, owner Jack Kent Cooke had begun to meddle in personnel decisions. Against Coach Fred

Schaus' objections, Cooke had pushed to get rid of his team's popular 29-year-old forward Rudy LaRusso. He thought LaRusso was a brute around the basket. He preferred more grace.

Tonight, with the Lakers in Detroit, many at courtside knew something was up when Schaus inserted the benched LaRusso into the starting lineup. Schaus, the whispers said, was simply following orders. The Lakers and Pistons had worked out a trade for LaRusso. But before all parties agreed on the three-way deal (also involving Baltimore), the Pistons wanted to see LaRusso in extended action to make sure that he'd recovered fully from offseason abdominal surgery.

Detroit gave the thumbs up after the game, and the following afternoon the terms of the trade were finalized: Los Angeles sent LaRusso to Baltimore in exchange for center Mel Counts. Baltimore then traded LaRusso to Detroit for veteran forward Ray Scott.

But LaRusso, an Ivy League grad, was no ordinary NBA player. He worked as a part-time stockbroker and had made a killing investing primarily in pharmaceutical companies. Although he enjoyed playing basketball, LaRusso no longer needed his NBA money to make ends meet and spoke openly about retiring in 1968 to better manage his portfolio. LaRusso also was concerned about his wife, Rosalind. She was seven months pregnant with their first child, and he didn't dare uproot her. She had a history of miscarriages.

With nothing to lose, LaRusso sounded off about the Lakers and what reporter Merv Harris later called "the nightmare season."[13] LaRusso described Jack Kent Cooke as a courtside menace. He said Cooke hurt the team's confidence, and Schaus, nicknamed "Furnace Fred," had become a foot-stomping wreck. LaRusso then told reporters that he'd rather retire than spend the rest of the winter shivering in Detroit. "I have no reason to uproot myself and leave town, especially considering that I like it here," he explained afterwards. "In football, you can at least play out your option. In the NBA, there are no options. You are a slave to the team that owns you. I'm not trying to change the system. All I say is, 'I quit.'"[14]

Within days, Piston general manager Ed Coil declared the deal kaput. But Coil, who had flown to Los Angeles to convince LaRusso to join the Pistons, was perhaps a little too diplomatic with reporters. In an unusual show of support for a disgruntled player, Coil praised LaRusso as a young man of integrity and said, "I respect his views."[15] Although most likely not intended, Coil had validated LaRusso's cause and cast Cooke, Schaus, and the team's general manager Lou Mohs as the villains.

Mohs quickly seconded Coil's sentiments. He lobbied Cooke to rescind the trade and take back LaRusso. Cooke agreed—but under one megalomaniacal condition. LaRusso had to publicly apologize for speaking ill of Cooke. Mohs hastily arranged a press conference, where LaRusso said sorry, tore up his retirement papers, and posed hand in hand with his smiling owner.

"I like his courage in apologizing," Cooke confabulated, anxious to declare victory in defeat. "Of equal importance is the fact that Rudy is now reinstated on the Laker roster ... As far as L.A. is concerned, the deal with Baltimore reverts back to its original status. My action does not set any NBA precedent. It's a personal matter between Rudy and me."[16]

But trades weren't "a personal matter" between owner and player. They were binding league agreements involving two teams, in this case Los Angeles directly with Baltimore. Cooke couldn't unilaterally cancel the trade to keep peace in Los Angeles. He also needed Baltimore's signoff. In their haste to arrange a press conference and put the LaRusso controversy behind them, Mohs and Cooke either forgot or failed to smooth things over with their Baltimore counterparts.

Herb Heft, Bullet co-owner and president, wasn't amused. "Cooke is not going to make a fool of us," announced Heft, apparently referring more to the communal "us," as in the

NBA, than his team. "How in good conscience could [Cooke] take LaRusso back on the team and say, 'Sorry, I traded you' and LaRusso in turn say 'Sorry I said all of those nasty things about you.' All of a sudden, they kiss and make up."[17]

On January 20, Heft filed a formal complaint with the NBA office in New York, and Detroit's Coil followed suit. Commissioner Walter Kennedy hemmed and hawed. "I'm greatly concerned over the matter," Kennedy bluffed. "I don't have unlimited powers, though. In any action I take I have to be guided by the league's constitution. It's an unprecedented action. No policy has been set up to cover the matter."

But the case really wasn't complicated. With retirement now out of the equation, the dispute boiled down to whether LaRusso could assign himself to Los Angeles. On this issue, league policy was abundantly clear. He couldn't. NBA players, like bushels of corn, were considered a commodity. NBA teams were free to purchase, sell, or swap their property on the open market as they pleased. Thus, an NBA player could no more set the terms of his use than could a lump of West Virginia coal.

"What are you gonna do?" quipped Boston Celtics general manager Red Auerbach, summing up the institutional thinking on the LaRusso's mess. "Can you let one player dictate policy to the whole league? Do I have to consult with a player before I trade him?"[18]

"But some of the blame has to be placed with the Lakers' management," LaRusso countered, reframing the issue as a matter of fairness. "If they had told me honestly what they had planned for me, I would have told them that I would retire before being traded, and the deal wouldn't have been made in the first place. I never wanted to be traded as a chattel of a ballclub," he said. "I wanted to start and finish my career as a Laker. And that's what I intend doing."[19]

A few days later, Kennedy suspended LaRusso to appease Heft and Coil. But to avoid a direct and likely losing battle with the contentious Cooke and his accomplished lawyers, Kennedy made the suspension temporary pending a vote of Cooke's fellow owners. Five days later, with Kennedy abstaining to vote, a jury of Cooke's peers ruled that the trade had indeed been consummated, and LaRusso belonged to Detroit. The Pistons promptly suspended LaRusso, and a disgruntled LaRusso threatened to sue the NBA. As the days passed, LaRusso thought better of his threat. He wasn't a labor-union crusader. Moreover, LaRusso had a far more lucrative job awaiting him with the Beverly Hills brokerage house of McDonnell and Company.

And so, with a heavy heart and still very much pulling for his teammates, LaRusso cried uncle. He quit the NBA.

Beverly Hills, Calif., Jan. 17, 1967—Two weeks until the ABA press conference. Mark Binstein, who learned of the ABA not even two months ago, was now its acting president and head of a "big-time" New York franchise. "Get outta here," as they say about a crazy sudden turn of events in his native Teaneck, N.J. God only knows what they'd say back home about the paper in his pocket. It was a contract for $250,000 signed by Wilt Chamberlain, arguably the game's greatest star, committed to play for Binstein.[20] Make that, Arthur Brown, the freight magnate who would soon partner with Binstein in New York and could afford to pay that kind of money.

Whether the contract was real or phony, only the 33-year-old Binstein knew for sure. But he clearly wanted to flash what looked like Chamberlain's signature to build enthusiasm heading into the ABA's next planning session, a three-day slog held again in the classy Beverly Hills Hilton. Binstein, short black hair, skinny tie, with dark rings around his eyes, surveyed the room considering his show-and-tell options. He called over his ABA cohorts, extracted the paper from his pocket like a winning lottery ticket, and mumbled something to the effect, "Take a look at this."

Eyes widened at the astonishing implications. Wilt Chamberlain was coming to the ABA. Binstein passed around the contract briefly, slipped it back into his pocket, and got down to league business. He talked about his progress, nearly wooing the millionaire Brown into the league to anchor New York and introduced Max Zaslofsky, the former NBA great and Brown's proxy for the meeting.

Though Phoenix and Seattle predictably dropped out, a half-dozen other cities were possibilities. In fact, things already had turned heated between Dennis Murphy and Gabe Rubin, the Pittsburgh theater owner who had just purchased a team. Rubin wanted the ABA to take in only so-called "big-league" towns like those in major-league baseball. For Murphy, whether the ABA played in Savannah, Louisville, or on Riker's Island, he didn't care. He needed teams and wealthy backers, wherever they called home.

In the audience observing it all was a handsome young man with sun-bleached blond hair named Gary Davidson. Though Davidson could have passed for a beach volleyball player, he was an up-and-coming Orange County attorney, whose office happened to be across the hall from McShane Associates. One of Murphy's gofers, who worked for McShane, had asked Davidson if he would like to buy into a new pro basketball league? Davidson, smart and ambitious, shrugged why not.

Davidson now sat parsing everybody's words. These guys, he concluded, were novices. They didn't understand the basics of incorporating a sports league. Chamberlain? He was under contract to the Philadelphia 76ers. The NBA's lawyers would eat these guys for breakfast. Davidson eyed the exit sign. But Davidson, a former prep basketball star, couldn't bring himself to leave. He loved the game. He loved the idea of entering pro sports for next to nothing down and, with his legal background and business acumen, reaping the rewards. By the meeting's end, Davidson was "in" and anxious to run this ABA outfit, Chamberlain or no Chamberlain.[21]

New York, Jan. 25, 1967—Eight days before the ABA press conference. The NBA's Old Guard scoffed at the rumored new kid on their block. "The ABA is ridiculous," bridled Boston's Red Auerbach. "Those people are throwing names around, trying to create interest. Who's going to play for them? Where are they going to play?"[22]

The NBA's tough talk went unchallenged, mainly because the league had yet to name a commissioner or an official spokesperson. But today, Mark Binstein, speaking as the league's acting president, tried to set the record straight in a formal newspaper interview, an ABA first. The interview read in part:

Q: How far is the new league from becoming a reality?

Binstein: Except for some minor details, it is a reality now.

Q: When does the league intend to start play?

Binstein: Also still to be settled, but I hope for the 1967-68 season.

Q: Can you tell me a little more about Constantine Seredin of New York and John McShane of Los Angeles, who were supposed to be the originators of the new league?

Binstein: They are both experts in the merchandising of sports and have that background. They'll have the same function in the ABA, merchandising our league.

Q—What about all the talk about Wilt Chamberlain as a player or owner or both in the ABA?

Binstein: No comment.[23]

New York, Jan. 31, 1967—Two days before the ABA press conference. Eight organizers and three prospective owners gathered at a long antique table in the elegant Louis XVI Suite of the St. Regis Hotel. A Waterford crystal chandelier dangled overhead shedding light on nothing but stacks of unfinished business.

The minutes read: "Meeting was called to order at 2:30 p.m. by Mr. Mark Binstein. Connie Seredin announced the presence of Joe Jares, a reporter from *Sports Illustrated*. The league gave him permission to attend all meetings and offer a 'behind the scenes' picture of the league for a special feature article he will write on the ABA."

Gary Davidson, his recently injured arm in a sling, sat next to his best friend and law partner, Don Regan. When Davidson told Regan about the ABA several weeks ago, they envisioned running the league through their law firm to boost their profile and business prospects. Now, they needed to bump the Binsteins and McShanes out of their way. The two spent part of the morning at the New York Public Library researching articles of incorporation. The afternoon minutes read: "Gary Davidson informed the members present that he had taken action to incorporate [the ABA] in the State of Delaware. [East Coast lawyer] David Kaufman did not think it was proper to incorporate without the entire organization knowing about it."

Davidson's take-charge, follow-me style grated on the East Coasters. "What you have to understand is the people on the East and West coasts never were happy partners," recalled Bill Erickson, a lawyer and close friend of George Mikan. "Both sides felt that they had founded the league, which gave them privileges over the other."[24]

While both sides struggled to find common ground in the St. Regis Hotel, Erickson and Mikan flew to New York to join the chaos. Mikan, with some prodding from Binstein and Murphy, said he might consider becoming ABA commissioner. But first, assuming an agreement could be reached, Erickson would negotiate Mikan's ABA contract. One non-negotiable point, per Mikan's orders, Erickson must serve as the league's general counsel, or exactly the position that Davidson envisioned filling to run the ABA's legal matters through his law firm.

McShane recessed the meeting at 4 p.m., announcing that they would reconvene tomorrow at 10 a.m. In the meantime, all were welcome for cocktails at Seredin's Manhattan townhouse. Cheers.

New York, February 1, 1967—One day before the press conference. After morning coffee and too many cocktails last night, the ABA organizers reconvened in the ornate rooftop conference room on the 20th floor of the St. Regis Hotel. The room offered a stunning, though windblown, view of Manhattan and its terraced skyline. Joining everybody for a brief hello was George Mikan, towering over the others like a portable New York skyscraper.

The minutes read: "The meeting was called to order by the Chairman, Mark Binstein, at 10:30 a.m. . . [Anaheim owner] James Ackerman made a report on the $5,000 deposits that had been received [to join the ABA]. Before a full report on the number of checks received was given, a general discussion was held."

The general discussion meandered into a shouting match that dead-ended in Cleveland. "Members were in doubt as to the status of Cleveland since both representatives were absent from this meeting. Mr. Gabe Rubin received a telegram from the Schmelzer brothers, stating that they definitely wanted to be considered franchise holders for Cleveland. Mr. Donald J. Regan objected, stating that he definitely wanted a franchise, was present, and had the $5,000 required as a deposit to secure a franchise. He would like a franchise in the eastern part of the country and would be willing to go into Cleveland with the Schmelzer brothers, if they were interested in getting together. Chairman Binstein stated that before going any further that they would hold a five-minute recess to call the Schmelzer brothers in Cleveland.

"A 10-minute recess was called while Mr. Binstein spoke to Larry Schmelzer in Cleveland. Mr. Binstein returned to the meeting . . . Mr. Schmelzer had stated that his brother was in Washington, D.C. and that every check written required their double signatures, he further stated that he would give his word that the check would be sent that day and would have it in our hands by tomorrow. Mr. Schmelzer further stated they have withdrawn officially from negotiating to buy the [NBA] St. Louis Hawks.

"Dennis Murphy moved to accept the Schmelzer brothers as the franchise holders in the city of Cleveland, under the terms set forth in the general discussion as stated above. Namely, a representative be present at tomorrow's meeting with [a $5,000 deposit]. Motion carried unanimously.

"Mr. Donald Regan returned to the meeting at 2:10 p.m., and informed the members that he is ready to deposit $5,000 with them, requesting the 11th franchise subject to his group and the league finding a mutually suitable location."

Then, as Regan recalls, fists started flying. The wicked right cross belonged to the little guy from Pittsburgh, Gabe Rubin. "He was about big enough to fit into your watch pocket," said Regan, "and he got into a fight with one of the potential owners who didn't like what he said or how he said it. It was literally like a meeting of the Egyptian Parliament, where the guys are punching each other out."[25]

Order was restored, and the meeting moved ahead to some big news. "Mr. James Ware [chairman of the Commissioner's Committee] stated that George Mikan would like to have $65,000 per year, oscillating $5,000 per year for four years with a guarantee of five years, non-cancellable contract with ABA. Committee members thought that $65,000 per year was too high, possibly $50,000 would be more in line, and with a possible bonus arrangement over $50,000 with three-year contract with the league. The bonus would be based on the profitability of the league. Mr. Ware stated that Mr. Mikan would not divest himself of his interests in his travel agency, etc., but would dedicate himself to the job on a full-time, 12-

months of the year basis. He would like to maintain his residence in Minneapolis and would prefer to have the league office located in Minneapolis.

"Dennis Murphy moved that we accept the recommendation of the Committee Chairman and have the committee ask Mr. George Mikan to become Commissioner at the Committee's suggested requirements, having Mr. Kaufman present as legal advisor. Motion seconded and carried . . .

"Recess was called to allow the Commissioner's Committee to speak with Mr. Mikan. The meeting reconvened at 5 p.m. There was no definitive word on Mr. Mikan's acceptance, but he will give his answer tomorrow."

New York, February 2, 1967—Hours before the press conference. More coffee, more vows to quit drinking alcohol, more chaos. The meeting was called to order at 10 a.m. by Mark Binstein and with no sign of the Schmelzer brothers. Cleveland was out. A roll call of the franchises was ordered: Anaheim, Dallas, Houston (absent), Kansas City, Minneapolis, New Orleans, New York, Oakland, Pittsburgh, and Don Regan. It's important to note that some cities, like Dallas, Houston, and Minneapolis, were wishes, not teams. They had no serious financial backing. In fact, one of Dennis Murphy's gofers was penciled in for Dallas.

The mood quickly turned dark. "Connie Seredin, carefully watching over each business session, read a proposed publicity release for the owners' approval, and it listed himself and McShane as the ABA's 'founders and organizers,'" wrote Joe Jares, still tagging along for *Sports Illustrated*. "The owners said no. Then Seredin suggested an 'assisted by Constantine Seredin and John McShane' phrase, but the owners killed that, too."[26] Both looked surprised, saddened even. Seredin and McShane were being written out of the league that they'd created.

The meeting moved on to nominating a league president. That brought more bickering, and Gary Davidson blew his stack. "We are in competition with the NBA, not with each other," he snapped, threatening to walk out on the ABA for good. Murphy grabbed Davidson's good arm and pleaded with him to stay. A few minutes later, Murphy had lined up the needed votes for Davidson to be elected ABA president.

Then the tension in the air turned to momentary glee. "Jim Ware returned from taking a phone call and announced that George Mikan had accepted the position of Commissioner of the American Basketball Association."

Now came the hard part. Erickson arrived with Mikan in tow to negotiate the terms of his contract. Erickson repeated Mikan's demands, one by one, and the members of the negotiating committee stalled for more time. "Take it or leave it," Erickson shrugged, gathering his papers and exiting the room with Mikan.

A few minutes later, Mikan and Erickson were seen glancing toward the nearest elevator. They would grab their suitcases at the hotel, catch a cab to the airport, and forget their silly trip to New York. But somewhere between pressing the elevator button and descending to the lobby, Mikan was buttonholed one last frantic time to take the job. Please! The news conference was minutes away.

There was no mistaking Bemelmans Bar in the lobby of Manhattan's five-star Hotel Carlyle. The walls are a whimsical mural wonderland of pink rabbits, swinging brass bands, and doe-eyed children all at play in New York's Central Park. It's Monet meets Curious George. A venue where fantasy softens reality and, two tall cocktails later, all seems possible.

The possible now preyed on the minds of many seated in the bar. They had just attended a press conference across the lobby in the hotel's Versailles Room to announce the latest wide-eyed, go-for-broke attempt to cash in on American professional sports. It was called the American Basketball Association, and those now clinking glasses in Bemelmans wondered whether a second American pro basketball league could turn a profit in a few years? Or were these ABA boys chasing another fool's errand?

Only time—and millions of dollars—would tell. If the press conference was any indication, the ABA would be one heck of a wild ride. The Versailles Room had been transformed into an impromptu Playboy Club. Young busty, big-haired women in hot pants pranced around the hall to greet the attendees with a giggle, distribute mixed drinks, and hand out press materials. Copy editors clearly were in short supply. The fourth paragraph of the official league press release mentioned the 10-team league might expand soon. In the following paragraph, the ABA listed just nine member teams.

Both statements ironically might have been factually correct. ABA teams were still more conceptual than real, and the proof sat at a long table near the podium, where each prospective owner had settled into his designated seat behind a white table card that named the city of his new franchise. There was Anaheim, Pittsburgh, Indianapolis, Minneapolis, New Orleans, Houston, Dallas, Kansas City, New York, Oakland— and Don Regan seated without any explanation behind a table card bearing a large question mark.

Shortly after 4:00 p.m., Gary Davidson stepped to the podium, his left arm still wrapped in a sling to start the session. Directly behind Davidson, the left side of a large white banner bearing the words AMERICAN BASKETBALL ASSOCIATION flapped lazily against the wall. The roughly 50 reporters in attendance glanced at each other, the guy with his arm in a sling, the bouncy babes still making the rounds, and the red, white, and blue basketballs that had been handed to them as souvenirs (yes, the famous ABA basketball was Seredin's idea). Were these ABA guys off their rockers?

Davidson introduced each team, and the reporters followed up with questions. Regan answered most of them, leaving reporters to wonder how a man behind a question mark had all the answers.

"George Mikan will be the commissioner of our league," said Davidson, who had a bad habit of talking fast and slurring his words.

"What are the terms of his contract?" asked a reporter.

"He'll be the highest paid commissioner," Davidson slurred.

"In all of sports?" followed up the reporter.

The all-knowing question mark replied, "In all of professional sports."

As Davidson slurred, all 6-foot-10 inches of George Mikan lurked in the shadows of the Versailles Room listening with disgust to Davidson butcher his way through the news conference. The ABA had caved to his contract demands, and Mikan had accepted his new title of commissioner moments ago. "This is all a bunch of crap," the Commissioner reportedly grumbled. "I'm gonna get up there and run this show."

Mikan, wearing his signature horn-rimmed glasses and a dark business suit with a plain white tie, reached the podium like a U. S. senator smiling to his constituents. "I've been in basketball all my life, and I'm sure this league will go," said the 42-year-old Mikan, breathing his credibility into the league with his every word and giving it life. He then told a calculated fib, "The men backing the ABA financially are men of considerable means. That's why I took the job."

The reporters scribbled down his words.

Mikan continued, "We don't plan to raid the National Basketball Association for players, but let's put it this way: I'll invite any player to join us if he is not under contractual obligations and if there will be no ramifications. We expect to compete with the NBA. It will be like General Motors competing with the Ford Motor Company. It's this kind of competition."

"Our intention is certainly not to get into any fights with the NBA. But we will strive to sign the college stars and, although we will not raid the NBA for its players, we certainly will invite them to come talk to us. I call that fair competition. And if you are expecting anything like the football [NFL-AFL] men, well, I'll tell you I wouldn't mind being 20- or 21-years old right now."

Mikan said he now planned to create a lively brand of pro basketball. The ABA would wow fans with a red, white, and blue basketball, feature a then carnival-like three-point shot to keep more six-foot, jump-shooting regular guys on the floor, and promote a wide-open game to allow the best athletes to wow crowds with their flashy moves. Pity the NBA. The ABA would now redefine pro basketball on its own terms.

Back at Bemelmans, Mikan's comments at the press conference hung in the air. To the left of the bar and its row of 120-proof colored glass bottles, a pink rabbit clutched an orange umbrella in one hand and an egg-filled picnic basket in the other. Nearby, an aristocratic cartoon dog, elephant, and rabbit gathered under a striped umbrella to sip champagne like gilded Central Park gentry.

Yes, all things were possible in this world. Ludwig Bemelmans, the artist who painted these Alice in Wonderland-like figures on the wall and who was better known as the creator of the Madeline children's book series, reportedly once told a friend that his epitaph should read, "Tell Them It Was Fun."

If George Mikan had his way, the same epitaph would greet the American Basketball Association in about four years when it merged with the NBA and brought needed innovation to his former league.

Endnotes

[1] Dave Anderson, "Sports of the Times." *New York Times*, July 1968.

[2] Steve Arnold, Interview with author, December 2011.

[3] Barry Murtha, Interview with author, April 2013.

[4] Murphy said he got the idea of starting a pro league while watching an NBA game on television in 1963.

[5] Dennis Murphy, *Murph*, 2002, p. 31.

[6] Murphy reportedly offered the league's L.A franchise to Klein and Schulman. Later, the Seattle franchise was offered to Schulman.

[7] Dan Hafner, "New Pro Cage League Plans Include L.A.," *Los Angeles Times*, November 15, 1966.

[8] Van Barbieri, "Van Fare," *San Pedro News-Pilot*, November 21, 1966.

[9] Don Regan, Interview with author, October 2020.

[10] Jim O'Brien, Looking Up Once Again, 2020, p. 82.

[11] Today, the down payment would come to about $9,600.

[12] Kim got wealthy providing the sham opposing team for the Harlem Globetrotters, starting with his Honolulu Surfriders in 1946.

[13] Merv Harris, *The Fabulous Lakers*, 1972, p. 97.

[14] Melvin Durslag, "The Ivy Way to Retire," *Los Angeles Herald-Examiner*, January 19, 1967.

[15] Merv Harris, "Detroit Gives Up on Rudy," *Los Angeles Herald-Examiner*, January 20, 1967.

[16] Merv Harris, "Lakers Take LaRusso Back," *Los Angeles Herald-Examiner*, January 20, 1967.

[17] Alan Goldstein, "LaRusso Suspended Again . . ." *Baltimore Sun*, January 22, 1967.

[18] Bob Sales, "Unborn Child Plays Part in Shaping LaRusso Future," *Boston Globe*, January 23, 1967.

[19] Alan Goldstein, "LaRusso Quits," *Baltimore Sun*, January 18, 1967.

[20] Merv Harris, "Rival for The NBA Due," *Los Angeles Herald-Examiner*, January 18, 1967.

[21] Regan, Interview with author, October 2020. Also distilled from Gary Davidson, *Breaking the Game Wide Open*, 1974.

[22] Will McDonough, "Auerbach Raps Russell's Press Critics," *Boston Globe*, January 24, 1967.

[23] Irving Marsh, "New Basketball League is a Reality," *New York World Journal Tribune*, January 26, 1967.

[24] Bill Erickson, Interview with author, June 2009.

[25] Regan, Interview with author, October 2020.

[26] Joe Jares, "Labor Pains of a New League,"*Sports Illustrated*, February 13, 1967.

3

While the ABA gestated in the early fall of 1966, the NBA prepared for its 18th season. It coincided with the arrival in the nation's bookstores of Red Auerbach's 370-page autobiography *Winning the Hard Way*. It was a chance for Boston's iconic coach-turned-full-time general manager to unload on how he overcame rotten officials, huffy sportswriters, conniving league presidents, unruly spectators, and, above all, Wilt Chamberlain to pilot his Celtics to nine of the last 10 NBA titles.

It was the Chamberlain part that mostly grabbed the court of public opinion. Journalists kept publishing their own 700-word ink blot tests that imagined whether they saw Chamberlain as mightier than Boston's Bill Russell. Or vice versa. And now with *Winning the Hard Way* in bookstores, no less an expert than Auerbach crowned Russell as the greatest of all-time "because he's a winner and a better guy to have around over the whole stretch—and in the big [game]—than a Chamberlain."[1]

Auerbach, in truth, never saw a potshot that he didn't like taking against Chamberlain. Part of it was psychological. He wanted to get into Chamberlain's head. He wanted Chamberlain to believe that the Celtics were unbeatable in a seven-game series. The other part was self-promotional: his Celtic Way was greater than the way of Chamberlain and his brute force around the basket.

But time passes slowly between final manuscript and a book's eventual release, and current events can take a provocative turn in the meantime from the norm. While

Auerbach shilled his book, Chamberlain's Philadelphia 76ers conquered the NBA. New coach Alex Hannum had shuffled the Philadelphia offense, placing Chamberlain and his brute force near the foul line on offense. The man who once scored 100 points in one game was recast as Hannum's innovative, pass-first "point center." "You know what happens if Wilt gets the ball—he merely holds it way up there, so no one except an astronaut could touch it, and waits until one of his mates has an opening to the basket," noted NBA coach Red Kerr. "Then he passes it."[2]

The passes whizzed into the able hands of Hal Greer, Chet Walker, Billy Cunningham, and all the other former errand boys-turned-scrappy scorers. The new-and-improved Sixers won 20 of their first 22 games, including a 42-point dismantling of the Celtic Way.

By February, the Sixers (47-6) were on pace to smash the NBA mark for most wins in a regular season and, barring a rash of late-season injuries, a sure bet to win the NBA title. The anticipated changing of the NBA guard from Celtic green to the red, white, and blue of the Sixers would be sweet vindication for Chamberlain. The Celtic monkey would finally be off his massive back, and his legions of critics, who spent way too much time cussing and discussing his perceived shortcomings, could all go to hell.

And yet, as settled as things were for once on the court, Chamberlain remained restless off it. Though a Philadelphia native, Wilt and his restless heart now resided in New York, where he owned a popular Harlem nightclub and could escape all the expectations swirling around him in Philly. According to Jack Chevalier, who covered the Sixers for the *Philadelphia Inquirer*, part of Hannum's genius was treating Chamberlain "like a man," letting him cavort off the court as long as he locked in on it. "Wilt would finish showering after a game in Philadelphia and his driver would always be waiting outside at around 11 o'clock to run him up to Harlem," said Chevalier.

"By 12:30, he'd be in his club partying. He'd wake up the next morning, and his driver would haul him back to Philadelphia for practice."[3]

Though Wilt enjoyed playing with his teammates, he loathed the front-office guys. Wilt swore that he had a handshake agreement with his trusted friend Ike Richman, the lawyer and former co-owner of the Sixers who ran the team until his sudden death in December 1965. That handshake agreement entitled Chamberlain to a 25 percent ownership stake in the Sixers and a cut of some racing horses in his retirement. Irv Kosloff, Richman's silent partner and a wealthy industrialist who now ran the show, told Chamberlain that he was sorely mistaken. Deluded even. With no written agreement (NBA rules prohibited players from owning teams, meaning a signed agreement could get everyone in trouble), Wilt turned testy, at times volatile, and could barely be in the same room with Kosloff, better known as "Koz." For Chamberlain, as great as this season was going, how could he play for a liar and a cheat who, in his mind, owed him about a million bucks?

His Sixers' contract was technically up at the end of the season, but Chamberlain couldn't just enter the free-agent portal and be done with Koz. There was no free agency in the NBA. Koz literally owned the rights to his basketball career, and no other NBA owner would dare buck this so-called reserve system, a pillar of the NBA and professional sports.

His only leverage and possible way out of the reserve was the ABA start-up. But Chamberlain walked a fine line between a soft threat to join the ABA and a public rush to judgment to vilify him for it. Nearly everywhere he went, Chamberlain had to fend off the same nagging question: Have you signed with the ABA? The more he denied it, the more people seemed to think he was hiding something. Chamberlain finally issued a full-throated public denial in the high-circulation *Philadelphia Daily News*, "I definitely have signed no contract with a new league," he told its ace sportswriter Jack Kiser. "If somebody is showing any contract around, it certainly doesn't have my true signature on it."[4]

Kiser and Chamberlain were on good terms, sharing a moderate addiction to betting on the ponies that ran daily at Philadelphia's Liberty Bell Park. That made them equally comfortable shooting the breeze about the top jockeys and the worst NBA referees. Their bond, more a symbiotic relationship, had Wilt opening up about his latest grievances. Kiser, known as "Jack the Ripper" for his poison pen, would then come to Chamberlain's aid to savage his enemies or, in this case, to bloody the latest ABA rumor.

Jack the Ripper's may have slashed the ABA rumors, but he didn't know his friend Wilt as well as he imagined. For within days, Kiser would do an about face in Pittsburgh that might have surprised even Scotland Yard.

Pittsburgh, Feb. 7, 1967—The Philadelphia 76ers were in town on this bitterly cold afternoon for tonight's NBA nightcap against the San Francisco Warriors. Though the 76ers had recently weathered a three-game road skid, they remained the team to beat in the NBA.

Lucky for the 76ers that they had arrived in Pittsburgh the night before. A blizzard now blanketed most of the Mid-Atlantic, shutting down airports and cancelling trains. Though the players were grateful not to be stuck right now on the turnpike somewhere outside of Allentown, climbing the walls of the swishy Penn-Sheraton Hotel wasn't any fun either. Several 76ers rode the elevator down to the lobby to beat the boredom, but Wilt Chamberlain wouldn't be joining them. The "Big Fella" remained cloistered upstairs, where he was expecting guests . . . ABA guests.

Chamberlain reportedly told his ABA guests that he would be "free" that afternoon. It's also unlikely that Chamberlain blabbed to his teammates about his afternoon tryst. It is likely, however, that Wilt whispered something to Jack the Ripper. How else to explain his lurking upstairs.

For Jack Kiser, catching Wilt talking to the ABA wasn't news. It was gossip, and he'd already crushed the speculation once. "There is much more mouth than money behind the entire [ABA] operation," wrote Kiser, "and if you think Wilt Chamberlain is going to be roped into a situation like that than you don't know Wilt Chamberlain."[5] Kiser also had nothing to gain. Standing watch on the league MVP without his informed consent was a lousy career move. Kiser needed Chamberlain as a source, not an enemy, during the 76ers' record-breaking season, this winter's lead sports story in Philadelphia. Being labeled a rat by the other players also wouldn't be pleasant. Kiser, like all beat reporters, traveled with the team.

And so, it was odd that the 38-year-old native Tennessean with the large ears, bony physique, and otherwise nondescript appearance, would risk it all to linger like housekeeping staff near the elevator on Chamberlain's floor. But there he was, likely at Chamberlain's urging. Kiser heard the elevator ding and observed three well-dressed white men tap on the door for room 1417 then scoot inside. Afterwards, Chamberlain handed Kiser the names of his visitors and their latest offer to jump to the ABA: a $50,000 annual salary, a $250,000 annuities package, and, importantly, a 30 percent ownership stake in the league's proposed New York franchise.

Philadelphia, Feb. 8, 1967—Today's edition of the *Philadelphia Daily News* was hot off the presses around lunchtime. Featured prominently at the top of the sports section was Kiser's exclusive. The lead paragraph read, "The rumors finally have become a reality. Whispers about Wilt Chamberlain receiving big offers to jump to the proposed American Basketball Association finally have taken a firm voice."

According to Kiser, those voices "involved ex-NBA star Max Zazlofsky, former West Point performer Mark Binstein, and an unidentified gentleman who looked very much like Art Brown, president of ABC Freightways Forwarding Company who is also president of the [ABA's] proposed New York club." He said Chamberlain agonized for 16 hours over the ABA offer, "then rejected it for the present time, but left the door open for further negotiations." As Chamberlain stated, seemingly speaking directly to Koz, "I will make some sort of announcement after the season is completed."

Jack the Ripper's scoop spread across Philadelphia, and the other NBA beat reporters spent the afternoon appeasing their editors and called Art Brown in New York for a follow-up comment. Brown scoffed. "We were interested in knowing his reaction. If he accepted, we wouldn't do anything about it anyway because he's under contract to the 76ers at the present time."[6]

Brown might not have wanted to do anything about it for another reason: The ABA still technically didn't exist. Its incorporation papers in Delaware and New York were being processed, and its bylaws were under internal review. More important, the ABA had yet to find wealthy investors for all 12 proposed franchises. For every mega-millionaire like Brown in New York and a moderately wealthy investor like Art Kim in Anaheim, there was a regular guy who flew coach and sent his kids to public school.

Matter of fact, the league's top priority after the New York press conference was to find a few more mega-millionaires. This make-or-break recruitment fell primarily to four good men: Dennis Murphy, who wouldn't relax until he had 12 viable owners; Mark Binstein, who had recruited Brown and was now working with investors in Indianapolis to shore up the ABA's 10th franchise; league president Gary Davidson, financially challenged and heading the Dallas franchise; and the financially challenged and presumed league counsel Don

Regan, anxious to secure the ABA's 11th franchise, which remained a question mark.

According to Regan, he and his buddy Davidson traveled to select cities alone or in tandem as smart, well-coifed salesmen. Sticking closely to Dennis Murphy's playbook, they would contact the local sports editor and reveal the ABA's interest in placing a franchise in their city. Once the story broke and the new pro team became the talk-of-the-town, Davidson and Regan started shaking hands and taking down names of prominent citizens who might be willing to invest in the ABA.

Regan said, "We'd say, 'Hey look, you want to get an expansion franchise in the NBA for $5 million. If you got one, you'll start with a bunch of NBA castoffs and it will be five years before you can build up the franchise and have a winning season to connect with your fanbase. In the meantime, you've lost all of this money and public support. What we'll do is go in and form a league and sign players against the NBA so you can win immediately. It will require the same $5 million over three years. But, at that time, we'll force a merger with the NBA."

In Dallas, Regan, Davidson, and a friend met with a prominent sports editor, waited for the news to break of the soon-to-be ABA team. Then they met with a staffer in the mayor's office named Bobby. The threesome said they needed 25 people to invest $10,000 each in the Dallas franchise, an arrangement that would allow Davidson and his limited finances to keep a small cut of the now $250,000 purchase price and remain league president. Bobby, a former point guard at SMU and warm to their pitch, advised, "To make it fly in Dallas, you've got to get Jimmy Ling."

Ling was the influential, Mark Cuban-like businessman and head of the conglomerate Ling-Temco-Vought. Regan gave him his spiel, and Ling agreed to kick in $10,000 for what would become the Dallas Chaparrals (today, San Antonio Spurs) with one stipulation: he would "carry interest."

"What's carried interest?" asked Regan.

"I am key to putting together this deal," answered Ling. "When you have another capital call, which you're going to have, then my interest in the franchise stays the same. I'm carried throughout the franchise. That's what I get for putting up my name."

Regan moved on to Louisville, where he met with the sports editor and made the acquaintance of a few small investors. Several newspaper articles appeared, and one caught the eye of Joe Gregory lounging on a yacht in the Bahamas. He showed his wife Mamie, an heiress worth an estimated $40 million, and they giggled about owning a pro basketball team in Louisville, Joe's hometown. Joe's follow-up phone call led to formal meetings, which led to Regan drawing up an ownership contract. It listed Joe and Mamie as holding the majority interest along with several smaller investors. Included among them was Regan, who kept a 5-percent cut of the team with carried interest. "None of them knew enough to ask what carried interest was," Regan laughed.[7]

With more substantive owners coming onboard in Louisville, Dallas, and other cities to join the high-profile George Mikan's ABA, the PR guys who created the league suddenly faded into the background. So would Regan and Davidson, the bright legal minds who incorporated the ABA. All had become expendable, and the first jettisoning of the ABA's founding fathers would come at the league's next organizing meeting, a three-day bender in New Orleans.

New Orleans, March 3, 1967—"Meeting was called to order at 2:25 p.m. by President Gary Davidson," the league secretary scribbled into his notebook. "Commissioner Mikan then welcomed the represented cities," which included newbies Indianapolis and Louisville, though the latter still had to be approved by the Board of Trustees as the ABA's 11th franchise.

About 20 minutes later, Davidson veered into a general discussion of performance bonds, the security checks that owners were required to submit to cover their expenses for the season. It was a tired and sore subject unresolved from past meetings, and the bickering was immediate. New York's Arthur Brown, possibly the wealthiest person in the room, belted out this double-dog dare, "We'll each put up a $50,000 performance bond, and then we'll go ahead with this venture."

"Motion 1 was made that $50,000 performance bond be in the Commissioner's hand of each franchise no later than April 1, 1967," the league secretary recorded. Brown, ironically, was the lone dissenter. He'd wanted the performance bonds submitted on the spot, not a month later. But the others agreed with Brown's broader assessment. It was time to put up or shut up.

Among those shutting up was John McShane. He made a final pitch for his own franchise in Honolulu, one of five cities vying for the ABA's 12th and final team. Cleveland got the nod (temporarily), and McShane got the boot (permanently).

Things also didn't go too divinely for Connie Seredin. In New Orleans, the owners decided they didn't want to be on the hook to his Professional Sports Management (PSM) for a hefty fee. He got the boot. Seredin moved on to chase two new divine concepts. One was the American Indoor Soccer League ("it's hockey without ice."), and the other was the International Professional Golf League, ("golf as a team sport"). Both went nowhere.

Dennis Murphy also lost his hold on the league. For months, Murphy had labored under the assumption that he and the wealthier top executives at his Orange County engineering firm would own the Kansas City franchise. His deal to play in the Kansas City arena fell through, and the franchise relocated to Denver. When his engineering partners discovered their side hustle might lose at least $250,000 in its first season, they bailed on Murphy. "Dennis took care of everybody but himself," said Don Regan, referring to Murphy's months-long quest to line up 12 wealthy ownership groups at any cost, including his own financial interests.[8] Murphy quickly slid down the ABA's organizational chart to publicity director in Denver.

With the PR guys out and the millionaires in, Brown and his wealthy new friends swept through a mumble of motions, approving Mikan's salary and okaying Louisville. Most interesting was the hold-your-horses motion "that the ABA not approach contracted NBA players." It passed unanimously, though eliciting several nervous chuckles. Most of those raising their hands "aye" had already followed New York's example with Wilt Chamberlain and were whispering sweet somethings to several NBA stars.

None had signed, leaving the ABA to contemplate rosters of mostly no-names and forgotten stars tainted by college gambling scandals. But, like Chamberlain, NBA players weren't fleeing down the fire escape either to avoid the ABA. "These people come to you, and they talk money-talk," said a nameless San Francisco player. "So, you got to listen."[9]

Cincinnati, March 12, 1967—Oscar Robertson, the NBA's triple-double machine in Cincinnati, was among those considering the ABA's sweet somethings. Just on principle, not from a strong desire. For now, Robertson was too preoccupied with fixing the NBA. The Rudy LaRusso mess, Chamberlain's unhappy situation in Philly, and another headline-grabber to come. Robertson, in his role as president of the NBA Players Association (NBAPA), was quietly rallying his union brothers for an unprecedented postseason strike. Their rallying cry: No pension, no playoffs.

The players already had a pension plan, secured three years earlier when the players threatened to sit out the 1964 All-Star Game. The late-breaking boycott caught the owners off guard and, with network television cameras waiting to broadcast the game to the nation in primetime, forced them to agree to the first player pension plan. It required that the owners and the players split the cost of purchasing an annual $1,000 insurance annuity that would double in value over time. Going forward, any player who retired after 10 NBA seasons would collect a $200 monthly pension (about $1,900 today), starting at age 65.

But the pension was prospective, not retroactive. The owners wouldn't credit players for their full body of pre-pension NBA work, and that irked Robertson. If he blew out his knee tomorrow, his pension would be $75 a month for three, not his full seven, seasons. That's why Robertson and the NBAPA pushed for a retroactive deal that covered all seasons, past and present. The union also insisted that the owners fund the full pension, not split the cost with players, and that meant bumping up their contributions to more than $2,000 per player annually. Based on this dollar figure, a retired 10-year veteran would receive a $600 monthly check at age 65, then more than enough to keep the refrigerator stocked.

The NBAPA had sent its pension request to the owners last June as part of a longer list, including health insurance and, for the first time, dropping the reserve clause that bound each player to the NBA team owning his rights without any hope of free agency. So far, the union had gotten nowhere working its way down its list of grievances, mainly because Commissioner Walter Kennedy and his owners had become so adept at dodging meetings and stalling the NBAPA with process. "All they do is negotiate," complained Boston's John Havlicek about the owners. "They never come up with anything concrete."[10]

Doing most of the proposing was the NBAPA's lead attorney Larry Fleisher, the architect of the 1964 All-Star Game boycott. The owners, having been burned once by Fleisher, now grudgingly returned his phone calls and sometimes even met with him. The thinking seemed to be it was easier to control Fleisher by tying him up in negotiations as tedious as a Mideast peace process than letting him take the offensive and terrorize their interests.

The NBA's administrative stall tactics weren't lost on Fleisher. He was on the phone constantly with Robertson, updating him on the latest hurry-up-and-waits and drawing comparisons to the slightly more-advanced labor policies in the National Football League. There, the owners had eased their restrictive career-long reserve on players to a mandatory option year that kicked in once a contract was completed. The extra season in limbo allowed teams, in theory, to evaluate an athlete "playing out his option" and whether to resign or let him go.

The NFL also paid for player pensions by tapping into the millions that the NFL banked each year from its network television contract. Why couldn't the NBA do the same? True, the NBA's annual network take came to just $650,000. But assuming the players and owners were business partners, as Bob Cousy had proposed in the 1950s, the television money amounted to a community chest available to all to make fixes, retroactive or prospective, for the betterment of the league.

The hard part, of course, was convincing the owners, whose counterargument boiled down to a familiar not-so-fast. Each owner would need to invest between $32,000 and $60,000 in the first year to upgrade the existing pension plans and then set aside $16,000 each year thereafter to remain current. "We have not remotely reached the stage of TV receipts by football and baseball," Walter Kennedy said. "Therefore, we cannot institute such a pension plan."[11]

Fleisher wasn't buying it. League attendance was up by double digits, and the owners were moving forward with unprecedented expansion. The NBA, just nine teams strong two years ago, planned to jump to 18 teams by 1970, in part, to claim the best remaining American cities before the ABA got them. Nine NBA newbies would fill league coffers with millions in expansion fees. All of the above and the television money would be more than enough to cover an improved, retroactive pension plan.

Last January, while Fleisher, Robertson, and his fellow NBAPA player reps lamented the owners' discussed runaround tactics, the word "strike" had entered the conversation. No pension, no playoffs. When the player reps reassembled at the end of February for another status report, Fleisher relayed what he termed the owners' "final" offer. They would pay $1,500 per year into each player's pension plan. However, all players must cover the remaining $500 per year to meet their requested $2,000 annual contribution, and the new-and-improved pension would not be retroactive. A loud grumble commenced, followed by an angry show of hands and the scribbling of the following telegram to Kennedy under Robertson's signature at 2:50 p.m., "Player association at a meeting today voted unanimously to turn down proposals of board of governors in reply to our request."

The NBAPA had dismissed other unsatisfactory proposals from the Board of Governors. But the union had mostly kept its collective mouth shut afterwards. Not this time. After sending forth the 21-word telegram, the contingent gathered at Mama Leone's Ristorante, where the NBA often held press briefings. In an angry break with league protocol, Fleisher stepped to the microphone, flanked by all 10 player reps in a show of solidarity. "First, we are immediately filing with the National Labor Relations Board to be the first player union to be certified," Fleisher promised. "Second, we will not participate in any playoff games this year."

If Mama Leone were still alive, she might have swooned. The NBAPA, as mentioned, had already rebelled once before the 1964 All-Star Game. But that was a mere exhibition game, a two-hour blip of solidarity in the middle of a long season. What made this strike sound so 1960s radical is American professional athletes had never walked off the job, playoffs be damned.

When informed of the player rebellion at Mama Leone's, Kennedy pleaded a familiar not-so-fast and warned that "the owners feel strongly about negotiating with a gun to their head." Drop the strike threat, and they'd talk. The players refused, and Kennedy called an emergency Board of Governors meeting in Chicago. There, the owners per usual cursed Fleisher and accused Robertson of grandstanding. Detroit owner Fred Zollner, chair of the board's four-man pension committee and no friend of unions, said he hadn't spoken to Fleisher for more than a week and had no intention of engaging him. Zollner encouraged his fellow owners to stand strong. If they stalled and Kennedy worked the phones to spin the dispute publicly in management's favor, the union would lose faith in no time and surrender.

The owners of the NBA's 10 teams chose to stand united. At their instruction, Kennedy sent his own now-hear-this telegram to the 118 NBA players. Though politely worded, his missive forcefully put all on notice that striking violated their contracts and walking off the job prematurely would be grounds for termination and legal action. Kennedy gave them six days, or until noon, March 15, to come to their senses. No resolution, and Kennedy vowed that he, not the players, would cancel the playoffs.

There was, however, one influential dissenting vote from Los Angles owner Jack Kent Cooke. He was the leading voice of the so-called "millionaire owner" wing. They were a new breed of sports entrepreneur that lived off of several income streams and viewed their basketball teams as potentially lucrative investments, not a one-night show to "make the nut" as the arena owners called paying their overhead. Whereas the arena owners stuck to whatever worked in the past, Cooke and his fellow millionaires wanted to try something different and built for the future.

Cooke considered the aging, staunchly anti-union Zollner to be the wrong man to solve labor issues. As was his style,

Cooke took matters into his own hands and summoned Tommy Hawkins, the Lakers' NBAPA player rep. "Jack said, 'Tommy, my boy, this whole matter is ridiculous,'" recalled Hawkins. "He said, referring to the owners, 'We're all business people who have a financial stake in the league, and we're going to turn around and destroy everything to prove a point? It makes no sense.'

"Jack said, 'You're in touch with Larry Fleisher, and you're in touch with me. I'll give you a message for Larry, and he'll give you a reply. I'll take the reply to the pension committee [namely, Zollner], and we'll go back and forth. Let's see what we can do with this format.' So, that's what we did."[12]

Fleisher already had his hands full with his mostly lukewarm union membership. For many, a union card meant shelling out their annual dues and attending a team meeting after practice once or twice a season, usually when Fleisher blew into town from New York. They left it to Fleisher to work out the administrative issues and advise them accordingly. They were just too busy playing basketball to worry about contracts and pensions.

In fact, most of the 118 union members were way behind on their union dues. If these half-hearted union members bailed en masse on the strike to avoid losing salary, sleep, and a record $280,000 playoff pool.[13] it would break the union and set back Fleisher and his pro-labor agenda at least a decade. It was a risk that he felt deep in the marrow of his bones.

"One of my father's basic tenets was a player strike wouldn't work in pro basketball," explained Fleisher's eldest son Marc. "He told me that many times. My father thought the NBA players lacked the history and the all-for-one mindset of baseball players to hang together over the long-term to achieve their objectives.

"But my father also said if you're going to strike, do it at a critical time. He felt that critical time hovered around television. My father always felt that television gave him leverage to negotiate with the owners."[14]

And now, Fleisher was about to own a protest chant: No pension, no playoffs—along with a nod and wink to the owners that said no postseason television and its cash inducements. All Fleisher could hope is the owners, 10 stuffed suits strong, wouldn't wink back in a few weeks to celebrate their busting of the players union into 118 embittered pieces.

El Segundo, Calif., March 13, 1967—Rudy LaRusso had sat in his house two months ago feeling the weight of the NBA world on his shoulders. Tonight, at a belated testimonial dinner on his behalf at the Hacienda Hotel in El Segundo, LaRusso finally would get to tell his side of the story to about 400 of his teammates, fans, and friends. To no one's surprise, the Laker management stayed home to remain on good terms with Jack Kent Cooke.

"I wanted the opportunity to say goodbye to all my friends," began LaRusso, wearing a black formal suit. At the word "friends," tears dribbled down his cheeks.

LaRusso, fighting to maintain his composure, recounted the intense pressure that the management of the Lakers and Pistons had placed on him to honor the trade. His voice hardened, "Fred Schaus was telling me, 'You owe it to basketball to report to Detroit. We'll be short a man, you'll hurt the game.'"

LaRusso rebutted Schaus as honestly as he could. "Basketball, to me, is the kid playing in the schoolyard someplace, it's not Jack Kent Cooke's balance sheet," he continued. "If going to Detroit would have meant that some kid someplace could experience what I have experienced in basketball, I'd have walked to Detroit—believe me.

"I feel so fortunate I could have so many friends here. I wish every ballplayer could have the experience of knowing he's done something people have enjoyed," he said. "I hope in my future life I will continue to gain your respect, perhaps your admiration, I hope in the end result, I'm worthy of my maker."[15]

LaRusso wept back to his seat beside his wife Rosalind. All in attendance rose at once and gave old number 35 one last standing ovation. Among them was emcee Dick Enberg, Jerry West, Elgin Baylor, and Tommy Hawkins.

While LaRusso received his huzzahs on this sleepy Monday night, West, Baylor, Hawkins, and their fellow NBA players were about 40 hours from the owners' deadline. If an agreement couldn't be reached before then, the season would be over. The players would walk out on their teams and the playoffs.

New York, March 14, 1967—As night descended over the Manhattan skyline, management's deadline for the NBA players reached 18 hours or else. Commissioner Walter Kennedy trudged over to the Roosevelt Hotel, where he'd spend the night just in case his services were needed. But he wasn't holding his breath. Fred Zollner, Mr. Pension, remained eerily silent, and with no communication, Kennedy had nothing to offer Larry Fleisher over the phone but chit-chat about the weather.

Thirteen hours before the deadline. Kennedy switched on the television set and, sometime between *The Red Skelton Show* and *Petticoat Junction*, nodded off. Then he was awakened by the phone ringing. "Hello." A familiar voice answered him with something along the lines of you're not going to believe this. The voice said Zollner had just told a reporter, "I'm willing to guarantee a $600-dollar-per-month pension retroactive for every player in the league." Jack Kent Cooke must have finally gotten through to him after all.

Kennedy started working the phones, and just after midnight, Fleisher arrived at the Roosevelt Hotel to begin distilling Zollner's quote into a binding legal document. Eight hours dwindled to four, and then as the sun ascended over the

Manhattan skyline, Fleisher, Kennedy, and labor attorney Howard Lichtenstein shook hands on a deal—in principle. The Board of Governors would agree to address the NBAPA's list of grievances, and that included having a retroactive pension ready to go by June. In exchange, the NBAPA would call off the strike.

The three combed their hair and straightened their neckties. A hastily arranged news conference awaited downstairs. In front of the cameras, Kennedy and Fleisher each declared victory. Kennedy announced the playoffs would begin on schedule, while Fleisher trumpeted his sweet success. The owners had promised to God and now 200 million Americans to adopt a pension plan "completely satisfactory to the players" no later than June 8, 1967. In the meantime, he and the league's lawyers would solve some unsettled tax issues that had stalled the negotiations.

Kennedy, as was his duty, disregarded Fleisher and spun victory back in the owners' direction. "I believe the NBA has reached a new plateau in player relations."

Today, NBA history books and websites rarely mention the catastrophe that nearly befell the NBA in 1967. It's a glaring omission, comparable to Cold War political scientists passing on the Cuban Missile Crisis because the whole thing turned out to be a false alarm.

Pro basketball's false alarm of 1967 marked a subtle, but significant, shift in the politics of American sports. The NBA players had gained a say in league affairs. True, the players already had claimed a pension victory at the 1964 NBA All-Star game. But the 1964 victory involved the equivalent of a sucker punch and a lucky first-round knockout. In 1967, the players stood toe to toe with the owners and earned the equivalent of a 15-round decision. As Fleisher correctly explained the significance, "Never since the turn of the century has a group of athletes joined together and remained united under such trying circumstances. That loyalty has now been amply rewarded." Players in football, baseball, and other sports were watching.

Fleisher, meanwhile, gained greater credibility. He had shown the owners that he could rally his troops and get them to hold the line. Adversarial though his relationship would remain with many of the owners, Fleisher had earned their respect. He wasn't going away.

In the NBA's old days, labor issues were so seemingly straightforward. Players stuck to playing basketball and blithely allowed the owners to exploit them as cheap labor. When a player asked for a raise, owners reflexively pleaded poverty. As former Philadelphia owner Eddie Gottlieb explained the economics, "We had to make money or get out of business. We earned what we could, and we paid out [to the players] what we could afford."

That's why the anti-union industrialist Zollner and the NBA's small-time arena owners and promoters, such as Gottlieb and St. Louis' Ben Kerner, reverted to type upon learning of the strike. They had to bust the union, banish the troublemakers, and preserve their nickel-and-dime operations at any cost. That's the way pro basketball worked.

But Cooke, by pushing past Zollner and bringing the pension issue to a climax, effectively unyoked the players from complete domination by the owners. Why? Rudy LaRusso nailed it in El Segundo. It was all about Cooke's bottom line. From Cooke's conquer-the-world perspective, the NBA would never reach its full financial potential as popular entertainment clinging to an archaic business model that gypped its players to squeeze out nickel-and-dime profits. The league had to look in another, more modern direction to boost its cash flow and accelerate its growth and prosperity. For Cooke, that other direction offered a landscape of continued league expansion to increase market share and defray operating costs with the now hefty seven-figure entry fees. It also involved negotiating an expanded national television contract and more aggressively mass marketing the NBA product.

That's why Cooke didn't feel particularly threatened by Fleisher and the players association. He recognized that labor organizers and unions came with the modern NBA territory. He also believed that unions, if handled properly, could be a vital tool in protecting his business interests.

"As the Laker player representative, I met with Jack every Monday at 10:30 Los Angeles time, whether by phone if the team was out of town or in his office," said Hawkins. "He wanted to have a state-of-the-team message and know everything that was going on with the Lakers. It wasn't that he wanted me to snitch on my teammates. Jack wanted me to understand that, from a business perspective, it was imperative for him to know everything that was happening with the team."[16]

Endnotes

[1] Red Auerbach and Paul Sann, *Red Auerbach: Winning the Hard Way*, 1966, p. 101.

[2] David Condon, "In the Wake of the News," *Chicago Tribune*, January 10, 1967.

[3] Jack Chevalier, Interview with author, November 2009.

[4] Jack Kiser, "Wilt Talks on Topical Things," *Philadelphia Daily News*, February 1, 1967.

[5] Ibid.

[6] No byline, "Wilt Offered 20% of New Club," *Philadelphia Inquirer*, February 9, 1967.

[7] Don Regan, Interview with author, October 2020.

[8] Ibid.

[9] Art Rosenbaum, "Basketball Going Up," *San Francisco Chronicle*, March 8, 1967.

[10] Jack Barry, "Parley May Avert NBA Playoff Strike," *Boston Globe*, March 11, 1967.

[11] Jack Saylor, "'I Will Not Be Bullied by Players'—NBA Czar," *Detroit Free Press*, March 5, 1967.

[12] Tom Hawkins, Interview with author, March 2010.

[13] The $280,000 playoff pool, in 2024 dollars, equals about $2.6 million. The playoff winnings would range from about $800 per player (about $7,500 today) on a low-ranking team eliminated in the first round to about $6,000 per player (about $56,000 today) on the championship team.

[14] Marc Fleisher, Interview with author, April 2010.

[15] Merv Harris, "LaRusso in Tears," *Los Angeles Herald-Examiner*, March 14, 1967.

[16] Tom Hawkins, Interview with author, March 2010.

4

Baltimore, March 16, 1967—Like all NBA general managers, Buddy Jeannette had followed the "no pension, no playoffs" saga. But Jeannette hadn't been worried about missing the playoffs. Why would he? His last-place, injury-laden Baltimore Bullets, now 45 games behind front-running Philadelphia, were easily the worst show in pro basketball.

Jeannette, a former pro star who hated losing and especially like this, threw in the towel weeks ago on the playoffs. He preferred looking ahead to the upcoming coin flip, the one that would settle whether Baltimore picked first or second in the next college draft. If Jeannette called the flip right, the Bullets would win the draft's top prize: Jimmy Walker, "the next Oscar Robertson" from Providence College. Walker and his nifty dribble drives, according to the pre-draft speculation, would change everything in Baltimore.

But change wouldn't be cheap. In the past, Jeannette could name his price to rookies. Take it or leave it. Since the NBA was their only good option to turn pro, they took it. Now, assuming the ABA was legit, incoming rookies had another option to turn pro. Jeannette would have to bid on his 1967 draftees like French paintings at auction. The bidding on Walker, college basketball's Monet, could spiral into Cazzie Russell territory. Maybe $80,000 a season.

If so, Jeannette needed extra cash. The easiest way to get it, as all NBA general managers knew, was to siphon off $5,000 here, $10,000 there from their veteran players. Most were on renewable, one-year contracts that could be easily reworked each summer and explained away with a few choice, sometimes bogus excuses. The players, after all, knew little about the pro basketball business, and nearly all had no agents to wise them up. It was, to garble a cliché, like taking candy from a seven-foot baby.

Up first this afternoon was his starting center, LeRoy Ellis. Jeannette, middle-aged, dark haired, with a gravelly voice, welcomed Ellis into his office with the cool determination of a used-car salesman reaching for a contract to close a sale. He rasped for his lanky center to have a seat, make himself comfortable. Jeannette explained to Ellis' surprise and sudden unease that he wanted to "take care" of his contract for next season. Steady rank-and-file players, like Ellis, renewed their contracts in late summer, not March, unless they were on the trading block. Jeannette reassured him that wasn't the case. The truth, which Jeannette was prepared to obfuscate, was he'd unilaterally cut Ellis' anticipated (and rightful) $15,000 raise to the bone to free up more cash to bid on Walker. He needed Ellis' *pro forma* okay to finalize the grift.

Jeannette launched into his story, the one every NBA general manager could recite in his sleep. The team was terrible this season. Attendance was down. Money was tight. The best that he could do for next season was a pitiful $1,500 raise. Ellis, his anger starting to well, wasn't buying it. Not again. He did the math in his head. He would make $20,000 next season, or well below market value for a five-year NBA veteran and especially one who logged career-best scoring and rebounding numbers in 1967. He was worth maybe double that.

"You can just sign here?" Jeannette said nonchalantly, pointing to a line in the standard NBA player contract on the table in front of him.

Ellis stared blankly ahead, biting his tongue. Telling off his general manager would be a bad career move. The NBA ran on compliance, which roughly translated to players professing absolute loyalty to team and trust in management. Protest and negotiation were highly discouraged. His only option was to stall. Maybe time would force Jeannette to reconsider and give him a real raise.

"I'm not ready to discuss a new contract right now," stammered Ellis, his 6-foot-11 frame rising from the chair and scooting toward the door. "I need more time. It's been a long season."

The door clicked shut, leaving Jeannette as the one now staring blankly ahead and finally reaching for a convenient fact. Ellis would be back. The Bullets owned his pro career like they owned the Wilson basketballs used during last night's game. Ellis had no choice but to resign.[1]

Oakland, Calif., April 1, 1967—The NBA owners could continue to scoff that the ABA's first season would equal a five-month death march. But they no longer could belittle those waiting to march. Their ABA counterparts, with a few exceptions, were now financially flush. The proof was in the latest performance bonds, the annual deposit to participate in the league, approved during today's planning session at Oakland's Holiday Inn, a resort-like oasis just off the freeway. The ABA's big spenders upped the performance bonds from the formerly plebian $50,000 to the more-elite $100,000 per team. That totaled a $1.1 million community chest for season one, today about $9 million. Each franchise also had to submit a certified bank letter guaranteeing at least a $250,000 line of credit.

Among those millionaires now doing the math was the filthy-rich Texas oilman Bud Adams, who owned the Houston Oilers pro football team and was considering whether to cast his 10-gallon hat into the ring for the ABA's Houston franchise. Nearby sat Herb Kohl, the Milwaukee department store mogul. He agonized over whether to bring the ABA to Milwaukee as the league's 12th and final franchise. Across the table sat the $40-million heiress Mamie Gregory and her dog trainer-extraordinaire husband, Joe. They were attending their first league meeting as the proud owners of the Kentucky Colonels. Meanwhile, the expansion committee had fresh inquiries from wealthy figures in Atlanta, Memphis, and another one from Cleveland.

For now, the millionaires put their full faith and trust in Mr. Basketball himself, George Mikan. In fact, they started day two in Oakland by approving a generous $190,000 budget (today, about $1.5 million) for Mikan to staff and operate the Minneapolis league office. Mikan rewarded their generosity by disclosing some good news. Movie giant Metro Goldman Mayer (MGM) Studios, hoping to branch out and sell syndicated sports programming across America, had expressed interest in purchasing the radio and television rights to ABA games. Nothing in writing yet, noted Mikan, but "they" were off to a flying start.

"Sell pride," Mikan encouraged one of his millionaire owners, who'd asked what the ABA had to "sell" to gain a competitive edge on the NBA. "Every time you open the arena, every time you come on the floor, every time you get off an airplane in another city, every time you win or lose, sell pride."[2]

Around 2:30 p.m., the meeting took a hard turn from pride to the impatient. Milwaukee's Kohl had missed a 2:00 p.m. deadline to submit his league application, including a $125,000 check, to secure his franchise. Kohl requested a five-day extension. The ABA millionaires told him enough was enough. They were moving ahead with their final cut of 11 starter franchises. The names, all subject to change, fell off the tongue like reading aloud the menu items at the local fast-food Burger Chef: Oakland All Americans, Anaheim Amigos, Denver Rockets, Minnesota Muskies, New Orleans Buccaneers, Houston Mavericks, Dallas Chaparrals, Indiana Pacers, Kentucky Colonels, Pittsburgh (soon to be) Pipers, and New York Freighters.

Gary Davidson, the young attorney who had eyed Mikan's job, remained in a leadership role as a bit minority owner in

Dallas which enabled him to remain as league president. Davidson still resented Mikan ("loathed" might be the better word) for dashing off with the ABA front office that he'd hoped to plant in his California law firm. He also thought Mikan had failed to manage the league in lockstep with his more-nuanced vision as ABA president. After all, Mikan worked for Davidson and the owners, not vice versa.

Davidson could take meetings into his own hands, and very much at Mikan's expense, and this afternoon was one of those pushy, but timely, moments. With the ABA's 11 starter franchises finally set in stone, Davidson advised his colleagues to move on to the next organizational phase: hiring players and building rosters. According to the league secretary, "a lively conversation ensued that ended in Motion 14: Made by Davidson, Dallas, seconded by Downey, New Orleans, college draft to be held April 2, beginning at 9:30 a.m. Carried." Glancing up at the room's overhead clock, that left about 16 hours to scribble out a draft list. Who said Rome and pro basketball leagues couldn't be built in under a day?

Oakland, Calif., April 2, 1967—George Mikan welcomed everyone to the first annual ABA college draft, held in the Holiday Inn's Crown Room. A reporter reflexively jotted down Mikan's greeting and later added to his notes. "There will probably never be another draft like the first ABA draft."[3]

What he meant is the draft couldn't have been more seat-of-the-pants. A hat containing 11 numbered slips of paper had circulated the room beforehand, and representatives from each team ceremoniously reached in and drew a number (the lower the better) to set the draft order. Teams worked from a complementary draft report that listed the name, rank, and statistical numbers of the top college seniors. Mikan encouraged everyone to pipe up and share their thoughts on any prospective player to help keep things moving, at least in theory. "A name would come up, and we'd get from 14 to 18 different opinions," said Mike Storen, the recently hired general manager in Indiana.[4]

When Indiana's number rolled around, Storen ambitiously nabbed Providence College's Jimmy Walker, the certain top pick in the upcoming NBA draft. Walker wouldn't come cheaply, if at all. In a sign of these changing pro basketball times, Storen didn't call Walker to introduce himself and the city of Indianapolis. He called Walker's New York agent, Frank Scott, about the bidding process.

Scott admittedly wasn't an agent. He was a sports publicist and the promotional gatekeeper to baseball's superstars. Scott also was a Godsend for Father Joseph Taylor, a Dominican priest and an administrative mastermind behind Providence's rise on the national basketball scene. Father Joseph, wearing a priest's white habit, had introduced himself two weeks ago to Scott during a basketball game at Madison Square Garden. They zipped through the small talk and landed in Father Joseph's plea for Scott "to help Jimmy" turn pro safely and equitably. Scott, who was Jewish, accepted it as a mitzvah, or good deed. After all, he worked with business contracts all the time. How hard could it be being an agent? Scott was about to find out.[5]

New York, April 5, 1967—Walter Kennedy didn't fly to Detroit this year for the coin flip, though he could have. The Detroit Pistons, a season removed from guessing wrong on the Cazzie Russell coin flip, were back tossing for the top pick in this year's college draft. But Detroit wouldn't be calling it in the air this year. That dubious honor belonged to Baltimore's Buddy Jeannette, who, by the way, was still waiting on LeRoy Ellis to sign his contract for next year.

Kennedy, seated in his office with the blinds drawn on the 23rd floor of 2 Penn Plaza, near the new Madison Square Garden, was waiting for his do-it-all secretary Connie Maroselli to arrange this newfangled thing called a telephonic conference call. These "millionaire owners," with their fingers in multiple income streams, didn't stay in one place long like the arena owners. These millionaires bounced around the country attending business meetings, and Maroselli had to patch in callers in Maryland, Ohio, New York, and Michigan. But Maroselli, slender, with striking dark eyes and black, shoulder-length hair, was a whiz at all things telephonic. Shortly before 11 a.m., Maroselli entered Kennedy's office with fellow secretary Barbara Atlas and delivered the okay to pick up the phone from its cradle.

After the obligatory "hellos" and "please speak ups," Kennedy breezed through the rules. He'd already deputized his secretaries as special proxies, or eyes on the ground that would blow the whistle on him should they detect any funny business. Maroselli, a lifelong New Yorker, now eyed her boss on behalf of Detroit.

Ten minutes later, the commissioner was ready to flip the shiny $20 gold coin gripped in his right hand. It was the same antique coin that Pistons owner Fred Zollner had handed over to Kennedy last year following the Russell flip. And no, Zollner didn't object to flipping it twice. Losing Russell may have been a blessing. Dave Bing, Detroit's 6-foot-2 consolation prize, was the NBA's runaway Rookie of the Year in 1967 and, if teamed with Walker next season, would give Zollner the best young backcourt in the league.

"Baltimore, what's your call?" Kennedy intoned.

The telephone line crackled with white noise followed by Jeannette's gravelly "heads," which he uttered more like an incantation than a sure thing.

As the coin twirled into the air, Baltimore co-owner Earl Foreman, on the line from Cleveland, called out a low, coaxing, "HEADS." The gold coin immediately twirled downward, glancing off Kennedy's right thumb and trickling waywardly under his desk. The proxies exchanged glances. Did they dare say anything?

"Hold on," Kennedy called out, placing the phone on his desk and straining to retrieve the miss.

"It's tails. Detroit wins."

New York, April 6, 1967—Frank Scott rented an office in Manhattan's stylish Biltmore Hotel, near Grand Central Station. The fancy décor wasn't exactly Scott, originally just a poor, working-class kid from Pittsburgh. But like his fancy suits, the Biltmore's snazzy Madison Avenue address impressed clients, even if the publicity business was pretty routine. The 49-year-old Scott spent most of his days on the phone and cursing at his typewriter. That included his latest hunt-and-peck tirade that yielded registered letters to the NBA Detroit Pistons and ABA Indiana Pacers. They informed both parties to have their final closed bids for Jimmy Walker on his desk by midnight May 1.

Mike Storen, Indiana's young general manager, arranged to stop by Scott's office a few days later and ask for a favor. About that May 1 deadline, Storen said he needed more time to convince his colleagues to bet the farm on Walker. Could Indiana submit its bid a few extra days later?

Scott, an engaging storyteller, may or may not have answered the question in between tales of his New York Yankees past. Either way, Storen departed the office believing that the favor had been granted. Indiana would submit its offer a few days after Detroit, ostensibly to learn the amount of the Pistons' offer and come in just a few dollars higher.

As Storen made his way back toward Grand Central Station, Scott got back to work. He either forgot or misremembered Storen's ask. In Scott's mind, the May 1 deadline remained as firm as ever for both the NBA and ABA.[6]

Brooklyn, N.Y., April 10, 1967—LeRoy Ellis spent a few days at his mother's house in his native Brooklyn hoping to let his frustration with the NBA ooze out of his system. While there, Ellis noticed a strange letter addressed to him from a team called the New York Freighters. He'd never heard of them. The form letter, sent to NBA players from New York, explained that the Freighters were in the brand-new American Basketball Association. If Ellis wanted to come home and play in New York, the Freighters wanted to talk to him. Ellis refolded the letter and shrugged, "Why not?" It couldn't hurt to listen.

A few days later, Ellis sat opposite Mark Binstein, the smooth-talking Jersey City stockbroker, ABA organizer, and bit owner of the Freighters. Binstein, though age 33, had a steep, receding hairline and premature dark circles around his eyes that suggested wisdom beyond his years. When he spoke, Ellis listened. "I'm willing to give you a one-year, $30,000 contract," explained Binstein, which equaled a 50-percent hike in Ellis' salary. The offer on the table wouldn't last long, Binstein confided. Several NBA players, whom he wouldn't name, might claim the money first. Ellis finally shrugged. "Why not?" He'd never make $30,000 in Baltimore.

Ellis scribbled his name on the contract, and Binstein said he'd be in touch with the date and time for the news conference to announce the deal. Ellis shrugged off the coming media attention. It wasn't like he was Wilt Chamberlain. But he was suddenly an unwitting trailblazer. He was the first NBA veteran to defect to the rival ABA. No wonder Binstein, the stockbroker, was on the phone afterwards with the big news, as though he'd just closed a major Wall Street trade.

No wonder Binstein couldn't zip his lip. The deal was leaked in the newspapers, and Ellis, though not brutalized in the press, saw his reputation take an ugly drag through the NBA mud. He was tagged in NBA front offices as a greedy, egotistical rebel, one of the real bums that general managers loved to hate. Of course, the tags weren't exactly true. Ellis had no intention of blowing up the NBA system. He just wanted equal pay.[7]

Baltimore, April 26, 1967—Before Baltimore could sue the Freighters and the ABA to kingdom come, LeRoy Ellis agreed to return to Baltimore and meet man to man with Buddy Jeannette. The irony wasn't lost on many old-time basketball fans. Twenty years ago, Jeannette had been in Ellis' shoes. He'd jumped the more-established National Basketball League for more money as the player-coach of the Baltimore Bullets of the Basketball Association of America, the NBA's organizational precursor.

But Jeannette wasn't feeling especially empathetic. According to Ellis, Jeannette huffed and puffed and threatened to bankrupt him. "I kind of got nervous in my shoes," said Ellis. "Jeannette said the Bullets would take me to court because I was still their property, and being young and not knowing anything, I got real worried. I said, 'All right, if you can take care of the New York contract, I'll resign.' Jeannette said, 'Don't worry, we'll take care of it.' The nice thing was the Bullets gave me the same amount of money as the ABA contract."[8]

The next day, Ellis was back in the headlines, this time for finding Jesus and the NBA. But in saving himself, Ellis had made out like a bandit. Other NBA players took note. Maybe Ellis was on to something good.

New York, April 27, 1967—It was nearly a year ago that the big brass of the New York Knicks gathered at Mama Leone's Ristorante, with its serenading tenors and campy Italianate artwork, to announce the signing of the NBA's next superstar, Cazzie Russell. For whatever reason—and every New Yorker seemingly had a pet opinion—Russell had mostly bombed in his rookie season.

This afternoon, the Knicks brass returned to the popular West Side eatery to make another Gotham-sized splash. The Knicks had signed Bill Bradley, their top college draft choice from two years ago. The former Princeton All-American, who played the same small forward position as Russell, had famously delayed his NBA career to spend two years as a Rhodes scholar in England and play pro basketball on the side in Italy.

Think Russell's rookie contract was obscene? The Knicks, though cagey about the final figure, signed Bradley to a whispered four-year, $400,000 contract,[9] placing him near the very top of NBA salaries before scoring a point as a pro. "To my knowledge, the contract is for one of the largest money amounts ever paid a professional athlete in a team sport," the Madison Square Garden's chairman of the board offered up in a prepared statement distributed beforehand and fully intended to make splashy headlines.[10]

Bradley, wearing a light-blue blazer and tie, entered the ristorante on this rainy evening a regrettable 30 minutes late. "He was waiting for the rain to inundate 48th Street, so he could walk on water," an onlooker wisecracked. Bradley brushed the rain from his blazer and squished upstairs to the designated meeting room, greeted by a blitzkrieg of popping cameras and recording devices ready for a juicy quote.

"I love the game of basketball," was all Bradley could muster for going pro, not to law school. "I know this may be considered trite but that is the way I feel."[11]

Hanging on Bradley's every word was Marty Glickman, the beloved Knicks announcer famous for his signature on-air shill after free throws, "made it like Nemitz." But Glickman wasn't here to welcome the newest Knick to town. Bradley was his client. Glickman had just launched a side business called All-Pro Sports and, much like baseball's Frank Scott, would work as Bradley's private publicist, admitting no future on-the-air conflict of interest for him or his other NBA client Oscar

Robertson.[12] More surprising, his business partner was none other than Larry Fleisher, chief counsel of the NBA Players Association (NBAPA).

Fleisher, seated near Glickman, hung more on the numbers than the words being bandied about. That's because Fleisher now doubled as Bradley's agent. With nobody questioning the ethics of the NBAPA's general counsel privately representing a future member of his union and potentially profiting off him, Fleisher planned to move forward as a full-time labor organizer who moonlighted as a part-time publicist and player agent.

What was Fleisher thinking? He never provided the answer, at least publicly. Greed admittedly could have a been a factor. "Cazzie Russell money" had arrived in the NBA and, for a 10-percent professional services fee, agents now pocketed a tidy profit. But that's a little too simplistic. Fleisher hadn't dumped the NBAPA for greater profit. His business card still featured his NBAPA affiliation and, as Fleisher quickly assured everyone, he was determined to reform the NBA's feudal labor system.

The better explanation is Fleisher was tired of clamoring for attention outside the NBA system. Though his threats of player strikes had secured a decent player pension for the time being, walking the picket line wouldn't work in the anticipated years-long struggle for the players' Holy Grail: free agency. For that, Fleisher needed to labor from the inside, and what quicker way to shake hands with management and forge relationships with the NBA's power players than to serve as the gatekeeper to a presumed major talent and attraction like Bradley. Sure enough, Fleisher had talked face to face for the first time with Knicks president Ned Irish to form, if not exactly a personal bond, a warmer working relationship with one of the NBA's dominant figures.

By representing Bradley (and more top players to come), Fleisher could also connect two critical dots that worked in his favor. One, Fleisher would hammer out the first collective bargaining agreement between the NBAPA and the NBA. As rudimentary as the agreement was, it entitled him to review every player contract. Remember, owners controlled their players by limiting their bargaining power. They did so, in part, by a close hold on all player salaries. NBA players, the vast majority of whom still represented themselves, had no idea what the next guy made. It was management that told each player what they were worth and what the market (a buyer of one) would bear. Think LeRoy Ellis. Now, the information was his. Fleisher could connect the dots of the NBA market writ large. He could for the first time compare player salaries with player production and spit out the true worth of his future clients.

New York, May 1, 1967—The clock struck midnight, and all bidding closed for Jimmy Walker. The offer from the NBA's Detroit Pistons had arrived a few days ago, whispered to be a four-year, $250,000 offer. Not quite Bill Bradley money, but not chump change either. What about the ABA offer? Good question. Frank Scott still had nothing in hand from Indiana's Mike Storen, and that surprised him.

Scott waited by the phone just in case, then finally called Indianapolis around 2 a.m. No answer. A few hours later, Storen called to say there must be a misunderstanding. Just as they'd agreed a few weeks ago in Scott's office, Indiana would have something in writing in a few more days. Scott interjected that, no, Storen was mistaken, followed by "so long" and a click.[13]

By 10 a.m. that morning, Walker was shaking hands with Walter Kennedy as the newest Detroit Piston and proof positive in this year's propaganda war that the brightest stars of the college game weren't interested in the ABA. "The NBA is the status league," Walker said, repeating a line drummed into his head by none other than Detroit's Dave Bing. By clever coincidence, Walker spent the previous weekend playing exhibition games with Bing cloistered in Schenectady, where they had plenty of down time to bond as future teammates.

Storen cried foul, claiming Walker and Scott were in the NBA's pocket. He may have been right. But Storen committed some rookie mistakes, starting with his complete misread of Scott. He was a publicist. He was in the business of punching out standard, one-time agreements as though he were loaning out athletes like Enterprise rents out cars. Delays and mother-may-I's weren't going to work. "Believe me, I was just interested in keeping my agreement with Father Taylor, and I didn't care whether Jimmy was the third-highest paid player in history or any other number," Scott said afterwards.[14]

To break the NBA's monopoly on the brightest college stars, the ABA had to come hard and bid God awfully high to steal a few All Americans. But, as an anonymous ABA figure summarized the situation, the new league didn't know how to start the bidding. As the next few days would show, the NBA wasn't going to help them to figure it out.

New York, May 3, 1967—It was like a story from *True Detective Magazine*. Two days ago, the gravelly voiced Buddy Jeanette planted the rumor that the Baltimore Bullets would select Sonny Dove, the wiry All-American forward from St. John's College, with the second pick in the NBA draft. Everyone took the bait. But Jeannette wasn't really interested in Dove, who had an agent. And not just any agent. Dove had hired Arthur Morse of Cazzie Russell fame and NBA fortune. The Bullets couldn't afford Morse.

With the Dove misdirection in play, Jeannette and three other members of the Bullets front office left late the day before for New York and today's draft. But at 1 a.m. this morning, the Bullets contingent skulked through the lobby of the Roosevelt Hotel and out to their car. All agreed, nobody of consequence had seen them exit the hotel. The streets now emptying on this quiet Wednesday morning, the foursome gassed it out of

Manhattan and down I-95 South until they started seeing exit signs for Philadelphia. After a few wrong turns, they arrived around 3 a.m. in gritty South Philly at the corner of South 26th and Manton Streets. They cut their lights and engine and, like cops clutching a search warrant, rang the doorbell at 1217 South 26th Street, an imposing, three-story house with a grocery story on the bottom floor.

Lights flicked on, and a sturdy middle-aged Black woman named Rose Smith looked out the door. She immediately recognized Jeannette. He was that generous white man from the pro basketball team in Baltimore. So generous, in fact, Jeannette had appeared on her doorstep two weeks ago to drop off a brand-new red 1967 Oldsmobile convertible for her son Earl Monroe to "test drive" for a while.

"Is Earl home?"

Rose and her groggy husband invited these crazy white men inside, explaining that Earl was still out for the evening with his friends. Around 3:30 a.m., Earl materialized, his glassy eyes widening at the unexpected sight of four NBA executives hunkered in his mother's kitchen. Jeannette immediately turned on the charm but kept the small talk brief. He said they were here on business. "Earl, you're going to be our first pick in the NBA draft."

Oh, how times had changed. Four years ago, Monroe was a $60-per-week factory shipping clerk whose life was drifting God knows where. Then Monroe got his break to play small-college basketball in North Carolina, where he lit up the competition for a record-setting 41.5 points per game last season. Now, by the grace of God, he was turning pro.

"We'd like you to be in New York when we make the announcement," said Jeannette.

"Cool. When do we leave?"

"Right now."

The Baltimore contingent, plus their sleepy top draft pick, rolled through the dark up I-95 North. Somewhere between Trenton and the sunrise over Newark, it dawned on everyone that they'd spun out of South Philly so quickly that Monroe, wearing dark green pants and a casual pullover sweater, wasn't properly attired for the big announcement. They'd need to get him something more becoming, and that's why everyone needed to meet on the double in the hotel room of the team's co-owner Arnie Heft.

Once inside Heft's suite, everyone started shedding articles of clothing and handing them to Monroe with the order, "Try this on." When the clothes swap was over, Monroe wore the white dress shirt of Bullets publicity director Herb Heft (who four months later would sadly die of a brain hemorrhage) and Jeannette's skinny tie and tight-fitting sportscoat with a twilled, checkerboard pattern.

Jeannette finally reached into his briefcase and pulled out a standard NBA contract and a pen. He handed the latter to Earl and pointed to the signature line at the bottom of the page. Earl didn't think twice. He signed on the spot after reading just enough to see that it was a one-year contract for $19,000.

For Jeannette, it was a steal. Jimmy Walker was asking $250,000 (though Detroit, as a matter of pride, insisted the top pick signed a four-year, $110,000 contract). Don't even mention Bill Bradley or Cazzie Russell. They'd gotten Monroe for an old sweet song before the ABA could muck around and start a bidding war. Jeannette had kept the Bullets' payroll right where it needed to be at the bottom of the NBA.

Then came a knock on the door. It was Clarence "Big House" Gaines, Monroe's 6-foot-5, 280-pound mountain of a college coach, who had flown to New York on the Bullets' dime. Gaines thought he was there to negotiate Monroe's contract. But when he saw Monroe dressed in celebratory formal attire, Gaines knew he was too late. After a private "what-did-you-just-do" conversation with Monroe, Gaines lit into Jeannette for exploiting the situation. When Gaines finished, Jeannette bumped up the contract to a two-year deal at $20,000 per season, still below the going rate for a No. 2 pick.

The NBA draft would kick off at 11:45 a.m. at the swishy Plaza Hotel, but Baltimore had gotten the okay to announce Monroe's signing beforehand. "How much did you sign for?" asked a reporter at the news conference.

"A substantial amount," Monroe fibbed, realizing by now he'd been snookered.[15]

New Orleans, May 12, 1967—Baltimore may have absconded with Earl Monroe, but the ABA's New Orleans Buccaneers swiped the Bullets' second-round pick Jimmy Jones. Highly regarded by pro scouts, but little-known outside of Louisiana and Black college basketball circles, the Grambling star got a three-year, $75,000 deal and a new car.

This small victory flowed right into a favorite ABA theme. "We'll develop our own players just like the American Football League (AFL) did," said George Mikan, meaning Monroe and Walker might be must-see young stars, but Jones would be, too, with some extra time in the ABA oven.

In fact, the league's 11 teams already had stocked their rosters with more than 70 mostly unheralded ballplayers who would need more time baking in that ABA oven. Many were college seniors taken in the mid-to-late rounds of the NBA draft. All were NBA longshots who thought that they'd better take their chances—and signing bonuses—in the ABA. Others were "free agents," a catch-all term for stubbly grown men with day jobs, many of whom were NBA castoffs and college dropouts with game, who scrapped in semipro and industrial leagues hoping to reignite their careers. As Mikan liked to assure reporters, there was enough basketball talent to go around in America to stock an exciting ABA show, featuring its innovative ball, wider lanes, and three-point shot.

All true, but Mikan fudged the facts a bit. The AFL may have developed a whole winged "T" of unsung gridiron stars. But the AFL owners were never too interested in developing the unsung. They craved stars, big stars, young men with sizzle to their names to sell America on the league fast, their bottom lines be damned. That's why the AFL audaciously elbowed the established NFL aside to sign the 1959 Heisman Trophy winner Billy Cannon and crown him the sport's first $100,000 man for big print in the newspapers.

That sizzle also helps to explain how the AFL landed a nearly $1.8-million contract ($200,000 per franchise) with ABC in its inaugural 1960 season, all sight unseen. As ABC's then-producer Roone Arledge recalled with some buyer's remorse, "And the first AFL games were a lopsided kaleidoscope of rarely completed Hail Marys, flung downfield in ramshackle stadiums before crowds so sparse they could easily have been seated in one of the Rose Bowl end zones."[16]

With a little more sizzle each year and a whole lot of network infighting, the AFL had jumped to NBC three years ago for a five-year, $38 million mega-deal, which handed an annual $1 million network subsidy to each franchise. The AFL was now *NBC Sunday Football*, as much a network property as its popular sitcom *Bewitched*. In fact, NBC even sent a form letter to all professional prospects in the college football class of 1964 that began, "Later this month you undoubtedly will be drafted by a team in the American Football League. Since the National Broadcasting Company is in 'partnership' with the AFL for the next five years in presenting a full schedule of weekly champion games, the league has asked us to join in the hope you will be part of the future AFL presentations on NBC."

The rest was pro football history. The AFL, enabled by its extra millions, went long to connect with more college stars and raid more NFL rosters. With interleague hostilities at an all-time high, the NFL unwisely agreed to the first Super Bowl to prove its gridiron superiority to God and a record 45 million

Americans watching at home on TV. With the pro football business turned upside down, the first serious merger talks ensued, followed by a little help from pro football's senatorial friends in Louisiana to quarterback sneak through an antitrust exemption that allowed a merger of the leagues and some semblance of peace on the gridiron.

The AFL's tale had ABA officials in rare agreement: A network TV contract was vital not only to send the league's red, white, and blue product into the nation's rabbit-eared living rooms, but to subsidize its survival until a Super Bowl of Basketball and a merger were in the works. The good news was Mikan and his lawyer Bill Erickson remained in negotiations with MGM Studios to put the ABA on the air. In fact, MGM had recently agreed to an August 15 deadline to decide whether to pay $600,000 for "exclusive national TV and movie rights" to the ABA's first season or walk away from the deal.[17] Though MGM's offer wasn't exactly AFL money, it was comparable to the NBA's network television contract. The bad news was MGM remained in the crosshairs of a hostile Mob-ordered stock buy-up and takeover that had its executives watching their backs and corporate expenses.[18] Though the ABA deal was miniscule compared to the studio's $11 million outlay for its latest blockbuster film Dr. Zhivago, the ABA's timing wasn't the best.

Whether or not the MGM lion would roar next season before ABA games, several teams were stepping up their efforts to follow the AFL's other swashbuckling word to the wise: raid the other league's rosters. In fact, unnamed ABA sources were dangling a no-money-down offer for Wilt Chamberlain and fellow top-drawer NBA superstar Elgin Baylor to join a star-studded ownership group, which reportedly included singers Frank Sinatra, Dean Martin, and Andy Williams. The ABA sources claimed Sinatra and crew were close to having the ABA-mandated minimum of $100,000 to operate the Denver franchise and, once the money was in hand, move it to Los Angeles. The plan, though discussed at a secret meeting in San Francisco, quickly flamed out.[19]

But the ABA had made some headway with some of the NBA's middle- and bottom-drawer talent. Three days after LeRoy Ellis made his temporary leap, center Bad News Barnes, who ironically had been traded last season to Los Angeles for Ellis, became the second NBA player to defect. He and his torn Achilles tendon limped to the ABA's Dallas Chaparrals for a two-year, $50,000 contract and an undisclosed signing bonus. Los Angeles predictably sued for the immediate return of its property, alleging that Dallas' wooing of Barnes took place in a "deliberate, malicious, wanton, reckless, and unjustifiable manner."[20] Before anything went to trial, Barnes hobbled back to L.A. to accept a handsome raise.

In early May, Chicago's center Erwin Mueller, a member of the NBA's 1967 All-Rookie Team, took the leap. He signed with the New York Freighters, then leapfrogged back to the Bulls for a raise. Other players bluffed,[21] and a few more jumped,[22] including Detroit's soft-spoken career reserve Wayne Hightower, who departed for the ABA's Denver Rockets. But as an aging journeyman, Hightower wasn't worth Detroit's time and effort to reclaim him, meaning Hightower and several other benchwarmers slipped through the NBA cracks to play in the ABA without any legal redress.

"All athletes are pieces of meat," Hightower later summed up the situation. "Some get treated like hamburger, some like steak."

The three might have been NBA hamburger. But two days after the Hightower signing, the ABA finally sliced into some sirloin. The news broke appropriately enough at an upscale Minneapolis steakhouse called Murray's: home of the silver butter knife steak.

Minneapolis, May 18, 1967—In these days of wall-mounted rotary phones, the waiter lugged Murray's portable telephone, its extension cord trailing on the carpet like bread crumbs, to the corner table and placed it in front of the young

Black gentleman everyone called Louie. Lou Hudson, last season's runner-up NBA rookie of the year with the St. Louis Hawks, looked surprised. Did people really talk on the phone over lunch?

Hudson glanced across the table for help to Eddie Holman, a short, trim white man in his late 40s with black, greased-back hair and a blustery, know-it-all affect. Holman, an eighth-grade dropout, had spent most of his adult life running various Minneapolis watering holes, earning a reputation as a gambler and card shark. But "Fast Eddie" had sold his last bucket of suds about eight years ago to gamble on Holman Oil and Gas Drilling Corporation. A big gusher later, Holman bought a 10-percent stake in the ABA Minnesota Muskies and, in between oil prospecting deals, ran the team's day-to-day operations. Holman's basketball credentials? He was a neighbor of ABA commissioner George Mikan.

Holman found the telephone number for Archie Clark. Like Hudson, Clark had starred two years ago on the men's basketball team at the University of Minnesota. Though the squad never won a collegiate championship of any kind, Holman and many folks around Minneapolis considered the Hudson, Clark, et. al years to be the school's finest. Holman hoped to turn back time in the pros, and Louie took the bait, becoming the first legitimate NBA star to jump leagues. Now Holman needed Clark, the starting point guard for the Los Angeles Lakers, to take the bait, too. Holman dialed Clark's number and handed the receiver to Hudson.

"Archie, I signed," Hudson confided into the telephone.[23]

Though Hudson didn't go into specifics, he'd signed a personal services contact with Muskies' majority owner Larry Shields. By signing with Shields, not the team, Hudson would draw a guaranteed salary next season, even if he didn't play a minute due to injury or a prohibitive court ruling. The agreement paid Hudson $37,500 in year one, $42,500 in year two, and $47,500 in year three. Throw in a $7,500 signing bonus, and Louie was sitting on $135,000.[24] As frequently happened in the ABA, Shields and Holman rounded up the total to $150,000 just for looks. Though the terms of Hudson's NBA contract with St. Louis weren't public, he signed a one-year deal, plus an option year. Knowing St. Louis owner and cheapskate Ben Kerner, Hudson was likely getting around $15,000.

Hudson handed the receiver to Holman, who hinted that the Muskies had a comparable contract waiting for Clark's services. Holman promised to be in touch, and the Muskies became the ABA's early team to beat with a lineup featuring outstanding young talent and some old college chemistry.

A week later, all that chemistry went poof. The Muskies were too low on cash to meet Clark's high asking price, and Kerner got revenge by filing federal cases in Minneapolis seeking an injunction to prevent Hudson from playing in the ABA and a fat $3 million in damages. "I'm glad to have a $3-millon piece of property," Holman wryly responded to the legal actions.[25] Hudson, however, was spooked by the allegations and all the zeros in $3,000,000. He abruptly flew to St. Louis and resigned with the Hawks for an undisclosed amount that almost certainly included a raise. "I'm a young man," Hudson leveled with a reporter about his ABA indiscretion. "And to young people, when you see the big dollar sign . . . that's it."

Though Shields and the Muskies could have sued Hudson and Kerner right back, they didn't. Make that, to save a few bucks they didn't sue right away. All this scrimping had the ABA right back where it started. Namely, with no bright, shiny NBA prize to show for its labors. The ABA needed a test court case that would endure the NBA's expensive slings, arrows, and half-cocked allegations of damages. The ABA needed a verdict on whether a pro basketball player could, under American law, switch leagues and, if so, when.

That's why the ABA owners woo-hooed last May over a possible test case. Clyde Lee, last season a rookie forward for the NBA San Francisco Warriors, had just signed with the ABA New Orleans Buccaneers. Lee, a quiet Tennessee kid, said he wanted to play closer to home. The Warriors promptly sued Lee, the Bucs, and the ABA in San Francisco Municipal Court for breach of contract and $1 million in damages. However, unlike the other jumpers, Lee seemingly couldn't return to the NBA. San Francisco had recently announced its no-return policy: Any player who signed with the ABA wasn't welcome back to the Warriors.[26] Since the Warriors exclusively owned Lee's NBA rights, his only remaining option was to fight in court for his right to become a Buccaneer.

According to Sean Morton Downey, Jr., the Bucs' vice president, he was prepared to go the legal distance for Lee.[27] So were his ABA friends. But between consulting with lawyers and filing the first motions in the case, money spoke again. A new team owner, whose bigger bucks gave him greater say than Downey, killed the lawsuit, calling the whole thing financially imprudent. New Orleans reneged on Lee's contract and told him to make peace, not war, in San Francisco.

Lucky for Lee, by then Warriors' president Franklin Mieuli had softened on his no-return policy. Mieuli welcomed back Lee, mainly because he needed him back. Mieuli's championship-contending Warriors were falling apart at the seams, compliments of the ABA and another Warrior just brash enough to pick up where the introverted Lee had left off.

Endnotes

[1] LeRoy Ellis, Interview with author, October 2009.

[2] George Ross, "Real George," *Oakland Tribune*, April 3, 1967.

[3] Ed Schoenfeld, "Daffy Draft—ABA Club Drafts Seagren" *Oakland Tribune*, April 3, 1967.

[4] Ibid.

[5] Joe O'Day, "Walker Takes Pistons' 300G," *New York Daily News*, May 3, 1967.

[6] No Byline, "Walker Was Set to Be a Piston," *Indianapolis News*, May 3, 1967.

[7] LeRoy Ellis, Interview with author, October 2009.

[8] Ibid.

[9] The dollar figure varied wildly depending on the source. The New York Daily News, for example, claimed Bradley got $600,000,and the Knicks weren't going to refute the high price tag and its publicity. But Marty Glickman, who helped negotiate the deal, has the terms as four years for $400,000.

[10] Larry Fox, "Knicks Land Bradley on 600G Bait," *New York Daily News*, April 28, 1967.

[11] Milton Gross, "Adulation Disturbs Bill Bradley," *Pittsburgh Press*, April 29, 1967.

[12] Marty Glickman, *The Fastest Kid on the Block*, 1996, p. 107.

[13] Joe O'Day, "Walker Takes Pistons' 300G," *New York Daily News*, May 3, 1967.

[14] Ibid.

[15] Clarence Gaines, *They Call Me Big House*, 2004, 233-235; Earl Monroe and Quincy Troupe, *Earl the Pearl*, 2013, 161-64; Gene Shue, Alan Goldstein, and Seymour Smith, Interviews with author; and coverage of the Monroe signing in the *Baltimore Sun* and *Baltimore Evening Sun*, April and May 1967.

[16] Roone Arledge, *Roone*, 2003, p. 63-64.

[17] Minutes of American Basketball Association League Meeting, June 14-16, 1967.

[18] For example: Arelo Sederberg,"MGM Management in a Real-Life Cliffhanger," *Los Angeles Times*, January 8, 1967; Charles Champlin, "Management Changes at Dream Factory," *Los Angeles Times*, August 6, 1967. MGM director Phil Levin had a long and deserved history of doing the Mob's bidding, when called upon.

[19] Lee Meade, "Trio Entertains Ideas on ABA Anaheim Entry," *Denver Post*, June 22, 1967; Fred Rosenfeld, Interview with author, November 2009.

[20] Phil Elderkin, "Rimming the NBA," *The Sporting News*, May 6, 1967.

[21] For instance, Boston's Bailey Howell and Philadelphia's Hal Greer and Billy Cunningham immediately bluffed an openness to switching leagues. "After all, money is what I'm playing for," said Howell.

[22] Including Cincinnati's then-unheralded forward Bob Love. He jumped right back to the NBA.

[23] Archie Clark, Interview with author, December 2009; Dick Jonckowski, Interview with author, May 2012.

[24] Minnesota Muskies, Inc. v. Hudson, United States District Court for the Middle District of North Carolina, Greensboro Division, January 16, 1969.

[25] Associated Press, "Hawks Seek $3 Million Damages Over Hudson," *Minneapolis Star*, May 25, 1967.

[26] Dick Friendlich, "Nate Signs with S.F.?" *San Francisco Examiner*, June 16, 1967.

[27] Bob Sprenger, "ABA Cage War Strategy," *San Francisco Examiner*, June 29, 1967.

5

San Francisco, June 17, 1967—It was just a gag. Rick Barry, the young star of the San Francisco Warriors, was downtown signing autographs at the Woolworths on Powell and Market Streets. Franklin Mieuli (mee-YOO-lee), president of the Warriors and an incorrigible merry prankster, thought it would be hysterical if he crashed the line of autograph seekers to present the face of the franchise with his contract for next season. Great photo op, free publicity, sneaky way to coax Barry into signing.[1]

And so, Mieuli scooted down to the popular five-and-dime store and scooched into place like an undercover boss, making small talk about Barry and the Warriors' amazing Nate Thurmond, the NBA's top young center. Going undercover wasn't tough for the 48-year-old Mieuli. He was working-class stout, tanned, with a nervous foreman-like energy to get things done. The energy was delivered in a mild, nasally voice punctuated with subtle inflections that, like verbal hooks, reeled in his listeners to share higher truths about the Warriors and their recent close-but-no-cigar trip to the NBA finals.

The undercover basketball boss finally inched to the head table, where Barry auto-scribbled his name on anything passing his line of sight. Surprise! "As long as you're putting your name on things, sign right here," began the inflection that Barry knew well.

"He didn't even look up," Mieuli said. "He just took the paper from my hand. Then I said, 'Sign it. It's a three-year contract.' I figured that would break him up. But he looked at me and didn't even smile [or sign the contract]. That's when I knew time was running out."[2]

That's when Mieuli knew the rumors were true: Barry was days, if not hours, away from joining the ABA's Oakland franchise. Thurmond had forewarned him the other day. Mieuli laughed him off, explaining that he and Barry had a "special" bond and familial understanding. The two understood that money was no object to keep Barry in San Francisco. As Mieuli told him recently, "That's the way it should always be with us."[3]

Mieuli, stung to the quick by Barry's silent treatment, loitered absent-mindedly in the shoe department, eyeing the real reason for today's autograph fest: Woolworths' roll out of Barry's brand-new shoe line. It was called the "Super Star Rick Barry Basketball Shoe" by Randy, a.k.a., Pro 24s. Truth be told, designer Randy had followed the standard molded rubber, white canvas, and nylon laces of Chuck Taylor court apparel, but stitched on the side of the high-top model was an oval Rick Barry patch. Retail price: $9 ($84 today). Oh, the power of the patch and an active imagination. Kids now could Be Like Rick in much the same way as the next generation would Be Like Mike in their Air Jordans.

Barry, tall, young, blond, and handsome, was considered the most marketable talent to hit the NBA since Boston's Bob Cousy. Last season, mainly because of Barry and his chart-topping 35-point-per-game scoring average, the formerly ho-hum Warriors were the NBA's third-best road draw, behind New York and Los Angeles. At home last season, attendance had spiked to a record 1.1 million, and the once ne'er-do-well Warriors banked $650,000, one of the NBA's best showings.

Then there was Brand Barry, pro basketball's new off-court glamour boy with the expensive salon haircut.[4] In just two pro seasons, Barry had endorsements hawking shoes, sportswear, Snickers candy bars, a washing machine, laundry bleach, and a neighborhood savings-and-loan bank. Barry, who hired his own publicist like the New York superstars, also had his own local daily five-minute radio program and was in negotiations with a national book publisher to tell his life story. A television documentary on Barry titled "Super Soph" had recently aired locally. Quipped a national sports pundit, "Barry ranks second in popularity in San Francisco only to the five o'clock martini."[5]

Mieuli, still stung by the silent treatment, needed something right about now with a green olive floating in it to calm his nerves. He exited Woolworths, where a Powell Cable Car 503 clattered by every few minutes. Old 503 could be a spine-jarring ride, but it was nothing like the thump-thump-thump of this offseason. The other league, like the other woman, already had stolen Clyde Lee for a month-long fling while whispering to Barry and almost every Warrior about playing for more money and without Bill Sharman.

The latter was Mieuli's hire last season to coach the Warriors. Great guy off the court, warm, personable, and a respected former all-star with the champion Boston Celtics. But on the court, Coach Sharman was all work and no play. He pushed his Warriors to the breaking point to get them to obsess over basketball all day every day. He wanted everyone to bounce out of bed each morning and limber up with challenging, state-of-the-science exercises, then dress down for a mandatory early practice (even on game days). Afternoons were reserved for team meetings and film study (an NBA first). For Sharman, one of the original modern, hyper-organized NBA coaches, this team togetherness turned single-mindedness would translate into the success that he'd enjoyed as a Celtic. For his players, the 41-year-old Sharman was a like a sadistic, know-it-all big brother. The season already was too long, too injury filled, too sleep-deprived, too consumed with travel. Sharman's all basketball and no play was an Rx for exhaustion. Barry told a friend that he'd never been so unhappy in his basketball-playing life.

Thurmond recently had thought long and hard about absconding with Barry to Oakland. Mieuli talked him off that ledge, reminding him that the ABA money was mostly unguaranteed. The no guarantee did the trick, and Nate the Great resigned with the sure-thing Warriors for a fat raise. Mieuli now would take the same sure-thing tack with Barry. No guarantee, no gain. But the clock was ticking, and Mieuli had to get to Barry before he did the unthinkable.

Pardon Mieuli for allowing the ABA to pass through his team like a virus. For the past month, "Franklin," as all called him, had been mostly incommunicado in these low-tech times, firmly believing all back home in Warrior-land was the way he left it. Just fine. He had been toasting high European culture with his daughter in Paris and Rome, breaking bread with relatives in Tuscany, and shopping for red chandeliers. Red chandeliers?[6]

That was Franklin. He was always good for a laugh and an offbeat something or other. Some of the something or others were classic. Like his creepy hand sculptures in the lobby of the Warriors' front office. Like the life-sized wooden statue of an Indian chief with the cryptic bubble caption "Pass interference." Like his exposed-brick office with its scattering of unopened wine bottles, miniature figurines, antique watches, pill bottles, and an ornate cable car figure in the corner that doubled as his radio. Above his desk, dominated by a pair of gold-plated French telephones, a sign honored his reported 15-hour days selling pro basketball to the Bay Area: "A great promoter never sleeps."

"Abstract clutter," one visitor wisecracked, unless Franklin was around to offer an interpretive tour of his artifacts. Good luck with that. Franklin didn't sit still for long. He had a way of vanishing in mid-conversation, barreling off on more business, more whimsy somewhere in The City, as San Franciscans called their metropolis. Other times, he disappeared for the peace and relative tranquility of his native San Jose, where he still resided, the proud son of Giacomo Mieuli, an Italian immigrant who had "made good" there in the flower/nursery business.

Franklin wove his flights of fancy into all things Warriors. He personally designed his team's cable car jerseys and stitched "The City" across the front (drawing derision from fans in New York, Los Angeles, and now Chicago). While traveling in bad weather, his boys wore flashy custom black raincoats with a Golden Gate emblem over their breast, considered over the top by the NBA's old timers who wouldn't even buy umbrellas for their players. At home games, wearing his lucky sky-blue blazer and hip turtleneck, Franklin loved to ring a cable-car bell like the town crier to rally the crowd noise.

"He's a big-fat showoff," muttered one of his NBA rivals.[7]

And those red chandeliers? He would hang them courtside at the Cow Palace, one of the Warriors' prime home venues, as the mood lighting for his latest oddball adventure: a luxury suite. "Franklin created the first luxury suite," said then-Warrior Tom Meschery. "It was right on the ground, not tucked away upstairs in a skybox. Franklin removed a couple rows of seats at courtside and replaced them with dinner tables. He slapped white linen tablecloths on the tables, hung his chandeliers above them, and had waiters and waitresses ply his season-ticket holders with champagne before the game."[8]

Part of Mieuli's oddball mystique was real. For Mieuli, two plus two equaled five groovy reasons to try something different than the usual NBA fare. But much of it was learned years ago as a young, entry-level advertising whiz with Burgermeister Beer. Mieuli, hoping to build the brand name, encouraged the small brewery to buy the football San Francisco 49ers. Instead, "Burgie beer" sponsored the team's local radio broadcasts, and as fate would have it, Mieuli managed the commercials. That's when he introduced himself to 49ers' owner Tony Morabito, who was so smitten with this passionate young fellow and his desire to enter the sports business that he sold 10 percent of the team to Mieuli at a bargain-basement price. Mieuli, who earned $250 a month at the brewery, now had a financial asset to leverage his imagination, ambition, ego, and, above all, keen anticipation of more East Coast-centric pro leagues relocating to the West Coast with the advent of the twin-engine plane and affordable commercial air travel.

Mieuli quit the brewery in 1955 and started his own pioneering Bay Area sports broadcast company. He built a network of local radio and TV stations to blast 49ers games and other local sports fare across the Bay Area. He also assembled an impressive stable of announcers and cleverly fobbed off most of his production costs on the teams, sponsors, and stations. Three years later, when the baseball Giants moved from New York to San Francisco, Franklin shrewdly scored their broadcast rights as well. Not only that, he yet again charmed his way into a piece of the team. By 1960, Mieuli ruled sports broadcasting across the Bay Area. He was rich, though hardly filthy rich, but substantial enough to consider the trifecta: buy into an NBA team.

In 1962, opportunity knocked when the NBA's Philadelphia Warriors were purchased and relocated to San Francisco by the Lemat Company, LLC. Lemat, the first-name portmanteau of businessmen Len Mogel and Matt Simmons, bet that the Warriors' superstar Wilt Chamberlain would be a huge hit in San Francisco, where city officials were considering whether to build a downtown sports palace worthy of an NBA team. As part of the San Francisco relocation, Mieuli managed to elbow in for a 7 percent stake in Lemat and, of course, the Warriors' broadcast rights. Mission accomplished.

Except the mission seemed doomed from lift off. Wilt and the Warriors lost big on and off the court that first season, dropping an unhealthy $250,000 (today about $2.5 million) and dividing home games among the city's subpar sporting venues like the Cow Palace, still sans the red chandeliers, and then very much an all-purpose livestock pavilion known for its swarms of flesh-eating horseflies. Or like the makeshift Civic Center, just down the block from the city's Tenderloin District and all things illicit.

Mogel and Simmons wanted out when the city dragged its feet on the new arena, and Mieuli obliged for $850,000. He assembled some local investors to defray his purchase outlay and took full control of the team, now his primary business.[9] It was a bit of a financial reach for Mieuli, but he muddled his way forward over the next several unprofitable seasons. His investors bailed on "Franklin's Folly," and he sold off some investments for needed cash to keep the team going. "They knew the college game," Mieuli explained the disconnect between Chamberlain and Bay Area fans, "and Wilt would dunk one ball after another. But that was too dull for the fans. They didn't come to see that."[10] He vividly recalled the night that his Chamberlain-led Warriors drew 328 paid admissions for a gate of $982, "which didn't even pay the Big Dipper's salary for the night."[11]

Behind on paying the Big Dipper and having lost $700,000 on the Warriors in three seasons, Mieuli admitted, "The roof fell in on me."[12] And so, he traded Chamberlain at the 1965 NBA All-Star Game for $300,000 in needed cash and three mediocre players. It was, hands down, the worst player-for-player trade in NBA history. But Mieuli reportedly had raced from hotel room to hotel room singing Chamberlain's praises like a door-to-door salesman trying to unload an expensive vacuum. "What?" answered then-Philadelphia owner Ike Richman and the eventual taker. "You don't trade a Chamberlain any more than an Elgin Baylor or a Bill Russell."[13]

Then, as if by sheer luck or divine intervention, everything clicked in Warrior-land during the 1966-67 season. Mieuli's former ho-hum Warriors were now the oh-wow talk of the NBA under the tutelage of young coach Bill Sharman. His Warriors, featuring the exciting young nucleus of Thurmond and especially Barry, still played in the creaky Cow Palace and the makeshift Civic Center. But Mieuli had moved his boys part-time into the brand-new 15,000-seat arena across the bay in, gasp, gritty Oakland. The bright, shiny modern arena brought bigger crowds and, critically, Mieuli's first profits in the basketball business. Franklin's Folly was now Franklin's Jolly Good Time.

Franklin was indeed a jolly good fellow to start 1967. He oversaw one big, happy, first-place basketball family built on old-fashioned Italian *amore* and *ama la vita*. Mention his name, and his players often chuckled like schoolkids at a kooky, favorite teacher. They broke bread with him, drank wine with him, and toasted his sappy dream of establishing the Warriors into a San Francisco treat worthy of the 49ers, Fisherman's Wharf, Ghirardelli chocolate, abalone, and the It's-It Bar.

And now, Franklin's jollies had morphed back to his follies. Like a tragic Verdi opera, if only Franklin hadn't been so proud and profoundly tone deaf to his players' grumbles about Sharman, his *amore* and *ama la vita* could have lived on forever and a sublime day.

Franklin Mieuli may have been down, but he certainly wasn't out. Call it his great contradiction. Though all giggles and stats on the outside, Franklin was as hyper-competitive on the inside as Barry driving to the hoop. Franklin was the great promoter who never sleeps. The great salesman with the golden touch. The great adman with the catchy idea, the winning innovation. Part of his inner-competitive self was hardwired into his DNA. Part of it was social conditioning from too many shut-up-and-listen board meetings with the NBA old-timers, the crusty arena owners and promoters who hadn't slept for decades. They shared their box-office epistles like numbered commandments, promising fire and brimstone upon any foolhardy promoter who disobeyed their Word on it.

"You leave a team to your goddamn manager, and he'll run up your salaries," the old timers told Mieuli. "Leave it to the coach, and he'll trade off your best player because he doesn't like the way he parts his hair."[14]

In other words, trust no one, call the shots, trust your gut. "He had to make all the decisions," former Warriors coach Alex Hannum said of Mieuli. "Everyone had to agree with him or he got upset."[15] In Hannum's case, he was fired for failing to comply with Mieuli's latest marketing brainstorm.

In Barry's case, remember their bond? Barry couldn't quit; the great promoter wasn't done with him yet. From Mieuli's perspective, Barry was just a confused, 22-year-old kid prone to making rash business decisions. He needed a lawyer or an impartial agent to walk him through the obvious: The Warriors could win an NBA championship next season. Barring a serious injury, Barry would be America's iconic Mr. Basketball through the 1970s, with all its fame and financial perks. Why throw it all away on a gypsy league that would be here today and presumably gone tomorrow?

Anita, Franklin's long-suffering assistant, called Barry and confirmed a special sit-down with the boss for next Tuesday morning. That's when Franklin would present Barry with a second offer for a $75,000 annual base salary. Guaranteed. Then he'd plead with him at this late hour, heart-to-heart, man-to-man, wise Italian uncle-to-confused, ill-informed kid, to please come home. Resign with the Warriors.

San Francisco, June 20, 1967—By 9:30 a.m., the coastal morning fog had burned off, leaving in view clear summer skies and the bustle of media activity up on Nob Hill. A light brigade of vehicles offloaded bulky equipment that rolled, bumped, and thudded into the Bellevue Hotel, where the Warriors lived. "You would have thought World War III was under way from the congestion and cameras, mikes, and newsmen around the morning Barry delivered his fateful choice," observed one among the inquisitive hoard.

"Are you still a Warrior, Rick?" a voice bellowed when Barry was finally spotted ambling down a narrow basement passageway leading from the parking garage to the Warriors' basement office, team flags and pennants displayed like an NBA embassy.

"I'll find out now," he mumbled and hurried into the office.[16]

By 10 a.m., Rick Barry had taken his seat in Mieuli's office, looking dapper in a navy-blue suit, pale blue shirt, and a red-and-blue striped tie. He was anxious to dispense with the pleasantries. First things first, Franklin insisted, and extracted several pristine sheets of paper labeled "Uniform Player Contract" from his desk drawer. This time, Barry looked up at Franklin and interrupted his just sign here. Barry informed him that he'd agreed to the meeting to offer an update. "I'm going to play for Oakland," Barry spilled.

"Have you signed a contract?"

"Yes."

Barry said he'd signed yesterday, and Franklin scoffed that the ABA money wasn't guaranteed. That the league was doomed. That it would never get off the ground. Franklin insisted for Barry's own good that he sign the NBA contract on his desk. His lawyers would fix his ABA indiscretion. Barry declined, and around and around they went.

About 40 minutes later, Barry spun out of the office and straight into a knot of microphones and a bright, disorienting bank of cameras, all rolling. "It was the most difficult decision of my life," he calmly told the mob. "I signed for strictly business reasons, because I thought the offer represented the best possible future for my wife and my family."

Oakland, now renamed the Oaks, paid Barry and family a then-astounding half-million dollars, which included a 15 percent ownership stake in the Oakland franchise and various incentives. To put this three-year deal in perspective, Boston's Bill Russell, the league's highest-paid star, made $125,000 per season as a player AND coach.

The money sounded way too good to be true—and indeed it was. Barry actually signed a three-year, $250,000 contract (or, $75,000 per season) plus the previously announced extras. But the ABA allowed the inflated figure, especially the word "million," to waft through the sports world like a song.

This date, with the NBA's equivalent of Pearl Harbor, would live in infamy. It wasn't exactly a sneak attack. But it was shocking just the same that the pint-sized ABA pulled it off. Barry, the half-million-dollar man and budding sports brand, lent desperately needed celebrity—and thus credibility—to the fledgling league. As George Mikan liked to tell the ABA owners, "Give me three years, and I'll give you a [viable] league." With Barry's "Golden Boy" image as their foot in the door with basketball fans, Mikan and his colleagues could now assume that, despite their initial stumbling and bumbling, they could bank on at least three years to put the ABA's innovative house in order.

Los Angeles, June 24, 1967—The Rick Barry signing quickly became the Rick Barry case. Franklin Mieuli had emerged from his office on that infamous morning to his own knot of microphones and vowing to file a $10 million ($92 million today) whopper of a lawsuit. It would be the sum of all his grievances with the ABA and his now-self-described "Prodigal Son" Barry. But first things first, Mieuli gave the green light to his trusted attorney Luther Avery to file in San Francisco Superior Court for an immediate injunction to block Barry from playing in the ABA until the $10 million matter could be properly litigated.

Avery, a 44-year-old tax expert with a disengaged personality that was once described to be "like talking to a cloud," had filed for a similar injunction just weeks ago in the ill-fated Clyde Lee case. Lee was summoned to appear in court while waiting with his wife at San Francisco International Airport before embarking upon a dream vacation to Hawaii, paid for by the ABA. Tonight, Barry was served at an equally inopportune time. He was a guest of honor at a highbrow fundraiser for the City of Hope medical center at the Beverly Hills Hilton, ironically where the ABA was born. While Barry mingled in his monkey suit, he was interrupted by the handing off of the summons to report to San Francisco Superior Court.

Barry, unlike Lee and the NBA's other medium-to-high-profile jumpers, shrugged off the intrusion. He'd expected the summons sooner or hopefully later in a less-public venue. He'd also remained committed to Oakland. Barry simply had more skin in the ABA game than Lee or the other jumpers. Bruce Hale, his college coach and now father-in-law, was the new headman in Oakland. What's more, co-owner and popular singer Pat Boone promised to help Brand Barry break into Hollywood as a side perk of joining the ABA.

Barry also was guided by idealism. "If an auto salesman walks off his lot and goes across the street and takes another job on another lot because it pays him $20 more a week, no one thinks anything of it, no one thinks he's doing wrong," he told writer Bill Libby. "If an insurance man leaves his firm and goes with another firm because it offers him more opportunity for advancement, everyone applauds his determination to get ahead . . . Well, then, why in hell can't a basketball player go to another team with another league, whatever his reason, without people calling him selfish and greedy and traitorous?"[17]

Such stay-the-course statements from Barry were music to the ears of the ABA trustees, especially the lawyers in the room who needed a test case to challenge the complex, multi-layered web of the NBA reserve system. At its core, the system reserved for each NBA team the exclusive league rights to any player it selected in the college draft, traded for, or signed as an off-the-streets free agent. In other words, NBA teams could claim to own their players like land, paper clips, nail polish, and any other commodity. These player commodities, unless released by their teams and thereafter unclaimed by rival franchises, couldn't switch teams or swap leagues on their own.

The NBA lawyers argued that the reserve system was backed by the U.S. Supreme Court as the law of the sports land. The Supreme Court allusion made the "reserve" seem as certain as death, taxes, and the laws of classical physics. Challenge the reserve system, and the courts would slam the offending player with million-dollar fines that he'd need to work off for the rest of his life. Think LeRoy Ellis. Only a few NBA players knew enough to question the legal basis of the reserve system. That was by design. Players played; the front office ran the business. But there was quite an epic tale to tell about the reserve system in pro sports. . . and a myth worth cracking.

The reserve system has its roots in America's Gilded Age (1870-1890s), a time when many a great American industrial fortune was made the old-fashioned way: through brains and bribery. Mark Twain dubbed these self-aggrandizing nouveau aristocrats as "robber barons" for bending laws and land claims to their financial advantage, then crushing labor and crippling competition to maximize their profits and power.

It was also during the Gilded Age that pro baseball captured America's imagination. Civic leaders in several Eastern and Midwestern amateur baseball hotbeds formed the first all-salaried pro teams to advertise their cities as "winning" places to live and work. These hard-swinging teams, operated by the players themselves, sometimes made their sponsors proud. More often, these teams descended into scandal as the shadier players in the bunch openly bet on games, jumped their teams in midseason for better deals elsewhere, and just couldn't seem to behave at the corner tavern. And yet, these summertime baseball extravaganzas, pitting rival cities in nine innings of high heat, could be profitable, and the more opportunistic investors in the bunch took note.[18]

Several saw an opportunity to get with these gilded times and corner the pro baseball market. Opportunity knocked loudest in February 1876 when several white-collar investors, convinced that baseball had to be saved from the foolhardiness of the players, organized an intervention called the National League of Professional Base Ball Clubs (today, the National League) to run the game like a "closed corporation." It featured its own corporate bylaws to promote parity among the teams, standard schedules, and standard league dues.

Importantly, the men around the table pledged allegiance to squeezing labor and making the National League more stable and profitable. They agreed to cap player salaries at $2,000 per annum and formed an unwritten pact to ban, really blackball, all variety of troublemaker. By 1879, they also tacitly agreed to allow each team to have dibs on, or "reserve as property," their five best players. That would prevent owners from competing amongst themselves to sign players and keep the salary cap firm. Four years later, the reserve was extended to all players. These agreements, mostly unquestioned, gave management near-complete control over players and the terms and conditions of their contracts.

By the early 1880s, the Gilded Age had spawned several bigger and bolder tricks of the corporate trade. That included a new management structure called a trust, a combination of independent businesses that answered to a governing board of investors. It's impossible in one pithy sentence to capture the trust's profound cultural implications. But one point is critical here. Trusts freed corporations from the longstanding prohibitions on owning businesses in any state but the one in which they were chartered to operate. Thus, corporate CEOs for the first time could vertically integrate businesses, or inputs, into the manufacturing process and dominate markets, or in the language of political economy, interstate commerce.

By 1900, magazine exposes brought into full light the democracy-diluting dangers of the all-powerful trust. Congress stepped in to pass antitrust reforms, such as the broadly worded Sherman Antitrust Act of 1890, and political hopefuls knew to tap into this populist sentiment and rail against the Rockefellers, Morgans, and Vanderbilts for manipulating the system and turning the American Dream to their unbending advantage.

The era's antitrust spirit eventually surfaced in professional baseball when the Baltimore Terrapins, a debt-ridden member of the defunct Federal Baseball League, sued the National and now American leagues, collectively Major League Baseball (MLB). The Terrapins alleged that the MLB operated as a trust of independent businesses (baseball teams) acting in league as a corporate monopoly (MLB) that thwarted members of the Federal Baseball League from participating freely in interstate commerce. That marketplace spanned multiple cities from Boston to Chicago, making it seemingly beholden to the Constitution's commerce clause and the federal government's exclusive right to regulate interstate commerce.

The Terrapins claimed in particular that had an open market existed to sign the best players, the Federal Baseball League could have survived and competed fair and square with the MLB. But the reserve system overseen by the MLB bosses ("highwaymen," they called them) stifled competition and literally trampled the liberty of the players, transforming them into property that belonged to these highwaymen like "chattel and slaves," stripped of their legal rights as American citizens to seek employment wherever they pleased.

The case banged around the lower courts for several years, landing in April 1919 in the Supreme Court of the District of Columbia. The jury awarded the Terrapins $240,000 ($3.8 million today). The decision was reversed on appeal, however, and the Terrapins petitioned the U.S. Supreme Court in 1922 for a final ruling in a case entered on its docket as *Federal Baseball Club of Baltimore, Inc. vs. National League of Professional Baseball Clubs*. This was the groundbreaking case that the NBA lawyers referenced, like death and taxes, to protect the reserve system.

George Wharton Pepper, the MLB attorney in the case and a newly elected U.S. senator, didn't waste the court's time debating antitrust law. His defense zeroed in on the same technicality that he'd presented in the lower courts with mixed results. While the federal government alone holds the constitutional power to regulate commerce among the states, Pepper contended that the Terrapins and their lawyers had blundered in their definition of interstate commerce. He later explained, "I raised at every opportunity the objection that a spontaneous output of human activity is not in its nature commerce, that therefore organized baseball cannot be interstate commerce; and that, it not being commerce among the states, the federal statute could have no application."[19]

Pepper's circular argument provided the court with a technicality, a debatable excuse to avoid blowing up the national pastime and its 40 years of profits. In the court's unanimous decision, Chief Justice Oliver Wendell Holmes wrote that the matter at hand "is giving exhibitions of baseball, which are purely state affairs." Holmes found that the interstate travel among teams "is a mere accident, not the essential thing. That to which it is incident, the exhibition, although made for money, would not be called trade or commerce in the commonly accepted use of those words."[20]

Like manna from on legal high, Major League Baseball had been awarded an exemption from American antitrust law. Gilded Age entitlement had survived to monopolize another day at the old ballpark. Even though the ruling was meant for baseball only, other professional sports dared to lay claim to the antitrust exemption in theory, assuming that, if push came to legal shove, Oliver Wendell Holmes had their backs. After all, football, hockey, and the rest served the same recreational purposes, only with different rules and equipment.

In 1946, the National Basketball Association of America (BAA), the forerunner to the NBA, hopped aboard baseball's antitrust exemption. Maurice Podoloff, the BAA president, drafted the league constitution and bylaws, lifting most of the text directly from the founding documents of the American Hockey League (AHL), where he also served as president. Included in his cut-and-paste was the AHL's reserve labor system and its restrictions on player movement patterned after pro baseball's reserve.[21]

In 1953, though acknowledging the 1922 decision was troublesome, the Supreme Court upheld baseball's antitrust exemption, though on the grounds that pro baseball had evolved with the antitrust exemption. To turn back the clock would destroy an American tradition. Four years later, in *Radovich v. the National Football League*, the court ruled that the NFL, unlike Major League Baseball, was subject to antitrust law. "If this ruling is unrealistic, inconsistent, or illogical," stated the majority opinion about its break from the baseball exemption, "it is sufficient to answer, aside from distinctions between the businesses [of football and baseball], that were we considering the question of baseball for the first time upon a clean slate, we would have no doubts" that the national pastime was subject to antitrust law, too.

Confused? Everyone was. The justices, however, proposed kicking this can of worms to Congress, stating it had the power to overturn baseball's antitrust exemption, if so desired. That was welcome news to a dedicated core of trust-busting congressmen. They began holding hearings and sniffing around for possible monopolistic business practices in professional sports, much to the chagrin of Podoloff. "I am firmly of the opinion that without certain rights, basketball cannot successfully operate . . . ," Podoloff testified in 1958, referring to the NBA's piggy-backing baseball's exemption and the reserve system. "These rights are the very foundation stones of the structure of professional basketball and any change in them will cause the structure to deteriorate and eventually topple."[22]

When Podoloff retired in 1963, Congress was still sniffing around, though with no progress on any legislative action. Podoloff could recall only a handful of minor court cases during his tenure that took up the NBA's reserve system, pro and con, or the Sherman act.[23] The former were inconclusive and settled on mitigating circumstances. For the latter, the judge presiding over the *Washington Professional Basketball Corp. v. National Basketball Association* case (1956)   delivered a preliminary ruling that served as a shot across the NBA's bow. "The business of professional basketball," he wrote, "conducted on a multistate basis, coupled with the sale of rights to televise and broadcast games for interstate transmission is trade or commerce among the several states within the meaning of the Sherman Act." Lucky for Podoloff, the case got thrown out of court soon thereafter on a filing error and was never resubmitted.

Challenges to the NBA reserve system weren't going away. The system was just too restrictive on too many players eager to make top dollar while their legs and jump shots were still able. For the NBA, as long as those occasional legal challenges involved individual players, lone wolves, chances were good that the reserve system would emerge unscathed. NBA lawyers were skilled at seeking injunctions and otherwise tying up these disagreements in court as simple, one-off contract disputes. Even if the lone wolves dug in and made federal cases of the reserve system, their chances of success would be wanting. The needed federal antitrust cases, with their potent legal decrees that could halt the reserve system, were out of a lone wolf's price range, in part because they dragged on expensively in an auto-churn of depositions, motions, countermotions, and unexpected delays. All while the lone wolf sat idle and stewing—no basketball, no paycheck, no assurance of winning the case. In fact, win or lose, NBA owners could be mobbish and vindictive toward those who crossed them. In the end, the wise lone wolf settled out of court or let filing errors stand, anything to get back to playing basketball.

However, combine a resolute player with a well-resourced rival league anxious to make him a near millionaire, and the NBA stared down the barrel of a loaded shotgun. That was the Barry injunction. True, Franklin Mieuli took the ABA to court to protect his "property." Where things turned double-barreled is Mieuli would argue as grounds for the injunction that Barry was subject to his NBA contract's option clause, part of the reserve system. This argument opened the door for a court to comment and possibly rule on the legality of the option—and the reserve—in an NBA contract. But Mieuli had no choice. Pointing to the option as the breach of contract was the only way for the Warriors or any NBA team to make their case to retain their property.

The option was listed in every player contract as article 24, ironically Barry's uniform number. When Barry signed his last NBA contact, he tacitly agreed that at the end of his one-year deal (September 1967), the Warriors had the option to retain his rights for another season, while paying him 75 percent of his former salary if he and Mieuli couldn't reach a new agreement. That bought Mieuli and the Warriors some wiggle room to assess Barry's true value to the team, in uniform or out (his choice), and ultimately offer him a fair contract to resolve the impasse.

Though clearly written, article 24 was profoundly confusing for what it left out. Namely, how long could the Warriors evaluate Barry's true worth? A day? A year? A career? Nobody knew for sure. The word-of-mouth answer, encouraged by management, was the open-ended: as long as it takes. The Warriors, after all, owned Barry's NBA rights through the reserve system, meaning they could renew his option each September for the remainder of his career. That was true in theory. However, no NBA team had ever tried it. There hadn't been a need. Until now, without a viable second league, nearly all players simply didn't dare buck the system.

If Barry and the ABA stayed the legal course, they would receive a first verdict on the legality of the NBA's option clause. It wouldn't be a sweeping federal ruling. Mieuli and his lawyers had been careful and, since the Warriors and Oaks were based in California, they filed for the injunction in the state court system. Assuming the ruling favored the Warriors under simple contract law, the ABA would get a bonus ruling. The judge would need to determine how long the option bound Barry to the Warriors. A day? A year? A career?

Both verdicts would be vital for the ABA moving forward. The NBA touted six legitimate superstars: Bill Russell, Wilt Chamberlain, Elgin Baylor, Jerry West, Oscar Robertson, and now Rick Barry. Capture them, like knights on a chessboard, and the ABA could make a powerful case for a network television contract and, like the American Football League before it, survive on an annual six- or seven-figure corporate subsidy that afforded national visibility and thus credibility and marketability. Of course, Russell and West weren't interested in the ABA. But Baylor, Chamberlain, and Robertson were mildly curious. That was a start. To reel them in, the ABA needed money and a verdict in the Barry injunction that liberated players from the option clause or finally clarified it.

Anaheim, Calif., July 10, 1967—George Mikan scheduled today's ABA Board of Trustees meeting believing the decision in the Rick Barry injunction would be out by now, and the league's next steps would be open for debate. Instead, the presiding judge delayed his decision, claiming a busy calendar, and Mikan and his trustees were left this afternoon at the Disneyland Hotel to ponder the pros and cons of Rick

Barry's feet. Make that, the Superstar Rick Barry Basketball Shoes, a.k.a., the Pro 24s, the same designer sneaker that had rolled out last month at Woolworth's.[24]

Bud de Recat, maker of the Pro 24s, had a business proposition. With Barry one fateful legal decision away from headlining the ABA, de Recat asked the trustees to consider naming his Pro 24s as the ABA's official shoe. De Recat then offered a free year's supply of Pro 24s to every ABA team. The trustees thanked de Recat, but took a pass on his offer.

From Barry's feet, the trustee's moved to Barry's signature. Would the NBA reserve system hold up in court? The consensus was the NBA had no legal right to restrict Barry from playing where he wanted or claim ownership of him in perpetuity, with its feudal overtones to slavery. To do so was a violation of antitrust law, and getting at the antitrust heart of the matter was where the mood in the room turned heated. Mikan and league chief counsel Bill Erickson proposed a wait-and-see approach to the injunction. Indiana trustee and lawyer Dick Tinkham wasn't buying it. He insisted that the league, via Barry's lawyers, file a motion alleging antitrust violations. Oh, but that was a longer conversation.

In San Francisco nine days later, presiding Judge Robert Drewes finally heard arguments for and against the injunction. "They would like to keep the old clause forever to stop competition," contended Barry's attorney John Cole, "they" referred to the NBA, calling its contractual devices "a millstone" around his client's neck. "To quote the chairman of a Congressional committee which investigated the baseball situation: 'The management can discharge the player, but the player cannot discharge the management.'"[25]

The lawyers for both sides gestured, objected, and Your Honored for three hours before Judge Drewes finally gaveled the hearing to a recess. They'd revisit the injunction next week.

San Francisco, August 8, 1967—Eight weeks ago, before walking out on the Warriors, Rick Barry handed over the keys to the red Porsche that Franklin Mieuli leased for him. That evening, Mieuli drove the Porsche to a remote hill, which he called "a cliff," and "bawled" his eyes out. Today, Mieuli's eyes spilled tears of joy over Judge Robert Drewes' unexpected approval of the Barry injunction.

Make that, the timing was unexpected. Barry's lawyers filed a last-minute motion asking for Judge Drewes to consider the case's implications for California antitrust law, an area of jurisprudence that the Warriors and the NBA wanted to avoid. So did Judge Drewes. A preliminary hearing was scheduled for this morning to take up the merits of the ABA's antitrust motion, a legal battle that could last for weeks and clog Judge Drewes' orderly court docket for months. Instead, Judge Drewes shocked everyone by issuing a prepared statement granting the injunction without considering the antitrust motion. "There can be no doubt that [the] defendant deliberately breeched the solemn contractual obligation to play for the plaintiff, and the court so finds," ruled Judge Drewes.

He elaborated that the reserve clause "appears to this court to be reasonably necessary to provide that stability and continuity required for the efficient management of such an enterprise [as the NBA]," adding, ". . . substantially identical league practices and contract provisions prevalent in professional baseball are not illegal as promoting monopolies, either as to cities or as to players."[26]

For the NBA, it finally had a court ruling to wave in the air that validated the reserve system. "I'm happy to hear the ruling," sounded off St. Louis owner Ben Kerner, one of the league founders. "This is what the NBA believed is right to keep a business in operation without creating chaos."[27]

Franklin Mieuli joked that he wanted the ruling tattooed across his hairy chest. He repeated the judge's words as proof that Oakland had acted improperly, and he promptly sued the

Oaks for $4.5 million, alleging the ABA team had indeed tampered with Barry. Mieuli's seven-figure bout of pain and suffering amounted to another game of legal chicken. Mieuli, assuming it was only a matter of time before Barry resigned with the Warriors, wanted to warn his rivals in the East Bay not to contest the inevitable.

It was Judge Drewes' second decision that put a crimp in the NBA's celebration. He interpreted the option as legally binding for one extra season. No more, no less. The ABA now had a workable answer to the option mystery. Chamberlain, Robertson, and every last NBA player were free to join the ABA in a year or two. If the ABA owners could tread water and option clauses for the next few years, they could bid their way to parity with the NBA, just like the American Football League had in its successful fight with the established NFL.

Endnotes

[1] This section is based on numerous sources, including: Phil Berger, "Why Rick Barry Switched Leagues," *1968 Pro Basketball Illustrated*; Rick Barry and Bill Libby, *Confessions of a Basketball Gypsy*, 1972; Al Stump, "The Fan Who Came in From the Cold," *True Magazine*, March 1968; Frank Deford, "The Education of Mr. Barry," *Sports Illustrated*, August 14, 1967, and interviews with Al Attles and Fred Hetzel.

[2] Berger, *1968 Pro Basketball Illustrated*; Stump, *True Magazine*.

[3] Deford, *Sports Illustrated*, August 14, 1967.

[4] Barry spent $6.50 (today around $62) for a customized razor cut and shampoo, then considered extravagant for a square-jawed athlete. "Wearing it this way does something for a person," Barry countered his critics. "It makes you feel like somebody."

[5] Jim Murray, "Frisco's Barry is Real Civic Hero," *Los Angeles Times*, January 11, 1967.

[6] This section is drawn from many sources, including: Al Stump, "The Fan Who Came in From the Cold," *True Magazine*, March 1968; Rich Wescott, *The Mogul*, 2008; Wells Twombly, "Capt. Mieuli Sank Valley with Ease,"

San Francisco Examiner, April 13, 1976; Rick Setlowe, "Franklin Mieuli," *San Francisco Examiner*, April 7, 1963; Frank Deford, "Will Franklin Mieuli Spoil Success," *Sports Illustrated*, February 15, 1971; Warren Wynkoop, "How Mieuli Took Over SF Pro Sports," *San Francisco Examiner*, May 26, 1964.

[7] Stump, *True Magazine*

[8] Tom Meschery, Interview with author, February 2011.

[9] No Byline, "Franklin Mieuli: Viewpoint," *Basketball Weekly*, April 2, 1981.

[10] Wescott, *The Mogul*, p. 251.

[11] Stump, *True Magazine*.

[12] Ibid.

[13] Ibid.

[14] Murray Olberman, "Phantom of the Hardcourt," *San Francisco Examiner*, p. 7.

[15] Rick Barry and Bill Libby, *Confessions of a Basketball Gypsy*, 1972, p. 94.

[16] James McGee, "As Low as You Can Get," *San Francisco Examiner*, June 21, 1967.

[17] Rick Barry and Bill Libby, *Confessions of a Basketball Gypsy*, 1972, p. 127.

[18] There are multiple sources on the origins of early American pro baseball. This section relies heavily on Harvey Frommer, *Primitive Baseball*, 1988, and Andrew Zimbalist, *Baseball and Billions*, 1992.

[19] George Wharton Pepper, *Philadelphia Lawyer*, 1944, p. 357.

[20] Federal Baseball Club of Baltimore, Inc. vs. National League of Professional Baseball Clubs, 259 U.S. 200 (1922)

[21] Neil Isaacs, "Maurice Podoloff," *Vintage NBA*, 1996, p. 232; Neil Isaacs, Interview with author, June 2020. Isaacs elaborated that Podoloff had mentioned the cut-and-paste origin of the NBA reserve system during their interview.

[22] Statement of Maurice Podoloff, U.S. Senate Subcommittee on Antitrust and Monopoly, July 31, 1958.

[23] Washington Professional Basketball Corp. v. National Basketball Association (1956); Molinas v. National Basketball Association (1961);

Central New York Basketball, Inv. v. Barnett (1961); Sears v. Graham-Paige, Corp. (1961).

[24] Minutes, American Basketball Association Meeting, Anaheim, Calif., July 10, 1967.

[25] Clint Mosher, "Mieuli Offered Barry $75,000," *San Francisco Examiner*, July 20, 1967.

[26] Lemat Corporation v. Barry, 80 Cal. Rptr. 240 (1969)

[27] United Press International, "Barry Can't Join ABA," *Boston Globe*, August 9, 1967.

6

Oakland, Calif., Oct. 13, 1967—California governor Ronald Reagan sent his apologies. He and wife Nancy would not be attending tonight's inaugural ABA game between the Anaheim Amigos and Oakland Oaks. No Gipper, no worry. There was still plenty of star power. Pat Boone, the popular crooner and Oaks' owner, would belt out the national anthem. He'd also crown Miss Oakland at halftime, right after pop singer Toni Arden dazzled the house, alternating in perfect pitch between English and Italian.

All were assembled tonight in the Oakland-Alameda Coliseum on this Friday the Thirteenth. There would be no vampire sightings to spoil the fun, though seated courtside was the slightly ghoulish countenance of Charley Hinkle. He was Oakland's 43-year-old publicity director and designated radio voice. Hinkle and his throaty Appalachian twang had a long and distinguished career behind the microphone calling harness races in his native southern Ohio.

When times turned tough in southern Ohio during the 1950s. Hinkle relocated to Pittsburgh, where he called races and moonlighted as the radio voice of Duquesne University basketball. But Hinkle started hitting the bottle, reportedly crashing an expensive car into a ditch and also struggling to stay ahead of his gambling debts. He needed out of Pittsburgh and sent audition tapes to, among other places, the brand-new Oakland Oaks; and damn, if he didn't get the job. Now, through the grace of God and nothing stronger than an occasional beer, he'd get his life straight out West.

Redemption was also the storyline for virtually all the tall guys warming up for tonight's ABA opener. There was number 33 Willie Porter, cut by the NBA Cincinnati Royals and trying to find another team that paid. He was known as "Fang" for getting his front teeth knocked out during an earlier exhibition game. Number 34 was Lavern Tart, a.k.a. "Jelly." The streak-shooting southpaw had bounced around the semi-pro Eastern League, hoping to reignite his pro career. Then Oakland called, and Jelly jiggled off to make some cash. Number 54 was the lumbering seven-footer Mike Dabich. Everyone called him "Frankie," short for Frankenstein. He backed up number 42, "Jumbo Jim" Hadnot, a local kid who played his college ball back East. Jumbo Jim couldn't crack the Boston Celtics' roster after college, and the Oaks were his last shot at drawing a pro salary.

Oakland's lone superstar Rick Barry was around the arena somewhere in street clothes. He would presumably join Jelly and the others next year after, judge's orders, sitting out his NBA option season. Funny, that wasn't the case for Anaheim's number 40, Ben Warley. He played last season for the NBA Baltimore Bullets, then Seattle grabbed him and his expiring one-year contract (including the added option season) in the NBA expansion draft. Warley signed with Anaheim instead, drawing a distracted shrug from Seattle officials.[1] And so, Warley and a few other low-value NBA ex-pats could play immediately, while Barry sat for a season never far from further legal jeopardy.

Hinkle was minutes away from gametime, while back in the Berkeley studios of KPAT ("1400 on your radio dial") host Al Edwards wrapped up his "Sound of Music" program, the best of the 1940s from Dorsey to Sinatra. Now came the hard part. KPAT had never broadcast a live sporting event, and, fingers crossed, the hookup would hold. Edwards bid everyone a pleasant good evening, followed by the tick, tick, tick of KPAT's iconic metronome to signal the next program, and then, presto, Hinkle was live with the Oaks and Amigos, Jumbo Jim and Jelly.

Hinkle read the starting lineups handed to him, and then "they were off" like the ponies. The first ABA game was up and down, back and forth, and occasionally side to side. Jelly to Jumbo Jim and out to Fang and Steve "Snapper" Jones. The Oaks scored 70 points in the first half and 134 for the game. That was good enough to edge the 129 points of the scrappy Amigos, led by their mad three-point bomber Les Selvage. He played last season for the Phi Beta Sigs of Southern California's Interfraternity Negro League and reportedly kept his fingernails long to better control the ball. They audibly scraped off the red, white, and blue on each of his three-point hoists.

"They said we wouldn't make it," told-you-so'ed ABA commissioner George Mikan afterwards. "Well, we've waited a long time for this night, and it has been a fine one. I think it's very good quality basketball and, like everything else that's new, it can only get better."[2]

Barry, after pointing out some defensive flaws and rookie mistakes, got with the effusive opening-night program. "That three-point shot is going to open the floor up because you have to defend against it, and that opens up the middle. Both these clubs run your legs off, and they're both big."[3]

When Hinkle called races back home, his signature line was, "Here they all come," delivered with a guttural flair and flourish. That line captured the awesome possibility on display tonight through the league's opening week. The ABA's 11 teams finally galloped forth, though mostly greeted by empty seats. In addition to the roughly 1,000 free admissions tonight in Oakland, just 4,826 people paid the two bucks to pull up a Coke and a hot dog and be a part of basketball history. Still, it was a start. Hinkle signed off from courtside, and KPAT returned to its regular programming with host Walt Jamond and his "turntable twirlings" until 6 a.m.

Minneapolis, Oct. 22, 1967—The ABA conjured itself forth with mostly by-the-book team nicknames, such as Oaks, Pipers, Colonels, and the edgier Buccaneers. ABA organizer Dennis Murphy, now doing publicity in Denver, pushed for naming the franchise after the Colorado state bird: Lark Buntings. Thankfully, Murphy was overruled in favor of the manly Rockets.

But there was one ABA team nickname that confused everyone—the Minnesota Muskies. What the heck was a muskie? Not even Larry Shields, the California construction magnate whom Murphy roped into purchasing 80 percent of the Minnesota franchise, seemed to know. A muskie, or "muskellunge" in Swedish, is a North American species of large freshwater fish with incredible strength and endurance. Or, more colloquially, a muskie is a big, honking pike that's hard to catch and tough to haul into a boat. Muskies are also notoriously, as they say in Swedish, *grim*.

How ugly was on full display at halftime of the Minnesota's opening game against Kentucky at the brand-new Met Center. Eddie Holman, who owned most of the other 20 percent of the team and served as general manager, stood fidgeting during a ceremonial presentation of a mounted 44-pound muskie caught last July in the foreign waters of Wisconsin. Hopefully, the thing didn't flap mechanically or play polka music. Holman offered the requisite, "oh my," and looked for somebody to take this beast off his hands. But Holman had almost no staff. His team had been advertising for weeks to hire a head of promotions and a crew of part-time salespeople. But, like landing a muskie, it was tough reeling them in.

Holman and his mounted muskie found their courtside seat, and the second half commenced featuring his greatest ABA accomplishment to date: rookie center Mel Daniels, his first pick in the first ABA draft. The University of New Mexico grad was the only college All-American to go ABA in 1967. But Daniels already threw around his body, hips, and elbows like a seasoned pro. For Holman, all pats on the back aside, signing Daniels was a classic case of beginner's luck aided by a cheapskate NBA general manager.

The cheapskate was Cincinnati Royals' GM Pepper Wilson, who lost four of his top five draft choices to the ABA taking care of business the old-fashioned way: this is our offer, take it or leave it. As Daniels remembered Wilson's one-year take-it-or-leave-it: "When [Wilson] said $14,000, I said, 'Is that the bonus?' 'No, that's salary.' I had to ask him again. I was hurt, shattered, completely destroyed."[4]

Daniels peeled out of Cincinnati ready to sell his hook shot to Holman for $35,000, a salary that simply popped into his head. Holman countered with $22,500 per season over three years, plus a $10,000 signing bonus. Enter John McManus, a prominent New Mexico district judge who advised Daniels: Take the ABA money, but on one condition. Holman had to type a no-cut clause into the three-year agreement and initial it.

From a business perspective, the judge's request fell somewhere between reckless and radical. What if Daniels didn't pan out in the pros? What if Minnesota had to release Daniels two months into the season and sign a free agent who could do his job right? Minnesota (and Holman as a part owner) would be legally bound to pay every last dime guaranteed to Daniels for services never rendered. Every seasoned general manager, especially in the NBA, knew that guaranteeing rookie contracts was a quick way to get fired for fiscal irresponsibility.

Not Holman, a sports neophyte and a high-risk, high-reward Minnesota oilman. He shrugged okay to the judge's request, scored Daniels, and helped to establish the ABA's most-potent early weapon against the NBA: the no-cut contract. For the players, the no-cut guarantee canceled their worries of the ABA folding and reneging on contracts. This put the league and its dollar signs on equal financial footing with the NBA. What's more, it forced mostly risk-averse NBA owners to do the same, making them bristle at the craziness and giving them a good first reason to merge and return to fiscal sanity.

Too bad Holman couldn't have also typed in a no-ejection clause into Daniels' contract. Players had been slipping all night on the brand-new floor, which had been pretreated with various industrial solutions. Just minutes into the third quarter, Kentucky's wiry Ken Rhine rear-ended Daniels. The rookie turned and whacked him. Peace was quickly restored, but the two referees tossed Daniels to teach him a lesson.

That was also all she wrote for the Muskies. Little Louie Dampier, on a weekend pass from the National Guard, and the sharpshooting Stew Johnson got hot from behind the three-point stripe, and Kentucky surged ahead for the 104-96 win.

"I'd liked to have had a full house," moped George Mikan about the mere 8,104 paying customers.[5] At league meetings, Mikan had pressed each team, come hell or high water, to pack their arenas on opening night. Holman had done his best, having declared the opener Kid's Night and raffled off a Shetland pony at halftime to one lucky youngster, come to think of it. Maybe he should have offered to raffle off the mounted muskie, too.

Eddie Holman toted all 44 pounds of his mounted muskie up to the ninth floor of Minneapolis' Farmers and Mechanics Bank building, a 10-story 1940s art deco edifice where the team rented an office. His desk was littered with bills, bills, and more bills. Another 30 feet further down the hallway in suite 902, large block lettering declared George Mikan's Viking Travel, Inc. Below, a more modest sign whispered "American Basketball Association." Through the double doors, past the travel posters declaring "Go Hawaii" and "Far East in the Spring," sat Mikan's two full-time ABA staffers.

One was angular Thurlo McCrady, the league's middle-aged executive director, a fancy term for jack of all trades. A better description was the administrative glue that held together the whole ABA operation. The Nebraska native, who'd spent most of his career in college sports coaching and running athletic departments, was most recently assistant to the American Football League commissioner. His acquired specialty: managing referees.

The other full-timer was Don Carr, a friend of Mikan's who served as head of publicity. Though the trim, 42-year-old Chicago native was bright and energetic, he had little or no experience in public relations. How ironic. The basketball league conceived by public-relations professionals was now in the willing, but unable, promotional hands of a management consultant. For the short term, Carr's previous consultations— and connections—with the hotel and sporting goods industries had come in handy. He was in negotiations with U.S. Rubber (official ABA shoe), United Airlines (official ABA airlines), Samsonite (official ABA luggage), Spencer Communications (official ABA magazine), and Rawlings Sporting Goods (official red, white, and blue ball and uniforms).[6]

All these negotiations were great, but they lacked the one thing that mattered most: a lucrative network television contract. That fell to Mikan and the ABA's chief counsel Bill Erickson, who characterized the wooing of television executives as "endless."

Their first whack had rolled foul. Metro-Goldwyn-Mayer (MGM) backed out of syndicating ABA broadcasts nationally, preferring to guide the ABA's quest for a national network. Thanks to MGM, Erickson and Mikan met with executives at CBS Sports, including its personable No. 2 man Jack Dolph (destined to be Mikan's replacement). Dolph said all the right things—then issued an internal memo recommending that his network take a pass on the ABA.

The "no thanks" boiled down to two factors. One, pro basketball was a ratings underachiever, which had become common knowledge in the industry after two decades of trying.

Two, the ABA had a scant presence on the East Coast, where the national media congregated, and this void created the perception among television executives that the league was too small-market for them to profit.

Adding to this perception, the ABA had no team occupying the all-important New York spotlight. The ABA's original New York Freighters started the season over the George Washington Bridge bivouacked in an old armory in the township of Teaneck, New Jersey. The New Jersey Americans, they were. The change of address wasn't by choice. Though team officials couldn't prove it, at least not beyond a legal shadow of a doubt, all strongly suspected the NBA and influential Madison Square Garden, Inc. had an invisible hand in making sure their pursuit of a suitable facility in Manhattan went nowhere.[7]

Inside Mikan's Viking Travel, it seemed at times like the ABA was also meant to go nowhere. McCrady and Carr fielded daily SOS calls requesting clarification of league policies and trying to stay calm about the zaniness befalling them. In Minneapolis, rain drenched several palates of opening-night game programs left on the delivery dock. In Houston, the inside of the visitor's locker room was visible from the arena's upper reaches. Rowdy women gathered there after games and a few beers to hoot and holler and watch some "real men" shower. In Anaheim, members of the visiting New Orleans Buccaneers got stopped for speeding. When the little brown bottle from which they'd been swigging was discovered, the players tried to bribe the cop. That's the way they handled things in Loo-siana.

And yet, like a factory conveyor belt, the ABA rolled out a weekly schedule of games. There were plenty of flaws bumping along that conveyor belt, but the finished products went into the scorebooks, warts and all, then crackled across the newswires just like the NBA games. Within a few weeks, the ABA had its own data, crunched into statistics and crafted into a self-identity.

A big part of that self-identity was the tri-colored ball. "It's hypnotizing to watch it rotating in the air," rookie Mel Daniels oh-wowed. "Kind of psychedelic."[8] Every sports-minded kid from Brattleboro to Bakersfield wanted one. Many had even internalized the ABA's obscure orbit of teams and statistical leaders. Since most sports-happy homes subscribed to the magazine *Sports Illustrated*, a highlight in the weekly mail stream, any full-color article that elaborated on the league with the cool ball was a must-read. The same went for the weekly ABA column in the popular *Sporting News* broadsheet.

Still, most pro basketball buffs, from habit and years of team loyalty, still turned first to the NBA, its seven-foot giants, and its myriad storylines. In Los Angeles, Elgin Baylor was back, and the Lakers were prepared to go as far as his surgically repaired knee—and sidekick Jerry West's jump shot—would take them. In Philadelphia, Wilt Chamberlain was back for the time being and ready to prove that the 76ers' championship season was no fluke. In Boston, could the aging Bill Russell and Sam Jones turn the tables on Father Time and return Boston to the winner's circle in 1968?

So far so good a month into the regular season. Boston stood atop the Eastern Division, and the Philly faithful had started their annual buzz to beat Boston. In the Western Division, injuries had slowed the Lakers. But St. Louis was off to a flying start, and San Francisco was fleet enough to give chase, kicking dust in the faces of the three expansion teams (Chicago, San Diego, and Seattle) at the bottom of the division.

In the NBA boardroom, expansion remained the most-debated—and divisive—topic. The pro-growth'ers stuck to two arguments. One, the NBA had to locate in a wider swath of America to popularize its product. More teams would make the NBA more of a national league—and grow its marketing and television revenues. The second argument was reactionary. The NBA couldn't let the ABA claim the best of the remaining Midwestern and Western cities. Neither could they let the ABA have free reign in the South. To control the pro basketball chessboard, the NBA had to limit the ABA's next moves and chances of controlling key open squares—Atlanta, Kansas City, Milwaukee, Phoenix. In fact, though they eventually backed down, the pro-growth'ers even considered expanding into a few ABA cities and claiming them by force and fiat.

The anti-growth'ers bah-humbugged that quality, not quantity, sold tickets. More expansion, they feared, would further dilute their base of talent, diminishing the product and its popular appeal. Or, as New York's Ned Irish argued, the Knicks had 41 home dates per season. Why would he want to schedule a rotten expansion team from Timbuktu when he could have guaranteed sellouts with Boston, Los Angeles, and Philadelphia?

Irish and the anti-growth'ers also called a spade a spade. They accused their counterparts of growing dependent on the expansion fees that were divvied up, each team banking roughly $200,000 per season in free cash to defray costs and limit losses. This addiction to easy money made annual expansion a selfish decision. It placed their individual financial interests before the league's general welfare.

As with any good debate, both sides were correct to various degrees. But there was another question worth asking: What about the quality—the wealth—of the new owners? The answer was not always as financially ironclad as it seemed on paper. Just ask Don Richman.

Don Richman was living the dream. Two years after graduating from the University of Southern California (USC), class of 1954, Richman fell into a dream job as the school's sports information director. He was just 25 years young, but a lightning-quick learner known as the little guy with the easy, low-key demeanor and zippy one-liners. By age 29, Richman jumped into another dream job promoting the Los Angeles Chargers in the brand-new American Football League.

He and his Bill Veeck-like entrepreneurial flair hit the ground running, selling within weeks 12,000 season tickets. "Which is fairly good," he quipped, "considering we don't have a team, we don't have any opponents, and we don't have a schedule."[9]

When the Chargers moved to San Diego in 1961, Richman stayed behind to chase his Hollywood dream: writing TV scripts. He had a gift for it, and soon his name rolled in the opening credits of episodes of "The Farmer's Daughter," "77 Sunset Strip," "The Man from U.N.C.L.E.," and his own creation "Rat Patrol." On the side, he took up writing radio jingles for corporate sponsors. That is, when he wasn't consulting for the NBA Los Angeles Lakers and winning praise from Jack Kent Cooke.

Yes, Richman was living the dream—except for one seemingly impossible one. Having his own pro sports team. Franchises cost an arm and a leg, and Richman, despite his surname, wasn't rich, not even close. He had bills to pay and a young family to feed. But one day in the spring of 1964, peer pressure got to him via the gregarious Dick Vertlieb, his former USC frat brother turned stockbroker and a certifiable sports nut. He was bored stiff trading stocks and day-dreamed on the job about having his own pro team, too. Vertlieb, a bright-side-of-life optimist and truly one of a kind, yakked into Richman's ear that if they didn't listen to their hearts, both would "spend the rest of our lives wondering why we didn't take the chance."[10] Richman hemmed, hawed, and finally said count me "in."[11]

Vertlieb and Richman were about to join a new generation of entrepreneurial dreamers, short on cash and willing to beg, borrow, and scam their way into pro sports. Football and baseball, with multimillion-dollar price tags to get in the door, were out of their price range of course. But the NBA, with an entry fee of about a million bucks, give or take a few hundred thousand, was a magnet for these dreamers (so was the ABA). What set them apart, though, Vertlieb knew his hoops, having played and coached, and Richman knew two influential NBA figures in Cooke and commissioner Walter Kennedy.

The two shared their dream with Kennedy, who offered some friendly advice. Find a big-league city with a big-league arena. Then, organize a group of wealthy investors to pay for most of the franchise. "We were both making a good living, but not enough to fly everywhere and stay in nice hotels to meet with [prospective] owners," said Vertlieb of their jaunts around the country in search of wealth.

"So, we would take overnight red-eye flights to a city to meet an owner, find the fanciest hotel, and—without checking in—clean up in their bathrooms. Then we'd call the owner, telling him we're staying [there], and don't call us. We'll meet you in the lobby."[12] The zaniness, like the Marx Brothers' "A Day at the Races," made for boundless hilarity. But in the end, the laughs were on them. No serious investors emerged.

In Jan. 1965, in a put-up or shut-up moment at the NBA All-Star Game, Kennedy reportedly told the two politely to apply for an expansion franchise, now going for $1.75 million, or quit bugging him. They settled on Cleveland or Pittsburgh. More zaniness. More disappointment. That brought them to their third choice, Seattle. Richman had spent a week there while traveling with the USC football team and liked the ocean views. Seattle also had a big downtown arena, and it checked the box for the NBA's latest expansion point of emphasis: Find a city without other big-league franchises competing for air time. More zaniness ensued, more tough luck finding an owner. "I'd walk down the street in Beverly Hills," said Vertlieb, "and people who knew me would jump to the other side because they knew I'd ask them for money to buy a team."[13]

By Aug. 1966, their NBA dream seemed doomed for lack of funds when Vertlieb, while perusing the morning newspaper, had a five-alarm brainstorm. Richman's old football Chargers had just sold for a record $10 million (about $100 million today). The buyer was a 21-person consortium led by Sam Schulman and Gene Klein, high-level executives of the multimillion-dollar conglomerate National General Corporation. Maybe they could spare a couple million.

Vertlieb cold-called the high-powered Klein who remarkably picked up the phone. It was a sign. In his most steady stockbroker's voice, Vertlieb said the purpose of his call was to share inside information on a promising pro basketball investment opportunity. Klein, not a basketball guy,[14] probably would have dumped the call, except his partner Schulman was in conversation with the ABA about starting a team in Los Angeles. Klein took the bait, and a few days later, the frat brothers had their face-to-face meeting to ask for two million bucks. Klein and Schulman interjected that they wanted their NBA opportunity to be in San Diego as an extension of their football team. Richman cracked a joke about San Diego and its glut of retirees, then turned serious, "I have another city—Seattle."

"Why Seattle?" asked a surprised Schulman.

Richman, the consummate PR pro, ticked off the whys, and Schulman admitted that choosing Seattle made sense.[15] He also admitted that he and Klein were temporarily overextended on the Chargers deal. They didn't have a million or a half-million to spare.[16] The four bounced around a few ideas and landed on an unorthodox one: Schulman and Klein could be the front men for the Seattle deal. Nothing illegal, mind you, just some old-fashioned deception that boiled down to this. Klein and Schulman would post the requisite $100,000 "good faith" bond with the NBA to buy the team.[17] The bond never would be cashed. It was earnest money, and the NBA wouldn't dig any deeper to question whether the heads of the high-flying National General could afford to buy into the league. Their extreme personal wealth was a given. Like a high roller in Vegas, they were good for it.[18]

Except Klein and Schulman wouldn't pay a penny of the $1.75 million entry fee. The frat brothers, abundantly clever and resourceful, promised to cover the cost. They just needed a few months, once the NBA approved their ballclub, to open a few revenue streams and collect the needed cash. In return—and, again, for no money down—Klein and Schulman would own the basketball team. All the frat brothers asked, especially from the more hands-on Schulman, was to be left alone to live their dream of running a pro franchise. "It's your decisions," Schulman answered in his blunt-spoken manner, "and you can go on making them until you make enough of them that don't turn out well."[19]

The four shook hands on their deal, and the frat brothers booked the next cheap flight to New York to wow their NBA friends with the latest. And yes, old habits—and necessities— died hard. They made sure to freshen up in the lobby bathroom of the Crown Plaza Hotel and wait out front for a free ride. "The NBA representatives would always find them there, waiting to be picked up," recalled J. Michael Kenyon, then a Seattle reporter whom Dick Vertlieb regaled with the inside story. "Dick said, always chuckling, 'We had to make everybody think we had money.'"[20]

They also had to make everybody think that Seattle was their second home. It wasn't. Neither had lived in the Pacific Northwest, and Richman clearly viewed Seattle as geographically remote and a giant step backward in time from hip 1960s culture. "Don and I had a little saying: 'When the world comes to an end, Seattle will still have a year to go,'" said Vertlieb.[21]

On Jan. 11, 1967, the day the NBA expanded to 12 teams, the names Klein and Schulman were rolled out as majority owners of the brand-new Seattle franchise. They were reported to have kicked in 70 percent of the $1.75 million purchase price. The purchase price, though still unpaid, was correct. The 70 percent figure should have been zero. "This is one of the real highlights of my life," Schulman monotoned at the Seattle press conference to announce his arrival in town as a sports entrepreneur like a conquering hero.[22] Maybe he meant it, maybe not. Either way, Schulman returned to Beverly Hills as the absentee team president and left Seattle to the frat brothers. They flipped a coin for their front-office titles. Richman won general manager; Vertlieb got business manager.

Their first item of business was to unloose those revenue streams and pay off the NBA. Richman, while working with the Lakers, reportedly had learned how those revenue streams worked, no money down. Season tickets started selling, eventually totaling $250,000,[23] and a local broadcasters paid roughly the same annually to air games on radio and television.[24] Richman then enticed Atlantic Richfield Company[25] to sponsor the team's broadcasts for a reported $2 million over five years.[26] The agreements gave the frat brothers collateral to borrow $500,000 from the local People's Bank.[27] But Vertlieb's *piece de resistance* was establishing the Delaware-based Seattle SuperSonics, Corp. in Jan. 1967 and issuing public stock in the team, reportedly an NBA first. The public offering produced another $500,000, bringing the team's bank assets to more than $3 million without the frat brothers dipping too deeply into their pockets or those of Klein and Schulman to pay the bills.

Cash remained tight, however, and the frat brothers scrimped in anticipation of the shortfall that awaited all first-year teams. The SuperSonics' 12-player payroll totaled just $240,000, which was now peanuts. Vertlieb bought bargain-basement equipment, booked the team on red-eye discount flights, and dumped the players into cheap, two-star hotels. On the court, the SuperSonics looked good for a first-year team. Walt Hazzard, the former slumping Lakers' guard, had rejuvenated his career and nifty playmaking in Seattle. Attendance hovered at around 6,000 per game, which, depending on your perspective, equaled either a half-full or a half-empty arena.

Richman, the consummate PR professional, chose half-full . . . and rising. Each week, he spoke on average at a dozen community breakfasts and luncheons to shill the thrills of Sonics' basketball. As Richman's reward for seemingly being everywhere at once in the Puget Sound, a local media association awarded him that winter the tongue-in-cheek "Most Overexposure" award at their annual banquet. But Richman's banquet-room schtick was starting to grate on locals. He joked that rainy, backward Seattle was "a 24-hour car wash" and "Forest Lawn with lights." The bada-booms always ended in the sunny realization that he and his fellow Californians were wrong about sleepy Seattle. But still. The digs grated.

But for Richman, the sunny realization was more wish than fact. Though he liked the people, Richman found Seattle gloomy and a long way from Sunset Strip. His 10-year marriage was on the rocks, in part over uprooting the family, and the phone continued to ring with job offers back home that might make things right again. His buddy Chuck kept offering him a partnership in his growing advertising business, and Richman was ready to chase another dream after the season: writing radio commercials. Vertlieb would remain in Seattle for another season.

Looking back, Richman had little to rue. He had outfoxed the "system," as everyone said in the 1960s, He had made his impossible dream come as improbably true as a zany Neil Simon comedy. But in the end, they outfoxed themselves. Sam Schulman, their front man, wanted to take control of the basketball team that fell into his lap. That made the frat brothers expendable. They weren't really from Seattle, were they?

"We'll try to give you a winner as soon as possible," Schulman had promised last January at the press conference announcing Seattle's NBA entry.[28] Time would tell that Schulman was dead serious when he uttered those words. Schulman's dogged pursuit of a winner in Seattle would soon place him at loggerheads with Walter Kennedy, his fellow owners, and the NBA bylaws. It would also turn this chance expansion owner into one of the main figures in the NBA-ABA War.

The hot topic on the NBA labor front through last season was Rudy LaRusso and his forced early retirement. "You ask if a pro has allegiance to his team," Wilt Chamberlain had leveled in January. "Well, did the Los Angeles Lakers have allegiance to Rudy LaRusso when they traded him—after all those years—in the middle of the season?"[29] Chamberlain's answer was hell no, and more players were starting to agree with him. The proof was in all of the leaps and near leaps to the ABA last off-season.

The funny thing was, LaRusso had landed on his feet. He put on a coat and tie and became a successful, full-time stockbroker for McDonnell and Company in Beverly Hills. But last March, soon after his teary farewell banquet, LaRusso met discretely with newfangled agent Fred Rosenfeld (a softball buddy and recent law school grad) and told him the retirement was off. At age 29, his body and spirit remained willing, and he wanted to play another season for the Lakers. Shortly thereafter, LaRusso sued the NBA for a then gaudy $485,000, charging the league with conspiracy and monopoly for allegedly blackballing him. His message to the NBA: Reinstate me with the Lakers, or I'll challenge the legality of the league's restrictive and quite possibly illegal labor practices in open court. By April 1, LaRusso turned up the heat when Rosenfeld met with the ABA Anaheim Amigos to discuss a possible contract.

Enter San Francisco owner Franklin Mieuli. He paid $20,000 to the Detroit Pistons to obtain the rights to LaRusso, and presto, last season's infamous Detroit-Baltimore-Los Angeles impasse was resolved. The only question was: Would LaRusso agree to play in San Francisco?

Ten days later, LaRusso dropped his lawsuit and signed a two-year, $40,000 per season contract with Mieuli. "I'd rather pursue a career than a lawsuit," he explained. The agreement was one of the more unorthodox in league history. Mieuli and the NBA allowed LaRusso to continue living and selling stocks in Los Angeles. They also allowed him to limit his time away from California, if needed, meaning LaRusso could pick-and-choose the road trips on which he accompanied the team. In return, LaRusso agreed to pay his own airfare to and from San Francisco to attend practices and home games.

"Practice is at 11 a.m.," LaRusso explained his daily commute from his home in suburban Playa del Rey. "I'll leave the house at nine, catch a jet commuter around 9:15 and be in San Francisco a couple minutes past 10. Then I grab a cab to San Bruno [where the Warriors practiced] and am suited up and ready to go by 10:45."[30]

Twenty-one games into the regular season, LaRusso couldn't be happier to call himself a Warrior and the same brute who controlled NBA backboards, just not with the grace that Jack Kent Cooke desired.

Milwaukee, Dec. 7, 1967—Marv Fishman should have been evaluating properties this morning. But the 43-year-old Milwaukee realtor, who specialized in building Cape Cod-style homes, couldn't concentrate. His mind kept drifting 90 miles south to Chicago. NBA Commissioner Walter Kennedy was there to attend an afternoon banquet honoring Dick Klein, an acquaintance of Fishman's and the majority owner of the NBA Chicago Bulls. Fishman had convinced himself that now was the time to make his pitch for an NBA expansion team in Milwaukee next season.[31]

Fishman also felt the ache and exhaustion of the winter flu taking hold of his bones and body. Fishman didn't trust himself behind the wheel on busy I-94, then wending through Chicago's insufferable traffic. When he couldn't find anyone to drive him to Chicago, Fishman finally sniffled off on his own to purchase a ticket on the next Greyhound Bus to the Windy City. His pitch to Kennedy couldn't wait.

In his haste, Fishman had forgotten his hat and an umbrella to fend off the steady rain soaking Chicago. After hoofing several blocks to the restaurant where Klein was now being hailed a jolly, good fellow, Fishman clicked the door open looking like a drowned rat and country cousin from Wisconsin. Thank God for his advanced receding hairline and a quick, easy comb-over. And thank God that Kennedy hadn't flown back early to New York. The commissioner sat at one of the white-linen tables looking bored out of his mind. Fishman pounced.

"Hello, I'm Marv Fishman from Milwaukee," he said in his gentle, almost confiding, voice. "And I'd like to buy a franchise in the NBA. All the readings appear to be right, and I think I can put a franchise together."

The sudden pitch startled Kennedy. But, as a former politician, he quickly turned on the charm and disarming small talk. Hearing out these pretty-pleases was part of his job description. In fact, Kennedy now had pretty-pleases stacked up on his desk from Atlanta, Cleveland, Kansas City, Phoenix, Portland, Vancouver, and a few other cities. Two cities would likely receive expansion franchises next season, even though the Board of Governors continued to bicker over more expansion.

Klein ambled over and announced that a Milwaukee-Chicago rivalry was a natural. Kennedy nodded half-listening and glancing repeatedly at his watch. "Oh my God, I've got to catch a plane," he finally interjected. Kennedy offered a perfunctory, "nice meeting you" to Fishman, then recited an immediate to-do list before applying for an NBA franchise.

As Kennedy gathered his things, he added, "There's somebody else from Milwaukee interested in a franchise." Fishman asked his name. Kennedy thought for a second. Funny, he couldn't remember.

Indianapolis, Jan. 9, 1968—In Minneapolis, the ABA's league office opened shop in a travel agency. In Indianapolis, the ABA Pacers opened its front office in a jewelry store on East 38ᵗʰ Street that was "closing its doors forever." The business owner, with months still left on his lease, agreed to let Mike Storen, the Pacers' young general manager, use the space for next to nothing. Storen hunkered down in a back office, all by his lonesome. He had a desk, a working telephone, and most recently two years of experience as director of publicity for the NBA Cincinnati Royals.

From that makeshift desk, Storen made some costly mistakes. The Jimmy Walker snafu was one. Another was his Oscar Robertson miscalculation. Robertson, an Indianapolis native, reportedly told an old friend and Pacers' operative that he would *consider* jumping to the Pacers for $150,000. Storen's job: mail the big honking check and let Robertson stew for a while. Instead, Storen sent a lowball offer of $115,000. Robertson winced and resigned with the NBA Cincinnati Royals. "Hey, that's the way you've got to play the game," Storen stood on his NBA laurels.[32]

But Storen had worked the telephones to assemble a decent opening-night roster. That included, per Robertson's suggestion, the high-scoring forward Roger Brown, banned from the NBA for life over a bogus college gambling allegation. It also included former NBA reserve guard Freddie Lewis, selected several months ago by the San Diego Rockets in the NBA expansion draft. Anxious for more money and playing time, Lewis signed a healthy three-year, no-cut deal with the Pacers, and Rockets' coach Jack McMahon promised not to sue. Oh, what a difference when that NBA name wasn't Chamberlain, Russell, West, Hudson, or Barry.

Now, from the back of this zombie jewelry store, Storen hustled to make good on staging the first ABA All-Star Game. According to Storen, he'd organized last season's NBA All-Star Game and would be happy to do the same for the ABA in its inaugural season. The Pacers "would take care of all the expenses," including complimentary gifts for the all-stars and a brand-new car to the game's MVP, just like he'd done in the NBA. In return, the Pacers could pocket any profit generated from the game.[33]

Storen and his small staff had attempted for weeks to move heaven and civic intransigence to put Indianapolis' best foot forward. No detail was too small. Flights landing in Indianapolis included these final instructions from the captain over the intercom, "Welcome to Indianapolis, site of the first ABA All-Star Game." From the airport, caravans of cars ferried all-star game participants to the Marott Hotel, a stately, 10-story brick edifice that served as the headquarters of the all-star game. The league trustees had checked into their rooms last night to get an early start on today's 9:45 a.m. board meeting and to wade through the usual stack of preparatory materials.

That included the latest attendance figures. The hopeful was Indiana's league-best 5,945 per-game average, followed by Denver (3,836) and Kentucky (3,227). The discouraging was league-worst Anaheim (1,057) and the wee-bit-better New Jersey (1,698).[34] How would the league ever finagle a network television contract bombing so badly in Southern California and New York?

And yet, thanks to Southern California and New York, the ABA would appear for the first time on national television tomorrow night. Well, sort of. The Los Angeles TV station KTTV-Channel 11 would send a broadcast crew to Indianapolis. KTTV wasn't just a local TV station, though. It was owned by New York-based Metromedia, Inc., formerly the Metropolitan Broadcasting Corporation, and ran the conglomerate's TV syndication division. That included sports programming, and KTTV, which already had a one-year deal with the ABA Anaheim Amigos, had cobbled together a one-time network including nine ABA markets (excluding

Indianapolis, Houston, and Louisville) and possibly adding in Akron, Dayton, and Washington, D.C.

Because the agreement was last minute, KTTV hadn't sold any ads. The ABA, not Indiana, would be on the hook for the $31,000 transmission fee, a point loudly debated in the trustees meeting. Eventually, the trustees acquiesced. After all, the trailblazing American Football League didn't hold an all-star game until its second season. The ABA had done it in one, and that was worth broadcasting to, if not the world, then about a dozen U.S. markets.

Conspicuously missing from the TV debate was Morton Downey Jr., the 35-year-old ball of energy behind the New Orleans Buccaneers and the wise-cracking life of the ABA party. The future talk-show pioneer, with a cigarette always dangling like an extra appendage from his bottom lip, had quit the ABA. He had a new radio gig in New York and couldn't bring along his rising basketball debt. Though Downey's wealthier, less-fun partners forged on in his absence, the Bucs were quietly for sale. So were Minnesota and Anaheim, both well on their way to losing more than $300,000 in their inaugural seasons.

"As you know, George," Downey wrote ABA Commissioner George Mikan in his letter of resignation as league secretary, "I wish you and the League all the success you deserve. It's just about a year ago that I fought like a madman for your appointment. I know that I will not be disappointed in having done so, however, at this juncture, I feel the League has not maintained proper faith with the owners through maintenance of an effective public relations program and we are doomed to the same basketball graveyard as the ABL [American Basketball League] if an effective program is not implemented immediately."[35]

Downey's wavering deference and resentment toward Mikan was shared by most of his fellow trustees. All admitted that the league needed Mikan. Or rather, his good-guy Mr.

Basketball image. But their financial losses were mounting, and the cult of Mikan was getting old. Mr. Basketball hadn't landed a TV contact to put the ABA, as anticipated, on equal footing with the AFL. Each trustee had definite opinions about how to run the league better and chafed at deferring to Mikan and his promise, as the only businessman in the room with a basketball background, "Give me three years, and I'll give you a merger."

The trustees' growing frustration with Mikan was mostly short-sighted. Mikan was more than a recognizable public face; he was the organizational will that propelled the ABA forward. Every big problem from Teaneck to Anaheim fell at his feet. Under the advisement of his lawyer and brainier other half Bill Erickson, Mikan muffled then managed the mayhem and put his public reputation on the line to build the public perception that the ABA was here to stay.

Solving the big problems of all 11 teams was exhausting—and increasingly thankless—work. That's why by late morning, Mikan had grown crabby at all the bickering. By noon, he, the ever-present Erickson, and the bickering trustees had grabbed their winter jackets. A ceremonial duty called, taking them prancing through the snow for an all-star luncheon downtown hosted by the Indianapolis Chamber of Commerce. Mayor Lugar, after wishing the ABA well with its big game this evening, handed Mikan an oversized key to the city. Mikan, still crabby from the trustees meeting, took out his bad mood on the local reporters forced to cover this cold-chicken event in the stark, rectangular hall called the Egyptian Room, modeled after the tomb of King Tut.

"I wish the press would get off our backs," he tut-tutted from the stage, about 700 people and several Egyptian slaves painted on the wall staring back at him. "I know I've made mistakes, and so has the league. But I'm tired of the press constantly making fun of us."[36]

Storen, seated in the audience, gritted out Mikan's cringeworthy vent and afterwards worked the room to put Humpty Dumpty back together again. "The press in Indianapolis and Indiana have been fantastic," he bowed and occasionally scraped. "His comments were uncalled for."

With fences mended and Mikan deposited back at the Marott Hotel, Storen moved on to the next crisis: ticket sales. They were as slow as ice cream purchases on this weather-alert day. Storen had promised the league and the Egyptian Room that tonight's contest would draw at least 10,000 fans to the spacious Hinkle Arena. Only about 5,300 tickets had been sold. Throw in 1,300 freebies to his season-ticket holders, and Storen was about 4,300 tickets shy of a sellout.

By 5:30 p.m., the evening darkness settling over downtown and just three hours from tip-off, Storen summoned his NBA experience and a trick that he'd already conjured to sell out on opening night. Storen and staff started calling police precincts, firehouses, community centers, and offered free tickets to the game. Remarkably, with the temperature in the mid-20s and dropping fast on this tired Tuesday evening, they had takers. Thank God, Hoosiers loved their basketball.

By 7:30 p.m., the pregame festivities began. Setting up at courtside, while the Halftime Honeys of Butler University, 16 beautiful young women strong, entertained the crowd by dancing to show tunes, was the KTTV broadcast crew of Tom Kelly, the third-down-and-a-cloud-of-dust voice of USC football, and Rick Barry, the ABA's superstar-in-waiting. Technical difficulties were inevitable, and KTTV's balky feed left the Halftime Honeys ringing the court at a standstill, smiles strained, gripping a court-sized American flag. Also standing at attention was the Marion College Drum and Bugle Corps in plumed white caps and uniforms, waiting to make Francis Scott Key proud on their mostly hand-me-down instruments from the American Legion.

When the KTTV producer finally gave the go-ahead, Barry couldn't help but notice former NBA star Cliff Hagan (he'd come out of retirement to try his hand as Dallas' player-coach) and NBA scrubs-turned-ABA all-stars: Ben Warley, Freddie Lewis, and Chico Vaughn. Again: Oh, what a difference when that NBA name wasn't Chamberlain, Russell, West, Hudson, or Barry.

The starting lineups finally took the floor, allowing Storen to heave a sigh of relief and take credit for the 10,872 leather lungs in attendance, the largest crowd ever to see an ABA game: The game raced back and forth through three quarters. Vaughn, one of the East's better three-point marksmen, nailed two from long range. So did the West's little Larry Brown, whose nifty passing elicited words of approval from Barry. But the fourth quarter belonged to the East's Mel Daniels. With 3:38 to go, the "rook" rattled down a five-footer from the baseline to put the East ahead for good, then added three more rattles and some caroms for a game-best 15 rebounds on the night.

Before the final buzzer blew, per Storen's orders, men in funny Shriners fez hats tossed exactly 100 regulation-sized red, white, and blue basketballs into the stands for souvenirs. Those lucky fans, however, turned on Storen when, thanks to a premature vote count, the MVP trophy went to little Larry Brown, not Daniels. While the leather lungs booed, Brown graciously accepted the shiny trophy and the keys to a 1968 Chevelle Malibu red convertible. Storen would have loved to pull "a Mikan" and tell the hecklers to get off his back. But there was no point getting huffy. Even if the attendance numbers were fudged just a little, Storen believed the ABA—or, more important, his Indiana Pacers—were on the rise.

So was the NBA, and its numbers didn't lie. Twelve. That was the number of NBA franchises in operation, up from nine two seasons ago. Though the NBA still hadn't driven down stakes into wide swaths of the American heartland, the league nevertheless had a solid bicoastal presence, turning the "National" in its name into an accurate descriptor for the first time in its history. Milwaukee and other cities were knocking on the NBA's door for admittance next season. The going rate for an expansion franchise was a record $2 million.

Then there was 2.9 million. That was the estimated number of NBA tickets that would be sold this season. That was up from 1.6 million in 1963 when Walter Kennedy took over as the league's top administrator. Kennedy attributed the uptick to several factors: the popularity of the sport, better arenas, and, of course, expansion. He also gave all hail to the NBA's return to network television, a deal he coordinated. The "NBA Game of the Week," which debuted in January 1965, ran 15 Sundays per winter, plus the playoffs.

Eighteen million. That was the approximate audience each Sunday for the Game of the Week. For Kennedy, the 18 million equaled a green blinking light that the NBA, stigmatized for its lackluster network ratings in the 1950s and early 1960s, had turned the corner as mainstream American sports entertainment. The Game of the Week aired in most American TV markets on Sundays, allowing kids in outposts such as Abilene, Boise, Cedar Rapids, and Shreveport to internalize the sounds of squeaking sneakers and bouncing balls and dream a little dream of Wilt, Russ, Oscar, Elgin, Jerry, and even Knicks rookie Bill Bradley, the NBA's latest projected white glamour boy who was off to a slow start.

Then, there was the number one. The NBA made sure to limit ABC to one game per week, expressing concerns about "oversaturation" of the market. Or, reading between the lines, because NBA franchises still made their biggest bucks at the box office, the arena owners in particular remained resistant to giving away too much product for free.

Airing one broadcast per week left the NBA vulnerable to the whims of local station managers, embarrassingly so. In Pensacola, with special coverage of the Winter Olympics underway and air-time tight, WEAR-TV bumped two weeks of NBA basketball in favor of old movies. In Los Angeles, the ABC affiliate frequently tape-delayed NBA broadcasts from the East Coast that should air live in the morning. Kids needed their weekend Rocky and Bullwinkle fix.

Such scheduling glitches sent the NBA's outspoken millionaire owner Jack Kent Cooke into orbit. Cooke, who reportedly believed the NBA was destined to play its games in television studios and survive on pay-per-view dollars, bent Kennedy's ear whenever a new indignity moved him. For Cooke, it was preposterous that Kennedy was doing business with ABC, the weakest of the three national networks, and handing it the exclusive two-year rights to the "NBA Game of the Week" for the trifling sum of $650,000. Pro football got $28.7 million per season in TV revenue. The NFL had also taken the brilliant leap into mass marketing, which sent Cooke into absolute entrepreneurial ecstasy. There was the innovative NFL Films, which grossed $1 million per year selling league highlight reels. There was also NFL Properties, which already raked in $600,000 per year (about $4.8 million today) selling NFL gear, pennants, and mascot dolls and granting corporate use of the NFL logo.

"I remember Walter walking past me at Cooke's first Board of Governors meeting and whispering under his breath, 'Out of the fire and into the frying pan,'" said Earl Foreman, then the Baltimore owner. Kennedy's fire was former Lakers owner Bob Short, who was always "about getting things done." Cooke, the frying pan, browbeat Kennedy and most of the other governors, reportedly trying to intimidate them as socially beneath his high station. Cooke, after all, jet-setted with Hollywood's finest and stayed in a penthouse suite at the ultra-highbrow Waldorf-Astoria whenever he traveled to New York on business. Eddie Gottlieb, a league founder turned influential special consultant, rented a modest office above a sporting goods store in Philadelphia.

Whenever the bombastic Cooke called to share his latest brainstorm, Kennedy could still afford to stare blankly out his office window. Cooke, though influential, wasn't the dominant voice in the room. That honor still belonged to the prickly, hard-to-like Ned Irish, president of the Knicks and the gatekeeper to the greater Madison Square Garden, Inc. and its corporate treasure. Kennedy and publicity director Haskell Cohen were on good terms with Irish. They were also unapologetic arena-owner hires, old-fashioned, seat-of-their-corduroy-pants publicity flaks, trained in the 1940s to be quick with a handshake and smooth when asking for favors. Launching a modern mass-marketing division just wasn't part of their day-to-day job descriptions.

Nevertheless, Kennedy had contracted with a modern production company called Winik Films to assemble an annual NBA season highlight film, narrated by ABC broadcaster Chris Schenkel. This season's working title was "Up, Up, and Away," a rip-off of a pop toe-tapper of the same name about a beautiful balloon then blasting over America's AM car radios. Whether a rip-off or an apt borrowed metaphor, Kennedy and the NBA seemed to be on the rise, or better, ready to capture a larger swath of mainstream American culture.

Indianapolis, Jan. 20, 1968—The television ratings were out for the ABA all-star game, and Mike Storen was thrilled. In New York, an estimated 2.5 million tuned in. "One man from New Jersey called after watching the game on television," raved Storen. "He said he had never thought much of our league before. But he said: You've got a fan now."[37]

Though the Pacers gave away $9,000 worth of tickets, Storen focused on two positives. One, this high-profile game established Indianapolis as an enthusiastic pro basketball town. Two, George Mikan now had viewership data to hand the television executives and convince them, hopefully for the playoffs, that a market existed for the ABA, with its three-point shot and exciting brand of basketball.

Storen tended to focus more on the first point. In fact, each day he updated a folder on his desk containing attendance figures from around pro basketball. "Only New York, Boston, L.A., and Philadelphia in the NBA have outdrawn us," Storen said with a straight face, knowing the Pacers' attendance figures were a little loose.[38]

Storen had his reasons for stretching the truth while still hunkered down in his office in the back of the former jewelry store. Most involved self-preservation. The Pacers had assumed the lease on the store, then brought in a few staffers, potted plants, and wall posters of red, white, and blue basketballs. But the makeshift team headquarters near the heart of sleepy downtown Indianapolis (they didn't call it "Naptown" for nothing) reminded Storen just how risky his career move had been. So did the pro basketball attendance file on his desk. Four ABA teams averaged under 1,700 paying customers per game; eight averaged under 3,000. If two franchises seized up, the league would land in intensive care. Four failures? The league would be on life support.

If the ABA flatlined in one season or George Mikan's allotted three, Storen needed to convince his former NBA colleagues along the way that Naptown was the right town for their next expansion franchise. That's why he pushed, peddled, and periodically prevaricated to put Indianapolis's best foot forward as a formerly overlooked, pro basketball-gaga Midwestern metropolis. That's partly why Storen and the Pacers willingly took a financial loss on the all-star game and still considered the evening a smashing success.

"We have an advantage here—no competition, no baseball, no football," Storen had said last November, echoing a criterion highly favored by Ben Kerner, current head of the NBA expansion committee.[39]

What Indianapolis lacked to turn NBA heads was a modern arena. The Pacers dribbled forth in a 9,000-seat gathering place at the fairgrounds. But lawyer Dick Tinkham, one of Storen's former Marine buddies and a hands-on part owner of the Pacers, knew lots of political movers and shakers. His vision, which he shared with others, was to convince those movers and shakers to clear the way for a modern downtown arena that would transform Naptown into Boomtown.[40]

That's not to say that Tinkham and Storen were hell-bent on joining the NBA. They weren't. Starting a league had its creative advantages over hitching onto an established, set-in-its-ways association, where they would be back benchers. But the two had to have a contingency plan on the ready if their current start-up league folded. That's what set the Pacers apart from day one in the ABA. The Pacers began with a deep community bond not only to help them survive but to help Indianapolis turn the corner and become a big-league town.

In fact, Storen recently fielded a call from an NBA Deep Throat, likely former team owner-turned-league consultant Eddie Gottlieb, inquiring whether the Pacers might be open to joining the NBA sooner rather than later? Similar Deep Throat calls were placed to Louisville and possibly Denver. They amounted to a premeditated attempt by the NBA to divide, conquer, and be rid of its weaker opponent. In the 1940s, Gottlieb's Basketball Association of America, the NBA's precursor, stole three top franchises (including player Mikan's Chicago Gears and Fred Zollner's Fort Wayne Pistons) from the rival National Basketball League. The theft was the decisive blow in the brief, but intense, BAA-NBL war that birthed the NBA.

Storen rejected the bait, and so did the others. The NBA entry fee would be in the millions, and their ABA partners would sue them for nearly as much for crashing the league. But the phone calls put Storen and the ABA on warning: The

NBA was now out to get them by any devious means necessary.

New York, Jan. 22, 1968—Toots Shor had hit the big six-five. But the jaunty former bouncer-turned-beloved, forever-young Manhattan saloonkeeper and restaurateur had no plans of slowing down. Why would he? Toots remained New York's drinking buddy to the stars. Since 1940, all the big shots, from baseball's Babe Ruth to crooner Frank Sinatra, had pulled up a barstool beside the boisterous, always engaging, and sometimes smashed Toots to swap manly insults ("being called a crumb, a bum, or a creep by Toots was a sign of affection") and tales of chasing "broads" and consuming alcohol. For some "crumb-bum" tourists, reserving a table at Toots' new three-story eat-and drinkery on 52nd Street to see who might swagger by was as obligatory as riding to the top of the Empire State Building.

On this tired Monday evening, those tourists swiveled their heads plenty at Toots' unusually tall, mostly dark, and mostly handsome clientele. Wilt Chamberlain ducked through the door and traipsed upstairs. So did Bill Russell, Elgin Baylor, and Oscar Robertson. The NBA was holding its annual pre-All-Star Game reception and dinner in a large banquet room upstairs. The shorter, older white guys were already upstairs firing up their cigars and latest grievances.

No knock on Toots' shrine to booze and sports, but several all-stars looked uncomfortable spending an evening with these older NBA squares. Chamberlain, for one, would have almost certainly preferred to hover in his Harlem jazz club. Wilt had reached a fragile détente last summer with Philadelphia owner Irv Kosloff. The latter forked over a one-year contract for $250,000—more-than doubling his previous salary—to get Wilt to forget about his alleged cut of the 76ers.

For Wilt's acquiescence, "Koz" privately agreed to ignore his expiring contract's option clause.[41] But Wilt wasn't exactly a free agent. Yes, he could choose his next team. But Koz would then have to negotiate a multi-player trade for his superstar—and here was the hard part—while getting that team to agree to re-sign Wilt at or above his now-seemingly outlandish salary.

And so, the clock was secretly ticking on Koz. There were reasons for hope that everything would work out in the end, though mainly because of the growing dysfunction among his fellow owners. Right now, they probably couldn't agree that the sky is blue. Their clash of ideas made it a good bet that one of the wealthiest would trade for Wilt and treat him to an NBA fortune.

Among the greediest was Jack Kent Cooke, the Los Angeles owner whose name his NBA colleagues often mocked in private with expletives stronger than crumb-bum. At today's Board of Governors meeting, Cooke so infuriated Detroit's Fred Zollner, the quiet one, that he stormed out of the room vowing to resign from the board. Though Zollner would walk back his threat, he skipped tonight's banquet, leaving his general manager Ed Coil to field the grumbles about that blankety-blank Cooke.

"It really didn't have to happen" Boston owner Marvin Kratter was heard siding with Coil.[42]

Most of the buzz, though, centered on the league's approval of expansion teams in Milwaukee and Phoenix for next season. That totaled five NBA newbies in three seasons. "Phoenix and Milwaukee, huh?" deadpanned former player Hot Rod Hundley, working on his first cocktail of the evening. "I'm making a comeback."[43]

By everyone's second cocktail, loose tongues sank Milwaukee, torpedoed Phoenix, and assailed the NBA's expansion plans. Several imbibers praised New York, Los Angeles, and Philadelphia for loudly voting no, arguing that too many bumbling expansion teams at once on the NBA circuit was bad for the league. In fact, during the meeting, the nays needed just one more vote to scuttle this year's expansion. Some thought San Diego, one of last year's expansion franchises, was in the bag to vote no, since it always voted with Los Angeles and that blankety-blank Jack Kent Cooke.

Not this time. "Well, we spent $1,750,000 last season to get in the league," explained a San Diego official. "And we figured to lose a lot of money this season. If we vote for the expansion, we get $333,333.33, and we just couldn't pass it up."[44] Put another way, New York, Los Angeles, and Philadelphia could operate without their piece of the lump $4 million in expansion fees ($2 million each from Milwaukee and Phoenix). The rest of the league couldn't so easily.

That's not to say NBA expansion had no overarching strategy. It did, and a big part of that strategy was to thwart the competition. Milwaukee could have gone red, white, and blue with some patience and further coaxing of the very wealthy Herb Kohl. He moved on to seek an NBA franchise in Milwaukee. In fact, it was Kohl whose name Walter Kennedy couldn't remember during his impromptu meeting in Chicago with Marv Fishman. Kohl forged full-steam ahead, and Fishman knew to defer to one of Milwaukee's more prominent sons. Then, Kohl was abruptly out of the running. He'd committed the NBA equivalent of a mortal sin by unwisely hiring the resented player agent Arthur Morse to twist arms and negotiate special terms and conditions for the new franchise. At Kennedy's urging, Fishman and his investors jumped back into the bidding for an expansion team in late December.

Now, four crazy weeks later, Fishman stood with his wife Janet in Toots' shrine to booze and sports looking rather sober-minded but trying to sound big league.[45] Many in the room recalled that Ben Kerner, a.k.a., Benny the Boob, lost his shirt 13 years ago in Milwaukee. Kerner fled town with creditors nipping at his heels and then, like a boob, set up shop in St. Louis, another presumed pro basketball boneyard. Kerner had survived there through his own hard work and the timely generosity of the mild-mannered Fred Zollner. Now, as the head of the expansion committee, the opinionated Kerner applied his school-of-hard-knocks past to guide the NBA's future. His struggles taught him that NBA franchises couldn't win hearts, minds, and dedicated fan bases in American cities already smitten with other established sports teams. For Kerner, to garble a Yogi Berra truism, the NBA had to "put 'em where they ain't."

"When I had the Hawks in Milwaukee, the [baseball] Braves came in," Kerner had been doctoring history all evening. "Both Milwaukee and Phoenix have no other major league sport now. That influenced us."

Kerner glossed over the obvious. After he bolted Milwaukee much the wiser, the baseball Braves paid off the city to break its stadium lease and bask in balmier Atlanta. Milwaukee lacked big-league sports because it wasn't a big-league town. Or so the guffaws went until dinner was served. At Toot Shor's, the banquet offering was as predictable as death and taxes: a salad, a steak, and a baked potato.

The Fishmans now worked their knives and forks wedged between the roly-poly NBA legend-turned-consultant Eddie Gottlieb and the ginormous ego of broadcaster Howard Cosell. "Isn't Milwaukee close to Sheboygan?" Cosell quizzed the Fishmans, purposely harkening the early NBA's failed attempts to tame small frontier towns such as Sheboygan and Waterloo.

The historical dig wasn't lost on Marv Fishman. He demurred politely, still thrilled to be NBA worthy but starting to wonder about the creeps who came with it. Downstairs, Toots held forth with his preferred brandy and soda. Times were changing, Toots told all. "Years ago, I had all the sports writers in my place," he would sometimes complain. "Now I got the fellas who do sports for the television stations, but it's a new type of business. Baseball writers used to go all night. These new guys don't go the distance."

Neither did these NBA guys upstairs. It was a new type of business with millionaire owners, lawyers, agents, unions. Hot Rod Hundley and the other old timers went the distance. The new guys were gone before the third round of drinks.

Anaheim, Calif., March 24, 1968—The Anaheim Amigos and the Oakland Oaks started the ABA regular season last October with dreams of winning a championship and spritzing champagne in the showers. Now, on a balmy Sunday evening five chaotic, brooding months later, the Amigos and Oaks would finally put the ABA regular season to bed. They entered their final fray with more than 100 losses between them, including the Oaks' current 16-game skid to nowhere. So dire was the mood for both franchises, as the *Oakland Tribune* aptly put it, "on the surface, it would seem to be a game nobody can win."[46]

Both teams should have been put out of their misery two nights ago. But officials at the Anaheim Convention Center, the Amigos' on-again, off-again home court, bumped the finale for a live closed-circuit showing of the UCLA Bruins in the semifinals of the NCAA men's basketball tournament. It had been blacked out on televisions across the Los Angeles area.

The delay left Oaks' radio announcer Charley Hinkle grounded back in Oakland, management's money-saving decision. That was okay with Hinkle. He needed to find a new job anyway. Pink slips would be forthcoming to all staff to help the Oaks save bucks over the offseason. The Bay Meadows Racetrack in nearby San Mateo was looking for a public-address announcer, and Hinkle could wrestle his tonsils far better down the homestretch than calling three-pointers.

Pink slips would also be waiting for most of the players on both rosters. The Oaks had secretly stolen Alex Hannum, the head coach of the NBA Philadelphia 76ers, and offered him carte blanche to rebuild the roster around superstar Rick Barry. The courts willing, Barry would be clear to play in Oakland next season.

In Anaheim, the Amigos front office in the Jolly Roger Hotel was already in boxes. Art Kim, who was Dennis Murphy's first "big-money" recruit, and his wealthy lawyer Jim Ackerman were also the first owners to head for the exits. They had departed about six weeks ago, leaving the team and its estimated half million dollars in debt in the hands of fellow owner Jim Kirst and general manager Jim Hardy, a hugely popular former USC football star. Both were eager in the gutsy, risk-oriented, profit-driven, must-win way of wealthy men to restart the franchise next season, just not in Anaheim and just not touting its current makeshift roster.

That makeshift roster now had its final date with destiny in the 8,000-seat Anaheim Convention Center, across the street from the fairy-tale world of Disneyland. It was truly "a small, small world after all" as just 1,108 customers paid their final respects to the dearly departing Amigos. At 7 p.m. sharp, a whistle blew and up went the basketball, twirling like a red, white, and blue beach ball. Anaheim's seven-footer Larry Bunce outreached Oakland's Jumbo Jim Hadnot for the orb, and tonight's lead official Ralph Stout trotted into position. Stout, a tried-and-true college official and basketball purist, continued to struggle with the league office's latest edict to cool it on the travelling calls. Fans wanted action, and ABA players got three steps, not the traditional NBA two.

But Stout wouldn't need to count steps or call a close game. Neither team played much defense. The Amigos put up 67 points in the first half, accompanied occasionally by the boom, boom, booms of the team mascot, dressed as a sombrero-laden amigo, firing blanks into the air from his pistol whenever the going got good. Possibly unnerved by all the gunfire, Oakland surrendered a team-record 31 turnovers. But the Oaks never quit until Les Selvage, Anaheim's designated mad bomber, drained two three-point daggers down the stretch followed by the final boom, boom, booms and a buzzer. Amigos 147, Oaks 145.

The Indiana Pacers bombed out early in the playoffs. Mike Storen quit fudging attendance figures, and Indiana's nightly headcount dwindled from 7,000 per game to just under 5,000. That still ranked as the league's best (the ABA's average attendance was 2,804 per game), on par with six NBA franchises. In April, the Pittsburgh Pipers defeated the New Orleans Buccaneers to bring home the league's first championship trophy. Pittsburgh's Connie Hawkins also took home the MVP trophy. Despite his NBA ban, now being contested in court, the slithery, 6-foot-8 Hawkins had people raving anew that he might be one of the best players in basketball.

With Hawkins in tow, Rick Barry in wait, and public enthusiasm for the league seemingly on the rise, Storen told reporters that the ABA had already surpassed its early expectations. "We thought we might go into our second season with about eight teams. We were wrong. Everybody still is in."[47] Storen may have been stretching the truth. Millions of dollars had dribbled down the drain in season one, and some wealthy owners, though not all, were anxious about putting more good money after bad, especially with no network television on the horizon. But a core group, which included Storen and his partners in Indiana, were already out and about and strategizing for the off-season. Strategy dictated that it was time to add more college All-Americans to the ABA fold and boost the league's talent level. George Mikan seconded that emotion.

Over in the NBA, Boston won its 10th title in dramatic fashion. After besting Detroit in the opening round of the NBA playoffs, the Celtics were in deep trouble in their annual best-of-seven grudge match against Philadelphia, trailing three games to one and teetering on elimination. But Boston, led by its retiring player-coach Bill Russell, battled back and won the series. In the deciding game seven in Philadelphia, Chamberlain attempted just two shots in the second half and afterwards blamed his poor showing on Coach Alex Hannum, *saying he preferred calling set plays for the other 76ers. Hannum diplomatically suggested otherwise.*

Either way, Chamberlain entered the off-season believing he was a free agent, the NBA's first, with no option year in his expiring contract to tie him to the 76ers. However, Wilt again had nothing in writing. He had to hope that 76ers' owner Irv Kosloff, whom he loathed, would be a man of his word.

Endnotes

[1] In November 1967, Seattle would seek an injunction in Los Angeles Superior Court to prevent Warley from continuing to play for Anaheim. The injunction would be denied over concerns for its belated filing (a month into the season) and naming of Warley, not the Anaheim Amigos, as the defendant. The ruling, counter to the earlier "granted" Barry injunction, demonstrates that the NBA option wasn't as inherently compelling to the courts as it was to the owners.

[2] George Ross, "Three Ex-NBA Superstars," *Oakland Tribune*, October 14, 1967

[3] Ibid

[4] Dick Denny, "Daniels Itching for Shot at NBA Stars," *The Sporting News*, March 27, 1971. P. 5

[5] Dwayne Netland, "Muskies Drop Opener 104-96 to Colonel Rally," *Minneapolis Tribune*, October 23, 1967

[6] Minutes, American Basketball Association Meeting, Denver, August 18-19, 1967

[7] Dick Schramm, Interview with author, April 2009

[8] Ira Berkow, "Mel Daniels Has Problems But No Regrets," *Lexington Herald-Leader*, November 1, 1967.

[9] Rube Samuelson, "Rube-Barbs," *Pasadena Independent*, March 23, 1960.

[10] Frank Deford, "The Sonic Boom in Seattle," *Sports Illustrated*, October 9, 1967.

[11] What follows about the origins of the Seattle SuperSonics is based primarily on three sources: Emmett Watson, "They Put the Team Together," *Sonics Magazine*, November/December 1979; Art Thiel, "Best Hustle in Sonic History Took Place Before Team Ever Took the Floor," *Seattle Post-*

Intelligencer, October 31, 1991; and J. Michael Kenyon, Interview with author, October 2009.

[12] Theil, *Seattle Post-Intelligencer*.

[13] Ibid.

[14] In his 1987 autobiography *First Down and a Billion*, Klein mentions the purchase of the "Seattle SuperSonics of the American Basketball Association." Wrong league. Clearly, as Klein even admits, he had no interest in basketball or owning an NBA team.

[15] Watson, *Sonics Magazine*.

[16] Kenyon, Interview with author.

[17] John Owen, "Calif. Cash for Seattle Pro Cagers?" *Seattle Post-Intelligencer*, December 21, 1966.

[18] As a *Seattle Post-Intelligencer* columnist would later write, "Gene Klein, who can buy and sell most of the other [NBA] owners, gave manager Don Richman a blank check and said —"Get a ballclub for Seattle." (May 8, 1967) That was assumption, not the fact, in Seattle.

[19] Watson, *Sonics Magazine*.

[20] Kenyon, Interview with author.

[21] Theil, *Seattle Post-Intelligencer*.

[22] Earl Luebker, "Sports Log," *Tacoma News Tribune*, January 13, 1967.

[23] Deford, *Sports Illustrated*.

[24] "To Our Shareholders," First Northwest Industries of America, Inc. 1971 Annual Report.

[25] Atlantic Richfield also was the proud sponsor of Lakers' broadcasts, thanks to Jack Kent Cooke.

[26] Associated Press, "Sonics, Richfield Ink Sponsor's Pact," *Tacoma News Tribune*, September 1, 1967.

[27] Theil, *Seattle Post-Intelligencer*.

[28] Luebker, *Tacoma News Tribune*.

[29] Sandy Padwe, Newspaper Enterprises Association, January 28, 1967.

[30] John Hall, "While Freeway Traffic Creeps, LaRusso Sleeps on Way to Work," *Los Angeles Times*, February 8, 1968.

[31] This section, including all quotes, draws primarily from Marv Fishman and Tracy Dobbs, *Bucking the Odds*, 1978, p. 26-28.

[32] Robin Miller, "Pacers Organized on Napkin," *Indianapolis Star*, December 15, 1991.

[33] Minutes, American Basketball Association League Meeting, Dallas, October 6-7, 1967.

[34] No Byline, "All-Star Coverage to Blanket Nation, *Indianapolis News*, January 9, 1968.

[35] Minutes, American Basketball Association Meeting, Minneapolis, December 14, 1967.

[36] Mark Montieth, *Reborn*, 2017, p. 154.

[37] Jimmie Angelopoulos, "ABA Crowing Over Sparkling All-Star Game," *The Sporting News*, January 27, 1968.

[38] Ibid.

[39] Jim Schottelkotte, "Cincinnatians Flavor ABA Leaders," *Cincinnati Enquirer*, November 17, 1967.

[40] Dick Tinkham. Interview with author, March 2014.

[41] Wilt Chamberlain and David Shaw, *Wilt*, 1973, p. 186-187.

[42] Roger Keim, "Milwaukee and Phoenix Join NBA Ranks," *Philadelphia Inquirer*, January 23, 1968.

[43] Sandy Padwe, "Quantity Valued Over Quality," *Philadelphia Inquirer*, January 23, 1968.

[44] Jack Kiser, "NBA Meetings a Wild, Wild Scene," *Philadelphia Daily News*, January 23, 1968.

[45] What follows is drawn mostly from Fishman, *Bucking the Odds*, p. 46-49.

[46] Paul McCarthy, "Oaks in Finale Tonight," *Oakland Tribune*, March 24, 1968.

[47] Bob Collins, "Sports Over Lightly," *Indianapolis Star*, March 24, 1968.

7

Reflecting on the ABA's maiden 1967-68 season, it's a wonder that more owners didn't follow Anaheim's Art Kim and New Orleans' Morton Downey Jr. out the door. All 11 teams hemorrhaged red ink, and the millionaires (and not-quite millionaires) who owned these bloody messes kept asking their commissioner and hired celebrity George Mikan to do something about it. "Something" translated mostly to negotiating a multi-year network television contract to subsidize the ABA's start-up costs, as all-but promised amongst themselves during the league's organizational meetings. Some trustees, though aware that sports ownership had advantages at tax time (more about that later), were still spooked by their spreadsheets and the thought of blowing a fortune on a damn basketball team.

And yet, that maiden season delivered occasional moments of Zen that this fledgling red, white, and blue Yankee-Doodle-Dandy league just might take off and fly.[1] One came last January in Houston during a board of trustees meeting. After a long day of discussing league matters, the trustees taxied to the Astrodome to attend college basketball's "Game of the Century," pitting the top-ranked defending national champion UCLA Bruins, winners of 47 straight, against the second-ranked University of Houston Cougars. Of course, UCLA had thumped Houston several months earlier in the 1967 NCAA men's basketball tournament. But that was a just game; this was a full-blown spectacle. More than 50,000 spectators—then an unfathomable figure for a sport born two generations ago in bandbox gyms built for hundreds—packed the cavernous football stadium. A Super Bowl-like halftime performance even awaited featuring the bubble-gum soul of Jay and the Techniques ("Apple, Peaches, Pumpkin Pie"), hot off their appearance on "The Ed Sullivan Show."

But first, all eyes and binoculars trained on a gleaming rectangle of hardwood, spread out like a picnic blanket in a field of green Astroturf. It was the makeshift, for-one-night-only basketball court. The stadium seating scaled up halfway to the domed ceiling and, just above the highest of the nosebleed seats, stretched a horizontal row of plush, red-carpeted skyboxes for Houston's 10-gallon glitterati. "Just under heaven," joked T.C. "Nick" Morrow, the oil tycoon and majority owner of the ABA's Houston Mavericks who hosted this group outing in his personal skybox.

From just under heaven, the historic game below looked like an epic ant fight. But the creature comforts were worth the eye strain. There was an open bar, and waiters toddled in and out with plates of flame-broiled beef slathered in tangy sauces. Mounted to the wall was the then-novelty of a large-screen color television set.[2] And that's when that moment of basketball Zen entered the booth. College basketball, like the ABA, had been written off by network television as a shaky, small-audience investment. Tonight's event proved every network executive wrong. More than 120 TV stations around the country bought into a syndicated network to air this Saturday night sports spectacular in primetime, a regular-season first for college basketball. And millions of American living rooms tuned in with rapt attention to see if UCLA, seemingly invincible with its All-American giant Lew Alcindor, "the next Wilt Chamberlain," could keep its winning streak alive against Houston's Elvin Hayes, the "Big E," and the greatest college basketball star ever in Texas.

In the ABA suite, the buzz began: Sign the senior Hayes for next season, then scoop up the junior Alcindor the following year. A network television contract would be waiting to repeat tonight's magic, which literally had advertisers calling in to the tiny syndicated network to see if play-by-play announcer Dick Enberg could mention their products between free throws.

Things turned downright giddy in the skybox when Hayes sank two free throws to put the Cougars ahead with 28 seconds left, then helped dribble out the final seconds of Houston's two-point glory, glory hallelujah. Morrow, square-jawed with broad features and as big as a mule, was a colorful slow-talker from East Texas who vowed right then and there that he would sign Hayes for next season. Money would be no object.

At the ABA's March 9, 1968 meeting in Louisville, Morrow made it official by drafting Hayes during a hush-hush, four-round college draft intended to help the 11 ABA teams get a head start on the NBA. But Morrow and his general manager Slater Martin had a problem. The Houston Cougars were still chasing a national championship and, as civic-minded Houstonians, they couldn't talk to Hayes about turning pro. It would violate NCAA rules and get everybody in trouble. And so, they waited like honorable suitors, declaring in the press their interest in Hayes and keeping at a safe distance

But the secret ABA draft, which George Mikan called an "evaluation session" and threatened heavy fines for any owner who said otherwise, predictably leaked to the press. The NBA countered by moving up its annual coin flip to assign the first two picks in its upcoming college draft. On March 25, San Diego owner Bob Breitbard fortuitously called "tails" to land the top pick and exclaimed, "We're going after Hayes."

Jim Hardy made that twinkle in his eye official on March 27, 1968. He was now general manager of the ABA's Los Angeles Stars. "The Amigos are dead," Hardy stated at the noon press conference. "The Amigos have been buried, and we burned their uniforms after the final game."[3]

Hardy stood flanked by ABA commissioner George Mikan and Gilbert Lindsay, president of the Los Angeles Sports

Commission, after signing a three-year agreement for the Stars to play in the Los Angeles Sports Arena. The 15,000-seat facility was the former home of the NBA Lakers, who moved eight miles down the freeway into their new pleasure palace in Inglewood. "The Lakers are now the Inglewood Lakers of the National Basketball Association," declared Lindsay, no fan of Lakers owner Jack Kent Cooke. "Los Angeles now has a team of its own—the Los Angeles Stars."[4]

The move marked the second time that the ABA and NBA would compete head-to-head in a major American market (the San Francisco Bay Area was the first[5]). For Hardy, the move wasn't about a declaration of war. It was a declaration of necessity. The Stars simply needed a big-league venue with ample open dates to accommodate its 40-something home games. The L.A. Sports Arena was it. But Hardy wasn't naïve. The Stars would need to pirate an NBA name or two for any chance of competing with Cooke's dynamic duo of Elgin Baylor and Jerry West.

Mikan nodded in agreement with the words from the podium, though this moment had to be a little surreal for him. He was the Lakers' original superstar, though in Minneapolis, and now he was helping to sabotage the franchise that he'd built. But all was fair in love and war . . . and signing top draft choices. For right down the freeway, the NBA's San Diego Rockets were holding their own presser. Two days after winning the coin flip for the NBA's top draft choice, team owner Bob Breitbard wanted to give the basketball world a heads-up: Elvin Hayes now belonged to him.

B ob Breitbard had collected a mountain of sports memorabilia over his nearly 50 years. Among his favorites was a rack of baseballs autographed by Ted Williams, the last of the .400 hitters and a schoolmate at San Diego's Hoover High class of 1937. Now Breitbard, a short, stocky man, square-jawed and still sporting an old-fashioned 1930s buzz cut, was about to collect his most-valuable signature yet: Elvin Ernest Hayes.

As the local television cameras rolled, the Big E leaned forward and scribbled his name at the bottom of a standard NBA contract. Flashbulbs popped, and Breitbard stuck out his hand to welcome officially the newest member of the San Diego Rockets. "He is one of the fine young men in the country," Breitbard said of Hayes. "You'll see a lot of him in San Diego."[6]

Breitbard, anticipating questions about his warp-speed signing of the most-coveted senior in college basketball, chalked it up to "good chemistry." As Breitbard explained, Hayes had flown into town yesterday morning, and the two met for a few hours behind closed doors in the San Diego International Sports Arena, bonding over sports, life, and family. Breitbard took Hayes on a quick spin around San Diego, the blue ocean waters shimmering seductively in the background. They stopped for lunch in Mission Bay and visited Sea World. The tour ended back in Breitbard's office at the Sports Arena, where the day's good chemistry bubbled over into the sweet alchemy of a handshake agreement on a contract. Within hours, its terms were written up and approved by Hayes' advisor Floyd Gee, a prominent University of Houston alum.

"What are the terms?" a reporter asked at the press conference.

Breitbard, also anticipating that question, said he wished to keep the terms private, which was odd. The New York Knicks felt no compunction telling folks from Fifth Avenue to Flatbush about the six figures showered on prized rookies Cazzie Russell and Bill Bradley. Why not the Rockets?

But the Big E, looking dapper in a navy-blue sports jacket and a cream-colored turtleneck, interrupted the inquisition and turned the conversation back to his choice and the NBA. "I want

to play against the greatest players, and they are in the NBA."
Made sense. Heads nodded, and pens scribbled.[7]

The news conference wrapped, and the terms of the Elvin
Hayes contract promptly leaked: a four-year deal for about
$440,000, roughly $110,000 a season and a huge, mind-bending
figure for a mere rookie. For the more skeptical reporters on
the beat, there had to be more to this story. Bob Breitbard was
no Rockefeller. His family ran a commercial laundry. What's
more, he was now leveraged to the hilt. In addition to owning
the Rockets and an expensive minor-league hockey team,
Breitbard had drained his bank account to finance the recent
construction of the $7.5 million San Diego International Sports
Arena. Word also had it that the city wasn't cutting him any
breaks on the arena's hefty tax assessment, soon to fall due.

In Houston, Nick Morrow seconded these suspicions. The
jilted ABA owner claimed NBA officials, shunning NCAA rules,
had contacted Hayes during the basketball season and handed
him $5,000, just because. Morrow also suggested there was
something fishy about Hayes' advisor Floyd Gee. He was a
sales rep for a chemical company, not a lawyer. Gee had
promised to meet with Morrow's Mavericks and pass along
their record-setting offer of $750,000 to Hayes. Instead, Gee let
Hayes race off to San Diego and advised him to sign ASAP for
far less money, which equaled financial malpractice. Or worse.

Morrow, however, had no hard evidence to prove his
suspicions. Neither could he point reporters in the right
direction to confirm his final bombshell: the NBA moguls had
pooled their money to help Breitbard get Hayes. Morrow said
he'd heard through the grapevine that Breitbard, though
paying part of Hayes's salary, would also get plenty of help
from his better-heeled NBA neighbors, namely Jack Kent
Cooke.

"We were acting like legitimate business people who
wanted to operate strictly within the codes of the NCAA
regulations," Morrow said. "And, as a result of our playing

according to the rules, we lost out and came in second. But, from this date on, it will be like [pro] football—all-out war."[8]

Hayes, Breitbard, and the entire NBA called Morrow's claims pure fantasy, a case of sour grapes. "It is absolutely false to intimate in any way that any NBA official ever contacted Hayes 30 days ago or that Hayes received any money from any NBA team or official before San Diego signed him," seethed NBA Commissioner Walter Kennedy.[9]

Kennedy was being truthful—to the best of his knowledge. Kennedy had been left in the dark about a secret NBA effort to sign this year's top college draft choices before the ABA could wow them with cash. The reason: plausible deniability.[10] If the underhandedness were ever exposed, Kennedy and his seemingly higher authority couldn't be blamed. In the NBA, like politics, perception was reality.

Irv Kosloff, owner of the Philadelphia 76ers, may have contributed to the Elvin Hayes NBA Fund. Then again, maybe not. He had other matters on his mind. The second half of the 1967-68 season had been a nightmare. A storm blew off large sections of the roof atop the Spectrum, the brand-new 15,000-seat public facility and the 76ers' home court, rendering it unusable for the final weeks of the regular season. While local politicians pointed fingers, slowing the needed repairs, the 76ers booked their final home games in any available venue with a box office, a basketball court, and a popcorn machine.

Popcorn sales should have been booming as the formerly high-scoring Wilt Chamberlain vied for, of all things, the NBA's assists crown. Yet, even as 76ers statistics whiz Harvey Pollack got caught fudging a few for Wilt,[11] Philadelphia mostly stayed away, seemingly to protest the embarrassment of the Spectrum and the 76ers' forced downgrade to all the old haunts. Koz lost thousands of dollars playing in these rinky-dink venues. Then, with the Spectrum still out of commission for the playoffs, Koz lost face. His defending NBA champions, banged up from the long regular season, built a commanding early lead in the Eastern Conference finals against the hated Boston Celtics, but stumbled in closing out the series and then choked at home in the deciding game seven. Fingers pointed in all directions, and Koz finished this miserable season at least $200,000 ($1.6 million today) in the hole.

Koz braced for more uncertainty to come in the offseason. His head coach Alex Hannum, keeping his vow to return to his native California, would soon announce his resignation. His two-year contract was up and, because coaches weren't subject to option clauses or reserve systems, Hannum already had a verbal agreement in place to lead the Oakland Oaks next season. Chalk one up for the ABA.

And, what about Wilt? He considered himself a free agent, the NBA's first, but he seemed to have backed off his "move-me-or-lose-me" demand. The goateed face of the franchise had just floated another option to general manager Jack Ramsay. "What would you think of the idea of me coming back next season with the 76ers as player-coach?" Ramsay remembered him saying. "You could help me manage the X's and O's."[12] Ramsay, a celebrated former college coach and a great one, ran the idea up the flagpole, and Koz pounced. He reasoned, because Wilt wanted to "put his name" on the team as coach and player, the Big Fella might be gearing up for his greatest NBA campaign ever.[13] Who in Philadelphia wouldn't pay to see that?

Ramsay said he informed Wilt: "We have a deal." While Wilt was away for a previously planned trip to L.A., Ramsay would consult with Wilt's lawyer and work out the financial details. They'd sign everything when Wilt returned in a few weeks. Until then, the agreement was hush-hush. Enjoy California.

Walter Kennedy moved up the NBA's college draft to April Fool's Day. That was in less than a week, and some in the front office of the Baltimore Bullets were starting to think the joke was on them. Neither scout nor executive could agree on their top draft choice, the second pick, and it now fell to their coach Gene Shue, a former NBA all-pro and a widely respected basketball junkie, to come riding to the rescue.[14]

Shue, known for his leftover flattop haircut from the 1950s, instructed his player-turned-assistant coach Bob Ferry to pack his bags. Time to high-tail it to Indianapolis, where officials with the U.S. Olympic men's basketball team would hold their college tryouts on March 25 and 26. They could take one last look at Otto Moore, the seven-footer from tiny Pan American College and their seemingly *de facto* selection.

But Shue was a picky evaluator of talent, and the "Big O," as Moore was known, had played very lowercase when Baltimore last scouted him. Shue nitpicked away at his game, but worried he might be acting too hastily. His peers kept predicting that Moore, with his long arms and unusual mobility for a big man, would be a star in the league, quite possibly "the next Bill Russell."

Two days later, Shue still wasn't sold on the next Russell. Shue worried that the Big O, long and extra lean, would be a clone of the Bullets' skinny seven-footer LeRoy Ellis, who, after nearly jumping to the ABA, had struggled last season jostling with the NBA's tallest and mightiest. Ferry turned the conversation to Wes Unseld, the University of Louisville center who was sitting out the Olympics. In Ferry's scouting report, Unseld literally walked on water, equating him with Jesus for his disarmingly high character.

High praise, but Shue hesitated. Unseld was maybe 6-foot-7. Shue couldn't imagine anyone that short, divine or otherwise, matching up against Russell, Chamberlain, or the Eastern Division's other seven-foot nightmares. Then, it hit Shue like a ton of bricks. All of those nightmares would soon either retire or be traded elsewhere. The Eastern Division would have a glut of shorter, bulkier centers. Unseld, built like a brick house, could wrestle for rebounds with the best of them. Throw in his catapult outlet pass to thrust the offense on the attack, and Unseld looked like a match made in heaven for Baltimore's open-court shooters, Kevin Loughery and Earl Monroe.

Shue called Baltimore. Arnie Heft, the team's personable part owner and a former NBA referee, scoffed at Unseld for all the obvious reasons. But Shue asked Heft to trust him. Heft turned to his general manager Buddy Jeannette, who'd scouted Unseld in person. He hemmed and hawed and slowly relented on one condition. Shue had to meet with Unseld and get a read on him, find out if he was leaning toward the ABA Kentucky Colonels, based in his hometown of Louisville.

Shue said that wouldn't be a problem. The Olympic tryouts would move to Louisville on March 28. To avoid tipping their draft hand to their snoopy NBA rivals, he and Ferry would tag along with the other scouts at the combine. Then, when the time was right, they'd scoot off for a secret meeting with Unseld, that rare 22-year-old who walked on water.

Wilt Chamberlain's West Coast trip was hardly a vacation. He cared for his ailing father, who lived in Los Angeles, and explored a few new business opportunities. But Wilt made time to walk the beach, sailboats bobbing in the distance, seabirds squawking overhead. Southern California and its live-and-let-live lifestyle were growing on him. So much so, Wilt had another change of heart. He couldn't return to Philadelphia, especially not after that ABC Radio leak.

Three days into his trip, ABC Radio broke the news: Chamberlain will coach the 76ers next season. Ramsay dutifully denied the leaked story, but a little too aggressively for Wilt's ego, stating the 76ers were "looking for a *successful* bench coach with pro coaching experience to *handle the Philadelphia situation.*" Handle? The Philadelphia situation? That was code for managing Wilt. He decided Ramsay hadn't been honest with him about the job offer. In fact, he strongly suspected that Ramsay wanted the job to return to coaching. (Ramsay denied Wilt's assertion to the grave, insisting that Wilt had the coaching job, if he'd wanted it.)

Infuriated, Wilt spent nearly four hours on the phone the next evening with assorted Philadelphia reporters rebutting Ramsay, not ABC's scoop. "Philadelphia situation—what's that?" Wilt yelped to a reporter. "Wilt Chamberlain, the problem player, and Hal Greer, the sulker, and Billy Cunningham and all the other problem men. Well, if we were such problems, how come we could win more games in the past three seasons than Red Auerbach and his nice, sweet boys ever won in three seasons at Boston?"

On the phone, as he was wont to do, Wilt mocked the NBA, noting rookies were now signing bigger contracts than proven 10-year veterans. He said the league was headed for a Titanic crash. "The NBA is a boat, loaded down to the gunnels with expensive salaries. So, the owners jam a couple of more heavy salaries aboard, and the boat starts to sink. Well, they're not going to tell Wilt Chamberlain to cut off a leg and throw it overboard so they can stay afloat. I helped build this boat, and I think maybe I've got a few more rights than the rookies."[15]

According to Wilt, his special rights entitled him to the NBA's first million-dollar contract.[16] Not annually, but cumulatively at $333,000-plus per season for three years. For the average working-class man on the street or hunched over a beer in the corner tavern, the thought of a tall, young Black man earning a million bucks for putting a leather ball through a metal ring boggled the mind. But that was Wilt's mystique. Like scoring 100 points in an NBA game or leading the league in assists, he just kept making the impossible dream come true. Whether dream or delusion, Wilt had put everyone on notice: Any team could have him next season for a cool, cumulative million bucks.

The freight elevator opened to the onstage thump, thump, thump of drums and bass guitar. Near the stage, what looked like narrow traffic lights suspended from the ceiling periodically flashed green, yellow, and red, piercing the darkness for split seconds and exposing a throbbing, wall-to-wall scrum of partiers. There were young, mini-skirted *femme fatales* in all Hollywood hair colors and styles dancing freestyle with cool dudes in sunglasses, checkered pants, and Nehru shirts. As the music thumped ahead, waiters in bell bottoms, light blue prison shirts, and red bandanas bound around their necks navigated the redwood dancefloor, delivering drinks and pocketing tips.

Wilt Chamberlain stepped off the freight elevator like Lurch into this madness known as The Factory, L.A.'s hottest night spot. The invite-only club was where Beverly Hills' finest came to see, be seen, and just feel groovy. Actor Paul Newman was a regular. So was entertainer Sammy Davis Jr. and writer Pierre Salinger. And so, too, was Sam Schulman, the five-foot-something owner of the NBA Seattle SuperSonics. He'd recently had a falling out with Gene Klein, his business partner, and they'd divvied up their sports properties. Schulman got the SuperSonics, and the NBA got Schulman's undivided attention and know-it-all business acumen.

Schulman spotted Wilt's famous goateed countenance silhouetted above the crowd in the flashing lights, and he wandered over to the NBA's hottest commodity. He ribbed Wilt about playing for him in Seattle. It was a throwaway line, about as likely as Schulman winning the Boston Marathon. But all things were possible in The Factory and its inebriated embrace of a better, peaceful, groovier world. Wilt bellowed surreally to Schulman that he'd love to play in Seattle. Schulman froze, not sure what to say next. That not-so-groovy world called the NBA would throw the book at him for tampering with Philadelphia's property if he didn't shut up, and so Schulman changed the subject.[17]

Wilt drove home that night with his ears ringing from the loud music and wondering whether Schulman might come to his million-dollar rescue. A few days later, Wilt received another unexpected ride to the rescue. He met with Alfred Bloomingdale, a department-store heir who'd recently bought into the travel business. Wilt wanted to join him as an investor in booking tours and joked to Bloomingdale that their business dealings would be much smoother if he played in Los Angeles.

"Jack Kent Cooke is a good personal friend," Bloomingdale teased, referring to the owner of the Los Angeles Lakers. "I'll see what I can do."

"Please do," Chamberlain replied.[18]

Bloomingdale relayed the message to Cooke, whose Lakers had recently lost in the NBA finals to Boston. Cooke, who hated coming in second even for a parking space, had taken the defeat hard and vowed to end his team's decade-long search for a dominant center, considered the game-changing key to NBA success. Wilt, more than any other NBA player, checked that box.

Cooke also had a more-expensive ulterior motive. He'd recently organized California Sports, Inc., home of his various sports properties. That included the Lakers, the expansion Los Angeles Kings hockey team, the grandiose arena called The Forum, a prominent stake in the Washington Redskins football team, and likely a pro soccer team in the not-too-distant future. As Cooke explained at cocktail parties, sports entertainment and its myriad marketing opportunities were the wave of the future. He planned to corner the sports market, starting with the NBA. As Cooke shrewdly calculated, assembling a for-the-ages Lakers team of Baylor, West, and Chamberlain would deliver the world championship and a pro basketball dynasty to L.A., all while teaching the ABA Stars an expensive lesson about treading on his turf.

Cooke soon called to have a chat with his dear friend Koz. Schulman already had tried. Koz dodged both calls, just as he'd avoided four other random inquiries about his superstar's availability. Koz had been through the wringer with Wilt. He squabbled with coaches, threatened to retire, claimed part ownership of the team, toyed with the ABA, demanded free agency . . . all while living a lush life in New York surrounded in his nightclub by gamblers and Gambinos. Through it all, Wilt remained a 76er, and Koz held onto the slim hope that the most-dominant player in the game would stick around a while longer in Philadelphia for old-time's sake.

When Gene Shue arrived in Louisville at the Olympic tryouts, he was greeted by a who's who of NBA scouts. Most were retired NBA lifers who'd entered the league hoping to play 10 seasons and boost their $5,000 standard rookie salaries to a more-respectable $20,000. That's why all were buzzing over Elvin Hayes. He was getting four and six times more to start than they'd pocketed at the peak of their careers. Hayes was set for life at age 22. Boy, did they ever play at the wrong time.

By evening, the NBA scouts had taken their seats in Louisville's Freedom Hall for a public scrimmage featuring the Olympic hopefuls and wealthy pros in waiting. Shue and Bob Ferry were notably absent. They had slipped away to Seneca High School. That's where Wes Unseld, a proud former Seneca Red Hawk, had committed that evening to playing in an alumni basketball game . . . and meeting Shue on the side.

When Unseld lumbered forward to shake Shue's hand, he looked as broad as an NFL offensive lineman. But animating this formidable physique was a disarmingly warm, Southern-tinged voice that could have belonged to an Eagle scout. Shue, an award-winning insurance salesman in the offseason, greeted the various Unseld family members and deftly turned the hellos to the NBA's comparative advantages. He hadn't gotten far when Unseld yes-sired that he preferred the NBA. Having cleared that hurdle, Shue headed down the homestretch to the all-important matter of money. The Bullets were prepared to tender their most lucrative contract in franchise history, a multi-year blockbuster that could reach $300,000.

Though flattered, Unseld politely said that the ABA Kentucky Colonels were offering more. Shue paused, having expected a full-throated wow at that stratospheric figure. The Bullets had pulled out all the financial stops to get there, and it was shocking that the ABA was already navigating a financial level higher in the mesosphere.

"How much?" Shue asked.

"Four hundred thousand dollars over four years."

Shue, a salesman's salesman and firm believer in the power of positive thinking, turned the conversation back to his product. The Bullets, he said, were prepared to match any ABA offer. Matter of fact, he would relay the latest information to Bullet co-owner Earl Foreman, a practicing attorney, whom he promised would make the NBA numbers work.

Everybody said their see-you-laters on this sleepy Thursday evening, and someone mentioned that Foreman should make the numbers work fast. Next Monday, per the Kentucky Colonels' request, Unseld's attorney Bob Maddox would draft a final contract with all of the revised terms and conditions, which he would read aloud, semicolon by tedious semicolon, for all to yeh, nay, and bring Big Wes into the ABA fold. Shue tried not to wince. His positivity told him that Foreman would come through. He had to, but how Shue had no idea. Neither did Shue want to let slip a chuckle. Rookies signing for $400,000. Boy, did he ever play pro basketball at the wrong time.

It was past 4 p.m., and the doors remained closed to the plush, walnut-paneled conference room at the hotshot Louisville law firm of Wyatt, Grafton, and Sloss. Inside, about a dozen people sat at a long wooden table listening to the firm's Bob

Maddox, dark-haired, broad cheeks, with a lawyerly flare for careful enunciation, read through the handwritten draft contract that he'd prepared for the parties of Wes Unseld and the Kentucky Colonels, Inc.

Hanging on his every semicolon were Joe and Mamie Gregory, the majority owners of the Colonels. Husband Joe was the basketball nut; Mamie, dirty blond and girlishly attractive and fidgety in her mid-20s, was the money. She was the heiress of a mining fortune estimated to be worth somewhere just north of $40 million. It fueled her flamboyant, anything-goes pursuit of whatever in this wide world caught her fancy. Lately, that included sitting courtside at Colonels games, her prized Brussels griffon Ziggy yapping in his green doggie game uniform, while she cheered tall men named Darrell and Goose. Last season, Darrell, Goose, and the other tall fellows managed just 36 wins against 42 heartbreaking losses. Mamie was told that with Big Wes snatching rebounds next season, that number would soar. And so would her Colonels in the ABA standings.

Maddox completed his enunciations, and Mamie and Joe shrugged okay. Type up the agreement, Joe declared, he'd sign it: four years for $400,000. Observing the foregoing was Unseld, dressed in an itchy Sunday suit and appearing outwardly as stoic as he did in college snatching rebounds off an enemy backboard. Inwardly, as basketball writers would later note, Unseld could get butterflies when his number was called on offense. Well, these numbers being called out—now personally guaranteed by the Gregorys—had his stomach flapping and his mind reeling. With the stroke of a pen, he stood to make more money than his father earned in a lifetime working nights at International Harvester.

Unseld eyed the dark-haired man with Italian features seated near him. That was John Dromo, Unseld's college coach, who had doubled as his agent since autumn. It's unclear whether the NCAA prohibited college coaches from representing their players in 1968. "Agenting" was a new phenomenon, and NCAA policy typically lagged behind the emerging realities on the ground and in the locker room. But common sense dictated that any major college coach who advised a player on turning pro entered an ethical gray area. College coaches arranging pro contracts just didn't look good, and most feared that openly mixing with the pros would suggest that their players were for sale, a sure way to land their programs on the NCAA's watch list and their coaching careers in hot water.

In fact, of the more than 200 college basketball players who were selected that year in the NBA draft, nearly all still heard second-hand that they'd been drafted. Nearly all still "negotiated" their own contacts alone. That translated to "sign here, kid." But Unseld was one of this year's first-round exceptions because Dromo, a longtime Louisville assistant in his first season as head coach, didn't fear the NCAA. Matter of fact, he "loathed" the NCAA, considered it a politically motivated organization that was out of touch with the daily grind of college sports. His loathing came from an earlier run-in. The NCAA fingered Dromo, then an assistant coach at Louisville, for arranging part-time retail jobs for two New York recruits to help them get home for the holidays. Dromo clung doggedly to his innocence, protesting Louisville's two-year probation but vowing to remain true to himself and his values.[19] That meant standing behind the good kids who came through the system like Unseld, whom he considered "the finest young man I've met in 30 years of coaching."[20]

Unseld, at the start of his senior year, had asked Dromo to shield him from all this pro stuff. Dromo thought instead about getting him an agent, but there were so few in Louisville. Attorney Bill Boone did some agenting on the side, but he now worked for the Colonels. In fact, Dromo started getting frequent calls from Boone. He wanted to know what it would take to get Unseld to sign with the Colonels, and the two floated a few whimsical dollar figures. Dromo finally threw in the towel and enlisted the help of Maddox, a tax law expert, who'd once assisted boxer Muhammad Ali and recently negotiated a pro football contract.

Maddox, like Dromo, was instinctively wary of the Colonels and the ABA. Though the Gregorys had money to burn, the league could go up in smoke at any moment. Even Boone seemed to admit as much. In conversations with Dromo, he kept floating the magic figure $400,000, Dromo's whimsical, pie-in-the-sky asking price for Unseld. But Boone wouldn't put anything in writing; In fact, he kept backtracking on the final figure. "They didn't want to make us a final offer that we could use to shop with in the NBA," Maddox explained. "But, at the same time, they asked us for the right to match any figure we could get" and, reading between the lines, lower the final sales price.[21]

Now, the backtracking was over. Hearing Joe Gregory's orders to prepare a final contract, the moment of truth had arrived to sign or not to sign. Indeed, that was the question. Dromo motioned for a short recess, like calling a timeout in the closing seconds of a tight ball game. He hastened to Maddox's corner office to huddle with lawyer and player. What about the Bullets? Maddox said Earl Foreman phoned two days ago but had yet to call back with a firm offer. Five minutes stretched to 10. Then 15. Then came their vow to stall the Colonels for another day, or until Foreman called with a counteroffer.

Feigning embarrassment, Maddox reappeared in the walnut-paneled conference room and explained that his client had "to go home and talk with his mother and father" before signing anything. The conversation then came full circle: Could the Colonels count on Unseld's services next season? After a soft yes and some mumbled maybes, a final meeting was scheduled for tomorrow, same time, same place, same contract to sign.

By lunch the next day, Foreman finally called Maddox with a firm offer. He said in his measured, lawyerly way that the Bullets would match the ABA contract. Dromo woo-hooed, and Maddox phoned the gentlemanly Joe Gregory at his sprawling 750-acre country estate to deliver the chilling words: "All negotiations are off." Gregory and the Colonels' top executive Bill Motsch who was out at the estate, raced off to Louisville for an emergency all-hands meeting. "What happened?" Motsch recalled asking Gregory. "I thought we had Unseld locked up?"[22]

Joe Gregory wasn't yet ready to throw in the towel on Wes Unseld. He telephoned Unseld, bypassing Maddox and Dromo, to up the ante to a cool half-million dollars. Team officials then upped the public pressure on Unseld. They took out a full-page ad in the *Louisville Courier-Journal* calling on "all basketball fans to tell Westley, by wire or phone, that they want him to play in Kentucky, before he signs with the NBA." The mayor even got into the act, offering to have a word alone with Unseld.

All to no avail. Unseld announced his decision was final and now miffed at the Colonels for dragging his father into their last-minute pretty please and, in his words, insulting him. In mid-April, as flashbulbs popped, Unseld signed with the Bullets. "The NBA has grabbed the two best collegiate seniors in the country," crowed Bullets' owner Arnie Heft, referring to Unseld and Elvin Hayes, while his friend and co-owner Earl Foreman boomed, "We're proud the great ones coming along are picking the NBA."[23]

Back in the Louisville Convention Center, Boone, Gregory, and colleagues gathered among the white office partitions to group-think about what went wrong. Unseld reportedly wanted to stay in Louisville . . . a final agreement had been reached . . . and the Colonels had outbid the Bullets by a long shot. The mayor was even calling him. How then did the NBA sneak in and haul off their hometown hero?

The answer challenged the popular perception that the NBA-ABA War was fought with money alone. It wasn't. There was plenty of sociology, too. As mentioned, with so few "basketball" agents out there, at least for now, Unseld and the other cream of the class of 1968 opted for the "personal advisor"—the trusted alumnus, coach, or friend who had plenty of business experience but little knowledge of pro sports and its inner workings. They got involved as personal favors. For them, helping out a buddy meant minimizing risk and going with the sure thing. And so they erred on the side of caution and the NBA's sure money.

Personal advisors were proving to be the ABA's kryptonite. They came with their individual quirks, or in the case of John Dromo, a clear conflict of interest. For Dromo, Louisville was a college basketball town, and the ABA was competing on his turf, the operative word now being "his." Dromo last season moved most of the team's home games into Louisville's grand 18,000-seat Freedom Hall, one of college basketball's Carnegie Halls. His boys in Cardinal Red now ranked as big-time college basketball entertainment, on a par with Adolph Rupp and the University of Kentucky, and Dromo recently signed a 10-year deal with Freedom Hall to keep the good times rolling.

Painting Louisville a deeper shade of Cardinal Red was also profitable. Dromo's program banked a record $450,000 profit ($3.7 million today) on the season.[24] The upstart Colonels, now holding court at the Convention Center, posed an existential threat to Dromo's hard work. The Colonels, though averaging only 3,168 fans per outing in season one, had the full support of the Junior Chamber of Commerce and had gotten equal time in the local press to legitimize the ABA. Locals loved the flashy tri-colored ball and the novel three-point shot, each conversion celebrated like a home run by pinging the Marathon Oil gong. That's why, while negotiating with the Colonels, Dromo reportedly asked them to agree, in writing, to refrain for 10 years from scheduling games in Louisville that conflicted with a U of L home game.

The Colonels declined, and Dromo continued advising Unseld to think big. Think NBA. Unseld dutifully heeded the advice. In the 1960s, coaches, like father, always knew best, and Unseld wasn't one to buck that cultural truism. Neither could the Colonels buck it with the power of cash alone. Unseld, thanks to his humble upbringing and Sunday school values, wasn't motivated by money. Sure, the six figures being bandied about made his head spin. But unlike future generations, Unseld felt no show-me-the-money greed or entitlement. "Money was important, but I had my degree," he later explained, "and I figured I could always make a living [as a school teacher]. You never miss money if you never had it, so I didn't lose sleep over money."[25]

The irony was Earl Foreman, the Colonels' NBA nemesis, had burned the midnight oil to make Unseld's contract work—and with good reason. His Bullets, like most NBA teams, operated in the red. The team always ranked near last in league attendance (then the major source of revenue) and was still trying to connect in a working-class town that loved its football Colts and baseball Orioles. To save cash, the Bullets had famously hijacked Earl Monroe, last year's second pick in the NBA draft, in the wee small hours of the morning to sign him to a below-market two-year, $30,000 contract before the ABA started the bidding war.[26] This year, of course, the Colonels had the jump on them for the same slotted pick. Lucky for Foreman, the Bullets would soon bank a one-time $325,000 payment of expansion fees (from Milwaukee and Phoenix), and like a government stimulus check, it would take some of the sting out of Unseld's team-record salary.

Also lucky for Foreman, he knew just where to go to remove the pain altogether. At a pre-draft NBA Board of Governors meeting, his fellow owners vowed, "We've got to fight the

ABA." A secret, never-to-leave-this-room pact emerged. "The owners created a secret fund that allowed teams to draw tens of thousands of dollars in order to sign the top picks in the draft," Foreman recalled. "It was pooled money from NBA sources, and it was absolutely, totally illegal. It was a violation of antitrust law.

"Jack Kent Cooke and Eddie Gottlieb, the two most unlikely people in the world, were selected to be the guardians of the money," he continued, the "unlikely" referring to their clash of personalities. "The thing that was so hysterical, from a legal standpoint, is they put the money in a trust account, and Eddie wrote the checks. The point I'm making is they tried to disguise what they were doing. That's how we got the money that enabled us to sign Wes Unseld."[27]

It's not clear whether anyone in Louisville was aware of the NBA's secret trust account, though Houston's Nick Morrow recently aired his suspicions. Either way, Baltimore's success showed how overmatched most ABA front offices were in experience alone. Take the Colonels. Joe Gregory was a dog trainer and a gentleman. His wife Mamie was a trust fund *bon vivant*, and Ziggy was, well, a dog. Bill Motsch, the team's number-crunching executive director, was a young accountant with no sports experience, and Bill Boone, though a recognized sports agent, represented professional golfers. He admittedly knew nothing about pro basketball. All counted their basketball experience in months, not years. "We were the blind leading the blind," Boone recalled years later.[28]

Conversely, the Bullets front office had seen it all. Gene Shue knew the pro game inside out as a long-time player and now coach. His boss Earl Foreman had four years in as an NBA owner and also had a financial stake in the NFL's Philadelphia Eagles. His partner Arnie Heft was a popular old-time NBA official with strong ties to the league's core figures—guys like Boston's Red Auerbach, Philadelphia's Eddie Gottlieb, St. Louis' Ben Kerner, Detroit's Fred Zollner, and New York's Ned

Irish. These old timers, equal parts wise and amoral, had survived two previous pro basketball wars and knew from past battles to combine their resources, a.k.a. collude, to win the coming war for the top college players.

So far wisdom and amorality were undefeated. Of the NBA's 14 first-rounders, not one strayed to the other league. The ABA, despite its best five- and six-figure intentions, was left with what passed for the crumbs. And yet, as bad as things looked during this rookie signing season, the ABA had scored a couple of direct hits on the NBA. One was letting Unseld name his price. Until now, NBA general managers set rookie salaries, not the other way around. True, the Knicks had certainly bargained with Cazzie Russell and Bill Bradley. But that was New York. That was its big-spender, king-of-the-hill image talking. The NBA's little guys couldn't afford to pay New York prices for their All-Americans. Now, with the ABA asking college kids to name their price, they had no choice but to bid high and pay Cazzie Russell money, not just for the ceremonial first pick but for the other high first-rounders. That was a hard check to write for NBA teams already awash in red ink.

Secondly, these inflated six-figure rookie salaries marked a tipping point that would attract agents. The inflated rookie contracts were now literally worth their while. These smooth operators were exactly the ones that NBA executives didn't want darkening their doorways with demands for guaranteed contracts, fatter signing bonuses, and whatever else they could squeeze out of them. Because agents had been banned for so long in the NBA from negotiating player contracts, with a few recent exceptions, general managers had no existing cozy relationships to manipulate and rig the college market in their favor. For Arthur Morse and other real agents, money talked, not league affiliation. Deals got done in a tug of war to maximize or minimize the final numbers, and that would give the free-spending ABA an opening to bolster its talent pool in a hurry and overcome its lack of stature.

For now, the NBA could crow about winning the battle of the 1968 college draft. "This is the year when the ABA has to put up or shut up," said Jerry Colangelo, the young general manager of the expansion Phoenix Suns.[29] He was referring to the ABA's promise to spend big and sign big this rookie season. Of course, the ABA had indeed been offering big, with no luck. Conversely, thanks to the Suns, having contributed disproportionately through expansion fees and the illegal trust fund, the NBA could afford to enrich Hayes and Unseld. Maybe all this money passing hands helped to explain an interesting behind-the-scenes trend. Most of the NBA's old-timers quietly put their teams up for sale. Maybe it was time to cash out before this cold war turned hot.

Earl Foreman hurried down the carpeted hallway, hung a hard right, and entered a familiar white choke of cigar smoke that confirmed he'd arrived in the right place for the NBA Board of Governors meeting. Puffing away at the card table on this May morning in 1968 were the last of the league's influential old timers. They sat per usual hunkered in their mostly frumpy, store-bought suits, puffing away and waiting for Walter Kennedy to roust them upstairs for the morning session.

Among those puffing on Roi-Tans was St. Louis owner Ben Kerner, the big news of today's meeting. "Bennie the Boob" had sold his St. Louis Hawks to an Atlanta group headed by Tom Cousins, a mega-wealthy young developer. Now, Kerner's fellow governors just had to approve the $3.5 million sale, and he'd retire a wealthy man at age 54 for his two-plus decades of NBA trouble.

While Foreman, a tall, distinguished-looking gentleman in his 40s, chatted up the Roi-Tans, Kennedy materialized and pulled Foreman aside. He needed a favor. Cousins would arrive shortly, and he was a rather prim-and-proper Southerner, a league first. Would Foreman intercept Cousins, engage him in urbane conversation somewhere away from the smoke and bluster? Kennedy mumbled something to the effect of God only knows how Cousins would react to investing millions to join a board of sloppy, card-playing old folks with their ties loosened and sleeves rolled up.

When Cousins appeared, Foreman turned on the sophistication and made a new friend. The affable Cousins confirmed in his slow, probing Southern intonations that he would move the Hawks to Atlanta. As part of his high-stakes efforts to revitalize the city's downtown, Cousins wanted to build a Madison Square Garden of the South. He called it The Omni. Foreman nodded along and eventually chaperoned the engaging white Southern gentleman upstairs to the boardroom, where he joined in the "ayes" to approve the sale and thus the NBA's first foray below the Mason-Dixon line.

All ayes then turned to the smiling Kerner, with his jet-black, Grecian formula hair combed back in a greasy 1950s style. Every board member had endured his cloying, stream-of-consciousness, let-me-tell-you-a-story brand of entrepreneurial persistence. As irritating as Kerner and his stories could be, he was a league fixture and would be missed.[30] "I got to do something for you before I go," Kerner was overheard persisting one last time.[31]

The hallway gossip soon turned to the juicier matter of Wilt Chamberlain and his offseason antics. Some chuckled at the Big Fella's nerve; others eyed the gray-haired gentleman from Philadelphia, Irv Kosloff, seated alone and presumably ashen over the prospect of hiring Wilt as his next coach. "I hear the 76ers need a coach who can handle Wilt," yukked former NBA star Red Kerr, the league's reigning king of the one-liner. "I've got one for them: Bill Russell."

A reporter eased over and asked Koz, "Do you get the feeling that you don't really own your team?"[32]

Koz looked up, bloodshot and unable to crack a smile. Neither could he spill on the latest in the Wilt saga, known only to a select few. Wilt returned from his California holiday disinterested in coaching and pushing a final ultimatum: Trade him immediately, otherwise Wilt would jump either to the ABA, rejoin the Globetrotters, or take whatever other action was needed to ensure Koz got nothing in return. Koz and his high principles had already tossed and turned for days over Wilt's brashness, finally reaching a morally acceptable decision. He called Jack Kent Cooke just before the Board of Governors meeting and announced in his soft, downbeat voice that he was ready to make a deal. Sign Wilt, and Cooke could have him, though officially in the form of a trade, not free agency.

The 76ers' Jack Ramsay and his Lakers counterpart Fred Schaus then worked out the trade: Wilt for the Lakers' young all-star Archie Clark, veteran Darrall Imhoff, and the promising Jerry Chambers. But there was a catch. All but Imhoff's contract were expired. Once Clark and Chambers resigned, the trade would go public. Until then, mum was the word.[33]

Mum may have been the word, but the still-pending Wilt Chamberlain trade didn't stay mum for long. The initial breach came on June 12 when a *Philadelphia Inquirer* reporter asked Jack Ramsey when he planned to call Jack Kent Cooke again about trading Chamberlain?[34] A member of the 76ers' small nexus of front-office staff had been speaking out of turn and off the record.

A week later, the tabloid *Boston Record-American* officially broke the story. According to its sources, Philadelphia soon would swap Chamberlain to Los Angeles for three players and one million bucks. The dollar figure was incorrect, which technically allowed both teams to deny the report. But the leaks continued. In San Francisco, radio personality Lon Simmons went so far as to name the three Lakers involved in the trade. Two days later, Cooke came clean and admitted his interest in obtaining Chamberlain.[35]

Getting all the players under contract, however, proved as exhausting as negotiating a Middle East peace agreement. Cooke regaled Wilt at his mansion over five evenings, three hours per meeting. "We talked about half an hour each time about a contract," Cooke said. "The other hours were spent discussing the playing ability of other players in the league, antiques, paintings, and politics."[36] Wilt finally tired of talking and committed to the Lakers, only to change his mind and team almost immediately. "I won't tell you where I'm going or how much they're paying me," he told Cooke. After a few well-placed phone calls, the jilted Cooke had his answer: Seattle. Sam Schulman had stolen Cooke's seven-foot prize.

Cooke and Schulman had history. Two years earlier, Schulman tricked Cooke into supporting Seattle's entry into the NBA.[37] Cooke didn't appreciate Schulman's deception then, and he didn't appreciate his sneakiness now. Cooke called Wilt's lawyer in righteous indignation and started throwing around his NBA weight and matching Schulman's higher offer.

"Shit, now what do I do?" Wilt asked his lawyer. Wilt told his lawyer to call Cooke and accept his latest offer and then phone Schulman and decline his offer. "Make it firm," Wilt added. "Tell them both this is final."[38]

Except Archie Clark had sniffed out the trade (confirming it earlier with Wilt himself). Clark shrewdly stalled on re-signing, hoping the Lakers would sweeten their offer to him. Until Clark re-signed with the Lakers, the trade couldn't be consummated.

Cooke, used to getting his way with players, threatened Clark. If the trade fell through, Cooke warned that he would see to it personally that Clark never played another minute in the NBA. But Clark, a steely Army vet, wouldn't budge. His stalling was a time-worn tactic right out of business negotiation 101, and yet Clark's move was gutsy, even revolutionary, for breaking with NBA culture, which dictated that rank-and-file players like him must be passive to management and its better financial judgment. Clark had another trick up his sleeve. He had arranged a last-minute meeting with the ABA's Los Angeles Stars. He hoped to wave an inflated ABA contract offer at Cooke and force him either to match it or sacrifice the NBA's then-trade of the century.

Ironically, the invisible hand of Wilt Chamberlain scuttled Clark's ABA ploy. On the morning of July 3, before Clark's afternoon meeting, ABA commissioner George Mikan and his staff had arranged a secret gathering with Chamberlain and his attorney at Los Angeles' Biltmore Hotel. The subject: What would it take for Wilt to switch leagues? At the table were officials with the L.A. Stars and Bill Ringsby, owner of the Denver Rockets, who served as a proxy for his fellow owners. Everything was on the sly with Mikan pretending to be in town to negotiate a network television contract for the ABA, while Ringsby checked into the hotel under an assumed name to ensure no leaks. Sunglasses were optional.

During the meeting, Wilt frivolously repeated his earlier extemporaneous pronouncement that he should be the first pro to sign a million-dollar contract. Cooke and Schulman hadn't gone quite that high, and Wilt remembered spouting off that there was "no reason the Stars should carry the burden for the whole league." He suggested the 11 ABA teams pool their wealth to subsidize his million-dollar contract. Lights went off in their desperate heads, and the roomful of ABA executives promised to be back in touch shortly with an answer.

For Wilt, it was another "oh shit" moment. "Oh shit" quickly became "oh no." Wilt's possible leap into a giant pool of ABA cash leaked to a Miami newspaper[39] and then dominated the day's sports news cycle. "Screw the ABA," Wilt told his lawyer and backtracked to Cooke and the Lakers, literally at Clark's expense. The Stars, thinking Wilt might jump, had nothing left to offer Clark.

On Friday, Clark arrived for a previously scheduled meeting in Cooke's office. He was prepared to cut his losses and sign the Lakers' offered $65,000 contract. The secretary asked him to take a seat in the waiting area. Mr. Cooke would see him shortly. Moments later, Cooke emerged. He appeared to be in a foul mood and approached Clark head on and without a hello.

"Well Archie, what do you want?"

The question surprised Clark. He thought Cooke had closed their negotiation at $65,000. The word "want" suggested that wasn't the case. His mind raced for a number. One popped into his head. He grabbed it.

"I'd like $105,000."

"Okay," Cooke answered. "Have your attorney contact my attorney. They can work out the contract."

Cooke grumped back into his office, his heart pounding. No counteroffer? Cooke, the master negotiator, had caved to a third-year guard from Minnesota. Clark called Fred Rosenfeld, his young lawyer agent. Shortly thereafter, Rosenfeld and Cooke's attorney Clyde Tritt huddled in the office suite behind closed doors. Clark remained seated in the waiting area, his mind whirling. He was a $100,000 man! He had reached the gold standard of sports wealth.

The door opened, and both lawyers emerged with furrowed brows.

"We've got a problem," Tritt said.

Clark's heart nearly stopped.

"You will be traded to Philadelphia," announced Tritt. "Philadelphia wants you to sign a standard, one-year NBA contract. But the 76ers are only willing to pay $55,000."

"Oh no, I can't sign for that," Clark interjected.

"Hold on," Tritt continued. "We can work it out. I'll add an addendum to your $55,000 contract for $50,000, which Mr. Cooke will pay. That puts you at $105,000."

Clark considered the plan and quickly saw the trap. He would earn $105,000 next season, and the 76ers would begin their negotiations the following year at $55,000, or at a 50-percent pay cut.

"No, I can't do that," said Clark, explaining the dilemma.

"Archie, I think we can solve the problem. If you resign with the 76ers the following season for less than $105,000, Mr. Cooke will personally pay the difference. Do we have a deal?"

Clark thought for a few seconds and answered in the affirmative. Tritt trundled into Cooke's office to share the good news.[40] Clark was in tow. Call Philadelphia.

The following Tuesday, Jack Kent Cooke held a press conference at The Fabulous Forum and officially revealed "the worst kept secret in NBA history."[41] Wilt Chamberlain was coming to Los Angeles. Cooke had matched the ABA offer, reportedly committing one million dollars to the 31-year-old Chamberlain over the next five years. Doing the math, Chamberlain may have taken a pay cut. He'd earned $250,000 last season in Philadelphia, which totals $1.25 million over five years. Nevertheless, Chamberlain technically was the first million-dollar man in professional sports.

"One million dollars," a boxing promoter once quipped, "the words tolled like a great bell . . ." And so it was for Chamberlain. As history would show, he wouldn't be the only million-dollar man in basketball for long as the fog of the NBA-ABA War wafted over the 1968-69 season.

Endnotes

[1] Based on notes in Minutes, American Basketball Association League Meeting, Houston, January 20-21, 1968

[2] Eddie Einhorn and Ron Rapoport, *How March Became Madness*, 2006, p. 57.

[3] No Byline, "Amigos No More—They're L.A. Stars," *Los Angeles Times*, March 28, 1968.

[4] Ibid.

[5] What about the New York Knicks and New Jersey Americans? The short answer is they weren't really in direct competition. The NBA had ostensibly blocked the ABA franchise from playing in Manhattan, home of the Knicks, and forced its banishment to out-of-sight, out-of-mind New Jersey.

[6] United Press International, "Elvin Hayes (Player of Year) Inks Three-Year Contract," *Hanford (Calif.) Sentinel*, March 28, 1968.

[7] The quotes drawn from coverage of the press conference in the San Diego Union, March 28, 1968.

[8] Rush Wood, "Mavs, ABA Declare $ War on NBA," *Houston Post*, March 29, 1968.

[9] Ibid.

[10] Carl Scheer. Interview with author, August 2013.

[11] Jack Kiser, "The Night Our Statistician Cracked," *Philadelphia Daily News*, March 16, 1968.

[12] Jack Ramsay, Interview with author, April 2011.

[13] Ibid.

[14] This section is based on interviews with Gene Shue, Bob Ferry, and Earl Foreman, as well as newspaper accounts from Baltimore and Louisville, particularly: Kentucky Colonels Athletic Enterprises, Inc., "Colonels Offer Unseld $500,000," *Louisville Times*, April 5, 1968.

[15] No byline, "Owner Kosloff Still Waiting for Wilt's Call," *Philadelphia Inquirer*, May 2, 1968.

[16] Jack Kiser, "Wilt Wants $1M to Play 3 Years; Will Coach for Free," *Philadelphia Daily News*, May 1, 1968.

[17] Wilt Chamberlain and David Shaw, *Wilt*, 1973, p. 196.

[18] Ibid, p. 195.

[19] John Dromo, Interview with Richard Cushing, December 1981, Oral History Center, University of Louisville Special Collections Room, Louisville, Ken.

[20] John Steadman , "The Unselds: Portrait of a Family," *Baltimore News-American*, April 19, 1968.

[21] Jim Henneman, "The Day Unseld Flew Louisville's Basketball Coop," *Baltimore News-American*, April 20, 1969.

[22] Bill Motsch, Interview with author, April 2019.

[23] Seymour Smith, "Westley Unseld of Louisville Signs Rich Contract with Bullets," *Baltimore Sun*, April 19, 1968.

[24] Dromo Interview.

[25] Dennis Klein, "How Wes Unseld Came On," *Pro Basketball Almanac 1970*, p. 41.

[26] Monroe remained unhappy about his NBA hijacking. "Rick Barry did the right thing in jumping to the American Basketball Association.," he said last summer, "and I would follow him for six figures. The only reason I signed with Baltimore in the first place was to see if I could play with the best. Actually, Pittsburgh of the ABA offered me more money. But I made a big mistake. And I'm paying for it now. If I could advise anyone coming out of college, I'd tell him to go where the money is. The less time I'm in Baltimore, the better." (Phil Elderkin, NBA Basketball, *The Sporting News*, September 14, 1968)

[27] Earl Foreman, Interview with author, March 2010.

[28] Gary West and Lloyd Gardner, *Kentucky Colonels of the American Basketball Association*, 2011, p. 33.

[29] Jack Murphy, "Speaking of Kemp, Stengel, Hayes, and Assorted Subjects," *San Diego Union*, April 4, 1968.

[30] Though his plans fell through, Kerner had intended to sell the Hawks and leap right back into the NBA. He was trying to assemble an investment group to start of expansion team in Houston. The investment group failed, and the San Diego Rockets eventually claimed Houston. Interestingly, in the summer of 1968, Kerner came very close to purchasing the Baltimore Bullets and moving the franchise to Houston, where he would have competed directly against the ABA. In the end, Kerner couldn't break the Bullets' contract with the Baltimore Civic Center. Otherwise, he would have consummated the deal. See Alan Goldstein, *Baltimore Sun*, January 14, 1969.

[31] No Byline, "Israel Sports Program Helped by Ben Kerner," *Buffalo News*, May 21, 1968.

[32] Sandy Padwe, "Wilt Thou or Wilt Though Not?" *Philadelphia Inquirer*, May 11, 1968.

[33] For more detailed information on the Chamberlain signing, see Bob Kuska, *Shake and Bake,* 2021.

[34] No Byline, "Wilt to Lakers? Report Denied by 76ers, LA," *Philadelphia Inquirer,* June 20, 1968.

[35] Roger Keim, "S.F. Announcer Latest Source to Say: 'Wilt to Lakers,'" *Philadelphia Inquirer,* June 22, 1968; Melvin Durslag, "Cooke Admits He Wants Wilt," *Philadelphia Inquirer,* June 25, 1968.

[36] Dave Anderson, "Wilt, Baylor, West—Can They Work Together," *True's Basketball Yearbook,* 1969.

[37] After agreeing to front the Seattle franchise (see chapter 6), Schulman also helped to get the team accepted into the league. Schulman's idea was to curry favor with the influential Cooke. That involved some deviousness. In November 1966, Schulman leaked a bogus rumor to the *Los Angeles Herald-Examiner* that he would form a rival ABA team in Los Angeles. "When Jack Kent Cook read that," Schulman said, ". . . he called me to have lunch. He asked me why I wanted an ABA team . . . I said I loved basketball, and I wanted a team. He said, 'Just tell me where you want to go, and I'll help you get into the NBA.' I told him Seattle, and he said, 'You've got it.'" From Blaine Johnson, "How He Became Mr. Sonics," *Sonics Magazine,* November/December 1976.

[38] Chamberlain, *Wilt,* p. 197.

[39] Luther Evans, "Chamberlain Negotiating Jump to Los Angeles of ABA," *Miami Herald,* July 5, 1968.

[40] Archie Clark. Interview with author, October 2010.

[41] Harry Hoffman, "Tales of Hoffman, Press of Atlantic City, Atlantic City, N.J., July 10, 1968

8

Life is full of surprises, just ask Lee Meade. Last summer, he was a rising sports editor at the *Denver Post* when he heard the fledgling American Basketball Association had placed a franchise in the Mile High City. The Rockets. He quickly discovered that the franchise's Southern California owners were undercapitalized and didn't know Denver from Cheyenne. Convinced the whole thing was doomed at liftoff and reluctant to stick his overburdened staff with another ill-fated team to cover, the 39-year-old Meade took one for the newsroom: He'd cover the Rockets until the franchise—and league—vaporized without a trace.

Several weeks later, the Rockets had a new owner, one of the richer men in Denver, and this rising editor flipped his opinion. Maybe the Rockets and the ABA would get off the ground? Meade, a Minnesota native, heard that the ABA was looking for a publicity director at its Minneapolis office and voiced his interest. After Thanksgiving 1967, Meade was seated across from George Mikan, his boyhood sports hero and public face of the new league, interviewing for the job. "How much do you want?" Mikan asked. Meade, who earned $220 per week at the newspaper, proposed double his salary.

"Okay, you got it," nodded Mikan. "When can you start?"

Meade answered Jan. 1, 1968. He then paused, "Wait a minute, we need to talk about my benefits."

"Fuck you," Mikan smiled. "You work for me now."[1]

So oppressive the ABA sweatshop wasn't. Meade hit it off with Mikan, reveling in his true-life tales of playing for the world-champion Minneapolis Lakers. He found Mikan to be the rare giant who seemed to enjoy the weather up there, smiling down and adjusting his trademark Clark Kent glasses sliding down his nose. He was always approachable, gracious, jocular, magnanimous. But, as Meade discovered, behind the pleasant facade ruminated a profoundly stubborn alter ego that was utterly fearless, willful, and wise.

"His stubborn disposition made it absolutely impossible for George to consider that the ABA might not make it," said Meade. "Sometimes, we operated with the league secretly owning a franchise and preparing to take over another. But George just refused to let it die. I can't stress this enough: Without George Mikan, there would have never been an ABA."

Shadowing Mikan that first season at league meetings was his close friend Bill Erickson, the ABA's chief counsel. Erickson possessed a brilliant legal mind that, according to Meade, made him the "brains" behind the ABA. "Bill was the kind of guy who would be talking to you," said Meade, "and he'd already be thinking five questions ahead."[2] Erickson told Mikan what to do. Mikan relayed the decision to staffer Thurlo McCrady, who carried out the orders often with Meade's assistance.

Then, last May 1968, Erickson resigned as ABA counsel after an unexpected turn of league events. A Miami group, in a true leap of faith, bought half of the insolvent Minnesota Muskies, officially $158,000 in the hole, to keep the franchise upright. When the new owners moved the Muskies to Miami, the ABA had no team in Minneapolis, and suddenly keeping the league headquarters there made no organizational sense. Erickson, thinking five questions ahead, could already hear the trustees asking for the relocation of the league office to New York, which Mikan refused to do for his own business reasons. Erickson's solution was to buy half of the Pittsburgh Pipers, the defending ABA champs who were teetering on insolvency for lack of a life-sustaining local television contract. Erickson adroitly coaxed Gabe Rubin, the team's owner last season and his new business partner, to move the Pipers to Minneapolis, promising lots of air time in the Twin Cities and providing the plausible deniability for keeping the league office right where it was.[3]

With Erickson officially moved to the trustee side, Mikan faced the summer of 1968 as the ABA's public face, administrative will, and, more than ever, its operational brains. He still oversaw the same skeleton crew tucked into the same row of offices in Mikan's Viking Travel Agency. Mikan had the choice corner space, next door sat Thurlo McCrady, followed by Meade's modest digs near the copy machine and never far from a landline telephone. "We could tell how well things were going around the league by how often the phone rang," said Meade.

Answering the phone was like a game of Russian roulette. Meade never knew if his head would explode at the news on the other end. "The players are forming a union," a voice warned. Another declared a proposed new ownership group DOA. All the bad news was relayed to Mikan, who had a strange method of crisis management. "If George came into the office facing a crisis, he would say, 'I'm going to play golf this morning, I'll check in with you,'" said Meade. "That left Thurlo and I as the only two people in the office. We'd sit there and do all the worrying. When George made his turn at the ninth hole, he would call into the office. We'd say this franchise is about to fold, and we'd tell him EVERYTHING—and it was ALL bad. George would answer nonchalantly, 'Okay, I'll call you when I finish.'"

After 18 carefree holes, Mikan would stroll into the office after lunch. "We'd say, 'Thank God you're here!'" said Meade. "Thurlo told him that we'd solved this and that problem, filling him in on all the dramatic details. George answered, 'See, I told you everything would be all right.'"[4]

Mikan's laissez-faire approach to crisis management had Meade and McCrady flustered. But they gave him the benefit of the doubt. He was, after all, George Mikan, the greatest basketball player ever. The same awe went for newspaper reporters. Mikan could still pull up a chair, wax nostalgic for a moment about the good old days, then confide, like an old family friend offering a stock tip, about his up-and-coming ABA. "One year ago, a franchise in the ABA was worth exactly ... zero, not a thing," Mikan told a Miami reporter in August, joining his thumb and forefinger to form a zero. "Today, it's worth a million bucks, and isn't that progress?"[5]

In September, he shared with a Minneapolis reporter, "It's a simple matter of economics. The leagues are not going to continue to bid against themselves for talent. The weak towns will fall out, and the strong will eventually form one huge pro basketball wheel," including the million-dollar ABA franchises.[6]

Back at Viking Travel, the phone rang and rang. Nothing too mind-blowing for Meade. Just the usual last-minute jitters before the start of the 1968-69 season. In Oakland, Rick Barry had finally cleared every NBA legal appeal and was ready for his ABA debut. In Houston, the Mavericks were quietly on life support and looking for a new owner. In Miami, the Muskies-turned-Floridians touted the arrival of "major-league pro basketball" in the Sunshine State. The Floridians had drawn up a cartoon logo featuring a boy wearing sunglasses dribbling ahead with an ABA basketball. Depending on one's perspective, the sunglasses made the boy either look way cool or totally blind. The same could said of the ABA dribbling ahead into its second season.

Miami Beach, Oct. 26, 1968—Blame it on Eric Clapton and The Cream. Tonight, the popular English rock-'n'-rollers would be blasting the Miami Beach Convention Hall, home of the Miami Floridians, forcing the Floridians to hit the road for their season opener. Coach Jim Pollard, who formerly starred with George Mikan on the world-champion Minneapolis Lakers, grumbled at Miami's welcome to the ABA. Not only would the Floridians be away tonight, they would be on the road for five games, in all over eight days. It was a lot to ask of his players, half of whom were new and still learning the plays.

Then again, the offense wasn't too complicated for now. Pollard's chalkboard doodling translated pretty much to get the ball to "Big Game." That was Lester "Big Game" Hunter, the team's top returning scorer. He was aggressive around the basket and an ABA legend of sorts for once elbowing Dallas' untouchable veteran player-coach Cliff Hagan and then reportedly finishing him off with a right cross. When someone compared his rough stuff to NBA hatchet-man Jungle Jim Loscutoff, Hunter demurred, "I've got a little finesse."[7]

Tonight, Pollard, Big Game, and the boys were in for a scrap against the New York Nets, formerly the New Jersey Americans. But the new address wasn't in bustling Manhattan, as the league desired. It was in Commack, a remote town on Long Island, 45 long miles from Madison Square Garden. Arthur Brown, owner of the Nets, had spent $150,000 over the summer sprucing up the Long Island Arena, his back-up facility last season and a house built for hockey. The court was laid over ice, which was fully exposed at the end of the court.[8] To prevent the ice from melting, the room temperature was kept around 30 degrees.

Brown had commissioned the composition of a team fight song, with the opening line, "The Nets, the Nets, the New York Nets/For action and thrills join the crowd." Well, not much of a crowd was on hand to belt out Brown's go-get-em. The Nets simply had no name recognition in a region of rhymed sports teams (football Jets, baseball Mets), and just 743 Long Islanders dotted the frosty (you could see your breath), 6,000-seat arena at game time. The disappointing turnout may not have registered with Pollard. He was too busy cursing the action on the floor. "We couldn't do anything right in the first half," said Pollard. His Floridians quickly trailed by 20 points and not even Big Game, raising his hand and calling for the tri-colored ball in the second half, could make up the deficit.

After the blowout loss, the Floridians caught the redeye to Minneapolis, where last season they answered to the Minnesota Muskies. Apparently, they'd now also have to answer for deserting Minneapolis last spring. "We want to show people like the Floridians," owner Bill Erickson spoke on behalf of God and Minnesota, "that [Minneapolis] is a great sports center, and taking away our basketball team was a mistake."

Erickson's comment was pure Barnum and Bailey, calculated hokum to assemble a crowd. "We've got quite a night planned for them," he blustered. "Instead of cheerleaders, we'll have booleaders, and we'll have all sorts of banners and horns to give away to fans." He'd already dubbed tonight's promotion, "We Hate the Muskies Night."

"We're going up there with sunglasses and sports shorts and a palm tree and just sit back and watch our boys win," a Floridians official blustered right back. "We've got some signs being made saying, 'Who Needs Minnesota?'" He floated another possibility: hand out oranges at the door, compliments of the Florida Citrus Commission.[9]

With the ginned-up tensions running high and ticket prices low, Erickson envisioned a sellout crowd tooting cheap plastic horns handed out at the door and merrily lobbing oranges at the Floridians. But the Florida Citrus Commission took a pass, and so did most of the Twin Cities, complaining of unseasonably cold weather. Just 1,943 buttoned up to boo, but their taunts and stray oranges weren't needed anyway. The Floridians looked lousy again in the first half, and the Pipers took control behind their slithery superstar Connie Hawkins, palming the tri-colored ball like a kumquat in his huge right hand. Midway through the third quarter, Pollard emptied his bench. Better luck next time.

Next time came two nights later in Duluth before a disappointing crowd of 1,600. There was no stopping Hawkins for a second-straight evening, though the game was more competitive. The next morning the Floridians departed winless for a rematch with the Nets, who drew just 384 Long Islanders for its last game a few nights ago. Roughly a 1,000 more Long Islanders dotted the arena this time around, and a hard-fought game tussled to the wire. With 13 seconds left, Big Game Hunter went for the kill shot, got fouled, and converted the winning free throw. The Floridians celebrated like school kids, then hurried from the locker room. The Kentucky Colonels awaited tomorrow, the final foe on their first spin around the ABA.

Getting to Louisville wasn't direct and easy, but playing there before an enthusiastic Saturday night crowd of 5,200 was a hoot and first glimmer of hope that the ABA wasn't ignored everywhere. The Colonels' sassy trust-fund owner and bon vivant Mamie Gregory, seated courtside with her yappy, ice cream-lapping lapdog Ziggy, kept the mood comical. She embarked upon a loud, running flirtation with Pollard, warning him to sit down or she might just get up and pour her beer over his head. Pollard bantered right back. Why not? Mamie's Colonels looked like they needed a beer break, shooting just 32 percent from the field. In the end, the Colonels were all wet, Pollard stayed dry, and his Floridians closed out their trek sporting a two-game win streak.

Landing back in Miami, Pollard and his players strolled into a magnificent 80-degree afternoon and open invitation to join a city in T-shirts and sandals to celebrate sun, sailboats, siesta, and South Beach—and that was the problem. Would Miami really want to come indoors to cheer tall guys in squeaky sneakers? "It's going to be a tough pull," admitted Dr. Tom Carney, who headed the Florida ownership group that moved the team to Miami. But Carney, a financier and investor who made a bundle on several East Coast dog tracks, was betting on ABA co-founder Dennis Murphy, a.k.a. "Murph," now the Floridians' operations manager and resident soothsayer.

"Can this possibly be love?" Murph cooed to a roomful of Miami reporters before the Floridians' home opener.[10]

The amore wafting through Murph's question was South Florida supposedly falling hard for pro basketball. Murph promised that he'd felt the love while out and about in Miami Beach, South Beach, and Coconut Grove and predicted the Floridians' home opener would be a sellout. Nine thousand love letters strong. Murph paused, then revised the prediction to a firm 4,200. Better safe than sorry. A reporter, not sure what to make of Murph's opening-night rapture, called Pollard for a plain-talk ABA update. "Not all the teams are drawing real well, of course" he admitted. "But what a difference a superstar like Rick Barry of Oakland or a basketball hotbed like Louisville can make to your league!"[11]

Officially, 4,317 turned out for the home opener in Miami's Convention Hall, though many reportedly entered gratis compliments of Murph. The half-filled hall applauded politely when the Floridians trotted out and formed a pregame layup line. By the fourth quarter, everyone "screamed" and "wailed" and came to their feet when the Floridians, led by Hunter, made a late comeback to sink the New Orleans Buccaneers. Murph kept up the freebies for several more games, and that pushed Miami to fourth in league attendance. "If we can hold our own until football season is over," Murph leveled, "I think we've got a chance—maybe to lose only $125,000 or so (a million in modern dollars)."[12]

Add the above number to the $158,000 owed from last season, and the Floridians in the best-case scenario would finish nearly $300,000 in the hole. But it was the worst-case scenarios already spiraling down, down, down that could sack the league at any moment. And that moment was about to come at the next ABA Board of Trustees meeting in Minneapolis' stately Leamington Hotel.

Minneapolis, November 19, 1968—Ask Bill Erickson about attending ABA Board of Trustees meetings in his earlier role as the league's chief counsel, and he offered a pained, post-traumatic chuckle, like remembering the passing of kidney stones. Some trustees were still stuck in the original East and West Coast cliques; others didn't respect George Mikan and openly rebelled against his leadership. All believed as successful self-made businessmen, lawyers, entertainers, and even dog trainers that everyone should just shut up and listen to them. When "them" spoke, sometimes all at once, the room filled with passion, idiosyncrasy, compulsion, narcissism, wit, wisdom, woe, and hubris.

"Every meeting was a roller-coaster ride just to get consensus," said Erickson. "I remember coming back from meetings all over the country [with George Mikan] and just wiping our brows and thinking, 'By God, we've got it together again' [to keep the league going]."[13]

All those roller-coaster trustee meetings were prelude to today's runaway, near-death Matterhorn ride in the Leamington Hotel. It came compliments of the Houston Mavericks, still technically owned by Texas oil tycoon Nick Morrow. "Technically" was a small tale in itself. Last summer, Morrow divorced his wife, and his new "lady friend" Phyllis (the reason for the divorce) told him she couldn't imagine what he saw in a silly, old basketball team, especially one that was costing him a small fortune. Her words stuck, and Morrow advised Mikan late last summer that he was abandoning the Mavs and moving on with his lady friend, two for the road.[14]

The Mavs were nearly shuttered a few months ago to give a Cleveland group time to purchase the franchise and relocate it there for the 1969-70 season. But the deal fell through, and efforts began anew to keep the team and pro basketball alive in Houston. Luck seemingly on the ABA's side, the trustees approved on Oct. 23 Houston's original three minority owners buying out Morrow's majority stake and taking over the Mavs. The agreement lasted a couple of days. The trio, having discovered that it would inherit all six figures of the Mavs' existing debt, nixed everything. No deal now sent the trustees back to Morrow with a pretty please: Would he hang on until a suitable buyer could be found?

As the trustees finished up their coffee and morning rolls, Morrow phoned Mikan from his lakeside duck-hunting lodge in East Texas to deliver his final hell no and to vow that he "wouldn't spend another penny" on the Mavs. Effective immediately, the team's front-office staff, players, payroll, and debt were the league's problem, and Morrow warned in parting, "Don't even bother to try and collect on the bond."[15]

Morrow was referring to the annual $100,000 bond that all franchises posted with the league as a security deposit and renewed proof of their solvency. Mikan, against his better judgment, had allowed Morrow to post this season's security deposit backed by an agreement between him and a third-party guarantor, not the ABA. With Morrow's hell no, the guarantee vanished with him, and the Mavs now faced the season with no owner, no money, and no real fanbase to generate revenue (three games into the season, the Mavs averaged a league-worst 754 paying customers per game, insufficient even to cover the rental fee on their gym).

Mikan interrupted the trustee chatter to share the bad news, including the vanished security deposit. If looks could kill. Mikan threw out the possibility of the league operating the Mavs this season. Translation: The trustees would pay Houston's bills, divided 10 ways. That aroused another hell no, this time from a spattering of trustees who preferred to terminate Houston as insolvent and unfit. The conversation accelerated from there, careening into old grievances (if they only had a network television contract) and heading head first into the same general problem that bedeviled the NBA. The ABA was headed toward an unequal class structure. There were the ABA haves, a few promising franchises (Kentucky, Indiana, Denver, and, for now, Oakland) that might just make it, and there were the have-nots, like the Mavs, buried deep in debt and dysfunction.

The inequality presented a dilemma. Did the trustees envision a league in which everyone rolled up their sleeves and helped their ABA brothers survive? Together they stood against insolvency and the NBA, divided they fell. Or, did they prefer a competitive, dog-eat-dog business culture? In this case, only the strong survived, and only the strong would be worthy of merging with the NBA. Two divergent paths, and with no consensus in the room on which course to take, the resource-starved Mavs were headed nowhere. Inertia ruled, meaning Houston would be the ABA's precedent-setting sacrificial franchise. Addition by subtraction.

Or subtraction by self-mutilation. Houston, the nation's sixth-largest city, was a major television market and a real selling point for the ABA. Losing Houston only bolstered the perception that the league was too small-market for network television. No network television, no future.

It was in this moment that J.W. (Bill) Ringsby, the wealthy owner of the Denver Rockets and president of the ABA Board of Trustees, had his epiphany: The ABA was over. The league had just entered its death throes, and it would be buried in the not-too-distant future in the same boneyard as the ABL, NBL, and all those three-letter pro leagues of yesteryear. He had to get out now before his financial losses multiplied and the bad publicity damaged his "Ringsby Rocket" Trucking System. After all, the Denver Rockets were a running-and-gunning advertisement for the hundreds of Rocket trucks plying the nation's roadways, sharing the same logo and orange-and-black color scheme.

Ringsby's players were already in Duluth for tonight's scheduled game against Connie Hawkins and the Minnesota Pipers. Time to act. Ringsby wandered off to find the nearest pay telephone.

"Bill, where are going?" asked Indiana trustee Dick Tinkham.

Ringsby mumbled something about the ABA being finished. He had to call his sons. They had to make arrangements to fly his players back to Denver immediately and begin dismantling the franchise.

"Without Denver, the league would have ended right there," Tinkham was later quoted in the book *We Changed the Game*, which he coauthored. The fear was Ringsby, respected by his ABA peers and one of the softer touches in helping the league out of its toughest financial pinches, would spark other epiphanies, cancel more games around the league tonight, and shut down more franchises.

Tinkham, a calm, cool, collected lawyerly presence, got Ringsby to hold off on calling his sons. There was still hope, Tinkham said, they had a possible investor en route, a U.S. Congressman no less. If he could be persuaded to purchase the Houston franchise, the ABA would continue with 11 teams. Nobody would be the wiser of the league's near-death experience, and the trustees could work to buttress the have-nots to avoid any carnage to come.

Enter the Honorable Jim Gardner, sitting U.S. Congressman from North Carolina. Gardner recently lost his reelection bid, and though a Republican from a staunchly Democratic state, he now had his eye on the governor's mansion in Raleigh. What better way to win friends and build name recognition than to barnstorm his own winning pro basketball team around the state?

Or so he had heard. Gardner had fallen under the spell of Don DeJardin, a former West Point cadet and basketball star who last season moonlighted as an ABA headhunter (he signed two players and a coach for Pittsburgh). DeJardin was also working on his master's degree in business, hoping it would be his ticket to run a pro basketball team. His schoolwork had him thinking outside the box, and his latest ABA brainstorm was called a regional franchise. Instead of limiting a team to one city, a regional franchise alternated its home games in three or four mid-sized cities. The combined populations of these mid-sized cities roughly equaled the census count of a big one, making them in theory equally choice markets for the national television networks. DeJardin's new view of mid-sized America opened it up for pro basketball. It also opened up the ABA to the mostly untapped wealth and ambition residing there, putting them in touch with funny-talking folks eager to get into "basket-BAWL" and transform their burgs into the next Green Bay.

DeJardin took his slide tray on the road, where Gardner's cousin heard his presentation on regional franchises. Something about regional franchises would work best in states like North Carolina that have strong high school and college basketball traditions to leverage. He passed the information to Jim, who followed up. "Don DeJardin was all West Point," said Gardner, father of the Hardee hamburger chain in Rocky Mount "He was a stand-up guy, highly organized, smart, methodical . . . I liked him a lot."[16] Enough for Gardner to recruit two other wealthy Rocky Mount businessmen to form the brand-new Southern Sports, Corporation. Enough for Gardner to fly to Minneapolis and inquire about the availability of an ABA franchise, unaware that the ABA's continued existence now depended on him saying hell yes to purchasing the troubled Houston Mavericks and carrying its boatload of debt.

Gardner proceeded past a grip of handshakes and a blur of names, then disappeared behind closed doors to meet with the league's executive committee, which included Tinkham and Ringsby. The latter may have needed a breath mint. He'd been drinking in the hotel bar to ease his frazzled nerves. The trustees talked up the availability of the Mavs, and Gardner explained that he wanted a regional franchise and hoped to bring pro basketball to Greensboro, Raleigh, and Charlotte. But not until next season.

The trustees, familiar with DeJardin's slideshow, nodded in agreement. After all, they could either abandon big-market Houston, which the NBA now had designs on, or fold up the league and go home. "How much for the franchise?" Gardner asked, a question the trustees hadn't yet discussed amongst themselves.

"Three-hundred thousand dollars," Tinkham ad-libbed.

With some further haggling on the price, Gardner said they had a deal. He'd return to North Carolina and dot all the i's and cross all the t's.

In Duluth that evening, Ringsby's Rockets defeated the Minnesota Pipers, 126-121, before just 652 paying customers. In Minneapolis, newspaper accounts of the Rockets-Pipers game tacked on a brief, *pro forma* mention of the trustees' meeting. The wire services, however, ran with Mikan's hurried announcement that Houston was sold during the meeting to an "anonymous" buyer for $165,000.[17] "The franchise will remain in Houston," he fibbed. With no further questions—and as Tinkham predicted—nobody in the press was any the wiser that the ABA nearly died a few hours earlier in the Leamington Hotel.

L os Angeles, Nov. 20, 1968—What a difference a superstar like Rick Barry makes. Unaware the ABA nearly imploded yesterday, more than 3,600 squeezed through the cranky turnstiles at the old Los Angeles Sports Arena to watch Barry's ABA-leading Oakland Oaks (11-2) defeat the Los Angeles Stars. That attendance figure may not have seemed like much to the uninitiated, but it more than doubled the Stars' most recent box-office disaster.

"I'm sure we're not going to break any attendance records the first year," Stars' coach Bill Sharman often stated the obvious, then reflexively threw his support behind the maverick league that he now called home. "Most people don't realize," he said, " . . . we don't lack great ballplayers,"[18] referring, of course, to Barry, whom Sharman of course coached two seasons ago with the NBA's San Francisco Warriors. Sharman swore his former pupil had never looked better than tonight, accounting for 35 points and joining his nifty teammates Larry Brown, Warren Armstrong, and Doug Moe in a second-half passing clinic that a serious-minded coach like Sharman could applaud.

Sharman also often turned philosophical, as if to answer the obvious question: What's a nice former Boston Celtic and future Hall of Famer like him doing in a struggling league like this? Sharman admitted that he'd burned out in San Francisco, but he couldn't find another NBA coaching gig on the West Coast, where he wanted to keep his family. When Jim Hardy, the Stars' GM called last spring with the coaching offer, Sharman had a warm, nostalgic feeling. Hardy, a former football star and big man on campus at Sharman's alma mater USC, had a well-deserved reputation for winning on and off the field. And sweet victory was already in the air for the Stars. Hardy's ABA friends assured him the Stars "will get first shot" next spring at landing UCLA's All-Everything center, Lew Alcindor, the game's next seven-foot must-see attraction.

"With Alcindor, there is no doubt that we would have it made," he said. "It would turn the corner for us real quick. That's all it would take—for us and for the whole league. You're gonna get your national TV contract, and you're off and running."[19]

However, the Stars' "first shot" at Alcindor was as empty a promise as peace in the world. Alcindor would call the shots on where he wanted to play in the ABA. "As for our draft rules, when it comes to Alcindor, we have none," George Mikan leveled a few months earlier, " . . . He's in college at UCLA, and if he wants to stay in Los Angeles, we'll award his rights to the Stars. If he wants to go back to his hometown, we'll give the rights to New York. If he wants to play in Oshkosh or on the moon—or anywhere in between—we'll establish franchises there. We want Lew, and we'll give him anything he wants."[20]

While Sharman waited for his seven-foot Godot, Lakers' owner Jack Kent Cooke anticipated. He anticipated epic NBA greatness this season from his "Dream Team" of Jerry West, Elgin Baylor, and Wilt Chamberlain. Sure, there were some rough edges to hew to start the season. Three superstars don't just fit together all at once. But Cooke anticipated his superstars would be at their level best within weeks. They would rewrite the league record book, steamroll the Boston Celtics in the playoffs once and for all, and claim the first NBA championship for his adopted city of Los Angeles.

Cooke anticipated celebratory suppers, champagne toasts, and half-cocked testimonials to his unflinching, go-for-broke leadership atop the Lakers organization, then a strange word to describe an NBA team, formerly defined as four or five guys and a secretary sitting around a cramped office. For the more sober-minded speechmakers, Cooke would remain the insufferable egomaniac whom they loved to loathe, mostly behind his back. He was the one NBA owner with the gall to plaster his name and photo, like a Central American dictator, five times in the first five pages of his team's media guide.

But for now, Cooke's popular image in the press remained mostly intact and unassailable. Citizen Cooke he was, an industrious Everyman who made good years ago investing brilliantly in the coming telecommunications revolution and mastering the fine art of marketing its creature comforts. As Cooke would sometimes confide, he started out in the 1940s as a penniless, wayfaring salesman slinging encyclopedias door to door in his native Ontario, Canada. He learned on those frigid doorsteps speaking through screen doors to smile and give the people what they wanted.

Or, at least let them believe they were getting what they wanted. Citizen Cooke now injected this sage life lesson like a narcotic into the marketing of his Lakers. In Southern California, the masses celebrated celebrity and the good life. And so, he gave them three basketball superstars in one spectacular nightly show cast in the red-carpet confines of Cooke's brand-new 17,200-seat Fabulous Forum, his $16 million (reportedly) self-financed shrine to sports, entertainment, Hollywood celebrity sightings, and conspicuous consumption. It was Cooke's version of Caesars Palace for sports, not slot machines.

The good life started with a dinner reservation way upstairs in the Forum Club, the arena's private five-star, Roman-themed restaurant. It was Beverly Hills circumstance meets Roman decadence. Jack was Caesar, feted by fawning friends while a swarm of seductive young women in gold and orange miniskirts that vaguely resembled Roman togas made the rounds. Maitre'd Jason reviewed the Forum Club menu, printed on faux antique parchment. He often recommended one of the featured "Dishes of the Gods," starting with the Gladiator's Reward (a petite steak) and culminating with the Vulcan's Sword (a medley of beef, lamb, Swiss sausage, breast of capon, mushrooms, fresh tomato, sweet pepper, pearl onions flambé). If the Roman faire didn't hit the spot, Chef Karl, a European-trained master of gastronomy, prepared an exquisite Filet of Beef Stroganoff, Roast Duckling Bigarde, or Breast of Chicken Kiev.

Even two years ago, the NBA's remaining small-time, hand-to-mouth arena owners would have howled at the very thought of opening a five-star, white-tablecloth restaurant in their peanuts-and-crackerjacks auditoriums. But the NBA's new breed of millionaire owners, led by Cooke, had begun to introduce luxury on a grander scale, a precursor of more upscale things to come. Cooke's thinking seemed to be that if he couldn't take the NBA to the country club, then he could bring the country club to the NBA.

Cooke had also started marketing walled-off exclusivity in the Forum's lower decks. For $8,500 per year ($72,400 today), some lucky so-and-so could lease an exclusive, glass-divided Terrace Box. "The boxes are carpeted, and each has six upholstered seats and a coffee table [with a phone]," wrote the *LA Times* of the 12-by-9-foot boxes. "An usherette stands by during all events ready to fetch food and beverages." Terrace Boxers also received two reserved parking spots at the Forum, free game programs and frequent in-game statistical updates, and six memberships to the Forum Club.

Though Cooke's greatest basketball show on earth wasn't yet selling out the Fabulous Forum, the parking lot was nearly full on most game days. The other night, nearly 16,000 strong packed Cooke's pleasure palace and cheered Wilt, Jerry, and Elgin onward in thumping the Celtics, a signature victory that extended the Lakers' early-season winning streak to nine games, evidence that Cooke's grand experiment was working, temporary rough edges and all.

What about the threat of the Stars? For Cooke, Sharman's Stars were like a piece of lint on his cardigan sweater, a temporary nuisance. Cooke scoffed that the Stars would never outshine his Lakers. Lew Alcindor? It was a pipedream. Cooke had on good intelligence that his fellow NBA moguls already had their feelers out to penetrate Alcindor's collegiate world and steer him their way. What's more, as a co-keeper of the NBA's secret rookie war chest, Cooke would personally pour in whatever it took to ensure Alcindor did the right thing. Just like he did for Wes Unseld and Elvin Hayes last spring.

Unseld was now proving himself to be a bargain in Baltimore, and Hayes was all the talk in San Diego. In fact, the Big E was on a rookie tear rarely seen in the NBA, averaging 30 points and 18 rebounds per game. *SPORT Magazine* and *The*

Sporting News already had flattering profiles of him in the works. Too bad others jostling in the press corps still hurled cynical questions at Hayes about his suspicious rookie contract and ghosting of the ABA. "Okay, let's get the worst out of the way," he groaned to a reporter recently. "You want to know why I didn't sign with Houston of the ABA, right? Everybody wants to know that. Why didn't I stay in my hometown when the Mavericks offered me so much money and all that.

"Houston never offered me a thing. That's all a big lie. They kept sending out press releases, telling people how they were going to make me the first million-dollar draft choice and how I was going to become the biggest star the ABA ever had. But they sat back and waited for me to come to them.

"If they had wanted me bad enough, they would have come to me. San Diego drafted me the Monday after the NCAA finals, called me five minutes later, and I agreed to talk to them. But I wanted to leave it open for Houston. They never called or even said boo to me."[21]

Houston's Nick Morrow, of course, wasn't around to dispute Hayes' claim. His boo didn't matter anyhow. Around the ABA, the verdict was in already. Eddie Gottlieb, the NBA's venerable behind-the-scenes fixer, cornered Hayes during the NCAA tournament in Los Angeles, slipping him a wad of cash and promising a lucrative league contract to follow. Even Sharman, who knew the NBA inside and out, said Gotty did it.

True or false, the alleged Hayes payoff became a call to ABA action. If Mikan and these white, middle-aged millionaire mavericks had any prayer of seizing the pro basketball market and bending it to their collective will, they had to sign Lew Alcindor in the spring, if not sooner.

In his confiding conversations with reporters, Commissioner Mikan kept reminding that an epic tug of war between the leagues was coming to secure the services of

Alcindor. "The ABA had a lot of boy scouts [owners] going around trying to coral talent," he said, referring to his league's inability to tie the knot with Hayes and Unseld. "Now, they're more aggressive; they have a better understanding of what it takes."[22]

For Mikan and the ABA, winning the hearts and minds of sports-loving Americans and stealing the NBA's thunder as the established league was about to get tougher. Much tougher. While Cooke's Lakers captured headlines out West, the New York Knickerbockers were making a low rumble on the East Coast. That rumble was about to harmonize into a very merry Christmas.

Detroit, Dec. 19, 1968—There were still five shopping days left until Christmas for most people. Not for NBA forward Dave DeBusschere. His Detroit Pistons were at home tomorrow night against the hot New York Knicks, then it was off to Atlanta, back home for a few idle days, followed by a Christmas Day clash in Milwaukee. By his own count, he was down to two days of shopping, unless he dashed out tonight. But it was bone-chilling, hat-and-glove weather, and DeBusschere still wasn't feeling 100 percent after his bout of "Hong Kong flu," the virus that had the world in its grip. Doctors were calling it a global pandemic.

The presents could wait, and DeBusschere settled in for the evening with his pretty, 22-year-old wife Gerri, a former airline stewardess, in their new house on Detroit's East Side. Big Dave, as he was known, wanted to hang a new painting, a wonderful splash of blues and reds depicting him slashing past New York center Walt Bellamy. Big Dave, after making the proper measurements, retrieved the stepladder, avoiding his fidgety Norwegian elk hound, and made his way up with nail and hammer. He'd nearly finished the job when the phone rang. Gerri answered, then called him over. It was Ed Coil, the Pistons general manager. He wanted to inform Dave that the

Pistons had just traded him to the Knicks for the guy in the painting, Walt Bellamy, plus swingman Howie Komives.[23]

The trade wasn't exactly a shocker. The Pistons were a struggling, backstabbing mess, and their new, ill-fated head coach was in the market for a scrappy center. Rookie Otto Moore wasn't working, and the seven-foot Bellamy, though moody, was a battle-tested veteran. DeBusschere didn't fault the Pistons for making the two-for-one upgrade. In fact, he was flattered. And yet, DeBusschere felt strange departing Detroit. It was his beloved hometown, where his working-class father sold beer for a living, where he attended high school and college, and where he'd played pro ball for the Pistons since 1962. Everyone in the Motor City seemingly knew his face, stopped to shake his hand when he was out and about, considered him one of their own. Then, with one phone call, it all ended. Even Gerri, a Long Island native, got weepy about leaving it all behind for the bustle of New York.

But pro basketball is a business first, not a fraternity, and the next evening at Detroit's Cobo Arena, DeBusschere made the unfamiliar turn into the visitor's dressing room to report for duty as ordered. Knicks' coach Red Holzman mumbled a welcome aboard and inserted DeBusschere right into the starting lineup. In the layup line, he slapped palms with his brighter future. It included Willis Reed, "The Captain;" savvy veteran guard Dick Barnett; the high-profile youngsters Walt Frazier and Bill Bradley; and swingman Cazzie Russell, whom the Pistons would have selected first in the 1966 NBA draft had DeBusschere called the coin flip correctly. Now, they were teammates. Small world.

DeBusschere navigated his early-game jitters, worried about making the right zigs and zags in the Knicks offense. But the offense proved "simple," and his new teammates knew their roles and shared the basketball. "They look for the open man," DeBusschere said, "and they're a good defensive team." Were they ever. Holzman kept yelling, "Dee-fense," not that he knew much about the subject before taking the head coaching job last season. Eddie Donovan, the Knicks' savvy general manager, advised Holzman to start there in rehabbing the ailing Knicks after nine losing seasons. Holzman's message had connected, and last season the Knicks logged their first winning record (43-39) since the early 1950s. In fact, the Knicks arrived in Detroit as one of the hottest teams in basketball, winning eight of 11 games so far in December.

The Knicks started the third quarter ahead by 12 points. DeBusschere just kept running the floor, setting hard screens, moving the ball, and crashing the boards. Then Holzman's virtuosos with the intuition of jazz musicians, eased into a smooth five-man groove, the harmonious sum of their parts greater than their individual skills. Midway through the quarter, the groove built into a 40-point blowout. A frustrated pro-Piston crowd booed and littered the court with paper airplanes. But when Holzman pulled his starters for the evening, they stood and gave their hometown hero a proper farewell. Big Dave plopped down on the bench next to Cazzie Russell, crossed his legs, and closed out the stat line of his Knicks debut at 21 points, 15 rebounds, and six assists.

"DeBusschere could be the biggest thing to hit Gotham since Joe Namath," a Detroit reporter speculated.[24] Gerri DeBusschere had a good laugh at that. Big Dave was no playboy like Namath, neither was he particularly brash. "He's All-American," she corrected. But the reporter was correct about something else. The Knicks with the multi-talented DeBusschere, the NBA equivalent of a Swiss army knife on legs, would soon be good enough to compete for an NBA championship.

Or, looking deeper into the NBA crystal ball, these new-and-improved Knicks would renew New York's larger basketball scene into a chest-thumping, we-got-game civic celebration of Gotham's legendary college teams, its prep powerhouses, and its hip playground legends. The Knicks would soon share the NBA spotlight with the legendary Celtics, the winningest franchise in the history of professional sports, and Jack Kent Cooke's "Dream Team" Lakers. All operated in major American media markets; all were natural rivals for national attention, its spoils, and its conceits. It didn't get any better than that for the NBA in putting its best foot forward in mainstreaming professional basketball—Rick Barry and the ABA be damned.

Commack, N.Y., Dec. 27, 1968—Rick Barry wasn't one to bite his tongue. Neither was his opinioned Oakland Oaks coach Alex Hannum, former skipper of the NBA Philadelphia 76ers. On road trips, the two often sat side by side, spouting off about their celebrated NBA's pasts and uncertain ABA futures. To cement his ABA future, Hannum proselytized hard on behalf of the league, even if it meant bending the truth. Barry wasn't so sanguine about the ABA. He'd reached the snap judgment that it was a "Mickey Mouse league" and already had compiled a lengthy list of gripes about its subpar facilities, low-budget travel, poor front-office business and basketball acumen, and, in his mind, grab-bag rosters.

Hannum advised Barry to get over it. Embrace his new role as the face of the ABA, sign every-last autograph and charm every-last fan in all 11 cities. Sell the league as an innovation, a vast improvement on the stuffy, grind-it-out NBA. Barry refused, saying he didn't believe it. Plus, he needed to conserve his energy to get through the physical demands of the season. Barry had plenty of bruises to show from overzealous opponents who roughed him up to win kudos from their teammates or coach. Barry, no shrinking violet, would slap, grab, elbow right back. If a defender took things too far, Barry would clench his fists and swing, much to Hannum's chagrin.

"I know you'd like to get tough, Rick," Hannum repeated. "But you've got hands like a violin player. You've got to protect them. Hold your tongue and just cool it."[25]

Hannum promised that his tougher teammates, like hockey goons, would get even for him. In the meantime, Hannum wanted Barry to simplify things, let the referees mete out justice. "I'm advising Rick to go to the basket more often," said Hannum. "He's bound to score, and if he gets fouled, it will put the other team in trouble."[26]

Barry's charge to the basket was working tonight against the New York Nets. Late in the third quarter, he had 37 points, many on drives and 11 from the charity stripe. With the Oaks comfortably in the lead Hannum was waiting for the next stop in play to sit Barry, hopefully for the remainder of the evening. But before the switch, Barry swiped a pass and dribbled blithely ahead for points 38 and 39. About 10 feet from the basket, New York's Ken Wilburn, a spot player whom the Nets would waive in two days, blindsided Barry just as he lifted into the air. Their legs tangled awkwardly, and Barry heard a pop in his left knee. The face of the ABA, the one for whom the league spent tens of thousands of dollars in legal fees, grimaced on the floor. Doc Turner, the Nets' trainer, said the play looked worse than it really was. Barry groaned to differ. "It's bad, I know it's bad," he repeated back in the locker room, briefly passing out from the pain. Hospital x-rays revealed torn ligaments and knee cartilage. The prognosis: Mr. ABA would be out at least a month.

Miami, Jan. 12, 1969—They said it would never happen. They said the American Football League's best would never win a Super Bowl, the new made-for-TV postseason extravaganza. They said the more established National Football League was just too good. It had the best players, best coaches, best teams. Comparing the two was like choosing between NFL sirloin and AFL hamburger.

But it was happening. With the final seconds ticking down in Super Bowl III, the NFL champion Baltimore Colts, a three-touchdown favorite to win, trailed the AFL New York Jets by two scores. Colts quarterback Johnny Unitas dropped back one last hopeless time and chucked long. "The game is over," announcer Curt Gowdy memorialized the moment for the estimated 60 million watching at home. "The New York Jets are the world champions. They have upset the Baltimore Colts and beat them handily here today."

Seated in the VIP section of Miami's Orange Bowl was the affable George Mikan. He was, as they say, in the moment. "It just shows you what a league can accomplish," Mikan told an onlooker. "Now, if the NBA . . ." and his voice trailed off in rumination.[27] When Mikan returned to Minneapolis, he filled in the ellipses, regaling everyone with his musings on Super Bowl III and the prospect of a pro basketball World Series. "We'd like to have a Super Basketball Bowl game at the end of this season," declared ABA publicist Lee Meade. "The sooner the better."[28]

Meade, though on message, was getting way ahead of himself and the NBA. The NBA wasn't interested in competing for superiority with the ABA. The NBA was intent on blowing up its rival, the sooner the better. In fact, the latest dirty trick, about to be rolled out at the 19th annual NBA all-star game, was emblematic of just how diabolical the league's governors could be.

Endnotes

[1] Lee Meade, Interview with author, September 2008.

[2] Ibid.

[3] Bill Erickson, Interview with author, June 2009.

[4] Lee Meade, September 2008.

[5] Fred Seely, "ABA Hunts Superstars for Survival," *Miami Herald*, August 2, 1968.

[6] Tom Briere, "Mikan Predicts Attendance Boom," *Minneapolis Tribune*, September 12, 1968.

[7] Charlie Nobles, "'Big Game' The Floridians' Hot Cat, *Miami News*, 1968.

[8] Oakland's Levern Tart would break his cheekbone in a few weeks after sliding and crashing on the exposed ice.

[9] Fred Seely, "Floridians Courting Minnesota Hate-Night," *Miami Herald*, September 15, 1968.

[10] Jim Huber, "Floridians Hope for Love-In," *Miami News*, November 6, 1968.

[11] Edwin Pope, "The Luckiest Coach,'" *Miami Herald*, November 6, 1968.

[12] John Crittenden, "ABA Three-Pointer Scores with Fans," *Miami News*, November 26, 1968.

[13] Erickson interview, 2009.

[14] Meade Interview, 2008.

[15] This section is based on the author's interviews with Dick Tinkham. It also quotes from Bob Netolicky, Richard Tinkham, Robin Miller, *We Changed the Game*, 2018, p. 75-77.

[16] Jim Gardner, Interview with author, July 2012.

[17] United Press International, Houston Rockets Sold for $165,000," January 3, 1969. Note: UPI revised its dispatch to ratchet up or down the sale price. Two were reported: a bogus $650,000 and a more realistic $165,000.

[18] Rich Roberts, "Alcindor—Like Shooting for the Stars," *Long Beach (Calif) Press-Telegram*, November 10, 1968.

[19] Ibid.

[20] Don Brown, "The Coming Battle for Lew Alcindor," *1969 Pro Basketball Almanac*, p. 12.

[21] Jim Huber, "A Tale of Two Leagues," *Miami Herald*, November 8, 1968.

[22] Briere, *Minneapolis Tribune*, 1968.

[23] Dave DeBusschere, *The Open Man*, 1970, p. 63.

[24] Jack Saylor, "Another Big Deal in the Works," *Detroit Free-Press*, December 22, 1968.

[25] Huber, "A Tale of Two, Leagues," *Miami Herald*.

[26] Ron Supinski, "Overweight Barry Still Eagle-Eyed," *Miami Herald*, November 6, 1968.

[27] Bob Fowler, "ABA Basketball," *The Sporting News*, February 1, 1969.

[28] Dean Eagle, "Did Joe Namath, Jets Give Psychological Aid to ABA?" *Louisville Courier-Journal*, 1969.

9

Baltimore, Jan. 13, 1969—Talk about bad timing. The NBA's 19th annual all-star game was set for tomorrow night in Baltimore, two days after the city's football Colts, a 20-point favorite in Super Bowl III, "choked" on national television in "The Biggest Upset of the Century." NBA officials, convinced like everyone else that the Colts couldn't possibly lose to the underdog New York Jets, had several days ago started shilling the All-Star Game as "Super Tuesday" to join in Baltimore's assumed championship revelry.

But on this dreary Monday morning, the city awoke and took a long, bleary-eyed look in the mirror. The Monument City had become Mudville. "The saddest thing that ever happened in the world, practically," a bar patron cried in his beer over on Greenmount Avenue.[1]

For the NBA officials now gathering in the city, Baltimore had better snap out of it by Super Tuesday night. The league needed a large, fashionable crowd to cheer on its basketball luminaries named Sweet Lou, Hondo, Sloan, and Earl the Pearl. The All-Star game was the one school night out of the year that the NBA had America's living rooms all to itself in primetime, without the other weekend sports faire to peel off viewers. It was the NBA's chance to wow the networks with a solid Nielsen rating and suggest to advertisers the league's potential for so much more.

But first, the NBA had blocked off Monday to hold its midseason meetings, including the Board of Governors' latest votes on the mundane and the top secret. The latter included today's surprising motion to admit the ABA Oakland Oaks into the NBA. No, the Oaks hadn't defected. Seattle owner Sam Schulman had a lead on obtaining the Oaks and, if the franchise was voted into the NBA today, he promised to find a buyer for the team tomorrow from his wide circle of Hollywood friends and tennis partners.

Schulman's power grab wasn't new. In the 1940s, Maurice Podoloff, president of the Basketball Association of America, the NBA's precursor, swiped three franchises from the rival National Basketball League. The big difference was Podoloff had schmoozed the three teams into joining the NBA; Schulman had deceived the Oaks' owners into selling their property without revealing his devious plan to transfer the franchise to the NBA.

He did it with help from his stockbroker, Lew Bracker. He was a rising, 32-year-old financial wizard to the stars and a cool cat to boot who raced sportscars on the weekends in the desert and formerly hung out with the late actor-rebel James Dean. When Bracker talked broads, whiskey, and smart investments, Hollywood types adjusted their Ray-Bans and listened. He was, after all, one of them.

According to Bracker, Schulman called him a few weeks back for a favor. "Sam wanted me to be his front man," said Bracker. Schulman asked him to pose as the head of a make-believe investment group that was interested in purchasing a pro basketball team. Bracker said he had lunch with comedian Bill Cosby, a minor investor in the Oaks, and inquired about buying into the ABA. That got him the telephone number for the more prominent Oaks' investor, singer Pat Boone. Let the con begin.

Though the Oaks weren't for sale, they would be soon. Not only was Rick Barry now injured and out indefinitely, the Oaks had almost no fan base to pay for their expenses. The team's debt had reached unsustainable levels on top of $1.9 million in loans owed to three banks. The team's mostly Southern

California investors saw the writing on the wall. They wanted out fast.

Having been prepped by Schulman on all of the above, Bracker floated the following offer: His "people" (Schulman) were willing to purchase the Oaks for a discounted $100,000. But they also would take over the team's outstanding $1.9 million in bank loans. That meant Boone, majority owner Ken Davidson, and the others could walk away whole from their ABA escapade.

The offer was soon verbally accepted—and that was Bracker the front man's prompt to stall. Raising some last-minute financial concerns, Bracker got a one-week extension to culminate or kill the deal. That gave Schulman just enough time to complete the caper's final make-or-break step: Get the Oaks preapproved to join the NBA, again completely unbeknownst to Boone or Davidson.

That's why Schulman now stood in Baltimore before his fellow members of the Board of Governors asking for their support. His exact plea is lost in time (Bracker wasn't there), but Schulman's motion reportedly passed almost unanimously. The Oaks were a preapproved member of the NBA for a couple of minutes—until the lawyers in the room spoke up. They said switching leagues couldn't be done for reasons that weren't in play during the 1940s. Among them, the ABA stated in its bylaws that all players, as human capital, revert to the ABA should any team jump to the NBA. Ironically, Oakland owner Ken Davidson reportedly was the source of the rule.

Schulman told Bracker to kill the offer, and he quickly bowed out and scrammed. But dribs and drabs of the Baltimore vote leaked and eventually reached Mal Florence, the *Los Angeles Times'* NBA beat reporter. He called Bracker, who fibbed and took full responsibility for the caper. "What was I going to do?" Bracker exclaimed years later. "I had nothing to lose, and Sam was my friend. I wanted to protect him."[2]

Schulman, smart and amoral, now turned his attention to another top-secret NBA matter: Signing God's next gift to pro basketball, UCLA's Lew Alcindor. Schulman headed a secretive subcommittee of owners tasked with winning friends and influencing Alcindor to sign with the NBA. Schulman's front-and-center involvement came with the expectation that even if Seattle didn't land Alcindor's NBA rights, the league would owe him big time for his headhunter services. It would be the start of a huge disagreement that would turn Schulman and his deviousness on the NBA.

Baltimore, Jan. 14, 1969—Mudville had snapped out of it by the 8:30 p.m. tip off of the NBA's now "Showcase of the Stars." A sold-out, coat-and-tie crowd oohed the spectacular and booed the seven-foot giant Wilt Chamberlain. Old Eastern Conference grudges die hard. ABC Sports filmed it all, unfortunately while time permitted. "At 9 o'clock, we go to Washington to bring you live President Johnson's State of the Union Address," play-by-play announcer Chris Schenkel kept interjecting. In this era of three major American television networks, each was expected to drop its regularly scheduled programming and air live all Presidential speeches of national importance. Johnson's farewell State of the Union address, hastily announced last week, was must-see democracy.

ABC and the NBA couldn't believe their rotten luck. But they didn't throw in the towel. "If we can get the guys [in Baltimore] to stall the start of the second half that long," ABC producer Chet Forte said, then the network could broadcast the second half in its entirety and save face with viewers.[3] And so, with 5:35 remaining in the first quarter, ABC cut to the thunderous applause on Capitol Hill and Johnson's "my fellow Americans," vowing to wait it out and return in about an hour for the second half.

Ruing the interruption was Roone Arledge, executive producer of ABC Sports who remained bullish on the NBA.

Arledge had spent the 1960s championing the idea that television must give America's living rooms the best seat and vantage point at live sporting events. That meant liberating the mounted, box-like, RCA TK 41 color television cameras from their traditional haunts in the stadium nosebleed seats and wheeling them like blinking, 200-pound steel robots as close to the action as possible in all kinds of fair and foul weather. For Arledge, basketball and its compact, weather-proofed indoor venues were sports broadcasting perfection waiting to happen. Cameras could get right on the floor, right on the endlines, to soak up the action and ambiance and, hopefully, convince millions at home that they'd spent the evening in Baltimore's Civic Center booing Wilt with Donnie and Doreen from Jessup.

Making Arledge's made-for-television NBA dream come true was Forte. He had been an All-American set shot artist in college and even topped Wilt Chamberlain for national player of the year honors in 1957. Wilt went pro; the 5-foot-8 Forte went into broadcasting, where he adapted his basketball instincts into a gift for capturing visually the pro game's power, grace, and tension. Before games, Forte, the perfectionist, personally positioned the half dozen cameras around the court with great care and precision to discover the right angle to capture Wes Unseld jostling in the paint or John Havlicek scooting in for a layup. During broadcasts, Forte disappeared to the control booth, a large van parked outside the arena, where he monitored the camera feeds streaming across six screens and two slow motion monitors, all the while chattering away into the ears of Schenkel et al. in a thick, high-pitched New York accent and always one imperfection away from a spontaneous meltdown.

Away from the booth, Forte liked to bet on games, including NBA contests, relying on the inside dope gleaned from coaches, players, and pregame buffets. Not sure if he had any money riding on tonight's outcome. Right now, his thoughts were on keeping the cameras rolling in the Civic Center to videotape for posterity the rest of the first half and, during the breaks in the action, playfully zooming in on a few of the many pretty women in attendance. Boys will be boys.

"Chet, Walter [Kennedy] says he'll hold it until 10 o'clock," color commentator Jack Twyman relayed to the control booth. "We'll start at 10 straight up."

On Capitol Hill, President Johnson wrapped up his speech just past 9:50 p.m. "Beautiful," Schenkel welcomed the next update relayed over his headset. "How much time do we have until 10?" Long enough for a blitz of commercials to make up for lost time and ad revenue. In the second half, the control booth signaled down 17 commercial breaks, several at inopportune moments in the action. "I think it's ridiculous," Chicago's Jerry Sloan grumped about the intrusions. "After all, TV doesn't own basketball."[4]

Watching in Minneapolis, George Mikan would have gladly endured all the complaints. At least the NBA had a network contract. No national networks would be on hand for the ABA's upcoming second all-star game. Just eight ABA cities, plus Chicago, would watch live. Minnesota's Connie Hawkins, the ABA's other superstar, would be sidelined with a blood clot in his knee. But Rick Barry promised to gimp out a few trots up the floor, prompting a headline in New York, where the game would be shown: "Rick Barry Saves TV Wasteland."[5]

Harsh, but it was mostly true. The infant ABA was wobbling through its terrible twos touting tall guys with mostly sketchy pro basketball resumes. Of course, many of these bottom-shelf pros formerly had been top-shelf collegians. They may not have been as splendid as Elgin Baylor or John Havlicek, but pair them with Barry, and anything was possible. Just ask Baltimore about Super Bowl III.

Louisville, Jan. 27, 1969—"Welcome to the ABA All-Star Game" read the handwritten sign posted in the lobby of the Stouffer's Louisville Inn, a busy 12-story motor inn located in the heart of downtown. The all-star game was actually tomorrow night less than a mile away at the Convention Center. Today, the ABA held its midseason board meeting at the Louisville Inn. Mamie Gregory, the vivacious hostess in the welcoming line, made sure everyone greeted Gaystock le Monsignor, a.k.a., Ziggy, her six-year-old canine decked out in one of his fetching outfits (he had 39 of them).

Most patted Ziggy, then followed the arrows to the four walls where they would spend the next nine hours skirmishing over the ABA's future. It would be George Mikan trying to get everyone to lower their voices and build consensus. "A lot of the focus was on shoring up the weaker franchises," recalled first-time attendee Jim Gardner, who received the expected approval to move the ailing Houston franchise next season to North Carolina.[6]

For the more legally inclined trustees in the room, discussion meandered to a recent court decision in the matter of the *Minnesota Muskies and Florida Professional Sports Inc. vs. Lou Hudson and Atlanta Hawks Basketball Inc*. Remember Lou Hudson, the young NBA star who had signed a legally binding contract two years earlier with the Minnesota Muskies, then backed out? The Muskies-turned-Floridians recently sued Hudson in federal court to force him to honor his ABA pledge. Their position was Hudson had fulfilled his NBA contact, plus the option ruled to be one year in the Barry case, and his ABA contract was the next contract in line for his services. They even filed the case in Hudson's neutral hometown of Greensboro, N.C., hoping a free-thinking federal judge would also question the legality of the NBA reserve system and, before handing Hudson to Miami, comment on its trade restrictive and antitrust implications, two ABA sweet spots.

There was nothing sweet in Judge Edwin Stanley's opinion. He sided with Hudson and the NBA, without addressing the elephant in the room: the legality of the league's reserve system:

> The injunctive relief sought by the plaintiffs must be denied, not because the Hudson-St. Louis contract was of "any legal force and effect" or is one that "the courts will enforce," and not because the merits of the controversy are necessarily with St. Louis, "but solely because the actions and conduct of the [Muskies] in procuring the contract, upon which [its] right to relief is and must be founded, do not square with one of the vital and fundamental principles of equity which touches to the quick the dignity of a court of conscience and controls its decision regardless of all other considerations."[7]

In short, the ABA's hands weren't clean. The Muskies shouldn't have tampered with a player under an NBA contract. Period. The ruling was a letdown for the now-Floridians, who badly needed Hudson's 15-foot jump shot to sell tickets, but it also served as a wake-up call to the ABA lawyers. If the courts preferred to ignore the NBA's reserve system in player contract disputes, the ABA had better do the job itself. It would file its own federal antitrust suit against the NBA, contending that the reserve system allowed the NBA to monopolize talent and limited the ABA's ability to compete in the pro basketball marketplace. Indiana's Dick Tinkham had been saying so much for months, and he now took the lead on preparing a blockbuster lawsuit to come.

By early evening, Mikan and the ABA trustees leaned back in their chairs and called it an exhausting day. They needed time to freshen up before riding the elevator up to the hotel's top floor for early cocktails in Stouffer's Cup and Stirrup Restaurant, site of the evening's all-star banquet. It would trigger a two-fisted exchange that would live on forever in league lore and demonstrate that pro basketball start-ups like the ABA were magnets for the most unusual characters.

The Cup and Stirrup offered an expansive view of Louisville's low-slung downtown skyline. Doing the gazing this evening were about 160 basketball-happy diners, all staked out at long wooden tables with varying views of the restaurant's makeshift podium. Seated at a head table was Jim Harding, coach of the East All-Stars.

It was impossible to be neutral about the 39-year-old Harding, the rookie coach of the Minnesota Pipers. His total obsession with winning preceded him. A Philadelphia sportswriter once called Harding, "a Prussian general, not a basketball coach" for being loud, belligerent, brooding, abrasive, volatile, paranoid, unrelenting, and, on top of it all, a pathological perfectionist. "I know more about this sport," he browbeat his Minnesota players during training camp, "than 99 and nine-tenths percent of the coaches in the country." Harding thought those who questioned his court expertise were fools.[8]

Halfway through the season, Harding had succeeded in rubbing just about everybody within his tyrannical orbit the wrong way. His players loathed him, reporters grumbled about him, and management worried that the new hire was too "high strung." They also worried about his physical and emotional well-being, since Harding suffered each defeat like a saber thrust through his right ventricle. In December, Harding's blood pressure had spiked to dangerous levels, forcing him to take a brief leave of absence. Now managing his blood pressure with medication, Harding returned in mid-January and picked up right where he'd left off: berating his lazy, no-good players and declaring his supreme fitness as a coach and leader of lesser men.

Harding, having drained a few cocktails before dinner, strode belligerently to the microphone when asked to introduce his East All-Stars seated somewhere in the audience.[9] All were expected to stand and nod with gratitude, starting with Harding's own Trooper Washington. No response.

"He's not here, Coach," a player blurted out. "He's sick."

"Sick?" Harding muttered, forgetting to cover the microphone "What do you mean 'sick'?"

Harding kept rolling through the names. He came to another of his players, Charlie Williams. "He's sick, too," somebody whispered.

"Those guys aren't sick," Harding shook his head. "This is going to cost both of them $150. They'll be able to pick up their paychecks with a teaspoon next week."

After the banquet, Harding wouldn't let it go. He called the players' rooms. "Meet me in the lobby," he seethed and then lit into them, upping the fine to $500 each. Minnesota owner Bill Erickson, trying to defuse the situation, told Harding to cool it. But he wouldn't. Declaring Erickson and his GM Vern Mikkelsen "gutless," Harding vowed that neither Washington nor Williams would play one second in tomorrow's all-star game.

After midnight, Harding brought his full rage upstairs to a post-banquet party, a wee-small-hours excuse for the ABA moguls to keep drinking. Harding, an anger-fueling cocktail in hand, spotted Gabe Rubin, Minnesota's other main owner and chairman of the board. Harding loathed Rubin, whom he considered weak, obnoxious, and, worse, a suck-up to his players. What burned Harding is his players had been calling Rubin behind his back to complain. Instead of backing Harding and the team, Rubin had taken the players' grievances to Erickson and seconded their calls for his ouster, though without success.

Harding excused himself to have a word, man-to-man, with Rubin. He glared his way over to the paunchy Rubin, 18 years Harding's senior and known for a hair-trigger temper, who sat at a table with the 6-foot-7, 240-pound Mikkelsen. Harding cut right to the chase, and the hot-tempered Rubin blasted right back. Harding lunged at his chairman of the board, ripping the breast pocket on Rubin's suit then thumped him a good one over his left eye. Rubin flailing his arms, scratched Harding's face sending a trickle of blood down his cheek. Mikkelsen quickly separated the two, but Harding continued trying to pull himself free for another go at Rubin.

By morning, Harding's fate was sealed. He'd been relieved of his all-star duties, while Erickson and Mikkelsen prepared to fire him. Down in the hotel diner, many gossiped like old women about the 1 a.m. confrontation. It made for lively conversation, but Harding's acting out also made a good segue into the anxiousness that gripped the league's trustees. If George Mikan wasn't twice their size, many trustees would have loved to have a go at him. He still hadn't delivered a network television contract, and with his calm, cool demeanor, many failed to appreciate his myriad contributions to the league's survival. But, as the second half of the season began, the most-committed trustees would work around Mikan and increasingly take the league's fate into their own hands.

Endnotes

[1] No Byline,"A City Swallows a Bitter Defeat, *Baltimore Sun*, January 13, 1969.

[2] Lew Bracker, Interview with author, July 2022.

[3] Jack Kiser, "NBA-LBJ Spectacular," *Philadelphia Daily News*, January 14, 1969.

[4] Ken Nigro, "Timeouts Slow All-Star Game," *Baltimore Sun*, January 15, 1969.

[5] Ed Comerford, "Rick Barry Saves TV Wasteland," *Newsday*, January 28, 1969.

[6] Jim Gardner, Interview with author, July 2012.

[7] Minnesota Muskies v Hudson, 294, F. Supp. 979 (1969)

[8] David Wolf, *Foul!*, 1972, p. 186.

[9] The account of the all-star banquet draws on Wolf's *Foul!*, p. 223-234, as well as articles in the *Louisville Courier-Journal*, The Sporting News, and wire-service coverage.

10

Miami Beach, February 2, 1969—A federal court had ruled. The Miami Floridians couldn't claim NBA star Lou Hudson, signed ABA contract and all. The Floridians, buried in fourth-place in the five-team Eastern Division, could have used Sweet Lou for this Sunday evening tilt against the Indiana Pacers and their stars Freddie Lewis, Roger Brown, and Mel Daniels, all NBA-worthy talent. Looking on the bright side, the Floridians still had the colorful Lester "Big Game" Hunter and their backcourt ace Donnie Freeman.

By early in the third quarter, aces were wild in Miami. Freeman wandered over in his slow, pigeon-toed gait to a young Floridians staffer, and within earshot of a middle-aged newspaper scribe at press row, barked, "Pay me or trade me!" Then Freeman loped off to rejoin his teammates.

Pay me? Trade me? The scribe scribbled it all down, and the Floridians staffer bounded over to have a word with his boss, Dennis Murphy, who now looked like he was having a Pepto Bismol moment. As both knew all too well, the Floridians were low on cash. In fact, they were three days delinquent on paying their players, and Freeman had just ratted out the front office to the press. With attendance already flagging, the Floridians couldn't afford any bad publicity.

After the final buzzer and Miami's surprising double-digit win, Murphy, or just "Murph" to most, scampered to the Floridians' locker room and shut the door. He needed a word alone with Freeman. On an established NBA team, Freeman would have been fined—and silenced—for conduct detrimental to the team. The team, not the player, always came

261

first. But Murph, the Floridians' operations manager (the guy who booked games and cooked up zany fan promotions), lacked the clout or the temperament to discipline Freeman. Murph opted to look on the bright side. Two years ago, Freeman was an unemployed pro basketball hopeful; now, he was playing in Miami Beach soaking up the rays on his off days at the Balmoral Hotel, where the team housed its players, and flourishing in the ABA.

Besides, Murph assured, paychecks would be in the mail next week. To the best of his knowledge, the players would get paid on Monday morning. The team's seven investors—its board of directors—had met on Saturday in Miami to discuss divvying up the team's rising stack of bills and when to pay them. They weren't deadbeat owners. They were a house divided, geographically and philosophically. The main bone of contention was the $158,000 in debt carried over from last season. Larry Shields, a Californian and the team's original and still-majority owner, wouldn't help pay down the principal. A leftover owner from Minnesota backed him. The new board members from South Florida didn't. They thought Shields was being unreasonable.

Studying the faces and parsing the acrimony was Jim Pollard, the Floridians' good-guy coach and general manager. "You can't put seven men together and talk about a lot of money and expect everything to be calm all the time," he minimized the verbal judo among the board members. The problem, Pollard stated, was the board lacked "a $50-million angel" to grant financial miracles.[1] He was right. There was no John D. Rockefeller in the room. But Pollard and crew didn't need $50 million; they needed a couple million to get them established in South Florida. The board could collectively cover a few mill—and then some. Shields was a prominent, self-made Southern California real-estate developer. Though his cashflow could be real tight, depending on where he was in building his latest subdivision, Shields wasn't hurting. Neither was the other major investor, Dr. Tom Carney, who owned his own bank in South Florida.

The real question was: Did the board members have the fortitude to keep shoveling their hard-earned cash into the start-up money pit called the ABA? Right now, they had little to show for it. They had no superstar attraction named Sweet Lou, no modern arena, no loyal fanbase, and no real tradeable assets to make the NBA envious. In fact, they were now projected to run at least a $200,000 deficit this season. Throw in last year's debt and interest payments, plus the annual league dues at $100,000. Then top it off with George Mikan's constant league-wide calls for cash to keep the ABA upright, and the out-of-pocket expenses bled down the bank accounts of each board member and put a crimp on funding their real-estate and other investments.

These successful businessmen and masters of finance should have known better than to throw their money around on a too-good-to-be-true pro basketball start-up. Or so you'd think. The writing was already on the wall in bold, 72-point type: Don't do it! Pro basketball didn't sell with the public like football or baseball. Though the better-off NBA last season set a season attendance record, half of its franchises still lost money, and those reporting a profit barely scraped into the black.

And yet, if pro basketball was such a financial bowl of gruel, why were so many masters of finance seemingly defying common sense? The answer: There were some magical ingredients in the gruel that had financial and personal benefits. Let's take a closer look.

That something started with a splash of old-fashioned American opportunism. As mentioned, owning a pro basketball team was capital-intensive in the short term. But over the longer haul, like holding onto a rehabbed real-estate property, a good return could be made in pro basketball.

Economists James Quirk and Rodney Fort calculated that a typical NBA team from 1950 forward doubled in price every four-and-a-half years.[2] With NBA teams now selling in the low millions, that came to a healthy profit five years hence.

Community boosting was another tantalizing ingredient. Cities with their own pro teams were in the news and often admired from coast to coast for their cool venues, rowdy fans, winning teams, or record-breaking superstars. A good pro basketball team could help boost an up-and-coming city (Atlanta) or state (North Carolina) to big-league status.

Then add to the soup something endemic to the new breed of pro basketball owner: extreme ego. Like buying a racehorse, a yacht, or some other ode to conspicuous consumption, owning your own pro team was a good conversation starter at the country club or city hall. Most owners also answered to the paunchy, middle-aged white male demographic. Their athletic exploits were either decades behind them or never happened. Owning a pro team gave them a do-over. They could live vicariously through the all-pros in their employ and pump their fists like they, too, could drain clutch 20-foot jump shots and wrestle with Wilt Chamberlain.

"The fact is that some—maybe most—sports franchises aren't especially well managed," said sport guru Bill Veeck, who made his mark in pro baseball. "Sensible, successful businessmen have been known to change once they become club owners. They do things they wouldn't dream of doing with the businesses that made them successful."[3]

All true. But there was one secret ingredient that was especially irresistible to the rich and famous, and Veeck knew all about it. Tax avoidance. Though known to lawyers and accountants, it was rarely, if ever, uttered in the popular press and served as the savory bouillon that helped make pro basketball and the rest of America's multi-million-dollar pro sports enterprise go around.

Most NBA teams, for example, kept two sets of books.[4] The first gave the basic accounting of a team's month-to-month revenue and expenses. These were the bottom-line numbers that made the old arena owners tick and general managers talk about their rising costs. Never mentioned was the second and far more meaningful set of books that addressed the team's tax liabilities. Every successful businessman loves a good tax shelter, and that's where the NBA and pro sports teams in general didn't disappoint. Their tax credits could be substantial.

To understand why means travelling back to the late 1940s and the creative mind of Veeck, who then owned baseball's St. Louis Browns. "I had always been struck by a basic inconsistency in the way we carried our players on the books," recalled Veeck. "When you buy a ballclub, you list your whole roster of players as a cash item, which means you cannot depreciate them. And yet, if you buy a player at any time thereafter, you carry him as an expense item, which means you can write him off immediately just as you would write off paper clips, stationery, or any other business expense."[5]

In 1949, Veeck's inconsistency reportedly found a four-legged solution. An acquaintance purchased a cattle ranch, and he mentioned to Veeck that the IRS allowed him to depreciate from his purchase price the value of the cows already grazing on the property at an amortized annual rate of, say, 20 percent. In other words, the IRS accepted cattle as tangible assets folded into the purchase price. But the IRS viewed those assets as depreciating rapidly on account of their short lives on the prairie.

"Bill came up with the idea that baseball players are a lot like cows," said sports economist Roger Noll. "They have a short, useful life. So, when Bill sold his baseball team, they tried it under the guise that the Browns were worth more if they could be a tax shelter as well as a team. And so, of course, they went for the home run. They allocated 95 percent of the pie [the team's total value] to the players. That then meant that 95 percent of the purchase price could be amortized over the average career length of a baseball player, which was about four-and-a-half years. When the IRS didn't question it, players-as-cows eventually became the standard throughout pro sports."[6]

Veeck's ballclub-as-tax shelter scheme only worked on one condition. The purchaser immediately had to reorganize the franchise as a new business. This switcheroo erased the previous owner's book value for the player contracts, assigning their value, like his acquaintance's cattle, as a depreciable asset that must be replaced every four or five years. The folly being, the owners of pro teams weren't long-suffering cattle ranchers. They were in the entertainment business and gave the hook to underperforming players by the week, month, and season. Or, they just didn't pay them.

Although reorganization could take multiple forms, depending on the ownership structure (public, private, group, or individual), the most common designation for federal income tax purposes was a Subchapter S corporation. Under this format, the owner has limited liability for team debts. But here's the trick. All Subchapter S corporate income flows into the owner's pocket. This puts our millionaire on the hook to pay taxes on the team's profits. Or, in a down year, write off the losses and save a few hundred thousand dollars on his personal income tax. Guess which outcome the owner preferred?

Preference became a sure thing in two ways. One, the owner went for the home run during the reorganization and assigned up to 80- to 90-plus percent of his team's value to the players. Two, the owner then took the incremental annual player depreciation to kill any book profit under the rule of thumb that the higher amortization, the smaller the taxable profits.

Sound too good to be true? Take a look at the 1968-1969 financial statement from the Seattle SuperSonics to its shareholders:

You will note that our financial report discloses a loss of $219,000 from the period covering June 1, 1968 to May 31, 1969. In fact, this figure is misleading, since the Seattle SuperSonics Corporation showed earnings of $46,734 before amortization of players contracts for the 1967-1968 season and earnings of $55,133 before amortization of players contracts for the 1968-1969 season.[7]

Or listen to sports economist Ben Okner. He and Roger Noll would serve in the early 1970s on a Congressional subcommittee that subpoenaed NBA financial records, subjecting them for the first time to outside scrutiny. While the stacks of documents that Okner reviewed were admittedly incomplete and lacking in proprietary specifics, he offered another telling example of the financial status quo from an early 1970s NBA expansion team, rendered nameless via a gentlemen's agreement between the NBA and the subcommittee chair:

One of the recent NBA expansion teams, for example, paid about $3.0 million for its franchise. It allocated $2.5 million, or about 83 percent of the total, to its player contracts and wrote off this amount over 18 months. Thus, nearly two-thirds of the cost was depreciated during the team's first year of operation . . . According to the books, the team lost $1.6 million during its first year of operation. But, in terms of cash-flow income, the situation is not quite so bleak. In addition to the $1.6 million depreciation cost, there was $0.3 million in deferred salaries and other noncash expenses for the year. By taking advantage of these deferred expenses and the player depreciation, the team turned the $1.6 million loss into a $0.3 million cash-flow profit. And if the tax benefit to the owners from the $1.6 million book loss is calculated at a modest 50 percent tax rate, the $1.6 million loss is converted to a $1.1 million profit![8]

The tax shelters, like Hollywood marriages, followed their own predetermined clock with the IRS. They typically expired in five years, the average length of a purchased player's career. Again, think cows. For a profit-driven owner, the plan was to enjoy the tax shelter while it lasted, then flip the franchise to the next tax-crazed bidder for double his money minus the capital gains tax.

All plans, of course, were subject to change. Detroit's venerable Fred Zollner and New York's Madison Square Garden Inc., owners of the Knicks, had been around so long that they predated Veeck's tax shelter. And in Philadelphia, Irv Kosloff was now going to keep the 76ers longer than the five-year mark.

Kosloff is noteworthy because he almost certainly had reorganized his franchise from the Subchapter S designation to a standard Schedule C limited liability corporation, landing them in the same tax position as, for example, Zollner. Why the second reorg? Kosloff couldn't afford to remain on the Subchapter S hook and pay taxes on team profits, presumably at an exorbitant 50- to 72-percent personal tax rate. The reorg redirected all team income into the corporate coffers of the 76ers, and player salaries were promptly reclassified as cash items, i.e., a cost of doing business.

Over in the ABA, the owners were on the same five-year clock, and it was ticking in all 11 cities and regions. That's why the Miami owners were silly to work at cross purposes and threaten their tax break. It was in their interest to get along, empty their pockets, share the immediate financial pain, and laugh all the way to April 15—until their accountants said to stop.

Miami Beach, Feb. 3, 1969—Too bad, Murph. After the Indiana-Miami game, the courtside scribe found Donnie Freeman, who explained his "pay me-or-trade me" disgruntlement. "If we are late to a meeting or a game, we get penalized," Freeman was quoted above the fold in the sports section of today's *Miami News* . "Yet, if the team is late with the paychecks . . ."[9]

Paychecks—and stocks. As it turned out, Freeman was miffed the Floridians hadn't purchased $3,000 in choice airline stock for him by Feb, 1, as stipulated in his contract. The guilty party, a team owner who excelled by day as a Miami stockbroker, apologized and completed the purchase.[10] Would Eddie Gottlieb or Ben Kerner have considered buying railroad stock for their NBA players in the 1950s? Hell no. What would this new breed of millionaire owners think of next?

None of the Indiana Pacers joined in Freeman's no-justice, no-peace. Why would they? All were getting paid on time, and conditions in Indianapolis were generally good. "Playing in Indiana was like playing for the Boston Celtics," said Ron Perry, traded from the Floridians to the Pacers early in the season. Indianapolis had embraced the Pacers, and Perry and his fellow Pacers paraded around town as local celebrities with all the perks. That included a sweet one from Marathon Oil, a team sponsor. For each made three-point shot, a lucky Pacer got a couple of free fill-ups at his friendly neighborhood Marathon gas station. Perry and his teammates sometimes bombed away for free gas, that is, until coach Bob Leonard told them to knock it off.[11]

The good times in Indianapolis hardly could have been predicted two years ago. The Pacers didn't trace their lineage to the ABA's founding Eastern group and its mass-marketing mania. Nor did they self-identify with Dennis Murphy and the founding West Coast group that sought to force a merger with the NBA. Indiana was simply an add-on franchise, like coaxing a friend's little brother into a pickup game to even out the teams, ensuring that the ABA would have enough franchises to form a full-fledged league. Same goes for Kentucky and Denver, the ABA's other early success stories.

All shared the same features. One, they were locally owned with firm roots in the downtown business community. That equaled plenty of local support. Two, all were the only pro game or one of the few pro teams in town. That made building a fan base less competitive than in New York, L.A., Minneapolis, and Oakland, where pro football, baseball, hockey, and basketball teams were plentiful. Three, Indianapolis, Louisville, and Denver were already basketball-friendly, unlike some of the late-addition Texas teams that struggled for attention in a land where football remained king. And yet, if the ABA failed, none of the three could be sure that the NBA would want them, especially Indianapolis. It still lacked a big, shiny modern facility that the NBA now preferred for its expansion franchises.

That's why, in the name of assured mutual survival, Indiana's Dick Tinkham hustled and ad-libbed to save the Houston Mavericks. That's why Tinkham volunteered for league committees. He and his general manager Mike Storen, two former military buddies, kept encouraging their colleagues to do things the Indiana way. Tinkham, for example, elbowed ahead of the other lawyers in the room, notably Bill Erickson and Gary Davidson, to take the lead on the ABA's antitrust suit. Tinkham already had lined up a leading antitrust expert, an old law school buddy, who was preparing the ABA's groundbreaking federal lawsuit. Tinkham firmly believed the lawsuit would be their yellow brick road to a merger.[12]

The Indiana way now dominated the ABA's first attempt to sign UCLA's coveted Lew Alcindor. Tinkham and Storen reportedly spent two nights in Las Vegas trying to coax the addled billionaire Howard Hughes, who'd taken up permanent residence on the Strip, into purchasing his own ABA team as broadcast fodder for his Hughes Sports Network. Hughes, or really his wealth managers, declined. Had they accepted on his behalf, Hughes would have received Alcindor's rights and likely become the league's ultimate sugar daddy, though with potentially dangerous consequences. Hughes, though reportedly too far gone mentally to realize it, was the Mob's latest front man in Vegas.[13]

Then there was the million-dollar check. At the all-star game, Tinkham and Storen got the league trustees to pony up $11,000 each, totaling $121,000, as collateral for a $1 million line of bank credit. Their plan called for an ABA official to sidle up to Alcindor and flash a $1 million check as his bright new tomorrow. "Wait a second," a voice piped up, "if you want to do anything with UCLA, you have to work through Sam Gilbert."

"Sam who?" the room answered.[14]

Sam Gilbert was a 56-year-old, self-described "fat, little matzo ball" of a man and the leading UCLA basketball supporter. The UCLA players called him "Papa Sam," an approving nod to his rich-uncle generosity and life-of-the-party exuberance. He sat courtside at UCLA home games in his trademark feathered fedora, his "rooting hat," ad-libbing in his punchy, up-from-the-streets argot. Papa Sam had their backs. He was family, friend, life coach, and their blustery, listen-to-me-kid financial advisor.

Rivals viewed Gilbert as corrupt to the core. He wasn't. However, Gilbert was no straight arrow either. He bent NCAA rules to make his Bruins—his boys—comfortable away from home and to feel privileged as the kings of college basketball. If the fat, little matzo ball felt good about the ABA, chances were excellent that Alcindor would second that emotion. But when the million-dollar check, typed out to Alcindor, was finally shown to Gilbert, he snapped, "Why are you showing me that? Lew doesn't want to play in the ABA."[15] Yet another slight from yet another personal advisor. These special friends had thwarted the ABA with Elvin Hayes and Wes Unseld. Was Alcindor next?

The brush-off forced Tinkham and Storen to brush up on Freud, Jung, and the power of modern psychology. They launched the basketball equivalent of a military counterintelligence effort. Objective: Win Alcindor's heart and mind with their targeted displays of ABA kindness. "We had both industrial psychologists and professional psychologists prepare questions for Alcindor," explained Storen. "Several different people interviewed Alcindor. We studied his activities at UCLA, talked to people from UCLA and people he knew from New York. We even hired a private detective to investigate him in California. We wanted to know who we had to get to in order to help Alcindor make the decision we wanted."[16]

They called their skulking around Operation Kingfish. The name smacked of Cold War derring-do, which satisfied these two former Cold War military men and cold-hard pro basketball survivalists. Operation Kingfish also marked a turning point in the ABA's self-identity and *raison d'etre*. Out with "the Lively League" and the promise to win over America with a zippier brand of pro basketball; in with "The Maverick League," a bunch of devil-may-care extremists willing to hit the NBA where it hurts, stealing the top rookies by any Freudian means necessary, inflating labor costs to unsustainable levels, and hopefully shredding its 1940s-style bylaws in federal court.

L os Angeles, Feb. 3, 1969—Guys in T-shirts and sunglasses liked to loiter at Phil's Newsstand on West Third Street and Fairfax Avenue, ("the biggest little library in the city"). Most pawed the merchandise, reading the latest magazines, and maybe strolling out with a 10-cent daily newspaper for the latest scores, and, of course, the latest word on the undefeated UCLA Bruins. The Bruins were a college basketball juggernaut, pure and simple, and the *L.A. Times* ran a piece this morning asking which Lew Alcindor-led UCLA team was the greatest, though demurring that such comparisons "may be tantamount to comparing Rolls-Royces with Cadillacs."

The UCLA story followed the bold headlines on page one about that Bentley idling in Inglewood, the Los Angeles Lakers. The Lakers, wearing their familiar Forum Blue and Gold,[17] lost yesterday in triple overtime in a wild one that included a phony bomb scare phoned in after the first overtime. But the real bombshell last week was on the cover of the latest *Sports Illustrated*, still on the rack at Phil's. It showed Wilt Chamberlain pointing into the great unknown framed by the words, "A Los Angeles Dilemma." Scribe Frank Deford, a.k.a., Frank De-Freud, put Wilt on the couch and scribbled down his clinical observations, starting with this concerning prognosis:

> When the Los Angeles Lakers got Wilt Chamberlain in a trade last summer, the immediate popular supposition was that they had dealt themselves a wonder team. With Elgin Baylor and Jerry West playing, too, every game would be a thrilling All-Star show and every box office would do boffo, turn-away business. The only problem, it was suggested, was that the big three superstars would be struggling with each other to see who could get the ball and shoot it the most.

> Now, as the NBA season moves into its last two months, it has become apparent that the results are exactly the reverse of the assumptions. The Lakers are, first of all, only a pretty good team with about the same chance to win the championship as last year's Lakers—who did not. Moreover, far from providing raging effervescence, the Lakers are dull almost to the point of tedium, and the slow realization of that fact may soon be reflected in attendance at the Inglewood Forum.

> The main problem on the court is not that Chamberlain, Baylor and West do not get the ball enough. It is that Chamberlain will not—or cannot—go to the basket when he does get it. In other words, the fantastic Laker juggernaut lacks a sufficient offense to carry it; the team has been reduced to depending on its defense.

None of that was news to Jack Kent Cooke. The Lakers, though comfortably atop the Western Division standings, were hardly the world-beaters that Cooke envisioned. He knew it, and so did the page-flippers at Phil's Newsstand. On top of the triple-overtime loss, Cooke's Dream Team fell flat last week to expansion Seattle and Philadelphia, the same outfit that unloaded Wilt the Dilemma on the Lakers.

Maybe Deford was right. Maybe Wilt was the problem. At age 33, he remained a dominant force in the NBA, and yet, he was aloof with teammates, grumpy with his coach, and fighting with his shooting touch. He snatched rebounds off the backboards, then he waved the basketball around like a speared fish for several seconds, killing the Laker fastbreak and slowing the action to the foxtrot that Deford mocked.

While Cooke dreamed up bigger-and-better marketing ideas and reportedly padded attendance figures to maintain the mystique of The Forum as a happening place, he let those in the Lakers' front office know in no uncertain terms that he expected an NBA championship. Maybe Deford had it right. Maybe Wilt "needs a challenge, for nothing else has served to make him go to the basket." Maybe he needs to finish out the season with the seven-foot brute force and panache that would make Cooke's Dream Team come true.

Los Angeles, Feb. 9, 1969—Dave Lattin sat dripping in the visitors' locker room, looking like he'd just been through the spin cycle trapped inside a Kenmore washing machine. Every bone in his muscular, 6-foot-8 frame ached. Same went for the 6-foot-10 rookie Jim Fox, who sat grasping for words to describe the futility of trying to stop a seven-foot man possessed, "I've never seen anything like it. I couldn't do anything about it."[18]

"It" was Wilt Chamberlain, and "the Dipper," as they called him now, dominated Fox, Lattin, and their Phoenix Suns this evening for 66 points, 27 rebounds, and, if the NBA had counted them, a double-figure night in blocks. It was an awesome muscle flex, as Wilt connected on 29 of 35 shots, 22 of which were dunks. If the Suns hadn't tripled-teamed the Dipper in the fourth quarter, he might have gone off for 80 points.

"This proves that the Dipper can not only score, but read, too," smirked Phoenix coach Red Kerr, the NBA's reigning king of the cheap one-liner.[19]

Kerr was referring to Frank Deford's broadside. Of course, Kerr would have preferred that Deford had kept his thoughts to himself. The Suns, through no bad blood of their own, had now fallen on the wrong side of Wilt's ego twice. The first time was on Christmas Day, the debut of this season's NBA Game of the Week. Jack Twyman, the color commentator and an ex-NBA star who should have known better, challenged Wilt during a halftime interview. "Why don't you follow your coach's instructions?" Twyman asked.[20] Twyman, of course, had a point. Wilt, who had been "standing around like a condemned building"[21] in the first half, refused to drift to the top of the key on offense and stand 15 feet away from his preferred spot near the basket. Coach's orders.

Wilt smiled, mumbled something forgettable into the microphone, and promptly lost his mind in the dressing room at the nationally televised indignity. In the second half, Wilt returned properly hydrated and properly determined to show the blankety-blank Twyman and millions of viewers at home who was boss. According to one observer, what followed was "the fury of an angry God," probably Jupiter, the god of thunder. Wilt blocked 15 shots in the second half (23 unofficially for the game), and his constant rumbling around the rim almost single-handedly zapped Phoenix's shooting percentage down to 24 percent. The Lakers won going away, as Wilt blocked one of every four of Phoenix's field-goal attempts in the second half. Such defensive dominance had to be seen to be believed.

And tonight, such offensive dominance had to be seen to be believed. Yet, in this game, Kerr's Suns somehow hung in there late into the fourth quarter. A weird bounce here, a lucky rebound there, and the Suns could have stolen the game, which would have been career highlights for Lattin, Fox, and crew, who bumped, pounded, and gave it their all inside to stop this angry 7-foot-1 God from throwing down his two-handed lightning bolts.

In truth, the Suns (13-46) weren't all that good. They weren't built to bump, grind, and beat the almighty Lakers—and that was no accident. First-year expansion teams inherited rosters full of hand-me-downs, borderline talent that the older NBA teams either didn't want or could live without. With no all-pros on the payroll, first-year expansion teams were doomed to lose for roughly the next five seasons. At least, that was NBA's in-house calculation.[22] It took expansion teams at least five seasons to shed the hand-me-downs and weave together a tailor-made winner via the college draft, the waiver wire, and good trades.

During those first five woeful seasons, expansion teams would descend into debt as their initially energized local fan base gradually quit on their tarnished losers and disgrace to their city. So, it was no surprise that the first-year Suns already were in deep trouble. Their average attendance had reached just 4,300 per game—and falling—and the team reportedly was on track to lose $175,000 (today, about $1.5 million) in year one.[23]

Lucky for Phoenix, the five-year calculation and curse wasn't carved in stone. There was a cross-your-fingers work around: hitting it big—Powerball big—in the college draft. And 1969 was one of those Powerball years. Phoenix, as the Western Division's worst team, had a shot at Lew Alcindor. But they didn't need Freud or an Operation Anything to get him. They just needed to win a coin flip with the Eastern Division's worst. If the coin landed right-side up, the Suns would be in the money for years to come featuring the next Big Dipper.

Suns president Dick Bloch figured the Alcindor payout at $5 million over the next few seasons, then a healthy NBA profit. It was a back-of-the-envelope calculation, but Bloch lived in Los Angeles and had seen Jack Kent Cooke dazzle Southern California with his Dream Team. He'd also followed the rise of the New York Knicks, now the industry torchbearer. The Knicks, since acquiring their glue guy Dave DeBusschere, were 24-5 and the toast of Manhattan. Through 27 home dates so far this season, the Knicks had sold 385,964 tickets for a league-leading nightly draw of 14,296.

And so, as difficult as it was for Bloch to watch Wilt decimate his Suns a second time this season, he looked to the future with hope. Heads, he wins; tails, he loses. By this time next season, the NBA could have four must-see attractions: the Knicks, Lakers, Celtics . . . and the Suns rising over the Arizona desert and sweeping across the NBA like a skyhook.

Minneapolis, Feb. 15, 1969—Lee Meade, the ABA's publicist, had stumbled onto an NBA bombshell: The Milwaukee Bucks, the worst team in the NBA's Eastern Division, already owned the draft rights to Lew Alcindor. It seems the NBA had held a secret coin flip last month for the first pick in the upcoming draft, giving Milwaukee a jump on the ABA to sign Alcindor.

Call Meade paranoid, but the head start aligned perfectly with the battlefield wisdom of his officemate Thurlo McCrady, a veteran of the recent pro football war. McCrady, an AFL foot soldier, shared his dark tales of the NFL lying, cheating, and, in some cases, temporarily abducting All-Americans to keep them from the grip of their rival.[24] The NBA, cut from the same dominant cloth as the NFL, had every reason to do the same to protect its pro basketball monopoly. So worried McCrady, and those worries had colored Meade's perceptions of the NBA.[25]

That's why the ABA front office organized today's top-secret emergency conference call to rally the ABA troops. After a round of I-told-you-so's, a perfunctory coin flip may or may not have taken place in George Mikan's travel agency. Either way, surprise! The New York Nets, awarded Alcindor's ABA rights at the All-Star Game to the dismay of the Los Angeles Stars, won the coin flip to make the charade official. (Alcindor recently said he preferred to turn pro in New York.) The league trustees then ripped through the first two rounds of their 1969 college draft, hopefully to get their own head start on the NBA. Let the bidding wars begin!

Unfortunately for Meade, the ABA was rotten at keeping secrets. His top-secret warning leaked immediately to reporters in St. Paul and Oakland,[26] who were quickly joined by their colleagues in Milwaukee in calling for more details. Meade said he'd read a story about the NBA coin flip in the early morning edition of the *Minneapolis Tribune*. The byline belonged to the trusted Tom Briere, one of the better sportswriters in town, quoting an anonymous NBA insider. But Briere's editor quickly yanked the story, realizing it contained a huge factual error. The Suns and Bucks, though bad teams, had yet to clinch last place in their respective divisions. The NBA couldn't hold the coin flip just yet, since it was still mathematically possible that low-lying Seattle and/or Detroit would be flipping for Alcindor in March.

Meade didn't apologize for running with Briere's oops. Who knew what the NBA was capable of? But the NBA's response was swift and unequivocal. Suns' president Dick Bloch protested, "There is not one iota of truth to that, and it is nothing more than a cheap attempt to get publicity." In Milwaukee, Bucks' general manager John Erickson railed, "The report is absolutely untrue and completely irresponsible." Enough said.

Milwaukee, Feb. 16, 1969—Oh no. The Milwaukee Bucks were suddenly winning a few ball games, and that included today's upset of, you guessed it, the Los Angeles Lakers, 106-97. "They were playing volleyball on the boards," Milwaukee coach Larry Costello praised his big men for battling Wilt Chamberlain inside, "and made it possible for us to get second and third shots."[27]

But don't blame Wilt. He was a force inside, snatching plenty of rebounds and picking up the offensive slack for the injured Jerry West. The problem was the Laker backcourt, sans West, couldn't keep up with Milwaukee's star of the game, Flynn Robinson. The shifty six-footer, a Cincinnati castoff formerly hidden in the shadow of Oscar Robertson, was on an offensive tear, pouring in 31 points today in the second half (41 for the game).

The win, before a chanting sell-out crowd, was the hands-down thrill of Milwaukee's maiden season. But privately, management was starting to get nervous about the Detroit Pistons. The Pistons, second worst in the East and seven games better than Milwaukee, had dropped eight of 10 games so far in February and showed no signs of pulling out of its nosedive.

Milwaukee owner Marv Fishman: "It was suggested at a board meeting that if this [winning] continued, someone should say something to Larry Costello (about losing a few for the Alcindor coinflip). But, of course, that was immediately dismissed as an absurd idea."[28]

Absurd it was because the Bucks were now a model NBA expansion team. They were projected to lose just $125,000 in year one, or $50,000 better than Phoenix. How'd they do it? The Bucks followed in expansion Seattle's footsteps and went public to multiply their first-year cash flow. About 425,000 shares of "deer meat" were issued, peaking at $12 a share. The Bucks also had been a hit at the box office, averaging an NBA expansion record of 6,246 fans per outing.[29]

Fishman and his associates had plenty to lose if a dumping scandal ever leaked. Why risk feast for guaranteed famine? And so, Costello coached to win, Robinson shot to score (including a 45-point gem in a victory over, you guessed it, Detroit), and Fishman crossed his heart and hoped to lose, though careful not to tank.

Minneapolis, Feb. 23, 1969—The marquee outside the Metropolitan Sports Center ("the Met") advertised tonight's game in block letters: Oaks vs. Pipers, 7:00. Not much else to say. Oakland's Rick Barry, the league's designated superstar, just had surgery on his damaged knee and was out indefinitely. Same with the Minnesota Pipers' Connie Hawkins, the league's other designated superstar.

Missing from the Sunday marquee was the 5 p.m. news conference now underway inside. Why the Pipers couldn't wait until Monday morning was a head-scratcher. But rumors were rampant that the Pipers would relocate next season to Cleveland or St. Louis. The Pipers wanted to nip them in the bud, especially the latest and loudest rumor yet. Three nights ago, the Pipers were preparing to play the Nets on Long Island when a certain Dr. Alan Levy introduced himself to a few players. Levy, the Nets' team physician, said he would be working for them next season. The Pipers, he explained, were moving to gritty Jersey City to play in the 6,300-seat National Guard Armory. Levy promised the blank looks that a deal had been reached last November, dropping the name of Mark Binstein as their new owner.[30] The name Binstein hardly registered with the players. But Binstein was one of the ABA's organizers, of course, part of the East Coast group and a name that kept reappearing.

Levy confided that Binstein was filing paperwork with the federal Securities and Exchange Commission for permission to sell 250,000 shares of the team. Like Milwaukee and Seattle, taking the team public would expand Binstein's cash flow and that of his three partners, which included none other than Gabe

Rubin, current minority owner of the Pipers. In fact, a Hackensack, N.J., newspaper even broke the rumor this morning of the ABA coming to town, though with a question mark.

And now, Bill Erickson, the Pipers' 38-year-old majority owner and his brilliant legal mind, stood at a podium down a rubber-carpeted hallway attempting to defuse the ticking question mark in a New Jersey newspaper. Erickson, dressed business-formal but sporting a full head of wavy brown hair that made him look windblown, got right to the point. The Pipers hadn't quit on the Twin Cities. Reporters scribbled down his pacifying words, but Erickson couldn't muster the one big defusing sentence that needed to be said: The Pipers will be back in Minnesota next season.

In truth, Erickson didn't know where the team would hold forth next season. To consummate the Jersey City move, one final, make-or-break approval was needed from Nets' owner Arthur Brown. Brown, having arrived in New York first, owned the league's territorial rights to a 75-mile radius of prime ABA real estate around Long Island. That included Jersey City, 55 miles away. If Brown said he didn't want company on his ABA turf, the deal was off.

That had Erickson et al. tiptoeing around to get the deal signed, sealed, and, belatedly delivered to Brown as a *fait accompli* that needed his rubber stamp for the good of the ABA. Now the cat—and Brown's ire—were out of the bag about a month too soon. "How come you've heard about it, and I haven't?" an exasperated Brown told the *Hackensack Record*. The reporter asked if Brown would veto the move? "That depends on who the team is and the owner is," he snapped. "They would have to be acceptable to me."[31]

Interesting way of putting it. Binstein and Brown, as they say, "had history." It went back three years when Binstein paused his career as a stockbroker to cast his lot with the ABA. "When I saw the money represented, I knew I was latching on to a good thing," Binstein said of the initial ABA meetings. "I went for broke to get a franchise [in New York]. But what I had simply wasn't enough—I got Art Brown interested, held on to a minority share, and now I'm in the big league."

Brown, an orphan who grew up fast and clawed his way to millions in the trucking industry, had heard it all in his nearly 60 years. Heard it all, but he'd almost certainly never encountered anyone like the calm, cool, and conniving Binstein, who had premature dark rings around his eyes that lent him an air of premature wisdom. "Mark Binstein's voice glides through the air on a thick, rich velvet carpet," a reporter later wrote. "The words don't run together so much as melt into a cloud of irrefutable logic. His voice can plunge the listener into despair or lift him into euphoria."[32]

The velvet voice convinced Brown that a "big-league" ABA team could outcompete the poorly managed Knicks. They just had to lease an arena in Manhattan. When that didn't work out, Binstein convinced Brown to move their operation just over the river to Teaneck, New Jersey and shared some additional inside information. Discussions were underway to build a 16,000-seat, multipurpose arena on a plot of nearby New Jersey swampland called the Meadowlands. When the arena was built in a couple of years, they could relocate their team there and wait for the NBA-ABA merger, which Binstein and his irrefutable logic presented as inevitable.

However, development of the Meadowlands would soon be tied up in court, and Brown's basketball dreams would soon be tied up in knots. Everything in New Jersey was subpar . . . the team, the players, the facility, the community support. Binstein blamed Brown; Brown blamed Binstein. With Binstein also now under a 23-count indictment for allegedly rigging stocks, the two agreed it was best to part company. Brown bought out Binstein and relocated his renamed New York Nets to faraway Long Island, where there also were rumblings to build a modern arena in a few years.

Last October, with his indictment out of the way, Binstein wanted his team back. He reportedly made Brown a bold offer. No go. Working his ABA contacts, namely Rubin, Binstein heard last fall the Minnesota Pipers, featuring New York playground legend Connie Hawkins, might be available for the right price. Phone calls and dollar figures ($1.2 million) were exchanged, and though he hadn't mentioned Lew Alcindor publicly, Binstein clearly knew the UCLA All-American hoped to play pro in his native New York. The Nets and his now-nemesis Brown, of course, had the ABA rights to Alcindor. But Jersey City was four miles from Lower Manhattan; the Nets' Long Island address was in the middle of nowhere. Maybe he could take a run at Alcindor, hopefully team him with Hawkins, and hasten the Meadowlands arena.

Back in Minneapolis, Erickson refused to cop to any of the above. He repeated that the Pipers hadn't quit on the Twin Cities, and they planned to finish the season strong. With no further questions, Erickson called the news conference a wrap.

There was a number floating like a metaphorical elephant in the room: $250,000.[33] That was the Pipers' projected shortfall for the season. For Erickson, though a muckety-muck by day with the Consumer Financial Group, a 1960s reinvention of the 1920s holding company, this figure bleeding into even higher estimates was gut-wrenching. He didn't have that kind of cash to throw around on a basketball team that, let's face it, wasn't connecting with his fellow citizens.

That's why he was getting out. That's why he needed the Binstein deal approved ASAP, even if it potentially set in motion a behind-the-scenes tug-of-war between Binstein and Brown for their rightful crack at Alcindor. Erickson felt no kinship toward Brown and the forever bickering ABA trustees, Gabe Rubin excluded. As Erickson prepared his swift exit, one had to wonder whether his good friend George Mikan might be right behind him out the door.

Detroit, March 5, 1969—"Well, our Pistons did it again: "They won!" a local sportscaster griped over the airwaves this morning stretching out each word in disgust, like discovering the neighbor's poodle has just pooped on his front lawn yet again.

The sportscaster, known around Detroit for starting the "Lose for Lew" campaign, urged the Pistons to dump the remainder of the season. Just roll over and play dead for a shot at Lew Alcindor in the NBA draft.

Mr. Lose-for-Lew had a point, but the Pistons front office had an image to uphold. Make that, restore. Three months after the DeBusschere goodbye, the office secretary was still digging out from the hate mail over the trade that should have never been. According to ex-Pistons coach Donnis Butcher, he'd agreed over Christmas week to swap Detroit's franchise-player-in-waiting Jimmy Walker straight up for Knicks' center Walt Bellamy. The next day, Butcher was fired for the Pistons' poor early-season showing, and his jaunty replacement Paul Seymour immediately renegotiated the trade. Walker was out; DeBusschere was in. It seems that DeBusschere was a confidante of team owner Fred Zollner, famous for his quick trigger in hiring and firing. (Just ask Butcher.) Seymour didn't want DeBusschere around and possibly badmouthing him to Zollner. The rest is New York Knicks and NBA history in the making.[34]

Though February had been rough for Seymour, losing 12 of Detroit's 16 games, the former NBA star had too much pride to roll over and play dead in season-ending March. So did Bellamy and Butch Komives, also part of the trade. Tonight, with the Knicks in town, "Bells" and Butch trotted onto the court to a shout of handmade signs taped to the upper balcony belittling them and hailing the return of the mighty DeBusschere. Between the paper shouts and adrenaline rush of facing their former team, Bells and Butch let their inspired play do the talking in leading the Pistons to the eight-point upset.

"If they keep this up, we'll lose our chance at Alcindor," raged Mr. Lose-for-Lew, blaming Komives and management by name like he was outing crooked politicians. In this case, the scandal was cheating Motown out of a blast of sky hooks, future NBA championships, and parades down Woodward Avenue.

The victorious Pistons (28-45) were now four-and-a-half games better than last-place Milwaukee in their dubious race to clinch worst in the Eastern Division. Just nine games remained in the regular-season. Make that eight. Two nights later, the Pistons beat the Cincinnati Royals, who had bested Milwaukee the night before. Milwaukee's magic number for futility was now three losses or less.

Indianapolis, March 9, 1969—Electricity crackled through the old Fairgrounds Coliseum. Human electricity. Almost 10,500 spectators of all shapes and sizes, which included 1,369 standing with overcoats in hand and clogging the aisles. This mass of basketball-crazed Hoosier humanity, the fourth legitimate sellout in a month, crackled with every defensive stop by their Pacers and sizzled with their every basket over the outstretched arms of Donnie Freeman, Big Game Hunter, and the Miami Floridians.

For a fledgling league that still entertained empty seats in most of its arenas, if only the electricity in Fairgrounds Coliseum could be bottled like Pepsi Cola and distributed to a New Generation of basketball fans in Long Island, Los Angeles, Oakland, Minneapolis, and Miami.

To be fair, Miami's New Generation of hoop enthusiasts was still under marketing development. In a sign of the music-thumping, cheerleader-bouncing, novelty-act-touting, giveaway-happy modern marketing departments to come, Miami's lead marketeer Dennis Murphy had spent the second half of the season turning two tickets to see the Floridians into a frolicking house of fun. There was Latin America Night, a discount *hola* for the team's Spanish-speaking friends; Nassau Night, a raffle for a free trip to the Bahamas; National Airlines Night, a pregame exhibition contest pitting stewardesses against local media celebrities. "Except for the fans these promotions brought in," Murph explained the method to his marketing madness, "we were getting only the hardcore basketball fan."[35]

Tonight, Miami guard Donnie Freeman took matters into his own hands, pinwheeling his 20-footers through the hoop one after the other to rally the Floridians in the third quarter from a double-digit deficit. Then with the game going down to the wire, the ball took a few favorable Pacer bounces, and Indiana had its sixth victory in a row. Just for the record, though attendance surged in Indianapolis late in the season, the Pacers logged in with a more modest, but still ABA-best, 5,400 per game That was better than 10 of the NBA's 16 franchises. Or, put differently, of the combined 27 NBA and ABA franchises, only seven averaged more than 5,400 fans per night.

Phoenix, March 10, 1969—The Phoenix Suns weren't too bad offensively. It was their defense that sucked. Like tonight against Baltimore. It was all score, baby, score in the second half, as Baltimore's Gus Johnson, Kevin Loughery, and especially the spinning, double-clutching Earl Monroe singed the nets for an NBA-record 84 points.

Most in the small crowd weren't so upset about the Baltimore blitz. The rotten defense was expected. Many bought their tickets, programs, and hot dogs to come to do their civic duty—of the basketball variety. With Phoenix (16-60) now guaranteed to be in the Lew Alcindor coin flip and possibly even call it in the air, general manager Jerry Colangelo wanted fans to vote on whether he should call heads or tails? Ballot boxes were located throughout the lobby of Veterans Memorial

Coliseum. Vote early, vote often, and the early returns already were in: Heads (60.2 percent), tails (39.8 percent)

Boston, March 16, 1969—Coffee, tea, or morning cigar? Red Auerbach, the cigar-puffing Boston general manager, always had a little breakfast buffet waiting in the Celtics front office suite whenever the ABC broadcast crew rolled into town for the NBA Game of the Week.[36] Broadcasters Jack Twyman and Chris Schenkel popped in on schedule, filled their plates, and pulled up their chairs around Auerbach. In his blunt, combative, and occasionally charming way, Auerbach wanted to set the record straight for his broadcast friends: The Celtics would be ready for the playoffs in 10 days. Guaranteed. The regular season was prelude; the playoffs were forever, and his battle-tested veterans rarely failed to bring home the top NBA prize. The proof fluttered from the rafters of Boston Garden: 10 NBA championship banners.

But Auerbach's record-straightening was more complicated this morning. His superstars Bill Russell and Sam Jones, now in their mid-30s, would retire after the season, and so far, their final opus hadn't been so hot. Both remained in their own right NBA virtuosos, but they weren't hitting quite the same crowd-pleasing notes anymore. Neither were the injury-plagued Celtics, mired in fourth place in the NBA's Eastern Division and about to log their worst record since 1950. In fact, showing no bounce-back in sight, the Celtics had lost six of their last 10 games, including a one-point heartbreaker last night to the first-place Baltimore Bullets.

Oh, the Bullets. The NBA's surprise regular-season studs were now right there with New York as playoff favorites. Just as Dave DeBusschere had been a Godsend for the Knicks, rookie Wes Unseld had been Baltimore's 6-foot-7 savior. His wide, bulky frame was immoveable inside, allowing him to handle all the dirty work around the basket. His aggressive rebounding and quick outlet pass, the best in the business, decimated retreating defenses.

Even if Auerbach and the other old-school general managers hadn't yet made their peace with these crazy rookie salaries, Unseld was proof that pooling NBA funds and going a little financially nuts had its rewards. So was rookie Elvin Hayes, the NBA's leading scorer as a rookie. The same went for Lew Alcindor, now just days from the fateful coin flip that would determine his prospective NBA zip code. Phoenix or Milwaukee? Yes, the Bucks recently clinched worst in the East after losing eight of their last 10 games. Sorry Detroit.

Chris Schenkel, an all-around good guy and one of the most recognizable play-by-play voices on television, nodded, sipped, and chewed. Schenkel had no interest in locking horns with Auerbach and his Celtic pride and prejudice. "Chris recognized that he didn't know a lot about basketball, and he let me do the talking," said Twyman, his broadcast partner and retired NBA star.

That included on the air. Schenkel would call the play-by-play action in his smooth, velvet-fog voice and "oh my" at colliding players. "They say basketball is a non-contact sport," was Schenkel's signature line and reflection of his limited basketball IQ. It also was Twyman's cue to sort out the collisions and do all the talking about rugged screens and other manly strategy in a passionate, modulating announcer's voice that often suggested he was sharing NBA trade secrets.

Somehow the Game of the Week and its fancy camera angles worked. Americans were tuning in more than ever for ABC's 12 regular-season broadcasts, plus the all-star game and five playoff games to come. Though still nowhere near the astronomical viewership of the NFL or MLB, about 19.5 million per week was the industry estimate for the NBA, up from 15 million five years ago.

The Los Angeles Lakers would play the Celtics this afternoon live and in color in what might be the last hurrah for the NBA's greatest rivalry and claim to popular-culture fame: Russell versus Chamberlain. Last hurrah? Bah humbug. Auerbach found the whole storyline preposterous. The two, he said, would meet again in a few weeks in the NBA finals. The proof fluttered from the Boston Garden rafters.

R ed Auerbach was right. The Rivalry continued into the playoffs. Boston snapped into peak playoff form, topping Philadelphia and besting New York for the Eastern Division championship. Waiting for Bill Russell and the Celtics in the 1969 NBA Finals were Wilt Chamberlain and the men in Forum blue and gold, much to the glee of Lakers' owner Jack Kent Cooke. The series climaxed in a game-seven showdown in The Forum. Cooke, convinced the Lakers' fabulous homecourt advantage equaled sure victory, famously ordered thousands of balloons to be suspended from the Forum rafters beforehand in preparation for the postgame championship celebration. Oh, the hubris. The veteran Celtics defeated the hobbled (and at times disgruntled) Lakers for their second-straight league championship, 11th in the past 13 seasons and one last Russell triumph over Wilt for the road. Cooke's balloons were later donated to a local children's hospital.

In the ABA, the Oakland Oaks took home the second league championship. They did it without their high-paid star Rick Barry, out with an injury, and relying on the lower-paid trio of little Larry Brown, rookie Warren Armstrong, and the controversial Doug Moe, banned by the NBA for life after allegedly consorting with gamblers. "There was a special warmth that radiated from the stands onto the playing court," a local sports columnist captured the championship feeling, "and right away you knew the Oakland Oaks finally had hooked the hearts of many people in this town."[37] Oh, the naivete. Sure, the Oaks had made lots of friends in Oakland. But remember the Hollywood stars who owned the team and blanched at its seven-figure start-up losses? They still badly wanted out of Oakland, hooked hearts, ABA championship, and all.

Endnotes

[1] John Crittenden, "Freeman: Pay Me or Trade Me," *Miami News*, February 3, 1969.

[2] James Quirk and Rodney Fort, *Pay Dirt*, 1992, p. 57.

[3] Frederick Klein, "Owning a Sports Team Looks Like Fun, but It Isn't Always Gold Mine," *Wall Street Journal*, September 9, 1969.

[4] Michael Burns, Interview with author, October 2012.

[5] Quirk and Fort, *Pay Dirt*, p. 91-92.

[6] Roger Noll, Interview with author, April 2009.

[7] Quirk and Fort, *Pay Dirt*, p. 110.

[8] Benjamin Okner, "Taxation and Sports Enterprises," *Government and the Sports Business*, 1974, p. 169-170.

[9] Crittenden, *Miami News*, February 3, 1969.

[10] Fred Seely, "Freeman Takes Stock of Floridian $ituation," *Miami Herald*, February 4, 1969.

[11] Ron Perry, Interview with author, July 2022.

[12] Dick Tinkham, Interview with author, June 2014.

[13] Terry Pluto, *Loose Balls*, 1990, p.191. The Mob secretly tapped into Hughes' fortune, moving properties into his name to throw off federal agents and expand the Strip and its bright lights and big casinos.

[14] Jim Gardner, Interview with author, July 2012.

[15] Ibid.

[16] Pluto, *Loose Balls*, 1990, p. 191.

[17] Jack Kent Cooke's highbrow color designation, though purple and gold it was in the cheap seats.

[18] Mal Florence, "Wilt Hits 66 in Laker Win; West Out 2 Weeks," *Los Angeles Times*, February 10, 1969.

[19] Joe Gilmartin, *The Little Team That Could and Darn Near Did!* 1976, p. 23.

[20] No Byline, "Wilt Turned On By TV, Leads Lakers' Rally," *Long Beach (Calif.) Independent*, December 26, 1968.

[21] Dave Hicks, "Santa Kerr Too Generous in Defeat," *Arizona Republic*, December 26, 1968.

[22] Michael Burns, October 2012.

[23] Dave Hicks, "Suns' Future Faces Lumps," *Arizona Republic*, May 7, 1969.

[24] For an excellent overview of the NFL's shenanigans, see Dick Weiss and Chuck Dy, *The Making of the Super Bowl*, 2003, p. 23-30.

[25] After signing with the NBA in March 1968, Elvin Hayes toured with a team of Texas collage stars mainly through New York. San Diego's young scout Max Shapiro coached the team and was asked to keep an eye on Hayes at all times should ABA figures try to get the Big E to reconsider. See, for example, *Troy (N.Y.) Record*, March 30, 1968.

[26] Paul McCarthy, "Lew to N.Y. in Secret ABA Draft," *Oakland Tribune*, February 18, 1969.

[27] Associated Press, "Bucks, Robinson Stop Los Angeles," *Racine Journal Times*, February 17, 1969.

[28] Marv Fishman and Tracy Dodds, *Bucking the Odds*, 1978, p. 104.

[29] Ibid, p. 88-89, 105.

[30] Tom Briere, "Rumors Shroud Piper-Oak Game," *Minneapolis Tribune*, February 23, 1969.

[31] Lew Azaroff, "ABA Team for N.J.?" *Hackensack Record*, February 23, 1969.

[32] Fred Kirsch, "Binstein Tells It Like He Hopes," *Hackensack Record*, February 8, 1973.

[33] Tom Briere, "Erickson: No Decision Yet on Pipers' Future," *Minneapolis Tribune*, March 11, 1969.

[34] Jerry Green, *The Detroit Pistons*, 1991, p. 73.

[35] Bob Fowler, "Promotion Develops Miami Into ABA Garden of Eden," *The Sporting News*, May 3, 1969.

[36] Jack Twyman, Interview with author, January 2011.

[37] Ed Levitt, "The Oaks' Love-In," *Oakland Tribune*, May 9, 1969.

11

John Erickson snatched up the telephone from its cradle, and the throng of reporters shushed for quiet in the conference room. The time was 9:57 a.m. Central. The big moment had arrived. Would Erickson and his Milwaukee Bucks win today's coin flip—the Super Flip—for the first pick in the 1969 NBA draft? Or would the Phoenix Suns take home this year's once-in-a-franchise prize: Draft rights to UCLA's 7-foot-2 college superstar Lew Alcindor?[1]

"It's some babe in New York," Erickson winked and gagged to the reporters, the telephone dangling from his ear.

The babe had placed Erickson on hold to dial in the other parties for the 10 a.m. conference call. Erickson, the Bucks' 30-something general manager, remained the smiling, glad-handing picture of confidence on the makeshift podium. Seated next to him was Wes Pavalon, Milwaukee's chain-smoking, nervous wreck of a chairman of the board. Two minutes later, Erickson hung up. The freaking connection had gone dead.

The phone rang again almost immediately.

Erickson snatched up the receiver again, and the intrusive, ill-timed voice of a Bucks fan asked, "Who won the toss?"

Erickson slammed down the phone.

The phone rang again. It was the babe in New York, who said she was ready to connect everyone: Erickson and Pavalon in Milwaukee; Dick Bloch, the Suns' millionaire owner, in Beverly Hills; Bloch's 29-year-old general manager Jerry Colangelo and Suns coach Red Kerr in Phoenix; and commissioner Walter Kennedy at NBA headquarters in New York.

Milwaukee was back on hold.

In New York, secretaries Connie Maroselli and Maryellen Burns continued dialing in Phoenix and Beverly Hills, while Kennedy, their paunchy, middle-aged boss, passed the time regaling a group of reporters in his office with memories of vaudeville.

"When I was 10 years old, I loved to watch [ventriloquist] Marshall Montgomery," Kennedy confided. "He would smoke a cigarette and talk while he was drinking a glass of water."

Nearby a glass of water stood beading on Kennedy's polished brown desk. The glass showed a cartoon mosquito stinging a horse on its rump and the word Skeeter's. To the more worldly in the room, Skeeter's was a men's social club.

"Don't we have any National Basketball Association glasses?" fussed Haskell Cohen, the league's media person.

"NBA Properties hasn't signed a contract for glasses," Kennedy answered. He took a sip of water and hid the Skeeter's advertisement under his desk, out of the probing glare of three television cameras and any potential awkward explanations.

Maroselli and Burns entered the room and nodded. It was time. Kennedy toddled over and raised the beige telephone receiver on his desk. His voice immediately transformed into the authoritative timbre of the NBA chief.

"I have two cards on my desk," he began, reaching for his reading glasses. "One has Phoenix written on it. One has Milwaukee. I will pick one, and that team will have the privilege of calling the flip or passing and allowing the other team to call. Understood?"

In Milwaukee, Erickson and Pavalon responded in the affirmative like game-show contestants. The telephone's audio was now being broadcast live over an intercom and filled the Bucks conference room with the procedural suspense.

"The card says Phoenix," Kennedy announced.

The voice of Dick Bloch responded within seconds that the Suns would make the call. His staff in Phoenix already knew the next words out of his mouth. The Suns had asked its fans to weigh in on the coin toss. The majority chose heads.

"I call heads."

"I'm going to flip a 1964 Kennedy half dollar in the air," the commissioner continued into the phone. "No, not a Walter Kennedy half dollar . . . in my right hand, catch it in that hand, and turn it on the back of my left hand. I'm going to put the phone down because I can't do it with my feet."

Kennedy executed the flip and removed his right hand covering the coin that he'd placed on the back of his left wrist. Observing it all were a gaggle of reporters. They had been deputized on the spot as eye witnesses to the coin flip's legitimacy, though without Bloch's fateful call blasted over the speakerphone. Phoenix and Milwaukee were muted.

"The coin has come up tails," Kennedy spoke into the phone. He then issued a few perfunctory words of parting and hung up the receiver as matter of factly as if he had just placed an order for Chinese takeout. Kennedy took a deep breath and smiled at the telephone. The reporters exchanged confused glances.

"So, who got him?" an impatient voice grumped.

"Oh, I'm terribly sorry," said Kennedy, "Didn't I say?"

"No."

"They called it wrong. Milwaukee gets him."

Kennedy flipped the half dollar a few more times for the mock benefit of any late-arriving television cameras. He smiled with each flip like the former politician that he was, until his secretary said to him, "You always keep getting tails."

"Oh, do I really?"

In Milwaukee, Erickson, a Protestant, explained that he was wearing his lucky Star of David, a gift from his wife's recent trip to Israel. Pavalon, a Jew, chuckled that his lucky charm was a St. Christopher's medal. Luck and religion worked in mysterious ways.

The next day in Louisville, the ABA's special assistant Thurlo McCrady arrived to attend the NCAA men's basketball tournament. A Milwaukee reporter cornered the blunt-spoken McCrady and asked for a comment on Wednesday's Super Flip.

"I knew Milwaukee won the flip, but I didn't know they'd announced it," said McCrady, an executive in the American Football League prior to taking his position with the ABA. "When did they do that?"

"On Wednesday," the reporter answered incredulously.

"You mean it was announced Wednesday," countered McCrady. "It was held three weeks ago."

The reporter explained that the coin flip had indeed been held yesterday before a multitude of witnesses who can confirm its validity. Why the conspiratorial tone?

McCrady offered a wry smile. "Let's say I knew a flip was held three weeks ago," he said. "We're talking to the same kids they're talking to, after all. Secrets don't stay kept forever."

McCrady left the reporter with these fighting words, "We'll do what is necessary to sign such a great player. I imagine Milwaukee will be rolling up its big guns, and so will we. Arthur Brown, who owns the [ABA New York] Nets, has a lot of money, you know, and he's willing to spend it."[2]

Arthur Brown had retained the ABA's exclusive rights to Lew Alcindor. Though Mark Binstein, his Jersey City nemesis, had tried to move heaven and the Securities Exchange Commission (SEC) to access Wall Street's capital markets and join the bidding, he was out of luck. The SEC remained an administrative black hole, possibly with cause. Binstein likely was on the SEC watch list for his previous 23-count indictment for rigging stocks, and so was the New York security's firm Kenneth Bove & Co. Inc.,[3] which Binstein had hired for the SEC filing. Either way, without the estimated $1.5 million windfall from the capital markets for the team's purchase, Binstein was stuck.[4] And so was Bill Erickson in Minneapolis. "It may take from 20 days to four months to become effective," Erickson clarified near mid-March.[5]

All eyes now turned to sunny Southern California and the roly-poly special advisor Sam Gilbert. Alcindor had agreed to allow Papa Sam to cut through all the seven-figure jive and negotiate *pro bono* a legitimate-and-lucrative pro contract for him. His qualifications: As a successful Los Angeles contractor, Gilbert had experience bidding on many a lucrative construction project.

Gilbert remained true to his contractor roots. He scrapped the art of the deal for the order of the application process. Gilbert advised both leagues that he, Alcindor, and Ralph Shapiro, a 37-year-old UCLA alum and successful Beverly Hills stockbroker, would travel to New York on March 23. They would meet individually with the NBA Bucks and ABA Nets and formally ask each to present its one-and-only contract offer. Importantly, neither team would be privy to the other's bid. The highest bidder got Alcindor.

According to public opinion, Gilbert and his call for order to protect Alcindor from a Conga line of agents and hucksters seemed as right as a Sunday sermon. "You might say we are the chastity belt for Lew," quipped Shapiro.[6]

But, when viewed from the perspective of Thurlo McCrady and the ABA, the unorthodox winner-take-all format seemed curiously scripted to serve the NBA's interests. Walter Kennedy sometimes quipped during the winter of 1969 that the NBA refused to participate in a bidding war for Alcindor. Gilbert's winner-take-all plan granted Kennedy's wish.

The NBA also won another absolutely critical consolation. The senior league could much more easily control the outcome of a single bid than the chaos of four or five secret counteroffers. That, of course, assumed the NBA had the inside track to outbid the ABA. According to those present when the ABA Nets presented its offer to Team Alcindor, the winner was already pretty obvious.

Sam Gilbert and Ralph Shapiro had just arrived. Waiting to greet them was a smiling, best-foot-forward ABA contingent led by Nets owner Arthur Brown. Joining Brown was his attorney Leon Rock and accountant Ralph Dolgoff. Towering over everyone at 6-foot-10 was Mr. Basketball himself, George Mikan.[7]

All parties settled into their seats. The view from Brown's 15th-story apartment at One Central Park West on Manhattan's West Side was anything but minor league. Below rustled the green of Central Park, further on rolled the blue of the Hudson River, and further yet raised the monochromatic gray of Manhattan skyscrapers. To think that 30 years ago Brown had started out in his native Chicago with a cardboard box as his desk and a hole in his pocket to pay for his freight-shipping company. Now the world was his oyster, and Brown was one million dollars and a scrawled signature away from also striking it big in professional basketball.

Leon Rock stepped toward Gilbert and Shapiro, placing on the table in front of them a certified check, the imprimatur Chemical Bank across the top.[8] The check read: Pay to the order of Lew Alcindor Payroll Fund. Printed in the box to the right was the figure one million dollars. All sets of eyes scanned the check but one. Alcindor was running late. The chuckle was he'd been on a date but would arrive shortly.

When Alcindor and his father appeared in the apartment, Brown scooped up the check according to plan. Brown and his ABA mates had left nothing to chance. Brown would start the meeting by talking man to man with the younger Alcindor. He would place his certified check from Chemical Bank like a gold bar in the middle of the table. Next to it he would place another gold bar—a million-dollar signing bonus from the league— and tack on a 6 percent ownership stake in the New York Nets, their team and basketball partnership. Accountant Ralph Dolgoff would take the floor next and explain a special brokerage account that Brown would establish that combined a mutual fund and a $250,000 life insurance policy for Alcindor. On Alcindor's 41st birthday, the account would mature and pay him $62,500 per annum over 20 years. The brokerage account, bonus, ownership stake, and base contract brought the Nets' contract offer to a then gaudy $3.5 million.

"When they started talking money, I left the room with [the Nets'] Max Zaslofsky," said the Nets' late-arriving assistant coach Dick Schramm. "You could just feel that something was wrong, and I remember thinking that we could offer Alcindor 50 million dollars and 55 blonds, and we'll still get nowhere with this negotiation."[9]

Brown stuck to the script at first. He asked Alcindor if he was open to playing in the ABA?

Yes.

Was his preference to play in New York or Milwaukee?

New York.

Brown handed him the certified check from Chemical Bank. Alcindor fingered the paper, eyed his name printed as clear as day across the middle, and handed it back. "Mr. Brown said to me, 'We'll give you a million dollars,'" recalled Alcindor, but without mentioning a timeframe.[10]

"I told him he could take it any way he wanted—over five years, 10 years, 20 years, or all in one year. I didn't care," Brown said afterwards.[11] That should have done the trick, according to the ABA's expensive psychological profile of Alcindor. "Our research showed that the idea of becoming an instant millionaire was something that would appeal to Alcindor," Indiana's Dick Tinkham said of the ABA's likely junk science.[12]

Brown then talked about the Nets, the team's $10 million future home Nassau Coliseum, and Bob Cousy. The former Celtics great had been interviewed by Brown the day before. If Alcindor signed with the Nets, Cousy likely would be his first pro coach.

Seated nearby, Mikan and Dolgoff exchanged nervous glances. Wasn't Brown supposed to place the bonus check on the table? He never did. In fact, a signing bonus wasn't mentioned. Brown reportedly advised them afterwards not to worry. As he had been prepped beforehand by Tinkham and his partner-turned-shrink Mike Storen, Alcindor would make the final decision, not Gilbert or Shapiro. Alcindor had just told him, man to man, that he wanted to return to New York, not shiver through a Wisconsin winter. Brown perked up. The ABA held the upper hand, and Brown started instinctively to hedge for a more economical deal. That's what good businessmen do. After all, factoring in the Dolgoff Plan and ownership stake, his total offer already reached a record $2.5 million. Why give Alcindor another million?[13]

Storen, Dolgoff, and others would share their "what about the bonus check" story through the years, allowing it to assume tragic significance.[14] According to one interpretation, Mikan was to blame for not handing off the check and sticking to the script. Another version blamed Brown for misreading Alcindor.[15] However, the real gaffe was about to come. Alcindor didn't offer a timeframe for the million dollars. He left it to Brown, who threw a few more-economical numbers at the wall for Gilbert's benefit: $200,000 over five seasons.

The numbers stuck, and that equaled the end for the ABA. Alcindor already had tossed around a few numbers with

Milwaukee's John Erickson and Wes Pavalon. Erickson explained: "We were in New York for what I thought was a get-acquainted session. [Alcindor] and his agent Sam Gilbert walked into the hotel room and asked us for an offer. Well, we didn't have an offer. But I noticed that Lew appeared hungry, so I said, 'We've got a plan in mind, but we'd like a little time to work it into a firm offer. Let's go have lunch. Then, give us a couple of hours, come back, and we'll present it to you.'"[16]

Erickson and his staff scribbled several scaled, back-of-the-envelope options and presented them later to Team Alcindor as strictly preliminary offers.[17] But scribbled offers are still offers. The best was a five-year, $1.5 million deal. It was an amount beyond Milwaukee's expansion budget—without some GoFundMe support from the league's pooled Alcindor fund.[18] They'd have to make a few phone calls and get back to Gilbert.

Instead of penalizing Milwaukee for failing to follow his one-bid rule to a T, Gilbert made a major and later oddly overlooked concession. He allowed Milwaukee's back-of-the-envelope hedge to stand as a space holder. Erickson and the Bucks would finalize their offer *after* Alcindor et al. met with the Nets. In short, the Bucks would get two bites at the apple; the ABA got one.

At Brown's apartment, with a rented Rolls Royce and Cadillac now idling downstairs to whisk Team Alcindor away, Gilbert turned to Mikan and asked if he had the Nets' final offer? Mikan nodded yes, believing correctly the package, minus the signing bonus, still totaled a record $2.5 million. Unbeknownst to Mikan, Gilbert and his financial expert Shapiro had done the math differently. They didn't include the Dolgoff Plan, considering the time-share brokerage account to be funny money. The same applied to the ownership stake in the iffy Nets, who could fold at any time. Gilbert and Shapiro boiled down the ABA's offer to Brown's $1 million certified check to be paid in full over five years. That came to roughly $500,000 below Milwaukee's preliminary offer.

"They [Gilbert and Shapiro] said if the NBA didn't renege on its offer, they would get back to us," Mikan recalled, confirming Milwaukee got a second bite at the apple to set the final price.

Gilbert paused and asked one final question. What about a signing bonus? He'd been told beforehand that the ABA had a healthy bonus check. Mikan shrugged no, following Brown's lead. Gilbert then called Erickson and locked in his high offer, now backed by the full faith and credit of the NBA.

"Back at our hotel, we sat and talked about it," Alcindor recounted. "I told Mr. Shapiro and Mr. Gilbert that I really preferred New York over Milwaukee, but not at that price differential. They agreed with me. The NBA offer was clearly superior. So we called Walter Kennedy and told him I'd be playing for the new Milwaukee franchise. He asked if this was final and if he could count on our word, and we said yes, it was, and asked him to start drawing up the papers."[19]

Indiana's Dick Tinkham and Mike Storen, apoplectic over the bonus check omission, tried to call Alcindor. No answer. He was out taping an interview with Chip Cipolla of New York's WNEW radio station to announce his decision. The NBA had hand-fed the story to Cipolla, an NBA favorite,[20] to lock in Alcindor to his decision.

"Guys went to the airport [later on Tuesday night] and found Alcindor and were telling him about the $1 million check and saying, 'Let's talk again, we'll raise the offer,'" said Tinkham. "He just said that he had made a commitment to Milwaukee and that was it."

According to Mikan, Gilbert then made a puzzling request. Fly to Los Angeles on Wednesday, and the ABA could continue its negotiation there. Mikan agreed and brought Tinkham and Storen with him. When the two sides finally met in a hotel suite around 1 a.m. on Thursday morning, Tinkham handed a mink coat to Alcindor for his ailing mother and finally presented the million-dollar bonus check. If you believed in the Dolgoff plan, the ABA's offer now spiked to $3.5 million, or more than double the NBA's offer.

"Gilbert kept repeating, 'Is that all? Is that all,' Is that all?" said Tinkham. "I'm thinking, 'Wait a minute. You're talking about a million dollars and a mink coat. You're acting like it's nothing.' Then Gilbert announces, 'I have to go make a phone call.'"

Tinkham and the others weren't sure whom Gilbert had to call at this wee hour of the morning, but they could guess. At the top of the list was Sam Schulman, who had befriended Gilbert and helped send him off to New York. Another possibility was Jack Kent Cooke, one of the ringleaders of the NBA money pool.

"Gilbert leaves the room for, I want to say, five minutes, comes back, and says, 'Milwaukee has topped the offer,'" Tinkham continued. "It was as though he already had his mind made up. We never had a chance."[21]

That was by design. Call it stage management. Gilbert had invited the ABA contingent to Los Angeles to keep them under wraps until Friday. Why Friday? Jack Kent Cooke had scheduled a press conference to announce the NBA's good fortune in grand style at halftime of a Los Angeles Lakers playoff game.[22] That's also when Cipolla had agreed to air his interview with Alcindor in New York and send out his nationally syndicated story.

"My decision was based mainly on the fact that it was the best situation for me financially," Alcindor told Cipolla over the airwaves. "It would have been a lot easier playing in New York, all things being the same. But, as it was, things were not the same."

"How could he say that?" an indignant Brown said after hearing the interview. "I know how much I offered. I have the figures right in front of me. Nobody in the NBA has even hinted that their offer is as big as ours."[23]

Brown was angry but certainly not shocked. In anticipation of losing the Alcindor sweepstakes, Brown had begun a few weeks ago to cut his pro basketball losses. He had secretly offered a 50 percent ownership stake in the Nets to a consortium of investors, headed by Roy Boe, a Long Island businessman. Boe countered that his group wanted full ownership of the Nets. Brown told his lawyer Leon Rock to draw up the papers.

Brown's decision to sell, however, was based on the realization that the Nets, as envisioned three years ago, would never conquer Manhattan. Indeed, Manhattan already had conquered the Nets. The NBA and their powerful Madison Square Garden business partners had successfully thwarted Brown from gaining even a toehold there.

"Arthur Brown had been committed to the ABA for the long haul," said Rock, meaning Brown believed the Nets would become profitable over time. "But we soon realized that for the ABA to have any chance of succeeding in New York, the Nets needed an owner who had the right contacts. Roy Boe was friendly with the owners of the Knicks and the [NHL] New York Rangers. That's why he sold the team to Boe."[24]

As Brown prepared to exit the pro basketball fray, he could claim one small moral victory. He may have lost Alcindor, but this time the NBA and those skulking figures behind the scenes had left a fingerprint.

Dick Tinkham, two days removed from lugging around a mink coat and a million-dollar check, had flown to San Francisco to serve as co-counsel in the *American Basketball Association et al. vs. the National Basketball Association et al.* in United States District Court. The Honorable Alfonso Zirpoli presiding. The case marked the first interleague antitrust suit in the history of American professional basketball, alleging that the NBA monopolized the marketplace and illegally limited competition. It also followed in the failed footsteps of the *American Football League vs. National Football League* (1962).[25]

Seated near Tinkham was the flamboyant Fred Furth, an old classmate at the University of Michigan School of Law. Across from them sat lawyers from the white-shoe New York law firm of Proskauer, Rose, Goetz, and Mendelsohn. The firm considered the NBA such a minor account that lead attorney George Gallantz viewed the case as a low-profile, low-risk training ground for the firm's latest law-school hires to learn the fine art of taking depositions.[26]

"The NBA lawyers were acting like, 'Okay, let's get this thing over with,'" said Tinkham. "They assumed the lawsuit was frivolous, and Judge Zirpoli would throw it out. They had flights to catch back to New York."

"When Fred presented his opening statement, he mentioned the note," Tinkham continued. "I looked over at the NBA lawyers. Their jaws had dropped."[27]

The note belonged to Boston's Red Auerbach. It was a one-page handwritten note that documented the NBA's pooling of funds to sign Alcindor. It seems that Auerbach headed the NBA's latest passing of the hat, and the note—the fingerprint and irrefutable proof of NBA collusion—had fallen into Furth's possession through sheer luck. His legal team had asked all 14 NBA franchises to provide some operational information, and Auerbach farmed out the request to Mike Burns, the bright college kid in the Celtics' front office whom he loved to haze. Burns scooped up the documents, including the one-page note, and blithely sent them to Furth.[28]

Burns' blunder enabled Furth to take what appeared to be a wildly circumstantial case and anchor it to a documentable act of collusion. What's more, he had named names, fingering Auerbach as the head of the NBA's patently illegal cabal. As the complaint alleged, the now so-called "Auerbach Committee" had among other things:

- Caused some of all of defendants [NBA teams] to enter into an agreement providing for the pooling of their economic power to bid on new players, including super stars, against individual member plaintiffs [ABA teams];
- Directed the exchange and trading of players between member defendants and other means of compensation between member defendants for such pooling of money;
- Agreed after the National Collegiate Athletic Association tournament on March 22, 1969 to jointly pursue a super star through the use of the defendants' combined economic power;
- Approached potential players with offers and potential offers of employment on a league basis rather than on a team basis.

Reporters asked Furth afterwards if Alcindor was the superstar mentioned in the complaint.

"I think that's a logical conclusion."[29]

Furth also snapped off the other elements of the case, and among the nine charges, four likely concerned Gallantz and his brilliant legal mind. The first alleged the NBA paid off the agents of the nation's best collegiate players to deliver their clients to the senior league. A second charge accused the NBA of directly paying off college players while they remained in school. While Furth lacked hard evidence on both counts, his ABA colleagues were confident a little digging here and a few subpoenas there might confirm their suspicions. Subpoenas soon would be served on Sam Gilbert and John Dromo, the college coach of Wes Unseld.

The third allegation claimed the NBA "warned, coerced and advised" its veteran players that joining the ABA would blacklist them permanently from employment in the NBA. Some ABA coaches knew this to be true from private conversations with NBA players, but they had yet to find one who would go public with the charge. None wanted to risk a blackball, given the ABA's uncertain future.

Finally, the lawsuit alleged the NBA had developed illegal contractual means to prohibit its players "from ever being free to move from the NBA to the ABA." To prove it, Furth took aim at the NBA's option clause that bound NBA players to their teams for one additional season after their contract had expired. Or, more to the point, it allowed the owners to control player movement like puppets on strings.

"The whole thing is ridiculous," Auerbach fired back. "I haven't been to the last three league meetings," ergo, he couldn't have headed a secret NBA committee.[30]

Auerbach and his NBA cohorts dismissed the lawsuit to reporters as the pro basketball equivalent of ambulance chasing. Others characterized the case as the final desperate act of a mortally wounded league. "To quote Shakespeare: 'The cup of hemlock is a bitter drink indeed,'" declared San Francisco owner Franklin Mieuli, anxious to end his own expensive lawsuit against the ABA and reclaim his star, Rick Barry.[31]

The NBA's perception became mainstream reality for two reasons. One, the ABA filed the lawsuit on the very same day as Alcindor announced his record-breaking contract. Alcindor stole the headlines—and the ABA's thunder—once again. Two, NBA reporters had zero inclination to pursue the ABA's allegations. Sportswriters in the 1960s covered teams and their championship runs. Secret committees and the arcane business of sports were out of bounds. Reporters, with a few exceptions, still crossed the line at their professional peril.

But in Judge Zirpoli's courtroom, facts were cold, hard, and utterly revealing. "The NBA was ordered to provide us with all of their records," said Lee Meade, the ABA's publicity director. "We got to see what they were doing, how they were conducting their meetings, and all of their secret arrangements.

We literally ran a Xerox machine out of business reproducing documents to send to other league officials."[32]

According to Meade, the documents revealed that the NBA employed the same self-serving tricks as the ABA. Both held secret college drafts, attempted to sign college players to league contracts, and otherwise colluded to sneak talent into the fold. But, for the NBA, there were two huge differences. One, the NBA had illegally pooled money to sign players. The ABA hadn't—or, at least, hadn't been caught red-handed. Two, as Furth would argue forcefully before Judge Zirpoli, the NBA held a monopoly on the pro basketball market. The upstart ABA didn't.

The NBA filed an obligatory countersuit to challenge the ABA's allegations. The bluff of the countersuit aside, the NBA was in a legal fix. If the lawyers of Proskauer, Rose, Goetz, and Mendelsohn couldn't make it all go away, the NBA had to hope that Franklin Mieuli was right about that cup of hemlock.

As a hectic March eased into April 1969, the NBA's other first-round valedictorians took a collective pass on the ABA—with one celebrated exception: Larry Cannon, La Salle College's star swingman. He went with the off-brand Miami Floridians. Pulling Cannon, a marketable white rabbit, out of its hat, the ABA had landed its first top five NBA draft choice (Cannon was selected fifth by Chicago) and added its second NBA first-round draft choice in three years (Mel Daniels was the first, ninth pick overall).

George Mikan, still blamed by some ABA trustees for botching the Alcindor deal, looked downright giddy at the impromptu signing ceremony in Miami's swishy Hilton Plaza Hotel. He also stepped to the microphone to switch the narrative from the doom and gloom of Alcindor to the happy days are here again of Cannon: "In the signing of Larry Cannon by the Miami Floridians, the ABA has signed its first Joe

Namath," he told reporters, harkening images of the brash, widely known face of the American Football League (AFL).

"When the AFL signed Namath," he continued, "it was the turning point in their short career. Signing a player of the magnitude of Cannon could very well be a turning point. Here is a boy who was very highly thought of around the NBA. We signed him, and by going with our league, he will encourage others to follow."[33]

Larry Cannon . . . the next brash, womanizing, shaving lotion-shilling, tabloid-darling Joe Namath?

Get outta here.

And yet, Mikan was oddly right about "a turning point." It just wouldn't be Cannon encouraging rising college seniors to take the road less traveled. The game changer was the little guy in the dark suit seated next to Cannon with all the wallflower appeal of a potted plant in this room dominated by tall people.

His name was Steve Arnold, a partner in the New York-based Pro Sports Inc. and Cannon's agent. Unlike Sam Gilbert and the other *pro bono* personal advisors, Arnold was a for-pay attorney who had been in the sports biz for several years, first mentioned several chapters earlier as a player publicist and now as a player agent. He'd seen up close and personal that pro teams, in his opinion, systematically gypped players to get ahead. His advice to Cannon was to sell his services to the highest bidder, the source of the treasury notes was irrelevant to Arnold.

Sound financial advice, but Arnold had a dirty little conflict of interest: He already had a deal in mind with the ABA Floridians. It dated back to last winter. While starting to negotiate the rookie contracts for two football Miami Dolphins, Arnold and his partner Marty Blackman also shopped around the city for some business leads. They made a contact in the Floridians' front office, and Arnold followed up with a call offering his professional services to Cannon, the Floridians' top draft pick. "Steve offered an all-expenses-paid weekend in

New York," said Cannon. "Of course, I took him up on it. It was New York."[34]

Cannon was impressed by Arnold, all of his degrees on the wall, and all of his big-name football and baseball clients, past and present. So impressed, in fact, Cannon nixed the offer of Tom Gola, his latest college coach and a former NBA star, to serve as his personal advisor.

That evening, the new face of the Floridians bellied up to the bar and ordered something stiff. His nerves were a mess. Cannon, a rugged, street-smart, tell-it-like-it-is kid from Philly, was raised on Gola, Hal Lear, Guy Rodgers, Wilt Chamberlain, and the lofty dream of playing in the NBA. He'd just deflated that NBA dream for cash.

Cannon, ready for another drink, replayed in his head the fuzzy swirl of events since he'd landed in Miami. The warm, welcoming handshakes from the unfamiliar businessmen, their disarming flattery, climaxing in a hard offer of $250,000 over a couple of seasons, more money than Cannon had seen in his life. "I want to do something special for you," team owner Tom Carney leaned into him. "I'll give you 5 percent of the team. The franchise isn't worth much now—we're losing money—but it will be profitable when the leagues merge."

Then came the hard close. This once-in-a-lifetime offer was good for the rest of the day only. Take it or leave it. Arnold brightened; Cannon disappeared to the nearest phone and dialed Chicago owner Dick Klein. "Look, you don't have to match their offer," he remembered telling Klein, "just tell me you'll get close to it."

"Larry, you should really go home and think about this."

"I don't think you understand. These people are telling me that the money is on the table NOW. If I come back later, it won't be the same deal. I need to make a decision."

Klein had nothing concrete to offer, and Cannon interjected a flustered good-bye. He hung up the phone, drew a deep breath, and announced he would take the ABA money. As Cannon would ponder, Blackman already was in Chicago to negotiate with the Bulls on his behalf. Arnold, if he'd wanted, could have stalled the Floridians. He could have updated Blackman on the ABA offer as classic negotiating leverage to force Klein's hand. But he didn't. Arnold got the deal that he'd wanted and earned kudos from the other ABA owners for delivering a top college prospect who now drowned his anxiety in something 180 proof.

The Cannon signing would prompt the ABA trustees several weeks later to call the game-changing Arnold with their own game-changing offer. "The ABA asked whether I would be its representative in signing players," said Arnold. "At that time, I was kind of tired of the players starting to get all of the advantage. We had done our job with that. So, I turned over the player negotiations to Marty, and I started representing leagues and teams."[35]

Endnotes

[1] This section draws from newspaper accounts in Milwaukee, Phoenix, and New York of the Super Flip.

[2] Terry Bledsoe, "ABA Official Doubtful About Flip for Alcindor," *Milwaukee Journal*, March 21, 1969.

[3] In May 1972, Kenneth Bove & Co. Inc. was in receivership, followed by convictions for fraud against its customers, including baseball's Ed Kranepool and basketball's Walt Frazier and Julius Erving.

[4] Jim Kaplan, "If It's in My Power Piper Will Stay—Says Erickson," *Minneapolis Star*, March 11, 1969.

[5] Tom Briere, "Erickson: No Decision Yet on Pipers' Future," *Minneapolis Tribune*, March 11, 1969.

[6] Stan Isaacs, "Alcindor's Now Playing in the Big Money Game," *Newsday*, March 24, 1969.

[7] Mikan had infamously suggested a few months earlier that Alcindor's pro contract rose to the level of a civil rights issue. Alcindor, he said, could save the jobs of 120 Black ABA players with one stroke of his pen.

[8] Leon Rock, Interview with author, April 2009.

[9] Dick Schramm, Interview with author, March 2010.

[10] Kareem Abdul-Jabbar, Interview with author, October 2009. Jabbar's recollection of "a million dollars," without mentioning a timeframe, matches Brown's account.

[11] No Byline, "Nets View Lew's Decision, Holler Foul," *Newsday*, March 31, 1969.

[12] Terry Pluto, *Loose Balls*, 1990, p. 192. About the junk science. Alcindor wasn't quite as bowled over at becoming an instant millionaire as the data led Tinkham and Storen to believe. Alcindor had been hearing about the big money ahead for several months. For example, NBA player Archie Clark was a close friend and mentor to Alcindor during this period. He advised Alcindor to ask for $2 million!

[13] As lawyer Leon Rock told me, "Brown was committed to do whatever it took to sign Alcindor." According to Rock and others who had worked for Brown, he was always level-headed and possessed uncanny business instincts. He also always pinched pennies and tried to save bucks. After all, he'd grown up poor.

[14] Ironically, Brown have gained financially by handing over the bonus check (pooled from the league trustees). Signing bonuses are treated as investments that must be amortized over the life of the contract. This is not a tax shelter—just a way to smooth the accounting cost over time. In the end, the amount of tax forgiveness is the same. The preferred alternative would have been to claim Alcindor's $1-milliion signing bonus as salary in the current year or possibly over the five years, deducting $200,000 per season. Owners prefer the former because it has a higher discounted present value.

[15] See Pluto, *Loose Balls*, 1990, p. 192-193. Oral histories often show that memory can be selective or limited. The cited pages seem to be a case in point.

[16] Don Fair, "Lew to Get Rough Test—Allen," *Seattle Post-Intelligencer*, July 8, 1969.

[17] See Bob Fowler, "ABA Basketball," *The Sporting News*, April 19, 1969. Fowler writes that after the first Bucks-Alcindor meeting, Erickson "was quoted

as saying, 'The meeting was strictly exploratory. He's [Alcindor] scheduled to meet with the ABA soon and he said if he had anything to discuss, he'd call us.'" Mikan said he had wanted sealed bids—one for each league—but Gilbert refused (See Bob Fowler, "ABA Basketball," *Sporting News*, April 19, 1969).

[18] See Paul Montgomery, "Top N.B.A. Stars Were Subsidized," *New York Times*, March 21, 1976. The arrangement was: The Bucks paid the first $500,000, the pool kicked in the next $300,000, and the Bucks picked up the remainder of Alcindor's salary. See also Peter Vecsey, "NBA Paid Part of Abdul-Jabbar's Salary," *New York Post*, January 28, 2011. The article quotes Ray Patterson, Bucks team president: "We could have never raised the kind of money that would satisfy him [Alcindor]. It's not like we billed other teams for it. We paid a percentage, and the league flowed the remainder through us."

[19] Lew Alcindor, "A Year of Turmoil and Decision," *Sports Illustrated*, November 10, 1969. p. 35.

[20] Cipolla was part of a three-man broadcast team for the NFL New York Giants that included Marty Glickman. Glickman was the radio voice of the New York Knicks and well connected to the team's influential executive vice president Ned Irish. Cipolla, sports director for New York's WNEW radio, previously got the scoop on the Wilt Chamberlain trade to Los Angeles.

[21] Dick Tinkham, Interview with author, October 2011.

[22] Alcindor told the *Los Angeles Herald-Examiner* (March 29. 1969) that the announcement originally was set for the following week, ostensibly to coincide with the NBA draft on April 7. "But," Alcindor said, "the ABA let it be known that I had signed."

[23] Stan Isaacs, "Nets View Lew's Decision, Holler Foul," *Newsday*, March 31, 1969.

[24] Leon Rock, Interview with author, April 2009.

[25] The upstart AFL alleged that the established NFL monopolized the pro football market and purposely expanded into new cities to claim territories and destroy the AFL. The court disagreed. It ruled that the NFL lacked the power to halt the AFL's formation or its operation in any American city. Moreover, expansion is natural to any business. On appeal, the ruling was affirmed.

[26] Howard Ganz, Interview with author, November 2018.

[27] Dick Tinkham, Interview with author, October 2011.

[28] Ibid. Tinkham related the story to me, but he couldn't remember Burns' name. I had to research it over the course of a year. Once I'd found the only person it could be—Burns—Tinkham confirmed that the name was indeed correct.

[29] United Press International, "ABA Files Suit, Cites Monopoly," *Baltimore Sun*, March 29, 1969.

[30] Ibid.

[31] No Byline, "Bucks Get Alcindor; ABA Sues NBA," *San Francisco Chronicle*, March 29, 1969.

[32] Lee Meade, Interview with author, October 2009.

[33] Jim Huber, "Larry 'ABA's First Namath'—Mikan," *Miami News*, April 18, 1969.

[34] Larry Cannon, Interview with author, September 2009.

[35] Steve Arnold, Interview with author, January 2010.

12

One day in early June 1969, Dick Tinkham answered the phone in his Indianapolis law office. The voice on the other end, unfamiliar and brusque, announced, "This is Sam Schulman."

Tinkham paused and thought, "Sam Schulman?"

The owner of the NBA Seattle SuperSonics, with whom Tinkham had never spoken, explained that he would be attending the upcoming NBA Board of Governors meeting in Detroit, and the matter of ABA star Connie Hawkins joining the NBA would be revisited. He needed Tinkham's help.

Under normal circumstances, Tinkham might have told Schulman to get lost. War is war, and fraternizing with the enemy, especially to help the NBA steal one of the ABA's finest, would be treasonous. But, as Tinkham knew, the NBA wasn't stealing Hawkins per se. The Hawk was forcing himself on the NBA, pleading for the Board of Governors to reconsider its decision eight years ago to ban him for life. His alleged crime: Helping New York gamblers to recruit college players and fix basketball games. Hawkins' scrappy lawyers, reportedly spending $36,000 out of their own pockets and logging a collective 10,000 hours on the case, were relentless in chasing down this perceived injustice.[1] They socked the NBA with a federal antitrust lawsuit asking for the then-exorbitant $6 million in damages and, more recently, took their grievance to Life Magazine and its popular court of public opinion.

As Schulman told Tinkham, the NBA's lawyers at Proskauer, Rose, Goetz, and Mendelsohn advised the league to settle with Hawkins rather than risk losing the case. Several influential owners bah-humbugged the legal advice. They scoffed at what they considered Hawkins' ambulance-chaser terms of settlement and harrumphed that the other dozen "lifers" would get the wrong idea and escalate their lawsuits.

Schulman wanted to break the board's stalemate by floating the possibility of some face-saving financial hocus-pocus. Or, tipping his hand, Schulman hoped to find some clever way to delay payment on Hawkins' damages for a few decades, when most of the board members would be long gone. That might ease the immediate pain in everyone's wallets and allow Schulman to line up the votes to shoehorn Hawkins into the NBA. That's where Tinkham entered the picture. It had come to Schulman's attention that the ABA had latched onto some financial hocus-pocus called a Dolgoff Plan. Schulman asked how exactly does a Dolgoff Plan work?

Tinkham hemmed and hawed about being put on the spot. But Tinkham, beneath his flat lawyerly, just-the-facts affect, was a born risk taker. That's why he joined the high-risk ABA in the first place. He decided to answer his NBA foe's question, explaining that everything started with a special brokerage account. It parked a mutual fund with a life insurance policy written in the prospective player's name. Twenty years later, the brokerage account matured and began spitting out payments to the now-retired player but at zero expense to the owner. As Dolgoff explained, time and money work hand in hand. While the money in the account grows, the owner simply pays the player a percentage of the interest and keeps all of the money to himself. What's more, because the owner pays into the brokerage account and legally owns it, he receives a tax break every step of the way.[2]

Brilliant, Schulman replied in so many words, sharing that Hawkins' NBA rights had been assigned to Phoenix, compliments of NBA commissioner Walter Kennedy. "Walter," as Schulman would say with irritation in his voice, was obsessed with upholding league protocol. Order, in Kennedy's strong opinion, dictated that league-worst Phoenix get Hawkins for missing on Alcindor. Nothing against Phoenix. In fact, one of Schulman's tennis partners was the Suns' majority owner, Dick Bloch. What bothered Schulman is the Board of Governors owed him the next available superstar—namely, Hawkins—for helping to steer Alcindor to the NBA. At the Detroit meeting, Schulman planned to formally raise his grievance and bring to a vote the matter of giving Hawkins to Seattle.[3]

Schulman confided to Tinkham that he felt philosophically at odds with the NBA status quo. The league operated like an Indian caste system. All tribute went to the white-haired Brahmin who operated the NBA's most-popular founding franchises (New York, Los Angeles, Boston, and, to some degree, Philadelphia). Bringing up the rear were Schulman and the expansion franchises in Chicago, San Diego, Milwaukee, and Phoenix. The Brahmin viewed them as a mere appendage, a necessary third arm to increase the league's market share and provide expansion fees to soften the bottom lines of primarily the eight top-tier teams. Within this organizational framework, expansion teams were free to run the show in their home markets. But the Old Guard controlled the NBA show and brand nationally. It was their intellectual property and absolute right to bend rules and bylaws as they deemed fit.

Walter Kennedy? Schulman didn't trust him. Kennedy answered to Ned Irish, the old-school president of the Knicks and part of the influential Madison Square Garden group. That brought Schulman back to the ABA and how he felt like a kindred spirit. Schulman had been a part owner of the American Football League's San Diego Chargers and cut his teeth in professional sports as the underdog trying to sabotage the established monopoly. Just as the football leagues merged, Schulman said the same would happen in pro basketball.

Tinkham remembered thinking Schulman wasn't such a bad guy at all. Sure, Schulman openly schemed to steal Hawkins. That was business talking. If the tables were turned, Tinkham almost certainly would do the same.

The two said their goodbyes and let's stay in touches. Schulman flew to Detroit a few days later to explain the Dolgoff Plan. The Brahmin balked, and the board again agreed to disagree on Hawkins. But Schulman got on the meeting agenda and aired his full-throated grievance. His woe-is-me ended in a compromise: another of Kennedy's curious coin flips. Tails it was . . . again, and Phoenix retained Hawkins' rights.[4]

Schulman, profoundly disappointed at all his hard work and no reward, was done kowtowing to the Brahmin. Come what may, he would fight the NBA status quo and build a winning team in Seattle on his own devious, laissez-faire terms, not according to the old-fashioned NBA bylaws. He later called his new ABA friend in Indianapolis with an update on the Detroit board meeting. Through all the four-letter vents about Kennedy, Irish, and that bombastic Jack Kent Cooke, Schulman and Tinkham agreed on a revolutionary idea. The two would continue talking and form their own secret interleague back channel for sharing gossip and strategy. This back channel, like a page out of a 1960s Russian spy novel, would open the first push for an NBA-ABA merger.[5]

Connie Hawkins scooched his 6-foot-8 frame closer to another unfamiliar middle-aged white man in a business suit and said cheese. A flash bulb exploded, and the newest Phoenix Sun moved away seeing a momentary shower of stars and feeling awkward. For Hawkins, feeling awkward was the story of these last few days in mid-June. He'd spent two terribly awkward ones in Los Angeles, where the NBA Board of Governors and their lawyers couldn't agree on his fate. The wrangling lasted at the Beverly Wilshire Hotel this morning until 2 a.m. when the head wrangler, New York's Ned Irish, finally relented. A jubilant Hawkins and his lawyers decided to grab a belated 3 a.m. dinner at the cafeteria in a nearby all-night drug store. En route in the hotel lobby, a bellman called out, "Aren't you Connie Hawkins?"

"How did you know who I am?" the Hawk answered.

"I just had to send out a telegram about you."

"But you didn't see my picture or anything. How did you know?"

"I knew, I knew," the bellhop sing-songed to his tall inquisitor with the gangly basketball physique.[6]

Now, in the light of day, the Hawk had flown 90 minutes east to Phoenix, where he delivered awkward gratitude to his supporters. He stood there like a wrongly convicted felon whose life sentence had been overturned by some shadowy supreme court of pro basketball.

"I still think it's a dream," Hawkins said. "It's kind of hard to believe I'm here now."

The first ABA player to jump to the NBA received a five-year, no-cut contract worth $410,000, which averaged out to $82,000 per annum. He'd earned $30,000 last season in the ABA. With his lawyers now willing to settle the lawsuit for damages in six figures, Hawkins would be made whole with a cash payment of $250,000, half of it paid out over the next five years; $35,000 to cover his legal fees; and, oh yes, a $600,000 Dolgoff Plan.[7] The NBA would fund the annuity with an annual payment of $16,861 ($1,347 for each of the 14 franchises), and Hawkins would start collecting on it at age 45.

Worried about the optics in Phoenix, Walter Kennedy released a bland, nothing-to-see-here statement blessed by his lawyers. Kennedy contended that he'd never closed his 1961 investigation of Hawkins, who had been banned out of an abundance of caution. Now that Hawkins finally had answered four key unresolved questions under oath, Kennedy could wrap up his investigation, and the Board of Governors could be satisfied of his moral fitness. Greater sanctimony to support a faulty premise the pro game had rarely seen.

In Minneapolis, ABA czar George Mikan played catchup. So did his pal Bill Erickson, still technically the owner of the Minnesota Pipers. "I'm sorry, we can give no statement," Erickson's beleaguered secretary answered the flood of press calls. "What can we state? He's gone." Mikan eventually sent a perfunctory telegram to Hawkins stating that the ABA would match any NBA offer. But like the late-arriving Alcindor bonus check a few months earlier, Mikan delivered the goods 13 hours too late.

In truth, there really wasn't much for Mikan to add to prevent Hawkins' exit. The ABA would survive without him. The Minnesota Pipers? That was a different question. Hawkins had been the franchise's prime selling point, an utterly unique basketball talent and New York playground God. Without Hawkins, the Pipers were a shell of a basketball investment for the next buyer, and this financial fact now roiled the thoughts and stomach of Bill Erickson. The Pipers at last count had lost $572,00 in Minneapolis (though Erickson wrote off $200,000 in depreciated player salaries).

Erickson could only blame himself—and Hawkins' lawyers—for the latest turn of events. Last season, Hawkins had been a no-show for the start of training camp, blaming the absence on his paltry contract. But rather than woo Hawkins into camp and a long-term, good-for-the-ABA deal, Erickson took the gracious way out. He agreed to void Hawkins' two-year ABA contract, at the lawyers' request, clearing the way for the Hawk last season to legally fulfill his option year and become a free agent. That's why the ABA couldn't sue him for breach of contract. "I was told playing without a contract would help Hawkins in his lawsuit against the NBA," explained Erickson. The idea being, if no NBA teams signed Hawkins as a free agent, it would demonstrate to the courts that he'd been blackballed by the NBA.

Erickson also claimed he had a handshake agreement with Hawkins that, after establishing the blackball and its antitrust implications, he would re-sign with the Pipers to show his gratitude. "I've been conned before, and I'll be conned again," Erickson concluded.[8]

Erickson also may have lamented his other handshake agreement and now seven-month ordeal to sell the Pipers to Mark Binstein. Internal league squabbling had nixed Binstein's best-laid plans to move the franchise to Jersey City. The Nets' Arthur Brown—and now Roy Boe—didn't want the competition. Pittsburgh, ironically Hawkins' adopted home city, was the latest proposed destination for the Pipers. The all-important Securities and Exchange Commission (SEC) continued to drag its bureaucratic feet on Binstein's questionable request to take the team public. Without this cashflow, Binstein couldn't afford to close on the Pipers' and their $1.2 million asking price. Binstein kept saying the SEC would release the stock prospectus any week now. Erickson wasn't holding his breath.

Sam Goldaper grumbled through the revolving doors of the Hotel Lombardy on Park Avenue in Midtown Manhattan.[9] Why in the world, he wondered, would his editor at the *New York Times* send him to cover day two of the ABA's Board of Trustees meeting in the dog days of July? There would be nothing to report. All of the news had come yesterday when the ABA's skittish owners fired George Mikan as commissioner for a perceived failure to lead. "Give me three years, and I'll give you a league," Mikan had famously vowed when he was hired. Two years, five months, and 12 days later, Mikan was finished.

And so too, assumed Goldaper, was the embattled ABA. The ABA had swung and missed on a network television contract to market its product nationally, whiffed with Lew Alcindor, and fouled out with Connie Hawkins. Even Rick

Barry had made whispers about returning to the NBA. What remained viable? Maybe the Indiana Pacers.

As Goldaper, a pudgy man in his late 40s, sauntered into the ABA's makeshift hotel press room, the league's publicity director Lee Meade stuck out his right hand in welcome. He knew the *New York Times* had mostly yawned at the ABA since its inception, reportedly with encouragement from NBA officials. The sight of a reporter from the nation's leading newspaper, even if it was the crusty Goldaper, was like manna from publicity heaven.

"I don't imagine much is going to happen today," Goldaper grumped.

"Sam, what do you want?" said Meade. "What would be your ideal story?"

Goldpaper thought for a moment. "Get somebody to say the ABA has been fooling around long enough with the NBA," he instructed in his blunt Brooklyn brogue. "Get them to say the ABA plans to start a bidding war next season for [college stars] Pete Maravich, Bob Lanier, and Rick Mount. And have them say that the ABA is willing to spend whatever it takes to sign them."

Meade told Goldaper to wait a minute, shuffling off to find the closest-available team owner. "Could you help me out?" Meade pleaded with an owner, telling him to fib that the ABA had just declared war on the NBA in the Hotel Lombardy.

The next morning, tucked away in the *New York Times* sports section, Goldaper announced the ABA "was here to stay," and Maravich, Lanier, and Mount were locked into its seven-figure crosshairs.[10] Though the story was concocted and not at all news fit to print, Goldaper's positive spin was indeed manna from heaven for the beleaguered ABA. The article recast the ABA from a 98-pound weakling on a deathwatch to a sinister force. Moreover, because the cooked-up story ran in a respected newspaper read by the sports editors of newswires and smaller East Coast broadsheets, Goldaper's narrative rippled across the country as an irrefutable new twist on the ABA's presumed demise.

Ironically, the ABA already had issued a post-Alcindor declaration of war back on May 21. The *New York Times* and its rivals simply hadn't covered it at the time. That day, the ABA had circled the wagons during a two-day league meeting at Minneapolis' Leamington Hotel and hammered out the broad outlines of its counterattack.[11] It boiled down to this:

Point One: The ABA was indeed here to stay for another season or two. The league had solidified itself with the arrival of well-heeled ownership groups headed by millionaires Roy Boe in New York and Jim Gardner in North Carolina. The ABA also was close to locking in Al Davis, commissioner of the American Football League (AFL). Davis wanted to purchase the struggling ABA champion Oakland Oaks for $400,000 and relocate the team to Portland. The ABA owners unanimously approved his offer and prepared to name Davis to the league's executive committee. Davis just had to write the first check.

Point Two: Collusion is a must. Even as they sued the NBA for collusion and otherwise playing unfairly, the ABA owners passed unanimously a hushed resolution to pool their money to sign future high-profile All Americans. The Leamington resolution would create a college draft fund with an annual $50,000 credit line open to each franchise as needed to sign "an ABA or NBA" first-round draft choice in 1969 and 1970. All teams would contribute equally to build the draft fund; but none would be on the hook to repay borrowed money. "Be it further resolved," the statement concluded, "that this fund when received by the Commissioner be kept separate from other Association funds and that this fund only be used for the purpose herein set forth."

Point Three: A new president, or lead owner, was needed. Their choice was the new millionaire in the boardroom, Jim Gardner. Ironically, chance, not ambition, landed the presidency for the 36-year-old politician. "Roy Boe called me after the meeting," recalled Gardner. "He said, 'You were the only owner not there, so we elected you league president.' I said, 'You're kidding, right?'"[12]

Now, in the wake of Mikan's firing yesterday at the Hotel Lombardy, President Gardner gained the temporary title of acting commissioner. Gardner brought a tougher, go-for-broke politics to the ABA that he'd honed as a one-term North Carolina congressman (1967-1969) and conservative Goldwater Republican in a Democrat-dominated state. Gardner was a suave politician, "smooth as glass," some said, but always looking for a fight.

Gardner applied the same smooth, fixin'-for-the-good-fight optimism to pro basketball. But with a major twist. Gardner admired ABA owner-in-waiting Al Davis for his attention-grabbing, bad-boy behavior as AFL commissioner. Gardner subscribed to the popular, sports-magazine narrative that Davis was the brains behind the recent pro football merger. It was Davis' gutsy decision to raid the enemy of two of its most popular veteran quarterbacks that prompted the NFL to wave a preemptive white flag and surrender to the demands of the AFL.

Unbeknownst to Gardner and most of America, the story was at best a half truth. The AFL-NFL merger talks, kept top secret from the press, commenced at least six weeks prior to the signing of the quarterbacks and were orchestrated by the AFL's more moderate leadership wing. Davis wasn't even at the negotiation table. In fact, he opposed the merger on the grounds that the price was too steep. The press, unaware of the larger story, inaccurately gave gobs of credit to Davis where maybe only a dollop was due.[13]

"Nobody in the AFL listened to Al Davis," Gardner thumped to reporters. "But he set up the pattern that we're going to follow." That left Gardner and the ABA to close out the summer of 1969 embracing a popular myth and promising to shake up the status quo. It would be Operation Kingfish times 10.

Acting Commissioner Gardner called an emergency meeting in late July to prepare for the coming season. Although the ABA had relocated its headquarters to Manhattan last month, suitable office space had yet to be found. In another of life's stranger-than-fiction moments, the only viable office space available in all of Manhattan was in the same building as the NBA headquarters. The ABA passed. Lee Meade, the ABA's public relations man turned urban pioneer, temporarily ran the ABA front office out of a rented house in the Long Island suburb of Rye. He didn't have enough chairs at the house to host Gardner's emergency meeting.[14]

Dipping into league funds, Meade booked a conference room with plenty of chairs at the Hotel Lombardy and plied it with a pot of coffee, breakfast rolls, and potted plants, just like these wealthy businessmen expected. Gardner introduced New York-based lawyer and agent Steve Arnold as the ABA's newly created director of player personnel. His official title aside, Arnold would operate as the ABA's agent at large. His job: Travel the country to locate and, if possible, sign promising college prospects for the ABA, preferably prior to the pro basketball drafts in the spring. If Arnold succeeded in signing a prospect to a league contract prior to the ABA's college draft, he would meet with the owners, share the good news, and hand over the signed contract to the first team that agreed to pay the player's negotiated salary.

As the ABA's agent, Arnold also carried a secret weapon in his back pocket. It was the Dolgoff Plan. Although Schulman had settled the Connie Hawkins case with deferred Dolgoff payments, Walter Kennedy and the NBA establishment continued to distrust the plan as falling somewhere between too good to be true and illegal. The NBA's mental block on all things Dolgoff meant Arnold and the ABA owners could negotiate with money that it didn't have (at least for now). In the NBA, the money on the table remained mostly real.

Gardner then proceeded to the meeting's top-secret agenda item: a one-round college draft. It would give Arnold and each ABA team a full nine months to work on signing next season's All Americans.

To get the draft rolling, Gardner selected Pete Maravich of LSU. A few more choices came, and Don Ringsby, the 30-year-old son of the Denver owner, was on the clock. "I remember I passed Denver's first turn around the table and postponed my pick to the following day. I went back to my hotel," said Ringsby. ". . . and called John McLendon, who was our coach at the time. I asked him, 'If you could draft any player in the country, who would you take?' He said, 'Spencer Haywood,'" mentioning he had Colorado roots. Sort of. Though a Mississippi native via Detroit, the 6-foot-9, freakishly athletic Haywood had starred two seasons ago at a junior college in the small Colorado city of Trinidad, about a three-hour drive south of Denver.

McLendon, a rare Black basketball coach on the national scene, mentioned to Ringsby that to reach "Wood," Denver would need to work through Will Robinson, Haywood's high school coach and legal guardian in Detroit. But that wouldn't be a problem. McLendon, formerly the chief scout for the 1968 U.S. Olympic basketball team, had been instrumental in getting Robinson's prodigy a tryout and launching his gold-medal acclaim. "We knew he was about to begin his second season at Detroit University [sic]," said Ringsby. "But we knew he'd prepped at Trinidad Junior College in Colorado, so we figured he had three seasons behind him."[15]

But Ringsby, admittedly not a huge basketball buff, had blundered. Haywood played only one season at Trinidad, making him a rising junior at Detroit and strictly off limits to the pros. Then again, maybe not. Arnold had been floating a truly revolutionary idea to break the NBA's lock on the best college talent. "I went to the ABA and said, 'Do you want to compete with the NBA?'" recalled Arnold. "Well, you've got to put in a hardship rule and sign the top young underclassmen."[16] The term "hardship" referred to underclass phenoms who would benefit immediately from a lucrative pro contract to lift their families out of poverty.

As Arnold explained, the hardship rule would give the ABA a one-and-two-year head start to flash gobs of head-turning Dolgoff money at the phenoms before the NBA publicly could join the bidding. The NBA long had followed its four-year rule, which mandated that all prospective players must complete four years of college before turning pro, unless they are willing to sit out a full season. This so-called Reggie Harding rule, named after the troubled seven-footer, provided a loophole for the NBA to sign players who academically weren't college material. It was a loophole that remained mostly NBA taboo.

The ABA owners balked at first, fearing the condemnation of the four-year colleges. But Arnold countered idealistically that if an MIT undergrad received a six-figure offer from a Fortune 500 company, he or she is not legally bound to graduate from college to accept the job. Why should promising young basketball players have to wait around?

"Are the NCAA rules legal," Arnold remembered telling his ABA colleagues. "Will they hold up in a court of law? What we are talking about here is equal opportunity. A kid plays basketball and wants to make some money and support himself and his family. That's illegal? We're not talking wholesale signings, just the select few we know can come into the league and make it at a younger age."[17]

The hardship tag fit Haywood like a seersucker suit. Back in Mississippi, his immediate family scraped by picking cotton for $2 a day. Hardship also fit Haywood's college life. After Trinidad, Haywood was supposed to attend the University of New Mexico, where Robinson had placed his former prep stars Mel Daniels and Ira Harge, both now in the ABA. But before

Haywood could become a Lobo, Robinson applied for head men's basketball coach at the University of Detroit. While interviewing for the position, Robinson promised to deliver Haywood and a national championship within two years. Detroit accepted Robinson's offer of Haywood—then hired a white coach. But not just any white coach. Detroit hired Jim Harding, the infamous college coach with tyrannical leanings who, during his brief ABA career last season, assaulted Minnesota owner Gabe Rubin at the ABA all-star game.

Haywood and Harding were a cultural match made in hell. "It was hate at first sight," Haywood said.[18] He wanted out, and Robinson, no fan of Detroit's double-dealing athletic department, was ready to move him elsewhere. But where? Some European teams floated a few numbers and scenarios. Not interested. The Harlem Globetrotters inquired. Not interested. And so did a shadowy go-between for the NBA's Cincinnati Royals. "He said Cincinnati wasn't in a position to play Spencer right away," said Robinson, "but they could pay him right away, sign him to a contract, get the rights to him, and use him as soon as he was eligible." He just had to sign a personal services contract with the Royals owner, then sit out two seasons in deference to the four-year rule. Not interested.[19]

Now, back at the Hotel Lombardy, another option was growing legs. Ringsby considered Arnold's spiel about hardship and the American way. If Arnold and his ABA colleagues had the guts to scrap the four-year rule, so would he. The next day, Ringsby went for the gusto. He selected Spencer Haywood, University of Detroit.

By early August 1969, chatter had picked up on the NBA-ABA back channel. Seattle's Sam Schulman, feeling bold and maybe devious, told his ABA friends to get ready for the NBA Board of Governors meeting on Aug. 6 in New York. He and Phoenix's Dick Bloch would force the merger onto the agenda on the final day and as the league's final item of business. Assuming they could convince Ned Irish, Jack Kent Cooke, and the NBA Old Guard to lay down their pride, Schulman advised Tinkham to have a small, but representative, ABA contingent on call in New York to launch merger talks.

On Aug. 8, Tinkham got the call. Schulman said the NBA owners had voted 13-1 to meet with the ABA. But he advised Tinkham not to be misled by the landslide vote. The owners still rolled their eyes at the ABA and doubted its long-term prospects. But they were willing to talk about a merger, in theory, to determine if there was anything worth pursuing.

By late afternoon, the two sides assembled at the negotiation table in New York's Waldorf Towers on Park Avenue. Representing the NBA on its new merger committee were Schulman and Irish. On the ABA side was Jim Gardner; Roy Boe, New York's new majority owner; and Joe Geary, a young lawyer and a minority owner of the Dallas Chaparrals. Alongside them sat NBA commissioner Walter Kennedy, the pinstriped lawyers from Proskauer, Rose, Goetz, and Mendelsohn, and Tinkham.

A few hours later, under the advisement of their lawyers, the leagues issued a perfunctory joint press statement to confirm the meeting and announce their interest in exploring the possibility of "cooperative arrangements," which translated to the following:

- The leagues should consider holding a joint college draft. Per Goldaper's article, the NBA didn't want to break the bank next year on the trio of Pete Maravich, Rick Mount, and Bob Lanier.

- The NBA had reservations about absorbing all 11 ABA teams through a merger. However, before a final number could be agreed upon, the ABA's Los Angeles and Oakland franchises must vacate established NBA territories and relocate to other viable markets for the merger to proceed.

The NBA's suggestion was to move the teams to Houston and Portland, Ore.

- Each ABA team would pay a $1.2 million indemnity fee to join the NBA. From the NBA's perspective, the charge was more than fair. Milwaukee and Phoenix, the most recent NBA expansion teams, had paid $1.5 million to join the league.

Although the session ended amicably the next day, the numbers didn't add up for the ABA owners. On top of the $1.2 million indemnity, the ABA teams would pocket no revenue from the NBA's network television contract for their first three years in the league. The lost revenue pushed the actual indemnity to an estimated $3 million per team.

While the prospective owners of NBA expansion teams might go along with paying this final tribute, the ABA moguls viewed pro basketball through a narrower ideological lens. Tribute equaled defeat. All had snapped up ABA franchises on the cheap, hoping to force a quick merger and flip their clubs on the open market at higher NBA values. Tack on $3 million to their already six-and-seven-figure losses, and the ABA moguls would end up bleeding money to get their foot in the NBA door. That was asking a lot.

Jim Gardner summoned his fellow owners to New York for another emergency league meeting. The topic: the merger talks. While running through the numbers on the table, Gardner exited the conference room to take an urgent phone call. The lilting voice on the other end belonged to a real-estate lawyer in the Washington, D.C., area named Earl Foreman. Gardner didn't recognize the name, but Foreman said he was a former part owner of the NBA Baltimore Bullets and wanted to get back into pro basketball. He'd heard the ABA champion Oakland Oaks were for sale. Al Davis had withdrawn his offer for business reasons. What if he purchased the Oaks and moved them to Washington, D.C.?

Gardner asked Foreman to join the meeting at 11 a.m. the next morning and make his pitch to the ABA owners. Foreman agreed, and Gardner returned to the conference room with the news. Oaks coach Alex Hannum immediately refused to leave Oakland. He requested his own expansion team to remain in the Bay Area, triggering another verbal boardroom brawl.

Everyone in the room knew things were bleak in Oakland. The team had lost about $2 million in two years. Bank of America demanded an immediate $1.3 million loan repayment from owner Ken Davidson. Everyone also knew that prominent Oakland owner Pat Boone, a devout Christian, seemed to be waiting on divine intervention to save him and the Oaks from the long arm of his creditors.

"Pat Boone kept saying, 'The Lord will provide, the Lord will provide,'" said Gardner. "But he had no plan to save the team from financial ruin when Earl Foreman called me."[20]

Foreman, tall and dapper, arrived the next morning with an unsigned proposal in hand to purchase the Oaks. There was just one hitch. The NBA had been adamant during the merger talks: No ABA teams allowed within a 75-mile radius of any existing NBA franchise. Washington was 35 miles from the NBA Bullets in Baltimore.

Gardner asked Foreman to step outside the conference room while the owners debated the sale and its broader implications. The owners quickly zeroed in on two choices. One, the ABA could make nice with the NBA and allow the champion Oaks to fold. With Oakland vanished, the ABA would have vacated an NBA territory (San Francisco) and likely would be forced legally to return Rick Barry, the Oaks' star and the ABA's only nationally known superstar, back to the senior league. According to the NBA, both were good-faith prerequisites for the merger to proceed.

Two, the ABA could remain on the attack. They could hand the team to Foreman, let him set up shop in Washington, and use the territorial issue as a bargaining chip to force the merger on more equitable terms.

After several hours of flipping and flopping, Gardner and his colleagues unanimously voted around 5 p.m. to hell with pacifying the NBA. Hit them where it hurts. Attack, attack, and plunder.

"Here I was this big-shot former NBA owner, and I was furious that they had kept me waiting," said Foreman. "But they had to make their decision. Finally, the doors opened, and they said they were going with me. They said I could help them force the merger."[21]

Baltimore Bullets owner Abe Pollin wasn't amused by the news. "As far as I'm concerned, the ABA doesn't exist," Pollin seethed.[22] He and Foreman, though not enemies, certainly weren't friends. Pollin called Walter Kennedy and retracted his vote for the merger. His message to Kennedy: Foreman had to go. The ABA trustees, for now, shrugged at the request. Long live, Al Davis. Attack, attack, and plunder.

Steve Arnold, the new ABA agent, took a few weeks before getting around to the Denver selection, Spencer Haywood. He contacted Will Robinson in Detroit, dropped John McLendon's name, and delivered his spiel: Robinson's former players Mel Daniels and Ira Harge were thriving in the ABA. Why not give the same opportunity to the 20-year-old Haywood? Arnold said he could arrange for Haywood to play pro basketball in Denver under the trusted McLendon next season.

Next season? Arnold explained the ABA's new hardship policy. If Haywood was ready to make history as the ABA's first hardship case, Denver was ready, willing, and able to make him a wealthy young man.

Robinson relayed the message to Haywood, who on his own volition called Denver and told Don Ringsby, "I'm tired of playing basketball for free. I've got a mother and family who need things right now."[23]

Haywood then flew to Denver with his guardian Robinson to discuss playing for pay. On Aug. 21, after pulling an all-nighter in Ringsby's office surrounded by lawyers and agent Arnold, Haywood "went hardship" and signed a pro contract.[24] It was a good, though not great, three-year deal with an annual base salary of $51,800 and a Dolgoff Plan that, starting at age 40, would pay him $15,000 per year for 20 years. Total lifetime value: $450,000. The deal also came with a temporary string attached. Silence. Ringsby needed to keep this hardship thing quiet for a few days while he sought final approval from the league.

Ringsby phoned McLendon in New York, where he was attending a two-day ABA meeting. He wanted his coach to meet privately with the league's leadership, including Arnold, to ensure the legality of the contract and the league's new hardship rule. Gardner slipped into Al Davis mode. Forget the NBA. Permission granted.

Not only would a hardship rule help the ABA corral talent in the short-term, it hit the NBA right where it hurt. For the past 20 years, the NBA had viewed the NCAA as a no-cost friend with extreme benefits. "We've got a built-in farm system in the colleges," explained Boston general manager Red Auerbach, "and most of the guys we bring in are already heroes because of the Olympics or the national recognition they've received." This built-in farm system was free to the NBA. Compare that to major league baseball and its labyrinthine minor-league system. The Baltimore Orioles, for example, operated seven minor-league affiliates, from Virginia to California. A recent study showed the Orioles had spent a total of $11.6 million (today, roughly $100 million) over the past 13 years signing, training, and working 1,305 prospects through its minor-league system.

The ABA's public exposure of the four-year rule for what it was—illegal—would force the NBA's hand. The league would have to adopt its own hardship policy to keep up with the ABA, and that would greatly weaken college basketball and progressively weaken its hero-making promotional machinery. In 1969, sabotaging the NCAA machine was as unfathomable to NBA executives as banning the jump shot.

McClendon called back Ringsby a short time later with the good news: Haywood was theirs. Ringsby asked his coach to fly to Detroit and accompany Haywood and Robinson back to Denver. They had a news conference to schedule.

The summer of 1969 would be remembered for astronaut Neil Armstrong uttering, "That's one small step for a man, and one giant leap for mankind," while walking on the moon. Haywood's premature entry into the pros surely paled in historical comparison. But within the wide world of sports, it would truly be one small step for labor rights, and one giant leap for the ABA.

On Aug. 23, the Ringsbys announced publicly Spencer Haywood was now a Denver Rocket. Newspapers across the country featured a jarring image snapped during the press conference of the well-tailored Haywood standing proudly while palming a red, white, and blue ABA basketball and holding it aloft. He towered over the two adults beside him. It was raw Black Power and pure underaged will on display. Jaws dropped at the photo, and the status quo chafed. "The decision [to sign Haywood] shattered a quarter century of peace between college and professional basketball," a Chicago newsman snapped, "and confirmed many in the belief that the new professional league has the morals of an alley cat."[25]

Or the courage of a lion to roam beyond the era's ethical barriers. "It's all I could do to keep it to myself," beamed Rockets coach John McClendon, holding up a yellow legal sheet of paper shortly after the Saturday afternoon press conference in Denver. McClendon was referring to his mum-is-the-word attendance at the ABA's two-day meeting in New York. While Foreman and the Oakland Oaks dominated the session, McClendon was asked to jot down Denver's proposed roster for next season. At the very bottom of the yellow sheet of paper, he had written the name Recneps—or, Spencer spelled backwards.

"I was going to tell anyone that asked that he was a new Polish center that I picked up," McClendon laughed.[26]

Haywood was actually the ABA's preliminary assault on the four-year rule. A mere hors d'oeuvre. "This has never been reported," said Gardner. "Right after Haywood signed, I met in New York with the lawyers of Pete Maravich. I remember the lawyers were from Pittsburgh. We shook hands on an agreement for Pete to sign with the Carolina Cougars before his senior season at LSU. I flew home to prepare to make the announcement, and the next day the lawyers called to say that Pete had changed his mind."[27]

The day after the Haywood shocker came more ABA plunder. Billy Cunningham, the face of the NBA Philadelphia 76ers, announced to a gaggle of reporters in Greensboro, N.C., that he was joining Jim Gardner's Carolina Cougars. "It was a big decision which my wife and I made," he answered in his slow, thick New York accent. "We weighed the pros and cons and decided it would be better if I played in Carolina. I want to spend the rest of my life here."

Cunningham had signed a three-year, $330,000 contract to join the Cougars. Although much of that figure would come from a 20-year Dolgoff Plan, Cunningham reportedly would receive a handsome $125,000 signing bonus plus ownership stakes in five franchises in Gardner's brand-new Lob-Steer restaurant chain.

As flashbulbs popped, a reporter asked Gardner to comment on the status of the merger in light of today's raid.

"There are still some problems involved in working out the merger," Gardner admitted. "There's the Los Angeles problem, the Baltimore-Washington problem, the Connie Hawkins problem, and Cunningham. But I believe all contracts will be honored effective the date of the merger."

Gardner then turned the answer back in a more scripted direction. "This is a major step in our three-year plan to develop a world championship team," he said of his Carolina Cougars. "First, we signed Bones McKinney as our coach. Now, we've added a superstar. Merger or no, we will have a good team."

"I might say," he added, "that we [the ABA] have been approached by approximately 20 NBA players. Until we sign a merger agreement, we're going to do everything we can to strengthen our league. And the longer they wait, the more we'll do to strengthen our league."

Then, Gardner unleashed a stunning prediction. "I think there's a good chance of a merger between the American and National Basketball Associations within two weeks."[28]

"That's impossible," Walter Kennedy countered a few hours later during the NBA's hastily arranged press conference in New York to rebut Gardner and announce that the merger talks now were kaput. Kennedy accused the ABA of a "breach of faith" over the past several weeks, including its fanning of rumors that superstars Oscar Robertson, Earl Monroe, John Havlicek, and others were soon to defect plus the wanton attempt by Gardner via his new coach Bones McKinney to hire Red Auerbach as the new ABA commissioner.

In Philadelphia, 76ers' general manager Jack Ramsay played to the cameras to deflate the story and its embarrassing implications. Cunningham couldn't go anywhere, he said, because every NBA player agrees in his playing contract to a reserve clause, not an option year. Ergo, the 76ers owned Cunningham like a coffee mug (or slave) as long as he played basketball or until they traded him—and his reserve rights—

to another NBA team. Only 76ers owner Irv Kosloff had the authority to make the transfer, and he wasn't feeling especially generous toward Gardner and the ABA at the moment.

A reporter asked Ramsay about Rick Barry's successful leap to the ABA. Hadn't a precedent already been set? "Franklin Mieuli GAVE Barry an option, but that is not in the terms of an NBA contract," Ramsay clarified with some basis in fact.[29] The NBA's reserve clause still had never been challenged legally. The 76ers could take as hard a line as their lawyers dared, and the dare varied from team to team.

But Ramsay had only himself—or really, Kosloff—to blame for letting things spiral out of control. Two years ago, while making the NBA equivalent of minimum wage, Cunningham received a contract offer from the ABA New York Freighters (now Nets). Intrigued, Cunningham telephoned former teammate and friend Gerry Ward. Did he know any lawyers? Ward suggested New York general-practice attorney Sheldon Bendit. His credentials? Bendit's son had attended Ward's summer basketball camp. Cunningham made the call, and, through sheer, stupid chance, Bendit became one of the original NBA agents and the lawyer of choice in the 76ers locker room.

Back then, Bendit finagled a decent offer from the Nets and, while driving back to Philadelphia with Cunningham, called Ramsay from the roadside hoping to leverage a healthy counteroffer. Ramsay agreed on the spot to increase Cunningham's $20,00-per-year salary to $50,000 per season. Ramsay said he'd have the contract ready to sign in the morning. Click. But when Bendit arrived several minutes late for the meeting, Ramsay seized the upper hand with Cunningham. He locked the door to his office and wouldn't let Bendit inside. When the door finally opened, Ramsay had talked Cunningham into signing a three-year contract for $40,000 per season, or $10,000 below his earlier offer. Ramsay's plea: All the money went to the team's star Wilt Chamberlain. There was nothing left to pay Cunningham.[30]

With Chamberlain now gone, Cunningham became the front office's chosen one. Last season, not only had Cunningham gotten the ball and posted career-best numbers, he had been the top vote-getter for the 1969 All-Star Game and earned All-NBA first team honors. But the 76ers had made no overtures to give him a raise in keeping with his superstar status. He was locked in at $40,000 per year for another season or as long as Kosloff felt like it.

Cunningham had hoped this summer to renegotiate his contract and get paid like Wilt. In the meantime, Dean Smith, his college coach at the University of North Carolina, had called him on Jim Gardner's behalf about joining the ABA. Cunningham, under Bendit's advisement, floated the ABA threat past Ramsay. He had nothing constructive to offer. "I was very open with them," Ramsay recalled the meeting. "I said that I'd be happy to give him the raise, but our owner [Kosloff] would never go for it. So, they said, 'We're going to see what we can get.' I told them, 'Well, do what you have to do.'"[31]

Ramsay sounded like old Eddie Gottlieb, cigar in mouth, reciting the common-sense economics of the NBA and the nickel-and-dime arena owners that got it off the ground. With the old Philadelphia Warriors as his main source of income, Gottlieb balanced his budget against actual revenue. To do otherwise was to risk losing his shirt.

Ramsay's retelling of the NBA's traditional nickel-and-dime narrative resonated with the sporting public, as sentimentally unquestioned as the good old days of Red Cap porters and the world-champion Minneapolis Lakers. But the narrative was no longer true. The arena owners were mostly gone, replaced by millionaires (including Kosloff) who had other income streams that, in a pinch, could rescue their NBA teams from sagging box-office revenues.

The heart of the NBA's problem was its old-fashioned business model, not its players asking for more. Push aside the tax shelter. Forget the periodic expansion fees that trickled down to established teams to defray their operating costs. What remained? A poorly marketed sport. The proof was in the bottom line. The NBA's reported five-year, $650,000 network television contract with ABC amounted to peanuts compared to the National Football League's $21.4 million annual broadcast boondoggle (local and national television contracts) and major league baseball's $8.8 million per year network television contract.

The merchandising of NBA T-shirts, shoes, and other official gear remained at best a cottage industry. While some owners pushed to expand NBA products across mainstream America, others cynically resisted. A major reason for their it-can't-be-done dismissals was race-based. The NBA had evolved into a predominantly Black league, and the owners remained skeptical that their best-and-brightest Black stars ever could be successfully marketed beyond the basketball court to connect with white popular culture like a Joe Namath or a Mickey Mantle.[32]

Until the NBA figured out how to market Black players to America and break the TV-and-merchandising impasse, gate receipts would remain the major engine of the league's growth with their inherent limitations. Basketball arenas are relatively small compared to football and baseball stadiums, which shrinks potential per-game profits. Neither could they blindly pass their rising costs onto ticketholders. League attendance, though on the rise, remained a promotional work in progress. Teams couldn't appear too greedy at the box-office window. Their customers would revolt.

That's what made the rival ABA such a pain in the NBA's neck during the summer of 1969. The NBA had yet to figure out a way forward, and here the ABA had the nerve to kick sand in their faces. The ABA had ramped up labor costs, stolen key players, raided college campuses, defamed the NBA in court, and otherwise created chaos in a pro basketball market that couldn't afford the turmoil.

"For two years now, the NBA has looked upon the ABA as a minor skin irritation that would dry up and go away," declared Jim Hardy, general manager of the Los Angeles Stars. "Well, now they must realize it's a genuine cancer."[33]

The stewardess announced over the intercom, "Welcome aboard United Airlines Flight 591 with non-stop service from Philadelphia to Washington's National Airport . . ."

Smith Barrier, a long-time sportswriter for the *Greensboro Daily News*, abruptly tuned out the stewardess on his three-o'clock flight when he noticed a large, young Black man lumber onto the plane and into first class just as boarding ended and the doors closed. He had to be an athlete. Shoot, the guy was about seven feet tall and built like NFL lineman Big Daddy Lipscomb. Flying with him was an attractive woman, probably his wife, who balanced a small child and a handbag.

Barrier's inquisitive mind started to race. That had to be Luke Jackson, the starting center for the Philadelphia 76ers. Make that, the Carolina Cougars. One of Barrier's sources in New York just told him that Jim Gardner had struck again. Gardner had a press conference scheduled for tomorrow, September 12, at 2 p.m. in Greensboro to announce that Big Luke had agreed to a three-year, $350,000 contract to join the Carolina Cougars. If true, that brought the ABA's late-summer wave of thefts to nine, which included today's heist of four veteran NBA referees.

Barrier filed away his random thoughts for the moment. Maybe he was mistaken. Maybe the guy was an NFL lineman. The 76ers, after all, had scheduled a dueling press conference to announce that Jackson would re-sign with the club. Maybe the 76ers knew something nobody else knew.

When they landed at Washington's National Airport, Barrier watched to see whether the trio boarded his connecting flight to Greensboro. Sure enough, at the very last minute, man, woman, and child boarded the airplane. Barrier had his confirmation.

"Hey, you're supposed to be in Philadelphia tomorrow for a press conference," Barrier joked after the plane touched down in Greensboro, sticking out his hand to introduce himself.

Jackson grinned like he'd been caught in a fib. "I've been dodging phone calls at the house all day," he said. "I don't guess they [the 76ers] know?"

Barrier nodded yes, explaining that a rumor had leaked out of New York earlier in the day. He asked Jackson what prompted him to leap to the ABA? Was it the money?

"I don't know. I haven't even signed a Carolina Cougar contract yet, going to do that in the morning."

"Did Cunningham talk to you about it?" Barrier continued.

"Oh no, I haven't seen Billy in two weeks," Jackson said as his handlers tried to push him along. Barrier overheard one tell Jackson, "You're checked in at the Albert Pick [Motel, and the site of the press conference]. You're W. B. McGinnis."

The next morning, Barrier answered his phone. It was Jack Ramsay. He had gotten Barrier's number from Bob Vetrone, a former newspaper buddy who now was on the 76ers' payroll as a publicist.

"Do you know where Luke Jackson is?"

"He's in Greensboro."

"You sure?"

"I came down on the plane with him yesterday."

"Where's he staying?"

Barrier sheepishly offered a few possibilities, including the Albert Pick.

Ramsay thanked him and vented, "This comes as a real surprise. What's this business coming to? He never talked with us about this. I've just got to talk to him before he signs anything. Can you find him?"

A few minutes before 2 p.m., Barrier meandered to the podium before the press conference got under way. Jackson, wearing a white suit with an open collar, sat next to Gardner. Barrier shook Jackson's hand and whispered that Ramsay had called. "He was really surprised about you coming down to Greensboro," Barrier said.

Jackson sighed, "I bet he was."[34]

Jackson's vanishing act had been a nightmare for everyone in the 76ers' front office. Ramsay finally had reached Bendit by phone late yesterday and then called Jackson. Big Luke was apologetic and promised to meet with Kosloff when he returned to Philadelphia.

That's also when Kosloff did an about face and opened his checkbook. Around 2 a.m., Kosloff had convinced Jackson to re-sign with the 76ers, Jim Gardner be damned. "Luke Jackson has been our property, never ceased being our property, and he remains our property," his sidekick Ramsay declared afterwards. For his misbehavior, Jackson got a guaranteed three-year, likely $350,000 contract, and a job with the 76ers' front office upon his retirement.

Jim Gardner never sued to reclaim Luke Jackson. Maybe it was for the best. Jackson had yet to fully recover from a severed Achilles tendon, and his left leg, entombed too long in a bulky white plaster cast, had atrophied badly in proportion to his otherwise chiseled physique. Big Luke faced an uncertain NBA road ahead with just one healthy leg to lean on. But he had a big contract, his poetic justice, for all of the nerve-numbing injections that, according to Jackson, put him in this compromised situation.

Gardner didn't call out the hounds and lawyers, in part because his administrative energy was needed elsewhere. The NBA secretly continued to negotiate a merger and, soon after the Jackson incident, NBA Commissioner Walter Kennedy called Gardner and Indiana's Dick Tinkham to make the following top-secret merger offer:

- Ten of 11 ABA clubs were eligible to join the NBA. The odd man out would be Earl Foreman and his territorially troublesome Washington, D.C., franchise. The NBA owners expected their ABA counterparts to buy out Foreman immediately and preclude any future lawsuits.

- The incoming ABA teams must pay a total of $15 million indemnity ($1.5 million per team) to the NBA within 10 years.

- Interleague play would commence with the merger. However, the ABA teams would receive no revenues from the NBA's anticipated new-and-more-lucrative network television contract for five years. Thereafter, each ABA team had the option to pay its $1.5 million indemnity in full and begin receiving its allotted portion of the television revenue.

- A common college draft would be held each year, effective immediately.

- No ABA team would be allowed in Oakland, and Rick Barry must be returned to the NBA's San Francisco Warriors.

The ABA contingent, unimpressed with the numbers and time frames, immediately countered with an offer more to its financial liking:

- Each ABA team would pay no more than a $1 million indemnity to join the NBA.

- Every ABA team would receive $100,000 per season from the network television contract for two years. Thereafter, the NBA and ABA teams would split the revenue 50-50.

- The merger would take place in two years, or at the start of the 1971-1972 season.

- Each ABA club had the option to pay its $1 million entry fee at the start of the 1971-1972 season.

- The "Super Series," pro basketball's equivalent of the Super Bowl, would commence at the end of the 1971-1972 season. In the interim, interleague exhibition games would begin immediately.

- ABA teams would receive the first six choices in their common draft over the next two years.

- The ABA's Los Angeles Stars would receive the rights to move to Portland, Ore., a market that was on the NBA's short list for an expansion franchise.[35]

Kennedy scoffed at the ABA's counteroffer, and Gardner promptly leaked news of the ongoing merger talks to *The Washington Post*.[36] He then blasted Kennedy in the widely read *Sports Illustrated* to smack the NBA yet again, Al Davis-style.

"All that's holding up a merger is Walter Kennedy," Gardner said. "I'll tell you why he's throwing up this smokescreen, yelling about procedures and all. He's hit—and hit hard—that's why. Kennedy is a bigot and a hypocrite. He acts so pious, when the truth of the matter is that the NBA had Lew Alcindor signed, sealed, and delivered long before he graduated. We didn't have a chance in the world at Alcindor. The NBA has done everything it could to kill off the ABA."

Left unsaid was Gardner had met Kennedy in person only once. Their strained relationship was more for public consumption than an honest, seething hatred. Still, Kennedy, more functionary than dictator, wasn't amused by Gardner's negative campaigning to force the NBA's hand.

"You see what we're up against," Kennedy countered. "This is a war in which we can't attack. If we did, what could we gain? There's nobody in the ABA that we want. Gardner is leading a harassment program designed to pressure us into merging cheap, and there's no way he'll succeed. You never know when to believe him. I have a few friends in Washington, and I've made myself familiar with his track record. He keeps running around, insisting there's going to be a merger in two weeks or three weeks. Well, I say there isn't going to be any merger for three or four years—if then."

Gardner: "Next year we will have a shot at 20 top-flight [college] ballplayers and six superstars. We think we can get four of those superstars for one big reason: The NBA couldn't afford them 'cause it's strapped financially. Ned Irish of the Knicks told me he has players making $50,000 to $60,000 sitting on the bench, and he just can't afford a bidding war. Why stay in business, he told me, when players' salaries soak up 110 percent of the gate? On the other hand, our people can afford one year of aggressive bidding—and most of them are willing to do it. Our money will be on the table next spring."

Kennedy: "Before they will consider merging with us, the ABA people say they want the first six choices in next year's draft, plus half of our existing TV contract—out of which they will pay their indemnity [to join the NBA]. Well, those demands are foolish. I repeat: There will be no merger with the ABA in the foreseeable future. And so, for all this stuff about NBA owners being unable to afford a bidding war, that's nonsense. We have always paid top dollar for our talent and will continue to do so."[37]

In late October 1969, Gardner stepped back—and down. He and his fellow ABA owners hired the affable, 41-year-old Jack Dolph to serve as the league's new commissioner. Dolph, a proud Philadelphia native and former director of CBS Sports, arrived with zero experience in running a pro basketball league. No problem. Dolph possessed something far more substantial. He had a viable plan to broadcast ABA games on his former network for a lot of money.

Endnotes

[1] Milton Gross, "Connie Hawkins, Million Dollar Player," *Hackensack Record*, June 24, 1969.

[2] Peter Dolgoff, Interview with author, September 2009.

[3] No NBA team had ever drafted Hawkins to claim his rights. That's why Kennedy could now assign Hawkins to the team of his choice.

[4] Chip Cipolla, the reporter to whom the NBA liked to leak, immediately ran with the "Hawkins to Phoenix" story. Cipolla was sports director at the New York radio station WNEW.

[5] Dick Tinkham, Interview with author, October 2011; the ABA Board of Trustees meeting notes confirm the Schulman-Tinkham back channel.

[6] Gross, *Hackensack Record*, June 24, 1969.

[7] Detroit's Fred Zollner paid for most of the Hawkin's Dolgoff Plan.

[8] Tom Briere, "Pipers Admit 'Con Job' in Hawks' Loss," *Minneapolis Tribune*, June 21, 1969.

[9] Lee Meade, Interview with author, July 2009.

[10] Sam Goldaper, "3 Stars Placed on A,B.A. Wanted List," *New York Times*, July 16, 1969.

[11] Minutes, Annual League Meeting, American Basketball Association, May 21-22, 1969.

[12] Jim Gardner, Interview with author, July 2012.

[13] See Dick Weiss' *The Making of the Super Bowl*. Weiss, an eyewitness to the merger, states, "Undeniably, he [Davis] stirred up lots of anger and accelerated discussions. But serious discussions [of the merger] had begun a good six weeks before he became AFL Commissioner. The trouble Davis triggered was a mere episode in an entire drama written and directed by Tex Schramm, Lamar Hunt, and certainly Pete Rozelle. Davis never participated in a single conversation." [p.37] This might explain Davis' comment in K Rappoport's *The Little League That Could*, "I didn't necessarily want a merger, but they [other owners] wanted it. And they got it." [p.159].

[14] Lee Meade, Interview with author, July 2009.

[15] Bill Libby and Spencer Haywood, *Stand Up for Something*, 1972, p. 188-189; Don Ringsby, Interview with author, April 2013.

[16] Steve Arnold, Interview with author, September 2013.

[17] Terry Pluto, *Loose Balls*, 1990, p. 181.

[18] Spencer Haywood and Scott Ostler, *Spencer Haywood*, 1992, p. 133.

[19] Libby and Haywood, *Stand Up for Something*, p. 66-67.

[20] Jim Gardner, Interview with author, July 2012.

[21] Earl Foreman, Interview with author, November 2011.

[22] No Byline, "NBA-ABA Far Away From Merger," *Philadelphia Daily News*, August 1, 1969.

[23] Ralph Moore, "Spencer Haywood: Mister ABA," *Sports All Stars/1971 Pro Basketball*.

[24] Libby and Haywood, *Stand Up for Something*, p. 67.

[25] Robert Markus, "Stops Along the Sports Trail," *Chicago Tribune*, September 9, 1969.

[26] Irv Moss, "Rockets Sign Olympic Star Haywood," *Denver Post*, August 24, 1969.

[27] Jim Gardner, Interview with author, July 2012.

[28] Larry Keech, "Cage Merger? You Take Your Pick," *Greensboro Daily News*, August 26, 1969.

[29] George Kiseda, "Ramsay Sees Legal Fight Over Billy Cunningham," *Philadelphia Evening Bulletin*, August 25, 1969.

[30] Sheldon Bendit, Interview with author, May 2009.

[31] Jack Ramsay, Interview with author, February 2012.

[32] Michael Burns, Interview with author, October 2012.

[33] Gary Ronberg, "Tossing Bombs Into the Hoops," *Sports Illustrated*, September 22, 1969.

[34] Smith Barrier, "By Smith Barrier," *Greensboro Daily News*, September 13, 1969.

[35] The NBA offer and ABA counteroffer were made on September 9, 1969. Both were recorded by ABA secretary Joseph Geary. He provided the handwritten offer and counteroffer to me.

[36] Mark Asher, "NBA Offers Merger If Caps Fold," *The Washington Post*, September 13, 1969.

[37] Ronberg, *Sports Illustrated*, September 22, 1969.

13

L os Angeles, October 9, 1969—"Good afternoon, and welcome to National Airlines Flight 42 with non-stop service from Los Angeles to Miami . . ."

Larry Shields buckled up for takeoff in first class. Six hours of sipping cocktails and flirting with stewardesses sure beat a day of sweating cost overruns on his latest Southern California housing development. Shields, in his mid-40s, well quaffed and supremely confident, couldn't wait to spend some well-deserved quality time in his newly purchased luxury apartment overlooking Miami Beach.

While there, Shields would check in on his ABA Floridians. Dennis Murphy, his old California buddy who ran the team's day-to-day operations, would prep him on the latest. Murph and ranking minority owner Tom Carney had recruited a wealthy land developer to load up on the team's newly issued public stock. Bob Howard, the land developer and an energetic 50-year-old part-time Miami resident, was just getting started. He planned to make an offer soon to buy out Shields' majority interest in the team.

For Shields, that was great news. it was time to sell. Cut bait. Three years ago, Murph had roped him into buying a franchise at an early ABA organizational meeting. Shields, who didn't know a pick and roll from a pick and shovel, had gone along with it to humor Murph—and reap the promised tax benefits. Little did he realize, the team also would make him an overnight public figure in Minneapolis and now Miami, where Shields, the successful California home builder, hoped to leverage his basketball credentials to cash in on South Florida's building boom. "It reminds me of the Los Angeles area 20 years ago," he said of all the foundations being poured.

Owning a pro team—and managing its death by a thousand invoices—wasn't for everybody. The owners came and went. In fact, Shields was struck recently that few faces remained from those early ABA meetings. Just he and Murph . . . and Gabe Rubin and now Mark Binstein. That's right, last July the Pipers had relocated to Pittsburgh with Rubin now calling the shots. Shields didn't interact much at league meetings with the middle-aged Rubin and his mercurial temperament. But Rubin had agreed to another ABA season for compelling financial reasons. He'd received belated federal approval to sell public stock in the Minnesota franchise as the newly reincorporated Pipers Basketball, Inc. Rubin, now with the controlling interest in the reincorporated team, gambled that he could sell the team before the extra cash from the stock windfall ran out and ate into his own bankroll.

What about Bill Erickson in Minneapolis? Erickson, like his buddy George Mikan, exited quickly a few weeks ago and never looked back. "We were glad it was over," Erickson explained. "It was like having had an affair with Marilyn Monroe. Thank God she's dead, so I can't do it again."[1]

But the post-Mikan ABA, unlike the actress, wasn't dead. Far from it. That's what kept Shields writing checks and heeding Murph's advice. Miami went nuts for the football Dolphins; why couldn't Miami go cuckoo for the Floridians? The Floridians had a near-monopoly on the winter sports market, with no hockey team to parry for publicity or arena dates like in Minneapolis. Through Murph's nutty promotions, public support for pro basketball was inching upward. This season, Shields had a potential superstar to trumpet in rookie Larry Cannon and a solid veteran core around him to chase an ABA championship. Coach Jim Pollard, the future Hall of Famer, was one of the true good guys in sports and a tireless ABA booster. Last season, Pollard made more than 200 personal appearances and was right there this season with Murph selling Miami on Cannon and tri-colored basketballs.

Shields, who had hoped to lose no more than $100,000 when he helped move the team to Miami, already had dropped more than that. But he was willing to go along with Jim Gardner's advice to attack, attack, and plunder. The attacks had continued into the fall with headline-grabbing precision. The Washington Caps (formerly Oakland Oaks) signed young NBA star Dave Bing with great fanfare, though he quickly backed out. In Louisville, the Colonels swiped promising NBA reserve and Kentucky native Tommy Kron.

In Los Angeles, NBA veteran Zelmo Beaty signed two days ago with the Stars. Beaty, following in the footsteps of Rick Barry and Billy Cunningham, became the third NBA all-star to commit to the ABA full stop. His agent? Strange but true— Larry Fleisher, chief counsel for the NBA Players Association. In San Francisco, agent Steve Arnold was out searching for more hardship cases. His fee: $25,000 per player. Also in San Francisco, the ABA had slammed the NBA with its federal antitrust case, and his NBA colleagues continued to squirm about it.

In New York, the new commissioner Jack Dolph promised that within two years the ABA would be live and in color every winter weekend on CBS. Dolph, as the former head of CBS Sports, had inside information that the network would drop the National Hockey League once its contract expired in the spring of 1970. Dolph was now lobbying his CBS colleagues hard to slide the ABA into the NHL's vacant time slot. The financial terms were yet to be determined, but the network money, finally, seemed bundled and a few signatures away from subsidizing the ABA.

On top of it all, the NBA had acquiesced over the summer to discuss a merger. Acquiescence today; acceptance tomorrow. There would be some bumps along the way, but the merger was as certain as this DC-8 now landing in Miami in, oh, about two more hours.

Shields sat back in his cushioned seat at peace with the friendly skies and nursing another cocktail. Then as the DC-8 bumped through the gathering darkness somewhere over Texas, a passenger stood, jabbed a pistol into the ribs of a passing stewardess and blurted out in a thick Spanish accent, "Havana, Havana." The two tangoed to the cockpit door, fumbled for the key, then slammed the door shut behind them. Twenty minutes later, the pilot announced over the intercom that the plane had been hijacked. Shields gulped down his cocktail and prepared for the worst. An hour later, the DC-8 touched down in Havana, and a hard charge of soldiers immediately nabbed the hijacker and hauled him off to God knows where. All passengers were ordered off the plane to answer some questions. "Sort of name, rank, and serial number," Shields described the process.

All 61 passengers were then herded into a large room, served a complementary chicken-and-rice dinner, and, after a four-hour delay, departed for Miami, where upon landing the U.S. authorities did their own name, rank, and serial number. Sometime after midnight, Shields finally fumbled for the key of his Miami Beach apartment. He'd call Murph in the morning and share with him his "you're-not-gonna-believe-this." Hopefully, this wasn't a sign of bad things to come for Miami and the American Basketball Association.[2]

Miami, Oct. 22, 1969—At the far end of the floor near one of the portable basketball goals, right where Larry Shields liked to sit close to the action, a roughly 20-by-20-foot white banner hung from the ceiling like a tapestry. It displayed the artsy outline of a basketball player and the words, "The Miami Floridians." Each word was its own bold row and shout, a warning to the visiting Los Angeles Stars that they had entered the house of Coach Jim Pollard, Larry Cannon, Donnie

Freeman, Willie Murrell, Skip Thoren, and the Miami Floridians.

Impressive it was, except this home opener wasn't really in the Floridians' house. Dennis Murphy had a falling out months ago with officials at the Miami Beach Convention Center, the Floridians' home base last season. No Convention Center had forced the Floridians to move its business operations, lock, stock, and basketballs, into Dinner Key Auditorium. They'd kill time there in Coconut Grove until the Miami International Sportsmen's Club, a planned 12,500-seat modern facility, opened in January. Fingers crossed. The developers still hadn't broken ground, but they seemed committed to doing business with the Floridians, co-sponsoring their radio broadcasts this season and agreeing to have the facility ready to host the next ABA all-star game.

Fingers crossed, too, for Dinner Key Auditorium. The hulking facility, about 150 yards from the waters of Biscayne Bay, had once housed Pan American Airlines' fleet of amphibious seaplanes that cruised the Caribbean. When Pan-Am left town, the terminal got a new lease on life as a makeshift exhibition hall, a vast consumer warehouse where the community milled on weekends at boat shows and impromptu music concerts.[3]

Basketball? Piece of cake, said the paunchy promoter George MacLean who rented the venue from the city to stage evening entertainment. MacLean spent most of yesterday telling Murph not to worry, while he and his crew sawed off and nailed down row after row of makeshift wooden bleachers, installed overhead lights, puzzled over the basketball floor (it was warped in places), and hung that dandy Floridians banner. By game time, Dinner Key was dusted off and mostly presentable. "As compared to our other alternatives—nothing—it's a nice place," one of the team owners looked on the bright side.[4]

True, but who wanted to drink a beer and catch a ball game in a decrepit airplane hangar rumored to be overrun by mice? Maybe that's why only 1,402 paying customers ventured through the turnstiles. But leave it to Murph. Though not much of a hands-on manager, Murph wasn't a bad marketeer. He'd organized a community-friendly, opening-night, thank-you-for-your-service promotion: free admission for Miami's more than 2,000 school crossing guards. By game time, depending on your perspective, Dinner Key was either half full or half empty. Either way, Murph was starting the season in the red. He needed to sell 3,500 tickets a night to break even in this cut-rate joint. He wasn't even close.

Following the national anthem and the swat of the opening jump ball, patron and crossing guard pondered the air conditioning. There was none. Murph and crew, fearing everyone might melt under the boil of the overhead lights, jammed open all available doors to let the stiff ocean breezes blowing off Biscayne Bay sough inside and occasionally whiffle shots. "You guys shoot so bad," Pollard bantered, "the wind probably helps your shots."

Through the wind and the raining down of jump shots, the home team came out on top, 119-98, though the debut seeded a post-game grumble about the rookie Cannon. Miami's "Joe Namath" managed nine shots. He made four for a pedestrian nine points. That wouldn't win them a championship or a Super Bowl.

Pollard told reporters to be patient. Cannon had game. Pollard was far more flummoxed by the site of Pittsburgh's Artie Heyman before the game. Pollard asked why he was in Miami? "I'm playing for you," Heyman answered. "One of your owners traded for me today" for cash and a future draft choice. The move was news to Pollard, who controlled the roster and earlier had nixed Heyman trade offers, twice, under the advisement that the ABA journeyman was nothing but trouble. But minority owner Sandy Rywell, a Miami stockbroker, couldn't resist. He was bullish on Heyman, a Jewish player from New York, thinking he would help connect with Miami Beach's lox-and-bagels retiree community. Maybe. But Pollard already had a Cuban forward sitting on his bench, compliments of Murph and his outreach to the Caribbean community. Where did the front-office's meddling end and a commitment to winning begin?[5]

For Pollard, the Floridians' greatest struggle this season wouldn't be with the Indiana Pacers or the Kentucky Colonels. It remained internal. It would be the wayward geniuses like Rywell who kept hijacking the team to the detriment of Pollard, the only guy in the organization with any real-world basketball smarts. As Pollard drove home, he could take heed that the ABA wasn't the only marketing mishmash. The NBA remained its own marketing work in progress, a point that was about to be made right now on the West Coast.

San Diego, Oct. 22, 1969—It was nearly two years since 50,000 people famously filled the Houston Astrodome for college basketball's "Game of the Century," featuring Houston's Elvin Hayes and UCLA's Lew Alcindor. Tonight, more than 13,600 people filled the San Diego International Sports Arena, anxious to watch Hayes and Alcindor meet again as pros. This Game of the Century Redux wasn't quite a sellout with football season still going strong, but as Hayes' San Diego Rockets and Alcindor's Milwaukee Bucks warmed up, the mood was electric inside the arena. A brand of electricity that the ABA sought to bottle two years ago, but which now was the exclusive, highly marketable property of the NBA.

But oh, that NBA marketing. Instead of waiting to milk the rematch for all it was worth after Christmas when the NBA Game of the Week started up again on ABC, the league scheduled it on a Wednesday just days into the new season. Instead of millions of people watching at home on TV like two years ago, the rematch was carried live on AM radio stations in Milwaukee and San Diego. Souvenirs? A complimentary glossy photo of Alcindor jostling with Hayes and a standard 50-cent game program.

As the starting fives gathered at center court for the opening tip, a voice in the crowd bellowed, "Eat im up, Lew,"[6] and that about summed up the ball game. Alcindor, who had four inches on Hayes, got to his sweet spot in the post, called for the ball, then turned for a jump shot or maneuvered for a hook. Over and over again. "I think Lew showed who was the superior player tonight," said Milwaukee coach Larry Costello, referencing his rookie's dominant 36-point, 19-rebound performance.[7] Just for the record, Hayes sat out the end of the game with a headache as Milwaukee rolled to a 13-point win.

Alcindor remained self-critical of his NBA transition. He'd come into the contest shooting just 41 percent from the field and fouled out tonight for a second time in three games. "I think I'm getting worse," he critiqued. "I keep fouling out, and that hardly ever happened to me at UCLA. I've still got a lot to learn."[8]

Though the NBA had dropped the promotional ball tonight, Commissioner Walter Kennedy had been busy for months consulting and rebranding the league. His committee of experts settled on "the New NBA." It was short, sweet, and a frank admission that your father's self-sacrificing, team-first NBA had gotten old. Bill Russell had retired. Elgin Baylor's knees ached, and Jerry West, badly outplayed in last season's playoffs by the young Lou Hudson, was winding down. The New NBA would celebrate the passing of the generational torch from Russell to Alcindor, Baylor to Hayes and the flashy Connie Hawkins, West and Oscar Robertson to Walt Frazier and Earl Monroe. It would celebrate this new generation for its young legs (Monroe excluded), superior one-on-one talent (Monroe very much included), and a fresh, above-the-rim athleticism with the potential to wow America.

That was the easy part. The heavier lift would be mass-marketing these young stars and their youthful values. They were the Me Generation—loose, cool, brash, go-it-alone, self-oriented, increasingly political, anti-war, and wary of authority. Many wore their hair and sideburns longer, smoked pot in college, and listened to their music blasting.

"I think [the Old NBA] should worry about me instead of me worrying about them," said Norm Van Lier, an unheralded second-year guard with Cincinnati. "I know they were all superstars. But I'm here to make it, and I want them to prove to me they're better."[9]

In the New NBA, Black was Beautiful. So was Black Power, Black music, and a rising Black counterculture that found its spiritual roots in Africa. Take Alcindor. He had converted to Islam during the summer of 1968 and now answered to a Muslim name: Kareem Abdul-Jabbar. He hadn't gone fully public yet with his identity switch, but a hyphenated "change was gonna come" that would align him (incorrectly) in the popular right-wing imagination with boxer Muhammad Ali, as a draft-dodging, Nation of Islam-affiliated subversive.

You thought selling Wilt Chamberlain in Peoria was tough.

But there was no alternative. Kareem Abdul-Jabbar would be the league's dominant figure for the next decade, even if he was still growing awkwardly into the role. "Until I've been around the league, it's going to be hard to evaluate situations," the athlete named Alcindor finished off his self-critique.[10]

His next learning situation would be against the physically imposing Chamberlain, then the savvy Nate Thurmond.[11] Every veteran wanted to test him. Every crowd wanted to jeer him. For the athlete named Alcindor, this NBA transition could be a lonely gauntlet to run. Sometimes, the gauntlet even infuriated him.

Philadelphia, Oct. 31, 1969—Luke Jackson, the almost ABA defector, would be back in uniform tonight for the Philadelphia 76ers in a limited role. Two weeks ago, during the season-opener against Los Angeles, Jackson had been jostling for position with his former teammate Wilt Chamberlain and caught a wicked elbow that partially collapsed one of his lungs. Jackson, anxious to live up to his big contract, hurried through the rehab. For his quick recovery, Jackson's reward tonight would be the sharp elbows of rookie Lew Alcindor.

Alcindor and his visiting Milwaukee Bucks were in Philadelphia for a second time in a month. In the first meeting back at the end of the preseason, Jackson and his backup George Wilson had partnered like a tag-team wrestling duo to thump the tall, gangly rookie. Now, nine games into the regular season, Jackson would tag-team mainly with veteran Darrall Imhoff to test the rookie's mettle.

At the start of tonight's game, Imhoff, a.k.a. The Axe for his hard fouls, whacked Alcindor a few times. Then Jackson got in his licks. Then Imhoff again. When the basketball glanced off the rim with 7:12 to play in the second quarter, Alcindor and Imhoff tangled. Imhoff shoved Alcindor in the back, and the rookie staggered a step forward, regained his balance, and winged a right elbow pointedly in the direction of the push. The elbow connected, briefly knocking out Imhoff and sending his 6-foot-11 frame crashing to the floor.

The Axe slowly rose to all fours, shaking his head to clear the cobwebs. The 10-year veteran located his rookie assailant about 20 feet away, smiling with hands on hips near the free-throw line. Imhoff made a wobbly charge but two players and a referee intervened to keep the peace and the infuriated crowd of 7,641 in its seats.

Message sent: Quit the bullying.

Alcindor had the same irreverent message for the mostly white, working-class crowds that heckled him each NBA night and treated him as a seven-foot freak of nature. They called him a pituitary case, surly, unpatriotic for boycotting the Olympics, and a radical Muslim with a new three-part secret handshake of a name: Kareem Abdul Jabbar. In the current issue of the magazine *Sports Illustrated*, its annual pro basketball preview with Alcindor and his new Afro hairstyle on the cover as the face of the New NBA, Big Lew talked openly of his "Black brothers" and "being fed up with white people."

When Alcindor fouled out with 31 seconds left in the game, the crowd booed the night's sharp-elbowed villain. Alcindor extended his right hand high into the air and held up a peace sign. The boos grew deafening. Alcindor, his head held high, then balled his hand into a Black Power salute. Strength, power, and resistance!

Owner Irv Kosloff, seated at courtside, was among those that Alcindor serenaded. Kosloff had attended the league's latest meetings. He had strategized on how to put the league's best marketing foot forward. And here was the seven-foot face of The New NBA declaring peace and resistance to its white fans. Oh, where have you gone Bob Cousy?

After the Bucks had eked out a 129-125 overtime victory, Alcindor and teammates Don and Greg Smith left the floor in a Bronx cheer of peace signs that drew more of the crowd's four-letter wrath. Reporters streamed to Alcindor's locker afterwards, notebooks in hand, for an explanation of why he decked Imhoff.

"I have no comment on that, you know," Alcindor mumbled. "There is no need to create bad feelings."

What about your gestures to the crowd?

"The people got on me for something," he shrugged. "I don't know why. I'm just playing the game."[12]

L os Angeles, Nov. 7, 1969—Wilt Chamberlain was just playing the game, too. That's the funny thing about it. His

Los Angeles Lakers were up big over the Phoenix Suns midway through the third quarter. He'd racked up 33 points already and was even running the floor tonight with the guards. On the next semi-break, Wilt reached for a pass from teammate Jerry West and felt his right knee buckle. Wilt, considered as sturdy as Mount Rushmore (he'd missed 12 games in 10 NBA seasons), couldn't unbuckle his knee and crashed awkwardly to the hardwood, where he writhed for several minutes of pure, fist-pounding agony.

Chick Hearn, the Lakers' beloved radio play-by-play announcer, described the scene as if he were covering a natural disaster. Owner Jack Kent Cooke watched from courtside in his own frozen, Edvard Munch-like scream, cursing his rotten luck. Cooke's Dream Team of Wilt, West, and Elgin Baylor was a clear preseason favorite to win the first NBA championship, post Bill Russell and the Celtic dynasty. But now, as five large, uniformed men struggled to help Chamberlain onto his one good leg, Cooke's Dream Team had become a nightmare. For West, no stranger to injury and agony, all he could wonder is what next would go wrong?

Also watching from the sideline was the NBA's newest preseason superstar Connie Hawkins. The Hawk certainly could feel Wilt's pain, having launched his belated NBA career this season in Phoenix with a stiff right knee that had yet to recover fully from surgery. The stiffness had Hawkins favoring the bad knee and managing his trademark swoops to the rim. On some nights, a Phoenix reporter quipped, the Hawk is "poetry in motion, on other nights a still life." Hawkins responded to his critics, "Opinions are like rear ends— everybody's got one." Oh, the New NBA.

Wilt was rushed by ambulance to nearby Centinela Valley Hospital, where the clinicians confirmed the preliminary diagnosis: a torn tibial tubercle tendon. He'd need surgery right away to fix it. The good news was a full recovery would be likely. The bad news? The recovery would take months, not weeks. Barring a miracle, Wilt was done for the season.

And so were the Lakers. But don't tell West. He'd started the season on a tear, leading the league in scoring at 29 points per outing in his annual, obsessive-compulsive quest for his elusive Holy Grail: an NBA championship. No Wilt put the onus squarely on West and the aging, oft-injured Baylor to keep the Lakers upright through the regular season and hoping for a miracle recovery and playoff run. It wasn't ideal, but, as the Celtics had shown so many times before, the Old NBA came with broad shoulders and an inexhaustible will. That is, if the usual injuries and fatigue of the 82-game season didn't consume Cooke's Dream Team first.

Miami, Nov. 29, 1969—Jim Pollard returned his tray table to its upright position and prepared for landing at Miami International Airport. He felt tired . . . tired of helping players manage their twisted ankles and gimpy knees. Tired of clashing with his mostly unimpressive rookie Larry Cannon, who booted a chair during a recent game to demonstrate his disapproval of Pollard's substitution patterns. Pollard also was tired of all his meddling owners. "Put in Cannon for heaven's sake," owner Tom Carney boomed over the crowd at Pollard last month in Dinner Key Auditorium. "What do you think we're paying him so damn much money for?"[13]

Most of all, Pollard was tired of losing. His young, injury-riddled team has lost 14 of its last 16 games, including last night's squeaker in Louisville. Pollard glanced at his watch. It was just before noon. That would give him time to drop off his luggage at home before departing again for Dinner Key and the Floridians' 4 p.m. game with the Pittsburgh Pipers.

After the usual thump, thump, thump landing, Pollard and his players straggled up to their entry gate, where waiting unexpectedly to greet them was the team's head of operations Dennis Murphy. This couldn't be good. Murph, not much for tact, marched forward, and within full earshot of the players, advised Pollard that he'd been relieved of his coaching duties. The Floridians would be going in a new direction.

Several players rallied around their now-former coach in a show of support. Pollard reportedly waved them off, noting he had several months left on his guaranteed contract. He'd be fine financially. By evening, Pollard had turned more reflective on his three years with the organization.[14]

Pollard leveled with a reporter, "They've got to decide right now whether they want to keep cutting corners all season and just getting by, or whether they want to make a real fight out of this thing." Since Murph moved the whole operation into Dinner Key Auditorium, things had gotten so penny-pinching that if Pollard needed to reach Murph in the front office during the day, he had to dial a nearby pay phone and wait for a passerby to answer and graciously find him. Why? Thinking the Floridians would be in Dinner Key temporarily, Murph decided to save a few bucks and forego paying for phone service.

"[Miami] is a fertile market," Pollard continued. "But people aren't going to come to us. We have to sell it to them, and it's not going to be done this season." Then Pollard muttered, "Howard is going to take a real bath."[15]

That would be Bob Howard, the millionaire land developer whom Murph had identified last summer as a potential buyer. Last week, Howard bought out most of the other owners for a nearly 70 percent stake in the Floridians. That included Larry Shields, the original owner, who kept just a token financial interest in the franchise just in case of a merger and its financial inducements.

Shields' farewell left just three ABA originals piping up at league meetings. . . Gabe Rubin, Mark Binstein, and Murph. Two East Coast groupers and a West Coaster. Rubin wanted out, Binstein wanted in. What about the West Coaster? Murph just wanted to make payroll.

New York, Dec. 15, 1969—The great spiritual teacher Ramana Maharshi once advised, "Let what comes come. Let what goes go. Find out what remains." By December 1969, what remained of last fall's New NBA brand was a hybrid of something new but fragile and something old but sturdy. Among the league's top 10 scorers were the time-tested names of Jerry West (30.1), Billy Cunningham (27.3, ABA bound but playing out his NBA contract), Oscar Robertson (26.5), Jeff Mullins (25.4), Hal Greer (23.5), and John Havlicek (23.0). Joining them were the new names and youthful ways of Elvin Hayes (25.8), Bob Rule (25.4), and Lew Alcindor (25.3). The top rebounder? Old Nate Thurmond.

Also remaining—or roaring for the first time in a long time—were the hybrid New York Knicks. They had melded their something new, something old into a pro basketball juggernaut, starting the season on an exciting 23-1 tear that included an NBA-record 18-game winning streak. The Knicks, now an NBA-best 27-5, were the toast of Manhattan and, by extension, the Moët & Chandon of America's New York-based corporate media.

In fact, today brought an NBA first. Move over Henry Kissinger, the NBA made the cover of *Newsweek Magazine*. Right there under the iconic *Newsweek* banner ran a photo of Knicks' center Willis Reed in action. A red slash across the upper right corner announced "Basketball's New Surge." Or reading between the lines, the sport had finally risen from the ashes of the college game's fixing scandals to re-emerge as popular mainstream entertainment. Basketball was once again a current event and societal trend worthy of polite conversation among the masses and the classes. And the driving source behind this surge into the media mainstream was the New York Knicks and, by association, the NBA's own rise from the ashes of its "bush league" past.

To think, not even a decade ago, rival periodical *Time Magazine* had chronicled a trip east by the Los Angeles Lakers much like describing itinerant factory workers moving from sweatshop to sweatshop. "Dressing Room 34 at Madison Square Garden was a dingy, bare place with peeling plaster walls, a row of coat hooks above a line of splintery benches and a bath and shower room that afforded no privacy. A bare-bulb overhead light shown down on the rippling brown muscles of the powerful Elgin Baylor, as he irritably wrenched his shirt over his head. 'Damn Garden,' he growled. 'You'd think they could give you better quarters than this, all the money they make.'"[16]

And now, the "damn Garden" was gone. Replaced by the new Garden and the new Knicks. And now, a leading news magazine embraced the game's classy revival in New York:

"The shiny, two-year-old "new" Madison Square Garden is the place to be when the Knicks play; the gamblers have been joined by a shouting, foot-stomping new breed of exuberant fans who are convinced that they are watching the best basketball team that ever played the game. The Knicks will have to maintain their present dazzling pace for some years before they can confirm that belief, but there seems little doubt that they are introducing a new era in pro basketball."[17]

In New York, 1969 had been a sports year like no other. In football, the Jets shocked the world and many a bookmaker with their Super Bowl upset for the ages. In baseball, the perennially inept Mets improbably won the World Series and a tickertape trip up Broadway Avenue. And now, in basketball, those formerly "knuckleheaded" Knicks were closing out the year on the cover of *Newsweek* and chasing New York's next world championship, selling out on most nights like a must-see Broadway blockbuster.

Five, four, three, two, one. Happy New Year! Champagne toasts and good cheer slurred merrily past the stroke of midnight from east to west until all the American time zones had finally passed out of the turbulent 1960s and into the waiting God-knows-what of the 1970s. And it was God knows what. America remained bogged down in Vietnam and at odds with itself at home. Up was down, down was up; right was wrong, wrong was right. The rise of the Great Society was the end of the American Dream. Everything was open for debate: White Flight and Black Power, the Warren Report and astronauts walking on the moon, Women's Lib and the Generation Gap, life in the Hamptons and hippies in the Haight.

But all this heavy stuff could wait. America stumbled off to bed, and then by mid-morning, plop, plop, fizz, fizzed to its feet and onto the couch for a date with the television set. "An orgy of football," a TV announcer described the New Year's Day roster of college bowl games. Wrote one social commentator, "The leisurely old custom of receiving friends, dispensing warming cheer, or making holiday calls has just about disappeared. Television-watching now starts with the morning coffee and the first of the bowl parades and continues without interruption until the last gun at the Orange Bowl football game—12 hours, broken only by circulation restoring stretch periods during the commercials."[18]

There was no New Year's Day orgy for the NBA. Just one game on tap in Seattle. But there had been a flurry of newspaper articles of late pegged to Walter Kennedy's recent State of the NBA media call. The commissioner predictably gave the league a clean bill of health under his watch, noting among other things that attendance had jumped from less than 2 million when he arrived in 1963 to 4.4 million last season. "We no longer have to go hat in hand to the TV people," boasted Kennedy. "Now, they woo us." Now, in fact, the league's contract with ABC paid each team $131,411 per season.

What about the ABA? "They pose no threat to us," Kennedy answered, then launched into an analogy approved by his lawyers. The NBA, he said, was like the trusted supermarket chain in town; the ABA was a just a pop-up challenger with no real roots in the community. What about the rumors of a possible merger? Kennedy stuck to his script: "The possibilities of a merger are extremely remote at this time."[19]

Several days later, Kennedy oddly sent a telegram to the league owners asking everyone to zip their lips about any possible merger talks. Loose lips didn't necessarily sink ships in the NBA, but they did provide some honest tells. Take San Francisco's Franklin Mieuli. When a reporter asked whether Kennedy's phantom telegram was meant to keep a lid on secret merger negotiations, he shrugged, "Where there's smoke, there's fire."[20] Mieuli had nothing more to tell, except he knew that some of the expansion owners were talking with the ABA. Or reading between the lines, Seattle's Sam Schulman and Indiana's Dick Tinkham had been swapping secrets again.

New York, Jan. 7, 1970—Dick Tinkham cut to the chase. He had good and bad news for the other 18 ABA trustees hunkered around the large conference table here at the Hilton Hotel. The bad news? The pro basketball merger hadn't moved one inch since the trustees last met in September. Their NBA counterparts were still sitting on it. Doing most of the sitting was the "Old Guard," the middle-aged cusses who operated the original NBA franchises. They still dominated the NBA from the inside-out, and they still remained cynical of the ABA's long-term viability and thus the need to merge.

The good news? The NBA's "New Guard," keepers of the six expansion teams, were open to the merger. All had bought into the league for six and mostly seven figures, and all at first had fallen into lockstep with the Old Guard. But all now were various shades of disenchanted. All, except Milwaukee, were disillusioned over their lackluster expansion rosters, their blow-out losses, their disappointed fans, and all their money down the drain while waiting the requisite five-plus years to build a competitive team, mainly through the college draft. For the New Guard, the NBA's 1940s-style system badly needed updating. A merger, though not the solution, might be a good start in that direction. It would bring more expansion teams, more regional rivalries, more New Guard owners like them to speak up at board meetings, and millions in ABA entry fees to boost their bottom lines.

Among the merger's staunchest believers remained Seattle's Sam Schulman, Tinkham's NBA Deep Throat. Bold, tenacious, media-savvy, and utterly amoral, Schulman was on a personal crusade since losing out on Connie Hawkins to make the NBA more laissez-faire. To raise his profile among the other owners, Schulman had volunteered for a few league committees. That included taking hold of the fledgling merger committee. His fingerprints were all over last summer's opening merger discussion and getting the influential Old Guarder Ned Irish to hear everybody out. Schulman said he planned to twist a few more arms and Old Guard egos to propel the merger to a yes-or-no vote within a matter of months.

Tinkham fielded several questions, and the trustees moved ahead with naming the ABA's first merger committee: Tinkham (a lawyer); New York's Roy Boe (really his lawyer Bob Carlson); Dallas' Joe Geary (a lawyer); and the new guy, commissioner Jack Dolph, who resided in Connecticut about five miles from Walter Kennedy. The two had known each other socially for years. They asked Dolph to contact "Walter" with the words: We're ready to talk.

While wrapping up the merger discussion, Dolph reminded everyone of the new "security measures" to prevent reporters from snooping in open briefcases and stealing the ABA's secrets. Heads nodded, but the coast was mostly clear. Just a few reporters were present at this two-day gathering, arranged in haste and primarily to finish planning for the upcoming all-star game. Or, as the trustees buzzed, to prepare for the ABA's breakthrough national telecast. About two weeks ago, Dolph convinced his former drinking buddies at CBS Sports to air the league's midseason showcase for an undisclosed amount of cash. The ABA, following in the successful footsteps of the American Football League, now had a toehold on network riches, which could sustain them for at least the next three years, the standard length of a TV contract.

In fact, Dolph said CBS also had an option on broadcasting a few playoff games this season and an agreement in principle with the league for next season to replace the National Hockey League. The agreement was, in Dolph's television-speak, "dependent on the economy of the marketplace." Translation: His CBS drinking buddies were still on the fence about whether the ABA checked enough demographic boxes to woo sufficient national advertising dollars.

Television or merger? Merger or television? CBS brought growth and self-sufficiency; the merger brought termination and incorporation into a league with an old-fashioned brown leather ball and an existing television contract. Yet, each was a potentially profitable pathway out of the financial desert of the Mikan start-up years and had all the trustees, like that old Ella Fitzgerald tune, imagining to varying degrees "nuthin' but blue skies from now on."[21]

Except for one. Jim Kirst, owner of the Los Angeles Stars. Kirst, a likeable, soft-spoken, 48-year-old Southern Californian, had skipped the New York meeting to sit at home and ponder a third possibility: Quitting the ABA altogether.

The quit in Kirst started last October soon after he signed veteran NBA center Zelmo Beaty to a three-year, $600,000 personal services agreement. The $600,000 didn't alarm his accountant. Kirst could afford it. He owned a prosperous heavy construction company that two years ago grossed about $28 million. The oh-my-God was over the terms of Beaty's pension, which Kirst agreed to fund through an insurance policy and its power of compound interest. In 25 years, as written in the contract, Beaty would be entitled to: "The sum of Six Hundred ($600.00) Dollars per month for each year of services as a professional basketball player, which sum shall be paid at age fifty-five."[22]

In other words, Kirst had grandfathered in all 84 months of Beaty's service in the other league and at 10 times the NBA pension rate. Tack on Beaty's coming three years of ABA service, and Kirst would be on the hook for a $72,000-per-year pension until Beaty's dying days.

Who cooked up this super-sized pension? It's hard to tell for sure. But it's easy to make an informed guess that the culprit was Beaty's agent, Larry Fleisher, lead attorney for the NBA Players Association. For several years, Fleisher's top priority was player pensions. Remember, Fleisher nearly cancelled the 1964 NBA All-Star Game to get the owners to support a pension for their players, and he nearly shuttered the 1967 playoffs for an improved pension.

Fleisher had certainly heard about the ABA's Dolgoff Plan, and it presented him with an extremely opportunistic move. By pairing Beaty's ABA pension to a Dolgoff Plan, Fleisher could inflate the monthly payouts to levels unimaginable in the NBA. If other superstars followed Beaty to the ABA's fatter pensions, the NBA owners would be sunk in future pension negotiations. They'd have to accept Fleisher's new Dolgoff-aided scheme as the industry standard or risk losing their grip on the game's top talent.

The plan was brilliant, though maybe a little too brilliant. Not all ABA owners understood—or trusted—the Dolgoff Plan. That included Kirst, who on second thought was uncomfortable with paying for Beaty's retirement for life.

Neither was Kirst comfortable with the summons due to be served any day for him to appear in Los Angeles Superior Court. Beaty's former NBA employer, the Atlanta Hawks Basketball, Inc., was suing Kirst, Stars' general manager Jim Hardy, and Beaty for $4.5 million for allegedly contriving "to destroy their business." Though Beaty was sitting out the season—his option year—just like Rick Barry did before his leap to the ABA, the Hawks claimed to have already exercised their option to renew his previous contract, or in NBA-speak,

Atlanta activated their indefinite reserve on his services. In fact, the Hawks alleged that Beaty had entered into a binding oral agreement to play for the Hawks through 1973, the length of the ABA contract, and they could prove it.

Based on the Barry ruling, which limited the NBA option to one year, the Hawks faced an uphill legal climb. Then again, maybe not. Sports law remained relatively new and unpredictable in America, with just a slender volume of case law for ready reference. The rulings often depended on the presiding judge's legal druthers, making the outcome of the Beaty case impossible to predict.

At his home in the lush foothills of Los Angeles County, Kirst also choked on the number $1.5 million. That's the dollar amount (today, $12.2 million) he'd lost in less than two years shilling an alternative to the NBA Lakers. "We'd be silly to think we're on par with the Lakers," Kirst once said, "but we think we've got an exciting club . . . We think people should enjoy the new venture in town."[23] But his new venture, which currently owned the ABA's second-worst record, were about as in demand as two tickets to the B-movie *Planet 9 from Outer Space*. Everybody and their Uncle Bob wanted to drive their tail-finned convertibles to the Fabulous Forum to watch the Fabulous Lakers with Jerry, Elgin, and Wilt and hang out, if only from afar, with the Hollywood glitterati seated courtside.

Kirst needed to fill 4,000 seats per home game to break even, but his team averaged about half that. Some nights he cheered with crowds in the hundreds. "If I want to see people play with a red, white, and blue ball, I'll go to the beach," an acquaintance explained missing many a Stars' game.[24]

Kirst toyed with relocating the Stars next season further out in the L.A. sprawl, preferably Long Beach. But the very thought of the Long Beach Stars drew a long face from Jack Dolph. To close the deal with CBS, Dolph needed ABA teams in big-market New York and Los Angeles, the bellwethers of his "economy of the marketplace." All of the above left Kirst stuck between a rock called looming bankruptcy and a hard place called the league's lucrative television contract. What about the merger? It, too, would come crashing down on him like a 300-pound anvil. Kirst would have to move the team to Portland, Albuquerque, or some NBA-approved Western outpost. The Lakers' silver-tongued owner Jack Kent Cooke already had spoken. He wanted the Stars gone before the merger could proceed.

Back in New York, as the trustees wrapped up their meeting, Dolph had one final matter of business. He was "taking action" against Kirst in absentia for failing to remain current on his league assessment, now paid quarterly in more manageable sums. Kirst owed the league $14,090.91. Dolph said he'd be in touch with him.[25] That is, of course, if Kirst wasn't in touch with Dolph first.

Miami, January 15, 1970—Larry Shields luckily hadn't been hijacked again flying to Miami. But with the word "merger" now hanging in the air, the future of the Floridians could very well be hijacked by the NBA Board of Governors. That was the rumor anyway at the latest trustees meeting in New York. The NBA wasn't keen on five ABA franchises, including Miami. These franchises, the rumor continued, would need either to relocate or accept buyouts from the surviving franchisers.

The NBA's dissatisfaction with Miami was based on the arena—or the lack thereof. Miami International Sportsmen's Club, proposed to open this month, still hadn't broken ground. That had new team owner Bob Howard crying foul amid all the merger talk. He'd been promised a turnkey basketball franchise ready to move lock, stock, and basketballs into the new arena. Dinner Key wouldn't cut it with the NBA. Neither would the Miami Convention Center, where staff were now making overtures to bring the Floridians back home next season. Howard, a builder's builder, wanted his own arena in

Miami on a choice 85-acre parcel and had begun stomping his feet to get it. But if the city council said no, Howard would be left with only the Floridians to stomp on. Or discard.

Jack Dolph suggested a workaround. Take the team statewide. Divide home games among Miami, Tampa, Jacksonville, Orlando, St. Petersburg, and West Palm Beach. "The formula has been proven in Carolina," Dolph explained, referring to the regional franchise model of the Carolina Cougars.[26] Playing in three North Carolina cities, the Cougars ranked near the top of ABA attendance at over 5,000 per game.

The regional formula also helped Dolph inflate the ABA's mostly small-market fan base to CBS Sports. For example, Miami was the nation's 41st-largest city (330,000), but Florida was the nation's ninth most-populous state (6.7 million).

Dolph, meanwhile, hadn't spoken with Walter Kennedy about the merger. But that didn't stop him, as part of his job, from selling the idea publicly. "Whether this year or next, I don't know," he told the *Philadelphia Inquirer*, "but I'm certain [the merger] will happen."[27] Dolph frequently noted that six ABA franchises were drawing decent crowds, which the NBA couldn't have boasted in its earliest years. Indiana even claimed to have turned a small profit, and the talent gap between the leagues was narrowing with Rick Barry, Roger Brown, and now rookie Spencer Haywood, who like Superman, leaped tall defenders in a single bound. Haywood's game remained raw in fundamental ways, but his gaudy rookie stat line was the stuff of a legend in the making.

The prospect of a merger also received a major boost today in federal court. Judge Zirpoli granted the ABA's protective order in its recently filed antitrust suit against the NBA. The case would proceed, much to the NBA's consternation. Dolph, learning his new job quickly, dashed off the following outgoing telegram to Kennedy, who'd just arrived at the NBA's midseason all-star game:

In view of proceedings held in Federal District Court for the Northern District of California on Jan. 15, 1970, and having met certain pre-negotiations [sic] conditions established by you, I hereby request as a representative of the American Basketball Association and its owners, a meeting with you, and representative owners of the National Basketball Association at your earliest possible convenience. A copy of this telegram is being sent to all NBA owners. The contents of this telegram will not be given to the press by the ABA.[28]

Left unmentioned was today's surprising incoming telegram from Jim Kirst. His dictated words were choppy, but his intention was clear. Kirst refused to pay his league assessment. He also planned to disband the Stars by no later than March. Dolph read then exhaled, his thoughts taking flight in opposite directions. No Stars to irritate Jack Kent Cooke was a win for the merger. For the CBS contract? No Southern California market may have just killed the deal.

Endnotes

[1] Bill Erickson, Interview with author, June 2009.

[2] No Byline, "'Havana, Havana,' Cried Cuban," Whittier (Calif.) East Review, November 9, 1969. This hard-to-find story details Shields' hijacking and includes his direct quote above.

[3] In March 1969, the legendary Jim Morrison and his band The Doors performed at Dinner Key. A angry mob rushed the stage and Morrison after he made lewd gestures. The mob didn't get Morrison, but the melee that ensued sparked a public outcry and concerns about those low-budget "hippie" shows at Dinner Key..

[4] Jim Huber, "Pollard Stunned by Heyman Deal," *Miami News*, October 23, 1969.

[5] Edwin Pope, "Dinner Key Auditorium Not Bad At All," *Miami Herald*, October 23, 1969.

[6] Jeff Prugh, "Lew Pours in 36, Paces Bucks, 115-102," *Los Angeles Times*, October 23, 1969.

[7] Dave Hoff, "'Big Lew' Shines," *Escondido (Calif.) Daily Times-Advocate*, October 23, 1969.

[8] Ibid.

[9] Alan Goldstein, "Better Defense Shue Resolution," *Baltimore Sun*, January 2, 1970.

[10] Hoff, *Escondido (Calif.) Daily Times-Advocate*, October 23, 1969.

[11] Thurmond would fly to L.A. on his own dime to scout Alcindor for the upcoming first meeting. Thurmond would dominate.

[12] This section is based on a compilation of the game's coverage in the Philadelphia newspapers; Darrall Imhoff, Interview with author, June 2011.

[13] Jim Huber, "Cannon-less Floridians Fail as Heyman Gets Late Start," *Miami News*, October 27, 1969.

[14] Jeff Pollard, Interview with author, July 2022, Harvey Steiman, "Pollard Fired as Floridians' Coach, GM," *Miami Herald*, November 30, 1969.

[15] Jim Huber, "Pollard May Stay as Personnel Head," *Miami News*, December 1, 1969.

[16] James Murray, "A Trip for Ten Tall Men," *Time Magazine*, January 30, 1961.

[17] No Byline, "The Dazzling Knicks," *Newsweek*, December 15, 1969; though no byline is listed, the article was penned by Pete Axthelm.

[18] Associated Press, "Televised Football Changes Nation's Holiday Customs," *Iowa City Press-Citizen*, January 2, 1970.

[19] NEA, "Walter Has Another NBA Challenge," *Noblesville (Ind.) Ledger*, January 5, 1970.

[20] John Horgan, "Pro Basketball Conspiracy Looms," *San Mateo (Calif.) Times*, December 31, 1969.

[21] Minutes, Special League Meeting, American Basketball Association, New York, January 6-7, 1970.

[22] I have a copy of Beaty's contract.

[23] Charles Maher, "He Guides the Stars," *Los Angeles Times*, September 25, 1968.

[24] Phil Musick, "Pipers Play Fallen Stars," *Pittsburgh Press*, March 15, 1970.

[25] Minutes, Special League Meeting, American Basketball Association, New York, January 6-7, 1970.

[26] Jim Huber, "ABA May Alter Plans for Floridians," *Miami News*, February 2, 1970.

[27] Sandy Padwe, "Next War for Survival," *Philadelphia Inquirer*, January 16, 1970.

[28] Author has a copy of the telegram.

14

Merion, Pa., Jan. 20, 1970—By the all-star break, the NBA governors had plenty to celebrate. Attendance was up 18 percent, Lew Alcindor (though not Kareem Abdul-Jabbar) was already a household name, and the storybook success of the Knicks had captured New York's popular imagination and sold thousands on the magic of pro basketball.

The governors also had plenty to jaw over at their midseason board meeting in the Marriott Motor Hotel, the NBA's all-star headquarters just over the Philadelphia line. Included on today's agenda: the merger, NBA expansion, and Walter Kennedy's lost voice. Yes, the commissioner appeared this morning in the hotel lobby mostly speechless and flashing a white index card. It read: "Hello there! I have an infection of the larynx. It's good to see you." The more cynical onlookers, mainly the NBA beat writers, belly-laughed that the governors okayed Kennedy's laryngitis by a 7-6 vote, with one abstention. Their joke was funny because it was true. The governors seemingly couldn't agree on how to change a coffee filter, but a plurality could agree that silencing their loquacious commissioner and his calls for order during board meetings might not be a bad thing.

Between Kennedy's silence and the governors' dueling decrees, the board meeting got off to a contentious start. Contentious item number one: Jack Dolph's telegram. The one requesting an interleague meeting on the merger. The one that Dolph promised "will not be given to the press by the ABA." Well, the telegram had leaked immediately to the press, providing Seattle's crafty Sam Schulman with an opening. He and four New Guard owners advocated for accepting Dolph's offer to meet, while the mostly Old Guard oy-veyed to let the ABA die already.

The governors agreed to disagree, then moved on to the equally divisive issue of expansion. Four cities were in the running, but the pro-expansion camp couldn't muster the needed 11 votes to pass the measure (though getting nine ayes), no matter how they sweetened the pot. As a scribe snickered, the owners were deadlocked over whether to sacrifice their "principles for more principal."[1] The latter being the $3 million entry fee per franchise. That totaled $12 million, or roughly a $1 million cut for each man sitting at the table.

Sticking to principle were five governors, including Los Angeles' Jack Kent Cooke and New York's Ned Irish. Cooke, who started the day as chairman of the expansion committee, insisted that the league had to drive a harder bargain. Three million was a "bargain-basement" price, he insisted. They should ask for $5 million per franchise. Cooke's argument: When the league signed its more lucrative national television contract in February, the expansion owners would double their investments overnight.[2]

For Irish, it was all about the league's competitive balance. He felt the earlier expansion had compromised league parity, much to the NBA's detriment. As Irish often complained, the Knicks had 41 dates per season in Madison Square Garden. He could sell out the games against Boston and Philadelphia; but good luck with drawing a crowd for lowly Phoenix and Seattle. Expansion was just bad for business.

By 2 o'clock, in keeping with all-star protocol, Kennedy hosted a press conference to share the league's latest news. Or, as the wags grumbled, say as little as possible. With only a labored whisper at his disposal, Kennedy stood at the podium and, like a ventriloquist, gently moved his lips or whispered into the ear of his new special assistant, Carl Scheer, who repeated his words into the microphone.

"Why was the NBA against the merger?" asked a reporter.

"The Board of Governors," said Kennedy/Scheer, "has set down rigid rules and standards about the merger, which can't be made public; until we are satisfied the ABA can meet these, there will be no meetings."

"How is the ABA supposed to learn what those standards are?" the reporter followed up.

"It could be a unilateral thing," answered Kennedy/Scheer.[3]

The reporters scratched their heads at the exchange, and Kennedy/Scheer moved on to announce something more concrete. The five members of the NBA expansion committee had successfully completed their terms and stepped down, effective immediately. They'd been replaced, effective immediately, by five fresh faces and thoughts on expansion. Or, reading between the lines, a procedural coup had sacked Cooke and his fellow no-votes on the expansion committee.[4]

"It's the consensus of opinion of the Board of Governors that a new approach and a fresh approach ought to be taken toward expansion," Scheer/Kennedy obfuscated. The reporters looked at each other. Huh? Philadelphia's Irv Kosloff later offered this clarification, "It means they'd like to fight it out to the finish" over expansion.[5]

By 4 o'clock, Kennedy/Scheer held a second press conference to declare the deadlock broken. A last-minute compromise proposal had emerged on the expansion question, and the Board of Governors had voted 12-2 to approve it, clearing the way for new teams next season in Buffalo, Cleveland, Houston, and Portland.[6] New York's Irish reportedly left the hotel "trailing sparks" over the pro-expansion tomfoolery. "The new committee is meeting with the franchise applicants and explaining the terms and conditions," ad-libbed Scheer.

By dinnertime, the new deal was dead on arrival. At least two of the would-be new owners walked when they discovered that the NBA entry fee had jumped to $4 million per franchise and came with seven deadly stipulations. They included no network television revenue for three years, no first-round picks in the upcoming college draft, no say in the league's upcoming divisional realignment, and building their teams from the shallowest pool of veteran talent yet in an NBA expansion draft. All demands were non-negotiable, and all four franchises must agree to the latest terms of membership or the deal was off.

"In all my 45 years of practicing law," protested Portland lawyer Moe Tonkon, "I have never been dealt with so shabbily."[7] Jack Kiser, the crack NBA watcher, called it, "one of the most greedy grabs in sports history."[8] Portland reporter Bob Robinson opted for pure opportunism. "It was as if the NBA was saying, 'We really don't want to expand right now, but if these four cities are suckers enough to go along with these terms, then, we will expand,'"[9]

Enter Abe Pollin, majority owner of the Baltimore Bullets and the newly appointed chairman of the expansion committee. Pollin was feeling the financial pinch in Baltimore. The Bullets had reported a net loss of $280,616 last season, and Pollin decided in November to take public nearly half of the franchise to help boost its cash flow.[10] He also decided that expansion and its sweet seven figures would be a big help, too.

Pollin, soft-spoken and far more diplomatic than Cooke, convinced the four expansion groups to give the league a chance to cobble together a more expansion-friendly final offer. A week later, the trusted Pollin had built consensus among his fellow owners to drop the purchase price to $3.7 million, grant each expansioneer a full-and-immediate cut of network television revenue, and reinstate their first-round choices in the college draft. While Houston eventually dropped out for other financial reasons, Portland, Cleveland, and Buffalo accepted the NBA's final offer.

"Nothing in this league makes sense—the inmates are running the asylum," San Francisco's Franklin Mieuli had muttered after the board meeting at the Marriott and just before dashing off to an obligatory league happy-hour.[11] A moment later, NBA scheduler and consultant emeritus Eddie Gottlieb trundled off to his hotel room toting his trusty copy of the 1970 Old Farmer's Almanac and several telephone numbers that he'd jotted down. He would reappear for the all-star banquet claiming that the Buffalo Auditorium, where the new expansion team would play, had just three open dates for next season. Oy vey.

Philadelphia, Jan. 20, 1969—Chet Forte settled into the ABC production van, punching buttons, testing camera angles, and tracking the live feed from New York. It showed the final scene of this week's episode of "Mod Squad." At 8:30 p.m. sharp, Forte three, two, one'd the broadcast live across the ABC network, followed by a hip, head-bobbing guitar riff. Then came the familiar adult voice of play-by-play announcer Chris Schenkel seated courtside:

"From the Spectrum in Philadelphia, Pennsylvania, it's the 20th annual NBA All-Star basketball game featuring the outstanding players of the Eastern Division taking on the extraordinary players of the Western Division."

Tonight's all-star extravaganza brought the usual early oohs and aahs from the 15,244 strong at the dream matchups. Jerry West versus Oscar Robertson. Billy Cunningham on Elgin Baylor. Willis Reed checking Elvin Hayes. But the excitement soon settled into an inescapable halftime fact: the extraordinary West squad didn't have a prayer against the outstanding East.

Jack Twyman, the broadcast's familiar color analyst, lugged his skinny, silver microphone onto the Spectrum floor for a live halftime interview with the injured Wilt Chamberlain. The Big Fella limped under the Klieg lights now sporting a modest

Afro and wearing a bell-bottomed, purple-velvet jump suit with a braided orange, green, and yellow vest. The latter, blinked one onlooker, "looked like an explosion in a paint factory." Or, as Chamberlain later chuckled, "I figure it will take 'em weeks to adjust those color TV sets."[12]

Twyman kept the conversation light and superficially friendly, and Chamberlain did the same. He mentioned his injury, vowed his return to action before the playoffs, and shared his approval of tonight's all-star excitement. Chamberlain—like all the players on the Spectrum floor—was also sitting on some top-secret news. The NBA Players Union met yesterday and voted to oppose the merger by any means necessary. Nothing concrete yet, but a legal challenge was likely.

Chamberlain finished up with an obligatory shout out to his West All-Stars to rally in the second half. But by the fourth quarter, the sellout crowd had begun to leak out through the side exits and into the snowy downtown streets to hail taxis. They missed a late West rally, engineered by Jerry West himself, but the East All-Stars held on for a seven-point victory. Each winning player pocketed $500 (today about $3,500), plus $50 in meal money. The losers walked away with $300 each and meal money.

The all-stars afterwards emerged from their dressing rooms in a scented fog of cologne, shaving lotion, and talc powder. And as a sign of their rising paychecks and looser style, behavioral and sartorial, some posed in their elaborate getups. As *the Philadelphia Bulletin* judged the fashion show, "In a finish closer than the ball game, Gus Johnson of the Bullets was a victor over Walt Frazier of the Knicks. Johnson matched Frazier sealskin-coat-for-sealskin-coat, pulled slightly ahead with his pin-striped mod-cut suit, but took the nod on his hat, a George Raft model with a brim like 747 wings. His shades had heavy silver rims that looked like an erector set."[13]

One stylish all-star game down, another yet to go. The ABA would soon hold its third annual all-star game in Indianapolis. The previous two were fun; this one would be special. Though Rick Barry was sidelined again with a knee injury, Denver's Spencer Haywood and the ABA would make their national television debut on CBS.

Indianapolis, Jan. 24, 1970—Jack Dolph, now three months on the job as ABA commissioner, had checked in two nights ago at the Stouffer's Motor Inn, the 13-story headquarters for the ABA all-star game. His first night there, Dolph bumped into two lawyers from Denver who asked for a word with him. They introduced themselves as representing the ABA Players Association and handed Dolph several mimeographed sheets of paper. It was a copied membership list with the typed names and badly scribbled signatures of players who had allegedly joined the union. Dolph's predecessor George Mikan, they said, refused to recognize the nascent union as the sole bargaining agent for the players. They hoped Dolph wouldn't make the same mistake.

Folding the sheets of paper into his pocket and as affable as ever, Dolph said he welcomed speaking with them upon his return to New York. As Dolph understood the law, that was his only possible answer as commissioner. If a majority of the players voted to unionize, the ABA had to accept their decision.

During yesterday's Board of Trustees meeting, Dolph shared this strange conversation with the trustees. "Not again," one groaned, then filled in the blanks for Dolph. Their names were Arlan Preblud (pronounced pre-blood) and Fred Epstein, and those blankety blanks nearly got the players to sit out last year's all-star game to force the owners to recognize the union. The players chickened out when the owners countered, "Fine, we'll shut down the league." But, as the trustees warned, Mikan was right. A union would burden everyone in the room with player demands that would escalate over time and, like a parasite, eventually kill its host. Besides, how did they know that the signatures weren't forgeries? Dolph passed the folded sheets of paper to Martin Heller, the ABA's chief counsel, and asked him to analyze the signatures. Dolph wanted to know for his own edification if any were forged.[14]

That's where things stood this morning as Dolph hunkered down for breakfast several hours before the big game. Thankfully, the Denver lawyers weren't around to interrupt his peace and calories while working over an ample breakfast plate. Dolph opened the local newspaper and found the coverage of yesterday's news conference at the trustees' meeting. The headline shouted: "ABA's Dolph, Sounding Like AFL's Davis, Declares War." A few inches down, Dolph found his money quote:

"We believe, on the subject of negotiations with the NBA, that the war is on. We have made our overtures to them, and we think it is sane and sensible to talk of a merger. To date, we have received no response, so we proceed with what might be called plan B—non-merger. That means the recruitment of any and all players from any and all teams . . ."[15]

Dolph's declaration of war made good copy, but it was mostly for show. Calculated bluster. The ABA owners were committed over the long term to plan A and the merger. And yet, as Dolph knew, he had been hired exclusively to carry out the calculated and short-term plan B. Really, the institutional leverage to force the merger. That leverage included prominently the high six-figure contract with CBS that Dolph promised to deliver.

This morning, everyone greeted Dolph with pats on the back for putting today's all-star game on national television. Today's broadcast on CBS, still about four hours off, would get the ABA's foot in the network door. Once the Nielsen ratings were in from today's action, assuming the numbers were decent, Dolph would do the rest. "I'm a salesman," Dolph had said when hired, "and I'm going to be selling the ABA."[16]

That's why the ABA needed this all-star game to pop on television. About three weeks ago, a committee was hastily formed to gussy up the Indiana State Fairgrounds Coliseum, the site of the game. It was like planning a frat party at your grandparent's house. The passé art-deco facility, erected in 1939 to exhibit livestock, was a good 30 years too drab for modern television.

And yet, the Fairgrounds Coliseum now looked alive and maybe 20 years younger. The bland 1930s concrete interior had been splashed in ABA red white, and blue. A tri-colored shout of balloons, basketballs, pins, pens, stickers, and saucy signage. "How does this grab ya NBA??" one shout-out read. On the upper balcony, a string of crepe-paper festoons hung like red, white, and blue roses. Then there was the "oh wow" of modern science: a camera that streamed live images onto a white mega-screen inside the arena, overwhelming this still relatively low-tech generation at the prospect of watching a home movie instantly (a nod to the Jumbotrons that were just starting to become technologically possible).

Ready to add some local color was a swarm of young women in miniskirts. They would greet spectators, manually change the numbers on the scoreboard, and toss red, white, and blue basketballs into the crowd. Also agreeing to show their legs and Hoosier spirit were local collegiate cheerleading squads. All this go, fight, win was minutes away as the anticipated overflow crowd started to arrive.

Then Dolph got the terrible news.

At 11 a.m., a pair of charter buses were supposed to transport 22 ABA all-stars from Stouffer's Motor Inn to the Fairgrounds Coliseum. It was about a 20-minute drive. But the buses were still idling, and all the players had just disappeared into Room 802. They were in with those Denver lawyers.[17]

Dolph lit a cigarette and started fidgeting. He needed the players at the coliseum pronto. If the 2 p.m. start of the game was delayed by even five minutes, CBS would cut to New York and run alternate programming in the time slot. As Dolph had been warned, CBS had to go live to a golf tournament in Akron at 4 p.m. sharp. It couldn't let a tardy basketball game delay the nation's tee time.

Dolph asked for an update from Bert Schultz, the league's red-headed publicity director. Nothing new. Dolph told Schultz to grab lawyer Martin Heller. They needed to go and talk some sense into Room 802. The time: high noon.

Arlan Preblud didn't necessarily have to say it. Everyone gathered in Room 802 already knew about the 1964 NBA All-Star Game, Wilt Chamberlain, Elgin Baylor, Tom Heinsohn, and all the big-name players had given the owners an ultimatum: Recognize the NBA Players Association among other demands, or there would be no all-star game. The owners caved. The NBA, which was then making its return to network television, badly needed the prime-time broadcast.

Now, those gathered in Room 802 could offer the same ultimatum to the ABA owners. Some were petrified that their basketball careers could be in deep trouble in a few hours if they proceeded with the strike. With the exception of NBA refugee Rick Barry and the heralded rookie Spencer Haywood, none came close to the fame of a Chamberlain or a Baylor to stand up to the owners with relative impunity. Strike in the ABA, and the owners could easily retaliate, fining players, benching them, or even terminating their contracts.

And yet, many in the room loathed the owners, not personally but for running the league with a slave-master mentality. The owners decided everything about the ABA, from the exact colors of the basketballs to the size of the championship trophy. The players had no recognized way even to offer a constructive idea to the owners, and that's why about half in the room pushed for the ultimatum.

Listening to the conversation grow more heated was Preblud. Though the ABA owners viewed him as a rabble-rousing labor crusader, Preblud was anything but. He had zero professional experience in labor or even antitrust law. Preblud was a criminal lawyer. In fact, he would have never in his wildest dreams attempted to form a pro basketball labor union, if not for a chance meeting about two years ago in a Denver men's store with Larry Jones, the star guard of the Denver Rockets. Preblud introduced himself to Jones as a gushing fan, and the two became friendly over the next several months.

Preblud discovered that his new friend was anything but the stereotypical, sentence-mangling dumb jock. Jones was well spoken and extremely personable, possessing a quick, analytical mind that not only dissected defenses but wore out textbooks. He held a master's degree in guidance counseling and spent big chunks of his off-season working on a Ph.D. Though "Dr. Jones," as some called him, loved playing in the ABA, he saw room for improvement.

"We don't have a players association for the ABA," Jones mentioned one day to Preblud. "Would you be interested to help organize it?"

With Preblud's why not, Jones mailed off a union questionnaire to the league's roughly 120 players to gauge interest. The mailing brought positive replies and a potentially career-crashing threat about his union-organizing activities. "I don't think it's something you should be doing," the general manager of the Denver Rockets advised Jones. "Don't you like playing in Denver?"[18]

Jones refused to be intimidated. In August 1968, he and Preblud held the first organizational meeting in Denver. Attendees were handed a flyer that read in part, "The American Basketball Association Players Association (ABAPA) must be a reality, only through your efforts can we achieve our goals." Those goals were extremely modest. The players wanted the right to add their input to a list of mundane things, such as the start date for training camp and the number of permissible exhibition games. As for more money or more of the hard-fought benefits now offered in the NBA, they didn't dare go there. "We realize the owners have already lost bundles of money, and we aren't going to be unreasonable," said Jones, claiming the union could self-fund player pensions via endorsements or specially arranged NBA-ABA games.[19]

Preblud sent a formal letter to then-commissioner George Mikan announcing the formation of the ABAPA. Mikan frowned, and Bill Erickson, his lawyer and the brains behind the ABA, offered the following tart retort, "The ABA does not employ players. Teams employ players," meaning a league-wide union had no jurisdiction or authority. Preblud countered, "If the league doesn't employ players, how can it hand out fines and suspensions?" Erickson repeated his contention that the ABAPA was a union built on a faulty legal premise.[20]

Around and around both sides went until now in Room 802. With game time approaching, about half of the players wanted to quit the rabble-rousing and get on with the game. Even Preblud was losing his nerve. "I was nervous as hell." As voices and tempers in the room rose, pro and con, Barry, the league's superstar, stood and sounded off like a seasoned veteran, "Look, you've got the owners by the balls. All you have to do is squeeze!"

That was the turning point. They would squeeze, dammit. "Yeah, screw these bastards," yelled Warren Armstrong, a radical rookie and a veteran rabble-rouser.

Then came a knock at the door. It was Dolph.

"What's it going to take to get the players on the court?" he asked.

Preblud stepped out into the hallway, and the two conversed for a few minutes. "Will they play if we promise to look into the matter?" asked Dolph.

"No way," Preblud answered. He stepped back into the room. If that was Dolph's vague final offer, the players would get squeezed. The owners could delay indefinitely their recognition of the union. Several minutes passed, then came another knock. It was Dolph.

He repeated, "All right, what's it going to take to get them to play this game?" Preblud extended a single sheet of paper, ripped from a yellow legal pad, that bore the handwritten words in ink: I, Jack Dolph, as commissioner of the American Basketball Association and on behalf of the league's team owners, hereby agree to recognize the ABA Players Association as the bargaining agent on behalf of all players on all teams in the ABA.

Dolph, scanning the text, grumbled, "Okay."

Larry Jones, the union president, signed at the bottom of the yellow sheet of paper, followed by Dolph. While the commissioner called his friends at CBS to confirm the broadcast, the players hustled out of Room 802 and boarded two idling charter buses. With sirens wailing from a full police escort, the buses roared unimpeded down busy Meridian Street to the arena, arriving out front with just under an hour to spare. The game—and the ABA—were back on the air, and the owners, general managers, and coaches were livid. "You fucked with my players," West coach Babe McCarthy shouted at Preblud. "I don't ever want to see or speak to you again."[21]

Before the 3 p.m. bewitching hour, the ABA wrapped up its first national showcase. Denver's Larry Jones shined as the game's high-scorer. But there was no way that Jones, the union organizer, would take home the MVP award. The honor belonged to his equally deserving teammate Spencer Haywood, the league's hottest young commodity. What was good for Haywood's growing court resume was good for the ABA's credibility and survival.

"As it turned out, the ABA tumble-around was a good show," wrote *Miami Herald* columnist Edwin Pope. "A national audience got a wide-eyed look at Denver's Spencer Haywood, who if not yet a superstar soon will be." Pope then wrote what so many were thinking. "A few more Haywoods" and the ABA could get its merger.[22]

Jack Dolph had a well-known taste for Scotch, and he needed something to toast the broadcast and drown his worries. Jim Kirst, the rueful owner of the Los Angeles Stars, made a cameo appearance in Indianapolis, as he told his friends, and "bailed out" of the ABA for good. Dolph and the trustees would have to operate Kirst's team for the remainder of the season. They had no choice. Perception is reality, in politics and sports, and letting the Stars fall out of the ABA firmament in public view might undo the pending CBS contract and give the NBA Old Guard fresh ammunition to nix the merger and let the ABA die already. The trustees, through their league assessments, would keep the Stars' shining for the rest of the season, while Dolph searched for a forever home for the franchise, almost certainly far away from Jack Kent Cooke to win his valuable vote for the merger.

Endnotes

[1] Phil Elderkin, "NBA Basketball," *The Sporting News*, February 7, 1970.

[2] Cooke's greed came at the expense of his trusted lawyer, Alan Rothenberg, who had applied for an expansion team in Houston.

[3] No Byline, "NBA Elects to Go to 16, Snubs ABA," *San Diego Union*, January 20, 1970. Despite the snub, some of the New Guard spoke out of turn. For example, Bulls general manager Pat Williams told the *Chicago Tribune*: "I believe merger is inevitable. It's got to happen. If you take the franchises going well in the ABA, like Indianapolis, Louisville, Denver, and the Carolina regional setup and put them in the NBA, the potential is unbelievable."

[4] George Kiseda, "NBA Votes to Expand to 18 Teams in 70-71," *Philadelphia Evening Bulletin*, January 20, 1970. The new committee members were: Baltimore's Abe Pollin (chairman), Chicago's Elmer Rich, Atlanta's Tom Cousins, Milwaukee's Ray Patterson, and Boston's Jack Waldron.

[5] Ibid.

[6] Murray Janoff, "NBA Sets Expansion Tag at $3.5 Million," *The Sporting News*, February 7, 1970. In the end, most owners compromised rather than fight. "I didn't change my vote for money," said Milwaukee's Ray Patterson. Patterson said he did so "to prevent a wide chasm from developing" among the governors. The main expansion naysayers remained Los Angeles, Cincinnati, and New York.

[7] Harry Glickman, *Promoter Ain't a Dirty Word*, 1978, p. 101.

[8] Jack Kiser, "Expanding the Asylum," *Philadelphia Daily News*, January 21, 1970.

[9] Bob Robinson, "Case Study: How Portland's NBA Bid Met Grief," *Oregonian*, January 25, 1970.

[10] See *The Sporting News*, January 24, 1970; *Philadelphia Evening Bulletin*, January 8, 1970; and *Baltimore Sun*, November 5, 1969.

[11] Kiser, *Philadelphia Daily News*, January 21, 1970. In the end Mieuli and Philadelphia's Irv Kosloff changed their no votes on expansion to yesses to keep the peace.

[12] Sandy Grady, "Wilt's Blinding Purple Suit is Smash of All-Star Fashions," *Philadelphia Evening Bulletin*, January 21, 1970.

[13] Grady, *Philadelphia Evening Bulletin*, January 21, 1970.

[14] Minutes, Special League Meeting, American Basketball Association, Indianapolis, January 23-24, 1970.

[15] Dick Denny, "ABA's Dolph, Sounding Like AFL's Davis, Declares War," *Indianapolis News*, January 24, 1969.

[16] Dick Klayman, "New ABA Conductor Sees a Pretty Picture," *New York Post*, October 30, 1969.

[17] Because all stars Mel Daniels and Bob Netolicky played for the host Indiana Pacers, they drove from their homes to the arena on their own and apparently knew nothing about the events brewing at the Stouffer's Motor Inn.

[18] Larry Jones, Interview with author, March 2009.

[19] United Press International, "ABA Star Helps Others," *Philadelphia Evening Bulletin*, February 23, 1969.

[20] Bob Fowler, "ABA Basketball," *The Sporting News*, April 5, 1969.

[21] Arlen Preblud, Interview with author, February 2009. The quotes and descriptions of the near boycott are from the Preblud interview unless otherwise noted.

[22] Edwin Pope, "ABA Needs a Few More Haywoods to Press NBA," *Miami Herald*, January 25, 1970.

15

The cities and times shuffled like playing cards on the giant departure board mounted overhead. A split-flap display board, they called it, and its audible whirr and up-to-the-minute accuracy were something to stand and ponder. Or grumble over delays. Walter Kennedy eyed the updated board, then continued his evening trudge through Manhattan's Grand Central Terminal en route to the tiled stairwell that led down to the departing commuter trains. Nobody waiting on the wooden benches would have pegged this Everyman in his late 50s as the titular head of the pro basketball world. Kennedy stood just 5-foot-8, needed to lose a few pounds, and walked with a noticeable limp.

The limp was the remnant of a childhood bout of polio that kept him off the sandlot in his native Stamford, Conn. But Kennedy, gregarious and ambitious, continued to pursue his love of sports in street clothes. At age 13, he became the scorekeeper for the local semipro basketball team and later served as the trainer for the local high school squad. Kennedy liked to tell the story of attending the University of Notre Dame in 1930 and asking the larger-than-life football coach Knut Rockne for a job.

"I'll do anything you want," he wheedled. "Heck, I'll even sweep out the press box."

Rockne turned to his publicity man Joe Petritz and said, "Joe, give this kid a broom and put him to work."[1]

Forty years later, Kennedy had worked up an impressive resume. He'd been Notre Dame's sports information director back in its glory days, travelled the globe as a publicist for the Harlem Globetrotters, promoted the Basketball Association of America (the NBA precursor), jumped into politics as the two-term mayor of Stamford, and, since 1963, kept the NBA ticking as its commissioner. Not bad for a kid whose Irish immigrant father drove a delivery truck for a Stamford dry cleaning store.

Commissioner Kennedy managed the league projecting a pleasant, welcoming façade that clicked with many. However, some dismissed him as an old-time publicity flak whose words were delivered in a soothing lather but were as slippery as wet bars of soap. "Walter is a kind, gracious, patient, cooperative individual who will speak to newsmen on almost any subjects," observed Phoenix sports editor Vern Boatner. "But he is a master of not telling you a thing."[2] His fickleness, especially among certain discouraged expansion owners, stirred up distrust, deep-seated irritation, resentment, and explained the mirth over his recent bout of laryngitis.

Kennedy located the New Haven Railroad commuter train waiting beside the platform. It would roll over the East River and 31 miles later drop him in Stamford. Kennedy proceeded down the aisle toward his usual car and cast of commuting characters. The man with the bad toupee was Howard Cosell, the ABC sportscaster with a brazen arrogance wrapped in a verbosity that America loved to hate. His Arrogance was off a few stops before Stamford. But the two seatmates often found time to "tell it like it is," or as much as Kennedy was willing to spill, off message and off the record.[3]

Cosell had returned recently from Super Bowl IV bearing fresh tales of the NFL milking its post-season cash cow. A record 60 million people watched the show on television. Meanwhile, the three national television networks were finalizing a record $142 million deal to broadcast the post-merger NFL, which included Cosell's high-profile gig on the new Monday Night Football with Giff and Dandy Don.

Those numbers were beyond Kennedy's wildest imagination. The NBA was only a few seasons removed from plying NBA beat reporters with cases of booze at Christmas to thank them for covering the league. But Kennedy could take a bow. The NBA's TV ratings were up 12 percent from last season, which came to about 18 million viewers each Sunday over a record 212 stations across the country. For Kennedy, these numbers were a source of pride. So was this season's rise of the New York Knicks. Want to start a casual conversation aboard Kennedy's commuter train? Just mention Walt Frazier or Dave DeBusschere. Five book proposals already were under contract to memorialize the mania. As *New York Post* columnist Leonard Lewin quipped, "Very interesting, since no one ever did a book before on any Knick in the team's 23 years."[4] New York's corporate community also had started to tap into the team's celebrity.

Frazier, for example, now made personal appearances for an air freight company; recorded radio commercials for Supp-Hose socks; posed for a Black magazine ad to sell sweaters; endorsed his own tennis shoe, basketball, board game, and camp in the Berkshires.[5] He also joined some of his teammates to film a mildly humorous national television commercial for Vitalis Hair Tonic. In the name of team unity, Knicks coach Red Holzman asked his eight cameo thespians to split the television booty 12 ways, or $500 apiece.

Today, pitching greaseless hair tonic for three figures seems quaint compared to the multimillion-dollar Air Jordan Empire that would overtake Madison Avenue 20 years hence. But the Knicks and their baby steps in mass marketing provided proof positive to NBA officials that pro basketball could be more than clicking turnstiles, consuming limp hot dogs, and downing tall cups of beer.

For Kennedy, the rise of the Knicks bandwagon was sweet vindication. He had spent seven long years tending to the team's petulant president Ned Irish and his almost daily demands to fix this and take care of that. Some NBA owners grumped that Kennedy had become Irish's toady. Kennedy shrugged. Or, more correctly, he viewed his subservience more pragmatically. Without Irish and his Madison Square Garden machine, Kennedy believed, the NBA was doomed to bush-league status. Pro basketball had to have a big-league presence in New York for any hope of catching up to the big profits of pro football and baseball. The Knicks mania proved it.

All of the business talk missed a larger claim buzzing in the background of the Knicks' success. New Yorkers viewed their metropolis as the Basketball Mecca of the World. New York had taken the lead in popularizing pro basketball in the 1920s, nationalized the college game in the 1930s with regional doublcheaders in Madison Square Garden, and nearly crashed the sport with the betting scandal of 1951.

But the Basketball Mecca claim went further. New Yorkers argued that the city had played host for decades to a vibrant playground subculture without equal in America. "Basketball is more than a sport or diversion in the cities," wrote Pete Axthelm, the author of *The City Game*, one of the four forthcoming books on the Knicks and New York basketball. (He also penned the earlier *Newsweek* cover story on the Knicks.) "It is a part, often a major part, of the fabric of life. Kids in small towns—particularly in the Midwest—often become superb basketball players. But they do so by developing accurate shots and precise skills; in the cities kids simply develop 'moves.' Other young athletes may learn basketball, and the city kids live it."[6]

The New York playground subculture had been portrayed in the first half of the 1900s as a white, ethnic proving ground, particularly in immigrant Jewish and Irish neighborhoods. When these immigrant sons began moving up and out to the suburbs in the 1950s and 1960s, perception shifted to the Black kids left behind in Harlem and Brooklyn. Axthelm took these previously invisible figures, their improvised moves, and gripping personal stories and made them rise from the asphalt like comic-book superheroes. Jumpin' Jackie. Earl the Goat. Herman the Helicopter. Funny Kitt.

Until now, White America equated Black basketball primarily with the Harlem Globetrotters whistling "Sweet Georgia Brown." The Black game was pure 1920s vaudeville with trick shots, crazy ballhandling, water-bucket gags, and little, if any, real game. For the more basketball astute, a Black game also existed on the other side of town. It dribbled forth each year during the state high school basketball tournament followed by the frank admission: These guys are good. But this Black game was viewed more as a stepping stone than a cultural scene. The top Black preps, if they wanted to get ahead in life, would have to accept full rides to the best white universities. Black kids, or so the thinking went, needed four years of UCLA's John Wooden to discipline their games and get them to straighten up and play right.

If the rise of Earl the Pearl and his popular Black playground game poked a hole in that white mainstream conception, Axthelm ripped it wide open. He melded basketball and sociology to give birth to a new literary and cultural archetype: the Black playground legend. In 1972, author David Wolf would follow in Axthelm's footsteps with his highly acclaimed *Foul!*, the story of playground legend-turned-NBA star Connie Hawkins. Journalist Rick Telander would deliver *Heaven is a Playground* and teach white suburban kids how to talk Black playground smack. All would validate a one-on-one style of basketball that in a few decades would resonate with the rise of a self-reliant, urban-cool, Black-dominated hip-hop culture that mass consumed all things NBA.

But all would unfold in the years ahead and certainly well beyond Kennedy's imagination and train stop. He was out at Stamford. He'd be back on the train tomorrow morning to do it all over again. Same time, same Howard Cosell, same bows, same scrapes, same God bless the NBA.

Pittsburgh, Feb. 1, 1970—Pick a number, any number. Fred Cranwell, the publicity director of the ABA Pittsburgh Pipers, scanned row upon empty row of the orange seats that ringed Civic Arena, capacity 12,500. Maybe 5 percent of the orange was occupied for this Sunday matinee between the Pipers (16-32) and Miami Floridians (14-34).

What was 5 percent of 12,500? Cranwell, a young dashing figure in his coat and tie, worked the numbers in his head and settled on 625. The league office didn't like announced crowds under 1,000, so Cranwell added on several hundred more as sugar on top. His final number of 1,026, an odd number at the end to make it more believable, was then scribbled into the attendance square on the stat sheet. Cranwell's dirty number would be passed after the game to league headquarters, where it would get laundered into the books as clean hard data, no questions asked. That book, if you believed its contents, had ABA attendance up by 40 percent from last season. That translated to more than 1.1 million tickets sold so far this season for an average game attendance of 3,823, again, assuming you believed it.[7]

Cranwell settled into his seat for the fourth quarter. Pipers 88, Floridians 79. He glanced again at all the empty seats. So much for today's star-spangled promotion: "Kids Day." All kids accompanied by an adult got into today's contest for a discounted 50 cents. Kids and basketball? The two went together like peanut butter and jelly. Can't-miss promotion. Right?

Wrong in Pittsburgh. "Pittsburgh watches Piper games only under severe duress," a local sports pundit wisecracked.[8] Duress and disdain. Pittsburgh was in no mood to grant the Pipers a second chance, not after the team deserted it a year ago for Minnesota. Not after the Pipers reportedly were only back in town to squat in Civic Arena for one season while the team's top stockholder-turned-general manager Mark Binstein worked the phones to find a qualified buyer to desert the city again.

Well, not exactly. Binstein and his partner local theater magnate Gabe Rubin, the team's recycled majority owner, started the season stuck in an administrative morass. Their team obviously was on the schedule and playing in the ABA. But because the league office had been in flux last summer, changing commissioners and locations, the sale of the former Minnesota Pipers, Inc., to the Rubin-led Pipers Basketball, Inc., hadn't been formally approved by the league trustees. Neither had the move to Pittsburgh. The league records still showed Rubin's franchise as belonging to the now-defunct Minnesota Pipers, Inc. What's more, Rubin wasn't clear whether the trustees, once they finally made the transfer, would stick him or any future owner with the Minnesota debt, estimated in the high six figures. Try selling that expensive can of worms to a prospective buyer.

All of the above had Rubin on edge and reportedly grousing, "What have I gotten himself into?" Rubin, a short, squat man who looked like comedian Buddy Hackett, and his taller wife, a lookalike for actress Carol Channing but with a potty mouth, loved palling around with these great, big athletes and following their own team in the newspapers. They just didn't want to lose any more money on pro basketball. Said Cranwell, "For everything I wanted to do, Mrs. Rubin would answer, 'We're not spending anything. It's my fucking money.'"[9] That went for getting the team on radio and TV, printing a media guide, traveling with the team on the road. Even the arena organist was prohibited from playing copyrighted tunes to avoid racking up trivial usage fees.

The real f'ing money behind the team this season came from the recent public offering of Pipers Basketball, Inc. But the stock purchases had fallen short of expectations. To make ends meet, Binstein borrowed $240,000 from his New York friends to cover the bare operational essentials—equipment, salaries, travel, and rent. Binstein, to his administrative credit, made payroll every two weeks.

Last month, or 36 games into the regular season, the ABA trustees finally approved a motion that "terminated" the defunct Minnesota Pipers, Inc., for failure to pay their league dues. With some procedural hocus-pocus, Minnesota's player contracts (already in Pittsburgh) were momentarily vested to commissioner Jack Dolph. Then, the trustees resolved unanimously to approve Rubin's on-the-spot verbal application for a new franchise and assigned Dolph's vested player contracts back to Pittsburgh. Critically, Rubin was liable just for "the debts and obligations incurred" by the Pipers "from this day forward," not the Minnesota debt. In return, the league asked for what boiled down to two conditions: Rubin must pay $45,000 to enter the league and provide proof of a $100,000 line of credit from his bank to pay for the remainder of the season. Done and done.[10]

Now, Binstein was ready to shop the team in earnest. The former college All-American and New Jersey stockbroker with the velvet voice waxed eloquent to his callers as though he were offering discounted shares of IT &T. Disregard the rumors, he assured, the Pipers would be in the merger. "First," Binstein pitched, "the arena, the population, and the television market are too big for a league to operate without a Pittsburgh franchise." He even let Cranwell run a low-cost advertisement for Kids Day in this morning's newspaper.

A lot of good the advertisement did. Cranwell glanced again at the empty seats, then the scoreboard. Miami had trimmed the Pittsburgh lead to six with 6:52 remaining. Time out, Pittsburgh. The arena organist launched into an improvised God knows what to God knows how many occupied seats. The Pipers in their home whites gathered around a tall, middle-aged man whose face was instantly recognizable to any long-time pro basketball fan. It was Buddy Jeannette. Yes, the former

NBA great and, more recently, general manager of the NBA
Baltimore Bullets. Yes, the same guy who read the riot act to
Bullets center LeRoy Ellis for jumping to the ABA. Jeannette
had jumped to the ABA this season to serve as Pittsburgh's
director of basketball operations and now its interim coach—
and a wily one he was at that. When Jeannette disagreed with
a foul call, he sometimes charged the nearest referee, yelling,
stomping his feet, swinging his arms, making a spectacle of
himself, whatever it took to incite the sparse crowds. Except,
out of the crowd's earshot, Jeannette wasn't questioning the
referee's vision. He was discussing American popular culture
to avoid picking up a technical foul. "I think Casablanca is the
best movie ever made!" Or, "I don't give a shit what anybody
says, fly fishing sucks! What do you think?"[11]

Jeannette wouldn't need to take down fly fishing tonight.
The Pipers were seven minutes from a second-straight victory,
and Jeannette told everyone to listen up and get the ball to
"Johnny." That was rookie swingman John Brisker, the one
player whom the Floridians to a man would rather not guard.
Over the last several weeks, Brisker had decked grabby Miami
defenders three times, sending the double-fisted message: one
false move, and, as they say in the playgrounds, it was on.

The buzzer sounded, and Brisker stepped onto the court
trailed by Miami rookie Wil Jones, nicknamed Slat. He was tall,
slender, and wasn't willing to mix it up with Brisker. A minute
later, Brisker had rained in three straight jump shots, and it was
all over except for calling the league office with the results. The
final? Pipers 122, Floridians 107. The attendance? Pick a
number, any number. How about 1,026?

Cincinnati, Feb. 5, 1970—Thursday afternoon in Cincinnati.
The New York Knicks checked into the Carousel Inn, a
sprawling 14-acre motor inn and entertainment spa for the
city's fashionable crowd. With their room keys in hand, the
players loped off two by two to their rooms, where by rote they

drew the curtains, unpacked their suitcases, called home, adjusted the TV set, and prepared to wait. They had about 30 hours to kill before Friday night's game with the Cincinnati Royals.

Reserve Mike Riordan wandered off to explore the downtown sights and sounds on popular Vine Street. Some distracted themselves at the Carousel Inn's clubs and restaurants. Dave DeBusschere and Cazzie Russell were spotted at a table for two scanning a Cajun-tinged dinner menu that included Pompano en Papillote and Baked Rockefeller. Russell looked across the table during their gastronomic feast as though he'd had an epiphany, "Dave, isn't this a great life? Can you imagine—traveling around and eating good meals and getting paid good money just for playing basketball?"[12]

They chewed on the epiphany and swallowed another hard fact of NBA Life. The Life giveth, but the Life tradeth away. The NBA brass traded players like baseball cards. Almost nobody was immune. Not Wilt Chamberlain. Not DeBusschere. Not even Cincinnati's Oscar Robertson, considered pound for pound to be the greatest player alive. This week, Cincinnati shocked everyone, including Robertson, by trading him to Baltimore. Almost as shocking, Robertson promptly killed the trade. Unlike the Lakers' trade-averse Rudy LaRusso a few years ago, Robertson had the right to say no. He was one of maybe a dozen NBA players with something new—novel, as they say—in his contract called a no-trade clause. Three years ago, during Robertson's contract negotiation, the Royals acquiesced to the clause, meaning the team legally couldn't trade him without his approval, mainly because the Big O was considered too good to trade. He was as Cincinnati as the Art Deco buildings downtown.

Three years is a long time in the NBA. Since then, Louis Jacobs took over Cincinnati Gardens and purchased the controlling interest in its primary tenant, the NBA Royals. Jacobs was a Buffalo-based multimillionaire with a decades-old monopoly on concession stands at major American arenas, race tracks, and myriad other sports venues. Last spring, his 32-year-old son Max took over as the Royals' chairman of the board. Max, who looked like an accountant, also acted like one. He reviewed the Royals' finances and blanched. In 1969, the Royals lost about $300,000 (about $2.4 million today), while also hitting a nine-year low in attendance. Max's solution was to rebuild the stumbling Royals in the winning image of the 11-time NBA champion Boston Celtics.

To do it, Max hired Celtic great Bob Cousy as his new coach and general manager. But Cousy didn't come cheaply. Max paid a then-astounding $100,000 per year for him to run his show.[13] "I was hired because I was a 'name,'" Cousy later wrote, "and Max knew that if there was any basketball interest in Cincinnati, it would have to be reawakened by a name that would get everybody's attention."[14]

In short, the Royals were now Cousy's team, not Robertson's. The new name in town wanted to play the same pressing, fast-breaking brand of basketball that made the Celtics great and got him the job in Cincinnati. That wasn't the forte of the ball-dominant Robertson, and Cousy quickly sensed his bad fit. He also started questioning his star's frequent injuries and missed games. In Cousy's NBA, unless a doctor intervened, players dressed down for every game. Cousy's growing frustration soon dead-ended in the realization that Robertson, at age 31, wouldn't age gracefully on the court. His contract was up at the end of the season, and Robertson reportedly wanted a then-gawdy $700,000 contract to finish his career in Cincinnati. Cousy and Max Jacobs had other ideas, Robertson's no-trade clause be damned.

After dinner, DeBusschere bumped into Robertson mingling at the Carousel Inn. "I don't want to play here anymore," he confided. "The club knew about the no-trade clause in my contract. They just lied to me."[15] According to Robertson, the Royals were now spreading lies in the newspaper about him, implying that he was selfish, greedy, difficult, a malingerer. All to taint his reputation and force him to leave. Robertson, a very proud man, wasn't having it. He started talking out of turn to the press, too. "I know I have to leave," he announced, "and they can have the team they want. But I'll pick the city where I go."[16]

Lost in the finger-pointing was a profound irony. Cousy organized the NBA Players Association in the mid-1950s. Robertson was now the president of Cousy's creation. He had fully embraced Cousy's historic call for a Players' Bill of Rights, sticking out his neck with the owners to secure better pensions, better health care, and even slip no-trade clauses into player contacts. And now, in the name of profit and building a better box-office attraction, Cousy sought to bypass the labor protection—a no-trade clause—that ailed him.

The next night, Robertson didn't dress for the Knicks game due to an injury. But Robertson clearly remained a bigger name in Cincinnati than Cousy. "The fans at Cincinnati Garden carried signs, saying things like, BRING BACK OSCAR and THE BIG O AND BOB WHO?" DeBusschere later wrote, "During the game, Oscar sat at one end of the bench in his street clothes, and Cousy sat at the opposite end. I didn't see them exchange a word the whole night."[17] Tonight's game was being televised live in New York, and Robertson huddled at halftime with broadcaster Bob Wolff to spill his frustration and repeat his vow to Walter Kennedy and those on NBA high: He would choose his next team.

Wolff thanked Robertson for his time and, following a long commercial break, the Knicks were back on court for the third quarter, just in time for DeBusschere, Russell, and their cohorts to shred a suddenly listless Cincinnati defense. The shredding continued into the final stanza, as both benches emptied, and the Knicks coasted to a 43-point triumph and NBA clinic on ball movement and finding the open man. "It's like sitting on a time bomb with that team, really," Cousy put a metaphor to the humiliation.[18]

The Life giveth, the Life tradeth away. Cousy and profit would get their way in the months ahead. The Big O would leave Cincinnati, and Cousy could commence building his Running Royals. But Robertson and labor would get their way, too, finding power in the pro-union principles that Cousy had championed. Robertson, not Cousy, would choose Milwaukee and dictated the terms of the trade. In Milwaukee, the game's greatest player pound for pound would team with the game's greatest young talent inch for inch, Lew Alcindor. The Big O and the Big A would produce a Bucks team to outrival the amazing New York Knicks. But that would be next season. For now, the Knicks had no NBA rival stalking them for superiority, except for maybe those bruised and battered Los Angeles Lakers.

New York, Feb. 17, 1970—Jerry West stared blankly ahead as though he'd slipped into a coma. His head suddenly shook, his pupils focused, and West formed the words, "What time is it?"

"Ten to seven."

West mumbled something to the effect that he couldn't believe it. He and his fellow Lakers had to start warming up for tonight's game against the New York Knick in 25 minutes. Tonight's contest was the 65th of the regular season. Right now, it felt like game 2,000. Standing there half-hunched in the visitors' locker room, West rubbed an orange heat-inducing balm wherever he remembered a muscle ached. Elgin Baylor did the same. Nearby, two teammates adjusted heating pads on their bruised thighs. The two would play tonight, mainly because they had no choice. The Lakers had just eight players still capable of standing upright. Hard to believe the Lakers (35-29) were knocking on the door of another Western Division regular-season title, just one game back of front-running Atlanta.[19]

The lobby of Madison Square Garden teemed like a Middle Eastern bazaar with offers of "programs, get your programs," Knicks yearbooks, Knicks posters, and all-variety of pens, pencils, magnets, key chains and other kitsch with an NBA logo slapped on it. Inside the arena, seats filled with businessmen in jacket-and-loosened tie, young hustlers in stylish polyester, women in tight pantsuits and furs, unkempt teens in letterman's jackets and sneakers, and balding, middle-aged gamblers chewing on their cigars and pondering point spreads. Tonight's game was the Knicks' 21st capacity crowd of the season. The Knicks, last season the first pro team to top 1 million in total attendance, were nearly 20,000 ahead of that record pace.

West finally pulled on his purple warm-up top and loped with the others through the gangway and onto the Madison Square Garden floor. A Hammond organ noodled through "New York, New York," "Satin Doll," or whatever copyrighted tune seized the nimble fingers of organist Eddie Layton. His day job was playing the duh-duh-duhs on three TV soap operas. The horn blared, and the golden voice of public address announcer John Condon brought 19,500 to attention: "Welcome to the magic world of Madison Square Garden Center. And now, for tonight's starting lineups."

West, his strained muscles loosened by all that orange stuff, trotted out to the center circle, slapped hands with his fellow starters, and went to work. But not Elgin Baylor. He remained too tired and banged up to muscle inside with Dave DeBusschere. West kept the Lakers close through the first half, then all the orange stuff in the world couldn't revive his tired jump shot. While West and his mates misfired, the Knicks went on an 18-4 run late in the third quarter, and that was it. The Knicks had won eight of their last nine games, 14 of their last 16, and were headed for their first Eastern Division title since

1954. Throw on roughly a dozen more of Condon's "Welcome to the magic world of Madison Square Garden Center" during the playoffs, and New York would have its next world champion.

As exciting as it all sounded, an even bigger story had been unfolding, mainly in New York, though also in Los Angeles. This story remained top-secret, and, if finalized, would end the pro basketball war and give peace a chance.

Back in the first week of February 1970, the merger talk had resurfaced during an NBA Board of Governors meeting in Los Angeles. Baltimore's Abe Pollin presented his revised expansion-friendly plan, and, sometime while approving more expansion teams into the fold, Seattle's Sam Schulman steered the conversation toward an unresolved question. What about Zirpoli?

That would be Alfonso Zirpoli, the seasoned, droopy-jowled jurist who presided over the ABA's antitrust case against the NBA. In January 1970, Zirpoli had rejected the NBA's motion to dismiss the suit and suggested that, before the case proceeded to trial, plaintiff and defendant should meet in private and attempt to resolve their dispute. The NBA owners weren't sure how to heed Zirpoli's advice. But the owners knew that they could no longer disregard the antitrust suit. The longer Zirpoli pounded his gavel in the ABA's favor—and he had a reputation for siding with the little guy[20]—the greater the chances that the NBA would spend the next decade filing expensive motions and countermotions and appealing his rulings. Or, more likely, the NBA would be forced to compromise on the reserve clause, grant its players free agency, and learn to inhabit a pro basketball world that had become one big court-ordered bicycle built for two.

San Francisco's Franklin Mieuli, sensing compromise working the room, grew irritated. The ABA had stolen his young superstar, Rick Barry. It had cost him a million dollars—

and counting—in legal fees to get Barry back. Let bygones be bygones? Never. The same went for Atlanta and its loss of center Zelmo Beaty.

Taking it all in with unusual equanimity was New York's Ned Irish. Agreeing to water down the NBA product with more expansion had nearly killed him. Considering a merger—and further diluting the NBA product with 11 mostly financially wobbly ABA franchises—strangely didn't get his goat.

Irish rationalized the contradiction, explaining that the merger was necessary to prevent the NBA from committing financial suicide. The median NBA player salary now was $35,000, an increase of $10,000 since the ABA appeared on the scene two years ago.[21] Twelve NBA players earned $100,000 or more per season, up from four two years ago.[22] The next college draft would bring more $100,000 men. Agents for this year's prospective crop of first-round draft choices already had floated no-cut, multi-year deals that rivaled and, in some cases, surpassed Lew Alcindor's landmark million-dollar contract. Jim Gardner and his swashbuckling ABA colleagues planned to take them up on their offers (though in deferred Dolgoff dollars) and further inflate the going rate for highly skilled basketball players. In Irish's opinion, this financial game of chicken was unsustainable, and the only solution was to merge and shove the ABA genie back into its bottle, deflate salaries, and return management to its rightful role of controlling team finances and splurging here and there on a Cazzie Russell, Bill Bradley, or Lew Alcindor.

Unbeknownst to most, Irish also had a less altruistic reason to pursue the merger. He wanted the ABA New York Nets to join the NBA for a tangle of financial reasons knotted around his Madison Square Garden, Inc. The latter was fighting a hostile corporate takeover.[23] It also had lost $2.1 million in the past fiscal year and paid $4.8 million annually in interest on its loans to finance the newly opened Madison Square Garden.[24] The debt's high rate of interest now had Irish and his MSG colleagues seeking additional income streams to improve their bottom line.[25]

One was to secure the operating rights to Long Island's publicly funded Nassau Coliseum, still under construction and about a year from completion.[26] Six other groups vied with MSG for the honor, including an entrepreneur who had written agreements to bring the Boston Celtics and NHL Oakland Seals to Long Island in two years.[27] That's when MSG made a calculated decision. Irish and colleagues offered to team with Roy Boe, owner of the ABA Nets and a trusted business partner of the committee chairman who would award the Coliseum contract. According to *Newsday*, MSG offered to bring the Nets and Boe's minor-league hockey team to the Coliseum as its winter tenants. Alternatively, Boe would operate the new venue but hire MSG as a $120,000 per-year consultant.[28]

Given all of the above, Irish had a sudden change of heart about the NBA-ABA merger. He offered to waive the Knicks' territorial rights for the Nets, a franchise that he secretly sabotaged three years ago, and also allow several of its ABA friends to join the NBA.

The Board of Governors finally put the Zirpoli question to a vote. All were in favor, except Mieuli. The motion passed, though with more of a shrug than it might appear. Most of the yes votes were willing to appease Zirpoli. They also were willing to contemplate peace and its advantages. But their musings came with no obligation to merge. All realized the devil remained in the financial details, and, as of now, no price tag for the merger had been discussed. There was nothing to take seriously.

That's also why none objected to the seemingly kind offer of Seattle's Sam Schulman to chair the resurrected merger committee. Most had multiple business interests, and booking additional flights to New York to wrangle with the ABA moguls would be a major time sink for a minimal return. In the end,

Zirpoli's best intentions likely would spiral right down the drain with nothing to show for them.

But Schulman's offer was more opportunistic than kind. He wanted, above all, to loosen the Old Guard's grip on the NBA, and Schulman thought he had a fighting chance to pull it off. He had Judge Zirpoli's blessing, the ABA's continued support, and now Ned Irish, arguably the most prominent member of the Old Guard on his side.

Jack Dolph is on the phone."

Walter Kennedy thanked his secretary for dialing the number and reached for the receiver.

"Jack, how are you?" .

Kennedy remained on good terms with Dolph, though he still had to wonder about Dolph's latest career move. Dolph had no experience managing a roomful of testy millionaires and running a professional sports league, let alone one that sailed under a pirate's flag.

Kennedy told Dolph that he had news from the NBA's meeting in Los Angeles. They needed to talk. They compared schedules and settled on a discreet meeting later in the week. Kennedy hung up the phone. He'd have to give Ned Irish an update.

The two commissioners met as planned somewhere in the shadows of New York minus witnesses. Kennedy said the NBA merger committee was back in business and had requested a secret meeting. Dolph answered that he chaired the ABA's merger committee. Kennedy waved him off. No commissioners. Owners only. The two floated some possible meeting dates and scenarios, and Kennedy said he'd confirm everything with Ned Irish.

Two days later on Feb. 13, the ABA's merger committee, minus Dolph, arrived amid the morning bustle of Midtown

Manhattan at a now-forgotten hotel, probably the Waldorf-Astoria. There was Indiana's Dick Tinkham, Dallas' Joe Geary, and New York's Roy Boe. Two lawyers and a dressmaker.

"Good to see you," greeted Sam Schulman, his voice still bespoke his native, up-from-the-streets Brooklyn, despite his years of wheeling and dealing in glamorous Beverly Hills.

Beside him was the salty Ned Irish. Abe Pollin, the third member of the NBA merger committee had been detained in Washington. He sent his greetings.

"The meeting was on a friendly basis and both men [Irish and Schulman] appeared to be very sincere," wrote Geary, who doubled as the ABA secretary. Tinkham concurred.[29]

Schulman said he thought the merger had a better chance this time around. Irish agreed with him, but he wanted the ABA, among other things, to drop its lawsuit as a precondition for the merger. Around the issues they went, each thorny and each potentially a deal killer, until the following six-point framework emerged:

Format: If the leagues ever agreed on a merger, the NBA wanted to circumvent the grindingly slow and uncertain process of seeking an antitrust exemption from Congress. The NBA's unorthodox solution was for the ABA to disband. The former ABA franchises would apply immediately to the NBA, flipping their established teams into NBA expansion clubs. All would be preapproved for NBA membership. Here's the rub. The NBA would accept no more than eight of the ABA's 11 teams. On the chopping block were the weakest ABA franchises Pittsburgh, New Orleans, and Miami. The NBA might accept Los Angeles and Washington. But they occupied NBA territory, and their owners must find suitable locations elsewhere.

Cost: Each former ABA franchise must pay the NBA a total of $1.25 million over 10 years. The sum equaled the latest NBA expansion fees. As Schulman and Irish explained, each NBA expansion team had added their cut of the NBA network television contract to the entry fee, bumping the total to $3.7 million. But the out-of-pocket expense for each expansion team was only $1.25 million. In this case, the former ABA franchises would not share in the NBA's network television receipts for their first three seasons.

League Structure: The former ABA franchises would play as a separate NBA division for three seasons. In the fourth season, full integration would occur.

Interleague Draft: All secret drafts of 1970 collegiate players will be voided, and a joint draft would commence, if acceptable to both leagues, in March. The two divisions will flip for first draft choice and then alternate picks until the seventh, eighth, ninth, and 10th choices, which would exclusively belong to the NBA's four expansion teams in each round.

Conflicting Player Contracts: Both leagues had to come clean about which college players already had signed secret pro contracts. These contracts would be renegotiated between the signing team and the drafting club. Contracts of players "jumping" from one league to another would be a matter of negotiation among the concerned clubs.

Payment of Defunct Franchises: The ABA clubs-turned-NBA expansion teams would be responsible for buying out the defunct ABA franchises. However, the first $2 million, accruing from further expansion in the NBA, would be paid to the former clubs to help defray the anticipated costs of buying out the non-joining clubs.[30]

The NBA's terms for the merger were out on the table. Both sides shook hands in parting, and it now fell to Tinkham, Geary, and Boe to sell some of their colleagues on the plan and buy out the rest. They advised Dolph afterwards on the negotiations, and he drafted a letter to each ABA owner. "You are hereby notified that a Special Meeting of the American Basketball Association has been called by the Commissioner and will be held at 9:00 a.m. Eastern Standard Time on March

4, 1970 at the Jockey Club, 1111 Biscayne Boulevard, Miami, Florida." Action item: To merge or not to merge?[31]

Endnotes

[1] Seymour Smith, "Kennedy Started Career Early in Basketball as Scorekeeper," *Baltimore Sun*, December 1, 1971.

[2] Verne Boatner, "NBA Chief Kennedy is Doubletalk Ace," *Arizona Republic*, June 21, 1969.

[3] Bob Kennedy, Interview with author, December 2010.

[4] Leonard Lewin, "Knick Team Picture Is a Study in Depth," *New York Post*, October 2, 1969.

[5] Walt Frazier and Joe Jares, Clyde, 1970, p.10.

[6] Pete Axthelm, The City Game, 1970, p. x.

[7] Fred Cranwell, Interview with author, July 2014.

[8] Phil Musick, "Battling Piper," *Pittsburgh Press*, February 4, 1970.

[9] Cranwell, Interview with author, July 2014.

[10] Minutes, Special League Meeting, American Basketball Association, New York, January 6-7, 1970.

[11] Cranwell, Interview with author, July 2014.

[12] Dave DeBusschere, *The Open Man*, 1970, p. 156.

[13] As America's Mr. Basketball, Cousy's highest annual salary as a player had been $35,000.

[14] Bob Cousy and John Devaney, *The Killer Instinct*, 1975, p. 105.

[15] DeBusschere, *The Open Man*, p. 157.

[16] Dick Forbes, "Oscar Says, 'I Have to Go,'" *Cincinnati Enquirer*, February 4, 1970.

[17] DeBusschere, *The Open Man*, p. 157.

[18] Barry McDermott, "Knick-ed, Heck! Humiliation, 135-92," *Cincinnati Enquirer*, February 7, 1970.

[19] Jeffrey Denberg, "Poor Lakers Show Up, Dave Shows Them Up, *Newsday*, February 18, 1970.

[20] Stanford Sesser, "Some District Judges Establish Precedents on Tough Social Issues," *Wall Street Journal*, December 14, 1970.

[21] James Scoville, "Labor Relations in Sports," *Government and the Sports Business*, 1974, p. 199.

[22] Ibid.

[23] Stanley Penn, "Contributions by Firm to Illinois DOP Follow Helpful Racing Ruling," *Wall Street Journal*, June 15, 1971.

[24] No Byline, "Madison Square Garden," *New York Times*, August 30, 1969.

[25] Frank Deford, "Merger, Madness and Maravich," *Sports Illustrated*, April 6, 1970.

[26] No Byline, "Coliseum Raises Conflict Issue," *Newsday*, March 25, 1970.

[27] Bob Waters, "Erdman: Big League Plans for You," *Newsday*, March 27, 1970.

[28] Drew Featherstone, "Coliseum Aims for Nets, AHL Team," *Newsday*, May 28, 1970.

[29] Minutes, Special League Meeting, American Basketball Association, Miami, March 4-5, 1970.

[30] Ibid.

[31] Author has a copy of Dolph's telegram.

16

Jack Dolph eased his way to the podium, a hastily hung ABA banner behind his 5-foot-8 frame, and eyed the reporters at the mid-afternoon press conference. Dolph hardly felt like a big-league commissioner at the moment. He had nothing juicy to leak or sweet to declare from the morning session of the ABA's emergency meeting. The commissioner scanned the ruffle of notebooks, started to channel a gravity that befit his title, and finally gave up the ghost.

"Welcome to the bomb, fellows," he smirked, meaning the press conference would be a dud.

A few chuckled at Dolph's dry sense of humor. Others were less amused by the implication that they were wasting their time on an otherwise delightful afternoon at Miami's posh Jockey Club, the white sails and turquoise waters of Biscayne Bay shimmering through the windows. Their editors wanted a headline.

"Will there be a merger with the National Basketball Association?"

"Possibly," Dolph deadpanned.

"Will the ABA expand?"

"Possibly."

"Will there be an all-out bidding war for the wealth of college basketball seniors between the warring leagues?"

"Possibly."

"Do you like your job?"

"Love it . . . I did yesterday anyway."[1]

Dolph lost that loving feeling several minutes later when Carolina's Jim Gardner urged his fellow trustees to craft a formal response to the NBA's merger proposal. All agreed, reluctantly, on the NBA entry fee. What about the buyouts? In an unexpected show of magnanimity, the franchises on the NBA's chopping block acquiesced to the buyout. Pittsburgh and New Orleans would get a million bucks. Miami would receive up to $1.5 million to pay off its larger debts. As for the troubled Los Angeles franchise, it had a possible new owner and could join in the merger, pending the NBA's approval of its request to relocate to Albuquerque. Yes, the NBA governors were approving the relocations of ABA franchises.

That left one final piece to the merger puzzle. The NBA had given two options to Washington owner Earl Foreman: Move his team or take the buyout. Foreman scoffed defiantly. His team would remain in Washington, D.C.

Dick Tinkham called Sam Schulman to relay all of the above as the ABA's formal counteroffer for the merger. In the meantime, Schulman said the NBA had no qualms about Bill Daniels, the proposed new owner for the Los Angeles Stars, but he suggested that the team move to Salt Lake City instead of Albuquerque. Ned Irish wasn't keen on a city that he couldn't spell.

Schulman called back the next day. Abe Pollin had put down his foot. Foreman must vacate Washington. No move, no merger. For Pollin, the matter was deeply personal. The two, though never close friends, had been co-owners of the Baltimore Bullets. After several seasons of the Bullets bombing at the box office, Foreman cut his losses about two years ago. Pollin gladly bought out Foreman and hung in there as the team's primary owner for one reason. Pollin wanted to build a modern arena near his hometown of Washington, D.C. and relocate the Bullets to its hopefully greener pastures. But before Foreman exited, he secretly re-signed a lease with the Baltimore Civic Center that kept Pollin and the Bullets chained there for four more years. As Foreman explained his treachery, he didn't want his native Baltimore to be without an NBA team.[2] This time, Pollin vowed to muscle Foreman out of Washington and get the last laugh.

Dolph and his fellow merger committee members recessed the meeting for 10 minutes and urged Foreman to name his price to vacate Washington. Foreman held his ground, claiming that the merger committee had placed the apple cart before the horse. Why surrender a prime piece of pro basketball real estate? The NBA had yet to commit to a merger; neither did it have the final say. Congress did. As Martin Heller, the ABA's lead counsel, had advised the merger committee, the NBA's proposal to dissolve the ABA was too risky. If the former ABA teams sued, the merger would be tied up in the courts for years.

The meeting reconvened, and Heller's warning came to early fruition. The owners of Pittsburgh, Miami, and New Orleans announced a change of heart. They now opposed the merger. So did Denver, calling it an NBA stunt to divide and conquer the ABA. Carolina and even Tinkham's Indiana backpedaled. That translated to five nos, four yeses, and two maybes.

After the meeting adjourned at 6 p.m., with plenty still to resolve in the morning, Dolph was spotted behind a tall glass of Scotch. He looked tipsy. "I haven't eaten dinner in two days," he explained, lifting the glass. "Lunch today was a half-glass beer. I'm beat."

Dolph still had nothing extra-juicy to report from the meeting, but the Scotch had numbed his brain and loosened his tongue. "Yes, it's inevitable," he said about the merger. "We will take these [ABA] conditions back to the NBA as soon as possible, and it remains to be seen how they accept them."[3]

He said this year's college draft might be postponed until the merger gets finalized. Whether postponement or merger, either eventuality worked in the ABA's immediate favor. The latest crop of college All-Americans feared the return of low-budget rookie contracts. As the NBA was about to discover, many were willing to take the ABA money and run while they still could.

The on-air light flashed, and the late-night announcer at WLWI-TV in Indianapolis enunciated his lines like a 50,000-watt oracle. "Eyewitness News at 11 o'clock has been preempted this evening, so that we may bring you this special sports presentation." The station's logo, the number 13 draped in the furls of a checkered auto-racing flag, dissolved from the screen into a live shot of the WLWI studio and the face of Don Hein, love or hate him, the station's tell-it-like-it-is sports anchor.

Hein introduced Jack Dolph, Pacers' executive director Chuck DeVos, and the team's general manager Mike Storen. Each nodded in sequence to the camera and offered a brief comment to the viewing audience. "When the American Basketball Association opened its doors three years ago, we named our club the Pacers because we wanted to set the pace," said Storen, the last to speak. "And we've done just that. Tonight, we're going to take another big step by signing one of the brightest stars in college basketball today . . . "

Out from behind a curtain emerged a figure who was about as familiar across the Hoosier State as a red barn. Rick Mount . . . The Rocket . . . Indiana high school basketball legend . . . two-time All American guard at Purdue University . . . and now one of the top pro prospects in America . . . decided to forego the NBA draft to sign a contract with the ABA Indiana Pacers. The marquee outside the station, capturing the thoughts of everyone, dubbed tonight's signing ceremony as being, "The Big Haul."[4]

The Rocket took a seat next to Storen, scribbled his name onto the five-year contract, and joined the ranks of the instant millionaire. Well, sort of. The Big Haul was: $40,000 per season, a $20,000 signing bonus, and a Dolgoff Plan that at age 40 would pay $50,000 annually over 20 years. That totaled $1.2 million, though Mount would see just $220,000 over the next five years.

"I don't know about everybody else, but this franchise is not going to sit around and wait for a merger," Storen added later. "We are going to sign players just as if there is going to be no merger . . . until there is one."[5]

Storen's fighting words captured the ABA's prevailing mood. Peace might reign one day, but until then every ABA franchise would fight tooth and nail for survival and continue to distrust the NBA enemy. That's why the Pacers openly defied the NBA's merger demand that "all secret drafts of 1970 collegiate players will be voided." They signed Mount, their secret draftee, even as his team's executive vice president Dick Tinkham schlepped to New York for another round of peace talks.

"I called [Sam Schulman] yesterday and told him about Mount," explained Tinkham. "He acted surprised, but not shocked. It's too early, really, to say how this will affect the talks, but they [the NBA] didn't say don't come."[6]

By morning, the transgression had faded into the background. Schulman (as time would tell) had never met a rule that he wasn't willing to break, and Ned Irish had no plans to draft Mount. The two greeted their ABA colleagues and began running through the ABA's response to the NBA's merger proposal. Pollin, the third member of the NBA merger committee, was vacationing in the Virgin Islands, and conveniently so. He missed a visit the next day from Earl Foreman, who presented his five acceptable merger scenarios for his Washington Capitols. Foreman's hard bargain kept the Capitols in Washington in all instances. He wasn't budging.

The committee members shook hands again. Now it fell to Schulman and Irish to convince their NBA colleagues to consider the ABA's counteroffer at the next Board of Governors meeting on March 16 at the O'Hare Inn, a stone's throw from the Chicago airport. The counteroffer consisted of four main points: All 11 ABA teams must merge, the $1.25 million indemnity fee per ABA team should be whittled down a bit, no joint college draft this season, and Earl Foreman would stay in Washington.

The large oval fountain, set to a soft burble and splash, lent an air of luxury to the entrance of the O'Hare Inn. Inside the lobby, the concierge directed customers to the inn's nine-hole golf course, health club, tennis courts, and the best in fine dining. That would be a table for two at Henrici's, a former landmark in the Chicago Loop that had been recreated here in the suburbs with the original 100-year-old grandfather clock famously tick-tocking in the entryway and the same mouth-watering Flaming Shish Kebab and Veal Cutlet Cordon Bleu.

But the O'Hare Inn's embrace of the good life went unappreciated by many who breezed through the lobby each day with the same get-in, get-out mindset. Chicago was the perfect geographic midpoint to hold national business meetings, and the inn and its ample conference facilities ("Where the Nation Meets") were just a two-minute drive from the sprawling O'Hare Airport. Once business had been transacted, the suits and briefcases breezed through the lobby again to catch the next flight back home.

On this frosty Monday morning in March, the thermometer stuck in the low 20s, a knot of middle-aged men in Brooks Brothers privilege appeared in the lobby with briefcases in tow. They needed directions to today's NBA Board of Governors meeting. By 8:30 a.m., the doors to the NBA conference room pulled shut, and Sam Schulman took the floor. He bid everyone good morning and began running his fellow owners, item by item, through the ins and outs of the ABA's counterproposal.

Outside several reporters had gathered in wait of breaking news. Morning passed into afternoon, and NBA commissioner Walter Kennedy finally emerged at around 3:30 p.m. from behind the closed doors. Nothing yet, he informed a cloud of cigar smoke, where several reporters camped out. Kennedy said he might have something in two hours.

Five thirty came and went. While the merger had made for provocative, pie-in-the-sky conversation at the last Board of Governors meeting in New York, it now carried a contentious, "what's in it for me" gravity. The Old Guard that dominated the league's internal politics offered some token principled resistance but now mostly favored the merger. Confirming this point, New York's Ned Irish introduced a motion to approve the NBA's latest counteroffer to the ABA. Seconding the motion was Detroit's venerable Fred Zollner.

The motion stipulated that "not less than eight but not more than 11 teams" would be admitted into the NBA. Continuing down the page were the following requirements:

- An entry fee of $1.25 million per team. The NBA wasn't budging. Each ABA team was expected to make a down payment of $125,000 to $250,000. The balance would be payable in 10 annual payments of an equal amount, secured by a bond with player contracts as collateral.

- Earl Foreman must vacate Washington, D.C., and he must agree to return Rick Barry to the San Francisco Warriors. All other former NBA defectors would be subject to the terms of a future negotiated settlement between their former NBA and ABA teams.

- ABA teams would receive no network television money for three years.

- The ABA antitrust lawsuit must be dismissed.

- Walter Kennedy would remain the NBA commissioner. In other words, Jack Dolph was working himself out of a job.[7]

By 8:15 p.m., the doors to the conference room banged open. Kennedy welcomed inside a few long-suffering reporters, choosing to downplay the incremental progress of the counteroffer and the past 12 hours of what-ifs. Kennedy knew all too well. Nothing was ever easy in pro basketball. Instead, Kennedy offered this brief formal smokescreen:

"The merger committee was instructed by the Board of Governors to meet again with the ABA [merger] committee, and they were given instructions by the league—instructions that the members felt had to be met before further merger talks can take place.

"We cannot divulge at this time what those instructions entail. That is all the action taken on the merger, and I will not be able to answer further questions on the matter. There was no vote. I can say that it was just a consensus that this was the way things should proceed."

Kennedy also mentioned that the NBA's college draft had been bumped up a week. Why? He mumbled something about the league wrapping up its college scouting sooner than expected. So, why not? Everyone knew that was bosh. The NBA had to be in a snit over the ABA's early signings. First Rick Mount, and now the highly touted Mike Maloy from Davidson College (ABA agent Steve Arnold strikes again).

Matter of fact, when the reporters finally called in their no-merger-yet stories to the sports desk, their editors almost certainly passed along an item that had run on the newswire earlier in the day. It had something to do with a big announcement in Washington, D.C.

I have a story to tell, and it will be told this afternoon." That's how Earl Foreman had advertised his 3:30 p.m. press conference at the Touchdown Club, Washington's venerable equivalent to New York's Downtown Athletic Club. Because his "story to tell" coincided with the NBA Board of Governors meeting in Chicago, the working assumption was Foreman would throw in the towel on cornering the pro basketball market in Washington. This storyline looked airtight a few hours later when a large bouquet of red roses adorned the podium of the Touchdown Club, ostensibly as a symbol of a loving farewell.

When Foreman finally strode to the microphone shortly after 3:30, he fell into a confiding tone about the intense pressure that he was under to fold his basketball tent. Foreman even hinted that his days in the nation's capital might be limited. Then, on a dime, his soft, confiding tone turned loud and irreverent. "This is the number one basketball town in the country," he thumped his finger. "If I'm wrong, I'll be wrong going down."

Foreman then craned his neck, and a side door creaked open. Out walked Charlie Scott, the thin All-American guard from the University of North Carolina in a black suit and gold tie. He gathered the bouquet of roses and presented them to two women who until now sat inconspicuously in the audience. One was his mother, the other was his wife, Margaret.[8]

Scott returned to the podium as the newest member of the Washington Capitols. His three-year take was a generous $133,333.33 per annum, with no deferred money.[9] How long Foreman, a moderately wealthy real-estate lawyer, could afford to pay top-dollar contracts to Scott and superstar Rick Barry with no possibility of recouping his money in the team's subpar 7,000-seat arena was anyone's guess.

"We have won the ball game," Foreman crowed on a day that the ABA also inked two other lesser college stars. "We're signing the draft choices, and they [the NBA] aren't."

Meanwhile, a rumor floating around the NBA Board of Governors meeting had the top college seniors—Bob Lanier (St. Bonaventure), Pete Maravich (LSU), and Dan Issel (Kentucky)—signing ABA deals by the end of the week. Sure enough, the ABA Kentucky Colonels announced the next day the signing of Issel for $1.4 million, much of it Dolgoff money, and his highly regarded college teammate Mike Pratt.

For the ABA, landing the 6-foot-11 Lanier too would be nice—real nice—but Maravich, a.k.a. Pistol Pete, was the grand prize. Every red-blooded, *Sports Illustrated*-reading American had heard of Pistol Pete. He was college basketball's 44-point-per-game scoring machine, the game's most entertaining young white player, and a love-him-or-hate-him 1960s fashion statement with his longish Paul McCartney hair and signature floppy gym socks. Just as Joe Namath and his winning playboy charm brought national notoriety to the upstart American Football League, the flashy Pistol Pete would suck attention to the ABA and serve as the final selling point for a national television contract with CBS Sports.

The ABA leadership hoped this early run of college signings would convince their NBA counterparts that the junior circuit (thanks to Jim Gardner, Steve Arnold, and Mike Storen) had figured out how to sign coveted rookies. That the pro basketball war was too expensive, too unwinnable to drag on for another year and college draft. Merger was their only way out. The more motivated the NBA was to make peace and save its cheap monopoly, the more the ABA could negotiate from strength, especially on one hypersensitive point: the entry fee. The ABA trustees, on second thought grousing amongst themselves, didn't want to pay $1.25 million each to get into the NBA. As a sweet spoil of their victory, they wanted full membership at a bargain-basement price or, better yet, for free.

Given all of the above, the NBA should have been plotting for the good of the league to prevent Maravich from spinning a red, white, and blue basketball on his finger next season. Remarkably, they weren't. As a clear sign that the NBA governors had lost their collective will to wage war, the owners took a pass on fighting for Maravich. They left his NBA future to whoever dared to draft him, and few front offices were willing to take the dare, at least enthusiastically.

The rap, really presumption, on Maravich was that bringing his Pistol Pete persona to town was like juggling loaded Smith & Wessons. Pretty soon, there would be a bang. Whether it was the bang of trying to manage the disruptive, circus-like atmosphere that followed him. Or whether it was the kaboom of Maravich's ball-hogging, razzle-dazzle style misfiring on the NBA court and in the locker room, especially his advance billing as the Great White Hope. When the bangs started, any unlucky general manager stuck in the line of fire would face a disillusioned fan base, a moping star, his enormous contract, dissension in the ranks, and no easy way out of the mess.

"You sit there and hope you don't have to take Maravich," said Cincinnati coach Bob Cousy, summing up the sentiment among many of his NBA colleagues.[10] Most didn't dare say it aloud and risk speaking truth to their excited fan bases.

And so it was. The Pistol-shy NBA versus the Pistol-whipped ABA. But life—and the NBA—sometimes can be stranger than fiction. Unknown to all but a few, a secret trade had gone bad several weeks ago and serendipitously placed the NBA in prime position to get Maravich. The unwitting architect of this zany turn of events was Franklin Mieuli, the chandelier-hanging, Rick Barry-coveting, ABA-hating owner of the San Francisco Warriors. As the draft approached and the stupid trade's implications would go public, Mieuli finally picked up the phone in mid-March 1970 and dialed for help.[11]

Franklin Mieuli is on the phone."

Walter Kennedy thanked his secretary and reached for the tan telephone receiver on the desk.

"Franklin."

"Walter, I need your help."

Kennedy listened as Mieuli started at the beginning. In late January 1970, he said, San Francisco center Nate Thurmond had blown out his knee. To salvage the season, Mieuli had decided to pursue Zelmo Beaty, the former Atlanta Hawks center who last fall jumped to the ABA's Los Angeles Stars and was halfway through sitting out his NBA option year. According to Mieuli's sources, the Stars were broke. Beaty had heard the rumors of his new team's demise and reportedly had toyed with jumping back to the NBA and its safer money. There was just one problem. Beaty refused to return to Atlanta. Mieuli assumed, once he smoothed things over with the Hawks, Beaty would be thrilled to leave his heart in San Francisco.

Mieuli explained that on Feb. 1, he'd called Marty Blake, the Hawks general manager, to ask if the rights to Beaty were up for grabs. "Sure, why not?" Blake told him. "He'll never play for me again. But Franklin, he'll never play for you either. Beaty's got a big ABA contract."

Mieuli disregarded the warning and asked Blake what he wanted for Beaty? Blake said San Francisco's reserve center Clyde Lee. No can do, Mieuli answered. He needed him to play center until Beaty signed. Blake paused. If he handed over Beaty's rights for nothing, Hawks owner Tom Cousins might accuse him of giving away the store. Blake remembered the new NBA rule allowing teams to trade their first-round draft choices. Until now, the Board of Governors had to pre-approve each and every trade of a first-round draft choice.

Blake also remembered that the Warriors were projected to have the seventh pick in the first round. That was good but not great for Atlanta. Still, it was something. "How about I take your first-round draft choice?" Blake said. "But if you ever sign Beaty, I get Lee, too."

Deal. Blake informed Cousins of the transaction and Atlanta's bonus first-round draft pick this year. But the trade was never made public. It hung undetectable in the air as a gentlemen's agreement.

A week later, the merger talks began anew. Beaty made peace with the ABA and informed the Warriors through a back channel (Mieuli and Beaty never spoke directly) that he was done with the NBA. The Warriors, meanwhile, suddenly imploded on the basketball court, winning just three of 15 games in February. March had been even worse thus far. San Francisco, earlier a borderline playoff team, now owned the

NBA's third most-feeble record. Or, in draft terms, San Francisco had the third pick.

As Kennedy listened, he could rifle through the projected first draft selections in his head. Detroit was committed to center Bob Lanier with the first choice. The second pick belonged to San Diego. The Rockets, still in a deep financial hole, couldn't afford Maravich without the NBA picking up a nice chunk of his salary, as the league already had done for Elvin Hayes two years ago. A second generous helping of charity wouldn't sit well with the owners. If the Rockets balked at Maravich, Mieuli would be on the hook with the third pick to take The Pistol. That is, if he hadn't jumped the gun on Beaty and traded away the pick. When the truth leaked out that Mieuli had given away a chance to draft Maravich for nothing in return, Warriors fans would hang him from the Golden Gate Bridge in effigy.

"Walter, how can I make this trade go away?"

Kennedy pleaded ignorance—and with good reason. Maravich had stated on numerous occasions that he preferred to spend his pro career in the South. Atlanta was the NBA's lone Southern franchise. What's more, Atlanta's Tom Cousins was the lone NBA owner who openly coveted Pistol Pete as the face of the franchise. For the NBA, it was a match—and blunder—made in heaven.

"Franklin, give Marty a call," advised Kennedy. "He'll know what to do."

Mieuli hung up the phone and called Blake in Atlanta. The two commiserated about the latest turn of events. Mieuli admitted that he didn't want Maravich in San Francisco. He just didn't want to look stupid. Blake replied that he didn't care about looking stupid. He just didn't want Maravich in Atlanta. The Pistol Pete Show would be too disruptive for his veteran, Western-Conference-champion ball club, which he believed was primed to win an NBA championship soon.

"Everybody loves you, Franklin," Blake ended the conversation, keeping the third pick that Cousins now coveted. "You'll come out of this okay. I'll figure something out." Click.

Blake saw only one possible way out of this mess. He called Pete Newell, San Diego's general manager, and "begged" him behind Cousins' back to take Maravich with the second pick. Newell refused. He couldn't afford Maravich, on or off the court.

Still two decades removed from the lights, camera, and action of the modern NBA college draft, Blake would break the news on the annual league-wide conference telephone call reserved for the draft. He didn't want to hear the shouts in his ear or have to defend the trade or the draft choice. Stealth would be the best policy.

He dialed Walter Kennedy in New York. "Walter, when you get to the third pick, I want you to say real fast, 'Atlanta selects Pete Maravich,' and move right on to the next pick. Got it?"

The NBA draft already had been delayed for 15 minutes. Walter Kennedy's secretary couldn't connect one of the teams to the conference call. Kennedy kept periodically reassuring the other 16 teams "any moment now." Then came the on-hold Muzak, followed by the screech of a gremlin in the line, more Muzak, and Kennedy's "any moment now."

"We seem to be having some trouble with Detroit," he finally clarified.

The delay gave teams a few more minutes to compare their notes. Who already had signed ABA contracts? Which players went with which agents? It was the dawn of a new NBA era. And yet, the dawning of this new era remained relatively unsophisticated compared to what the NBA would become just about 10 years later with the arrival of Larry Bird and Magic Johnson.

At the Warriors office in San Francisco, Franklin Mieuli was hearing voices in his head. Do it, do it. Mieuli raised his right arm, flogging himself mockingly over the head for show and mouthing in his best operatic tenor, "Mea culpa, mea culpa, mea culpa." Now that he had everyone's undivided attention, Mieuli announced to his staff that he had traded away the third pick.

"I know Atlanta will get Maravich on the first round," he concluded his soliloquy. "I will have to take my lashes."

Detroit finally joined the call, and Kennedy hurried through the draft's dos and don'ts, finishing with the good, old-fashioned warning, "Watch your language."

Kennedy managed to get the word "Detroit" out of his mouth when a voice bellowed "Bob Lanier" over the rest of his sentence.

"San Diego is next."

"Rudy Tomjanovich of Michigan" came the rapid reply.[12]

Now, it was Kennedy's turn to shine. In Atlanta, Blake braced for Kennedy's magic words. In San Francisco, Mieuli waited for the word "Atlanta." But the line continued to crackle with dead air. Blake, growing impatient, finally spoke up.

"Atlanta drafts Pete . . ." his voice trailed off nervously.

"Can't hear you," someone shouted.

"ATLANTA DRAFTS PETE MARAVICH OF LSU."

"Okay, Boston is next," Kennedy jumped in.

According to Blake, none of the other 16 NBA teams on the call questioned when, where, why, or how Atlanta landed the third pick and a chance to grab Maravich. The draft continued without incident—or any bad language.

"Could you imagine that happening today?" Blake laughed 40-plus years later over such a mysterious trade. "Amazing, just incredible."

In Atlanta, a small gathering of reporters and staff at the Hawks' headquarters erupted in spontaneous applause. Pistol Pete was coming to town. Who would have known?

Certainly not Jim Gardner, owner of the ABA Carolina Cougars. The Cougars held Maravich's ABA rights, and Gardner thought he still could sweet-talk his way out of a misunderstanding with father Press Maravich and seal the biggest deal in the league's three-year history. The 11th-hour entry of the NBA's only Southern team suggested otherwise. Gardner, assuming incorrectly that the NBA was up to its old tricks, called a reporter at the *Atlanta Constitution* and blasted off this verbal warning.

"Tom Cousins will think Quantrill's Raiders were a bunch of rank amateurs if Atlanta lucks out and signs Pete Maravich," he said. "If we don't get the kid, we're going to take the money and [Hawks stars] Lou Hudson or Walt Hazzard or both of them. Yes sir, I'm absolutely serious, dead serious."

Gardner was absolutely blowing smoke, at least for now. The leagues were under a self-imposed moratorium on raiding players during the merger talks. That Gardner would have to morph into a rhetorical, Al Davis-loving Quantrill's Raider so late in the Maravich sweepstakes spoke to a larger issue. The ABA, for all of its strategic counterattacks on the NBA, had badly botched a very winnable battle when victory mattered most.

Last year, the ABA had Operation Kingfish. It was the ABA's secret plan to enlist the credentialed help of psychologists, accountants, and even a furrier to woo Lew Alcindor to the New York Nets. Although unsuccessful, the individual owners recognized the necessity of marshaling their resources, come what may, to land that one big name that would bring instant credibility to the ABA.

After the Alcindor debacle, ABA officials had turned introspective. They had whiffed on signing college superstars

Elvin Hayes and Alcindor in successive seasons. In the meantime, they had made pitifully little progress in cracking the NBA's monopoly on the nation's best college talent. Instead of embarking upon another epic bidding war for Maravich, the owners opted for a more laissez-faire, win-some, lose-some approach to the college draft. That's why the ABA staged a secret one-round college draft last summer and voted to establish a common fund with a $50,000 credit line open to each franchise. The draft gave each team months, not days or weeks, to woo its top draftee away from the NBA, and the common fund allowed them to make uniformly inflated contract offers that might just win the day. That was the plan, and Indiana's Rick Mount signing in particular suggested its wisdom.[13]

And yet, had the ABA simply dusted off Operation Kingfish and made a true highball offer, placing most of the cash and frills up-front, as Earl Foreman had done with Charlie Scott, Maravich almost surely would have been headed to Carolina. The NBA, after all, had been largely dismissive of Pistol Pete, and, unlike the Alcindor negotiation, Maravich's lawyers had no preconceived notions about which league was best for their client. The ABA would have recouped its historic outlay for Maravich, who'd also grown up in North Carolina, with an almost-certain CBS television contract, plus all of the other residuals from its greater national exposure and popularity.

Instead, Jim Gardner and his officious general manager Don DeJardin had spent eight months alternately irritating and never quite connecting with Press Maravich, Pistol Pete's protective father and college coach. The same went for Pete's lawyers. The two Pittsburgh-based lawyers had warned Carolina to direct all communication through their offices. Gardner and DeJardin selectively ignored them.

Gardner and DeJardin called, fussed, and finally got their way on flying to Pittsburgh to present their first contract offer personally to Pete. For Gardner and DeJardin, the hope was Pete and father Press would swoon at their humongous offer (more on the offer in a second) and sign on the spot. If not, the humongous offer would at least scare off cash-poor San Diego, then assumed to be Pistol Pete's NBA taker. Should San Diego and the NBA match the ABA offer, Carolina could still counter with extra cash and half the Piedmont Mountains.

Gardner, DeJardin, and their four expert financial advisors arrived in Pittsburgh four days before the NBA draft to make their pitch.[14] Father and son already were aware of the proposed Carolina offer from a blabbing acquaintance (now a Cougars employee) while LSU was in New York recently for the National Invitational Tournament.[15] For Pete, a broke college student who drove a beat-up Volkswagen bug and scrimped to afford the airplane ticket to Pittsburgh, Carolina's initial $2 million offer, new cars, a possible movie deal, and promises of joining Gardner in the restaurant business, were mind-blowing.

"When Dad took me into the hall for a breath of fresh air and privacy, he almost had to anchor me to the floor," said Maravich on receiving the formal ABA offer in Pittsburgh. "I was so excited by the offers, I was ready to sign then and there!"

While father Press tried to talk his son back down to earth, their lawyer Art Herskovitz suddenly appeared in the hallway.

"What do you think?" Press asked. The two had known each other since the 1930s, growing up in nearby working-class Aliquippa, Pa. The senior Maravich considered his opinion to be the Gospel truth.

Herskovitz motioned them out of earshot of the Carolina contingent. "I think they're a bunch of phonies," he said.

Herskovitz and his partner Les Zittrain were mystified by Carolina's claim that the offer totaled $2.3 million. They weren't buying the math. Like most ABA deals, a large chunk of the money belonged to a Dolgoff Plan and, from the lawyers' perspective, was unguaranteed. If the ABA vanished, so did the Dolgoff money. "Totally inadequate," Herskovitz summed up the ABA offer. Ergo, Gardner and DeJardin must be "phonies."[16]

"Naw, are you serious?" Pete protested.

Herskovitz nodded and advised father and son to commit to nothing tonight. Stall the Cougars. Tell them that they'd mull over the offer and meet again next week.

That wasn't the answer that the Cougar contingent wanted to hear. But what could they do? The all-night meeting finally broke up after 4 a.m. A few hours later, father and son dragged out of their hotel beds, gathered their things, and hurried to the lobby for check-out. They had a 9 a.m. flight.

"And how will you be paying?" the clerk at the front desk asked Press.

"Paying?" Press grumbled. "No, no, the room was paid for by the fellows from the ABA."

"I'm sorry, sir, but nobody paid."

As Pete summed up the stiff: "If we ever needed a sign as to which offer [league] to take, that was it."[17]

The Cougars couldn't get another meeting with Maravich after their hotel gaffe, and that's when Gardner called out Quantrill's Raiders—and Earl Foreman. "I had a reputation then for signing players, so the Carolina people asked if I could help them get Maravich," said Foreman. "I talked with the father, and he said it was a personal affront the way that the Carolina people had treated him. The father said he wished that he'd talked to me first and all of that, but it was over."[18]

On Sunday, the day before the NBA draft, Atlanta owner Tom Cousins landed his private jet in Baton Rouge with Maravich's lawyers in tow. Soon after Marty Blake shouted that the Hawks would draft Maravich, Cousins secured a commitment from Pete to sign a reported record five-year, $1.9-million agreement once the lawyers finished dotting the i's and crossing the t's.

The ABA got more bad news soon thereafter when Bob Lanier agreed to sign with the NBA Detroit Pistons. For the ABA, much of the problem was once again the Dolgoff Plan. As Norman Blass, Lanier's agent, sniffed at its annuities and deferred payments, "Bob wanted to do his own investing."

Despite the victory, Detroit's general manager Ed Coil chased his jubilation with a hard shot of reality. In 1967, Coil signed Jimmy Walker, the top pick in the NBA draft, to a reported four-year, $250,000 contract. Three years later, Coil signed Lanier to a reported five-year, $2 million deal. "We just can't afford to sign any more Laniers," he said. Coil predicted the merger was inevitable and likely would be announced in "three or four days."

Coil was off by a little over a week and a crank telephone call.

Welcome to Palm Springs, California: Golf capital of the universe. Sam Schulman kept a condo in this high-desert playground for the wealthy, and he had invited the two merger committees to town in early April 1970 in the hope that the peace and poolside tranquility of Palm Springs would be a kumbaya for compromise on all of the remaining major issues, especially the Washington mess.

"What would it take to get you to move?" Schulman asked Earl Foreman, a special guest at the proceedings.

"I don't want to move," Foreman answered.

"Would it take $600,000?" Schulman asked.

"Sam, I don't want to move."

Schulman, knowing that every owner has his price, kept ramping up the figure by comfortable increments. Irish sat nearby. He looked pained at the numbers being bandied about to appease a former junior NBA owner.

"Would it take $900,000?"

"I'm not moving."

"How about a million dollars?"

Foreman, known to be a shrewd negotiator, finally buckled but only momentarily.

"I'll think about it," he mumbled.

Schulman suggested that they take a short break to give Foreman some extra time to reflect on the seven-figure offer. As Foreman recalled, he walked outside onto the baked earth of the Coachella Valley, the brown, jagged outline of San Jacinto Mountains in the background. Joining him was Indiana's Dick Tinkham. The two were on good terms and could speak candidly.

"You know, I came out here with every intention of supporting your right to keep the franchise in Washington," Tinkham started in.

"So what's changed?" Foreman answered.

"You just set your price in there," Tinkham continued. "That changed everything as far as I'm concerned. Earl, you've got to take the money now and move. Let the merger proceed."

Foreman said the comment confused him. He hadn't really affixed a price tag to his franchise. Sure, an offer of $1 million had given him pause. But who wouldn't pause at such a large figure?

The meeting reconvened, and Foreman decided to go for broke. Foreman said he had bounced around Schulman's generous offer and arrived at two non-negotiable demands in order to vacate Washington. One, when the merger takes place, Foreman said he would have his $1.25 million NBA entry fee waived. His team would join the NBA at no cost. Two, Foreman wanted his moving costs covered.[19]

Schulman, anxious to remove the greatest impediment to the merger, told Foreman that the NBA was open to his request. "I'll never forget," Foreman remembered. "Ned Irish got up, went into the bathroom, and sounded like he was throwing up. That's how upset he was about the deal that I had just made."

By evening, the meeting had adjourned with an agreement in principle on the Washington move. But principle is only as strong as its underlying consensus, and there was none to sustain it. Schulman also lacked the authority to grant Foreman a waiver on the NBA entry fee. He would have to argue Foreman's case at the next Board of Governors meeting, with little or no support from the retching Irish. Who knew which way the vote would fall?

The next morning, Tinkham met privately with Schulman at his Palm Springs condo. What next? The merger negotiations continued to be two steps forward, three steps back. Schulman looked at his friend Tinkham. He had a sneaky, borderline-diabolical proposition.

"I'll just call the *Los Angeles Times* and announce the merger," Schulman said. "Once the merger goes public, they [opponents of the merger] won't be able to stop it."

Tinkham remembers feeling hesitant. But Schulman reached for the telephone and dialed a number with a 206 area code. That was Seattle, not Los Angeles. Schulman, the mighty little owner of the local SuperSonics, immediately had a captive audience on the other end. He said: "How would you like the biggest scoop of your career?"[20]

Don Fair, the NBA beat reporter for the *Seattle Post-Intelligencer*, told him to fire away. Schulman offered background on the merger committees, their 90-day marathon of meetings and telephone calls, and the issues on the table. "We met in Palm Springs this week and cleared the final stumbling block," he announced triumphantly. "That was the moving of the Washington, D.C. franchise. This the ABA agreed to."

Fair followed up with several questions. "It [merger negotiation] wasn't easy," Schulman leveled. "But I think everyone knows it's wiser to try and live together and enhance the sport rather than be destructive. In some ways, sport is only one step removed from a [public] utility. And a utility must be under some type of general control."

The next day, Fair's newspaper ran the banner front-page headline: "Pro Basketball Merger 'OKd'" Below it ran a second banner headline: "Apollo 13 Blasts Off Today." Would Schulman's trial balloon meet a similar, near-disastrous fate as the infamous Apollo 13?

The *Seattle Post-Intelligencer* story pinged to the wire services and immediately entered the nation's news cycle. "NBA, ABA on Verge of Ending War." "Report ABA Set to Pay Indemnity." By the next day, reporters in the various NBA and ABA cities contacted their trusted sources to confirm the story. Predictably, it didn't hold water.

In Pittsburgh, the well-connected former Baltimore general manager Buddy Jeannette, now with the ABA, stated, "All of this talk may be a little premature."[21]

"I'm not aware of any agreement reached between the two merger committees, and I was there every minute," Earl Foreman told a reporter in Washington.[22]

In Indianapolis, Dick Tinkham came clean, "We still have problems. Washington hasn't agreed to anything despite what Sam Schulman said."[23]

Walter Kennedy, blindsided by Schulman's rogue tactics, offered no comment. He was waiting to read the meeting notes. Not San Francisco owner Franklin Mieuli. He broke ranks to declare publicly his profound frustration with the Schulman-led merger negotiations. Instead of kneecapping Sam the Sneak, Mieuli broke with taboo to single out New York's Ned Irish and directly accuse him of enabling Schulman's antics.

"Irish doesn't care what trash he brings into the NBA so long as the Nets survive and rent his building on Long Island," he railed. "It makes me laugh because Irish has always been against expansion. He isn't thinking about what's good for the league, only what's good for the conglomerate he's fronting for.

"I've got three votes to block this merger," Mieuli thumped. "And I hope to have a fourth, which would guarantee defeat [of the merger's passage]."[24]

While the NBA boardroom fractured into factions, the ABA factions pulled together. On April 14, three days after Schulman's bluff, the ABA issued a two-page press release that accepted the NBA's merger recommendations from the Chicago meeting and added, based on the Palm Springs session, seven workable recommendations. Among the high points were:

- All 11 ABA teams will merge.
- Ten ABA team will pay a total combined $10 million to join the NBA. Per the Palm Springs meeting, the NBA entry fee will be waived for Foreman's franchise. (The $10 million figure may have been a typo. All subsequent media reports list the figure as $11 million.)
- Although the Washington, D.C. issue remained unresolved, Foreman is open to exiting "under certain circumstances." Translation: Charge Foreman no NBA entry fee and cover his moving expenses, and the Washington problem would go away.
- Beginning in 1971, the leagues will hold a joint all-star game and postseason "Super Bowl" of basketball.

The NBA Board of Governors would meet on April 24 in New York to review the ABA's latest recommendations. By all indications, Schulman wouldn't need to pull another fast one. "The ABA statement closely parallels the resolution on what the NBA said would be acceptable," said Irish. "It's not verbatim, but it's very close."[25]

"NBA approval is virtually a formality," Tinkham told the *Washington Post*.[26]

Or was it?

The NBA Players Association had voted at the All-Star Game in Philadelphia to consider filing an antitrust suit to block any future merger plans. Their vote had hung in the air for the past three months as a threat without a clear target. They had one now. Prevent the NBA Board of Governors from slipping through the merger while lawmakers weren't looking.

Endnotes

[1] Gary Long, "Dolph: An Answer to Every Question—Possibly," *Miami Herald*, March 5, 1970.

[2] Earl Foreman, Interview with the author, September 2009.

[3] Jim Huber, "ABA Stiffens Demands in Merger Talks," *Miami News*, March 6, 1970.

[4] Gene Conard, "Instant Millionaire: Mount," *Kokomo Tribune*, March 10, 1970.

[5] Dave Overpeck, "Pacers Sign Purdue's Mount to $1 Million Pro Contract," *Indianapolis Star*, March 10, 1970.

[6] Dick Denny, "Pacers' Signing of Mount May Hurry ABA-NBA Merger," *Indianapolis News*, March 10, 1970.

[7] Minutes, NBA Board of Governors Meeting, Chicago, March 16, 1970.

[8] Thomas Yorke, "Caps Awaiting Merger News; Scott to Sign," *Washington Evening Star*, March 16, 1970

[9] No Byline, "Gentleman Farmers Take Action on Auction," *Newsday*, March 17, 1970. According to Foreman, he didn't understand the Dolgoff Plan and refused to use it. Foreman also picked up the tab for Scott's two brand-new Cadillac convertibles. He had agreed to only one, but Scott special-ordered a second Cadillac and charged it to the team. As Scott reportedly rationalized the second purchase, "Well, they were different colors."

[10] Barry McDermott, "Working in the Market," *Cincinnati Enquirer*, March 24, 1970.

[11] The section that follows is based on my interviews of Marty Blake, the general manager of the Atlanta Hawks in 1970. Blake told me his Maravich story twice, first in March 2004 and then in March 2009. Same story, consistent details.

[12] The description of the conference call is based on: Barry McDermott, *Cincinnati Enquirer*, March 24, 1970.

[13] The verdict on the ABA strategy remained out. All four big signings to date—Rick Mount, Mike Maloy, Charlie Scott, and Dan Issel—were hastened by the merger rumors. Mount wanted to stay in Indiana. Maloy had fallen into the ABA's lap. His agent was ABA co-founder Connie Serendin, then Steve Arnold. Scott received a phenomenal contract offer from Washington. Money talked. Issel was represented by his uncle, a life insurance agent who reportedly grasped the Dolgoff Plan and was smitten by its formula and yields. According to Peter Dolgoff, son of the plan's originator Ralph, Kentucky also sweetened the pot. "My father told me that one of the Kentucky owners pulled him into his office and asked, 'How much money do you think you will make on commissions on the life insurance [part of the Dolgoff Plan]?' My father looked at him and said, 'Well, off the top of my head, about $15,000.' The owner said, 'If I write you a check for $15,000 right now, will you let Issel's uncle be the agent?' I don't think my father had ever seen a check for $15,000 in his life. But that's what happened." Interview with author.

[14] In his autobiography *Heir to A Dream*, Pete Maravich remembers 15-plus years later the negotiation taking place in New York. However, a two-part series in the Pittsburgh Press in early April 1970 shoots down Pete's recollection. "For some reason," said Lester Zittrain [Maravich's lawyer], "the Cougars wanted to make the first offer . . . Jim Gardner came to Pittsburgh with an entourage—his two partners, a lawyer, a tax man, and another man he said was his financial consultant." Gardner also remembers Pittsburgh as the site of his first offer.

[15] Francis Essic, Interview with author, May 2013. Francis Essic was a Cougar employee who ran the team's office in Charlotte. He also was a former small-college basketball coach and an old friend of Press Maravich. Press even had been the featured speaker at Essic's summer basketball camp. Much has been made elsewhere about Bob Kent, another old friend of Press', teaming with Atlanta's Tom Cousins to gain an advantage over the Cougars. While Kent certainly was influential, the picture was more complex. Essic's dinner in New York to informally unveil the contract offer shows this. So does the fact that Cougars' folksy coach Bones McKinney had known Press Maravich for more than 20 years.

[16] Roy McHugh "Pressing Pistol Pete," *Pittsburgh Press*, April 9, 1970.

[17] Pete Maravich and Darrel Campbell, *Pistol Pete Heir To a Dream*, 1987, p. 139-140.

[18] Earl Foreman, Interview with author, September 2009.

[19] Ibid; Dick Tinkham, Interview with author, March 2014.

[20] Dick Tinkham, Interview with author, August 2009.

[21] No Byline, "No Reaction From Pipers on Merger," *Pittsburgh Press*, April 12, 1970.

[22] Associated Press, "Foreman Denies Caps Will Move," *Baltimore Sun*, April 13, 1970.

[23] Dick Denny, "Merger Seen As Pacer Win," *Indianapolis News*, April 14, 1970.

[24] Wells Twombly, "Mieuli Will Torpedo NBA Merger," *San Francisco Examiner*, April 14, 1970.

[25] Larry Fox, "Judge's Order Stalls Hoop Merger Plans," April 18, New York Daily News, April 18, 1970.

[26] Mark Asher, "ABA Owners Unanimous on NBA Merger Terms," *Washington Post*, April 15, 1970.

17

L os Angeles, April 9, 1970—Wilt Chamberlain glanced at his right knee. The one that he blew out running up the court last November. The one that was immobilized in a cast for eight weeks. The one that he spent 10 hours daily strengthening after the cast was removed so that he could rejoin the Lakers at the tail end of the NBA regular season. The one that held up just fine tonight in the Lakers' blowout victory of the Phoenix Suns in the seventh-and-deciding game of their Western Division semifinal playoff series. The one that helped Wilt roar for 30 points, 27 rebounds, about a dozen swatted shots, and which anchored a defense that limited the Suns to 30 percent shooting from the field.

Not bad for his 10th game back in uniform. "No, I'm not all the way back," Wilt answered the reporters gathered around him like mere mortals. "But I feel fortunate that I'm playing the way I am."[1] Down the hall, Suns' superstar Connie Hawkins cut to the chase. "With Wilt playing defense like that, they will go all the way."[2]

Three thousand miles to the east, necks stiffened. Lakers? Go all the way?

Until now, fate had dictated that the 1970 NBA postseason would be a New York moment, time to start spreading the news that the New York Knicks, the best team during the regular season (60-22), were King of the Hill, top of the heap, just like the football Jets and the baseball Mets. Only better. Nineteen years after the city's infamous college basketball betting scandal and after two decades of futility chasing an NBA title, New York would reclaim its rightful place as the hub of American basketball, the proud purveyor of The City Game, the incubator of the world's finest players, and home to basketball's greatest fans.

Two weeks ago, the city that never sleeps had been up for days in anticipation of the Knicks' playoff opener against Baltimore. Everybody and their cousin from Yonkers needed tickets, and scalpers outside Madison Square Garden winked and worked fast at obscene markups. "Can't talk long," said one playoff hookup. "Gotta get these tickets ready for tonight. It's the biggest thing we've ever had."[3] That included the 1969 World Series. Even corporate Madison Square Garden got into the act, gouging Knicks' season-ticket holders nearly double for playoff seats. In the neighborhoods, hard-core and penny-ante gamblers referenced the tabloid *New York Post* daily for the latest point spread and roster updates. Cazzie Russell had deferred his inconvenient National Guard call-up. Willis Reed, the Knicks' captain, was good to go, though his injured right knee, hip, you name it were killing him.

Against Baltimore, the Knicks triumphed in a thrilling, seven-game nail-biter. At one point, while Baltimore's star Earl Monroe lit up the Knicks with his spinning, double-clutching, try-and-stop-me-now trick shots, the Garden faithful spontaneously combusted into a bold, New York-Strong chant of "DEE-fense, DEE-fense," eventually accompanied by house organist Eddie Layton. And so a signature basketball cheer was born during the Knicks' historic playoff run.[4]

At ABC Sports, the NBA's network home for a recently extended three years at $17.5 million, the men in suits marveled that the once-lowly Knicks, playing in the new 19,500-seat Garden, were the hottest ticket in town. For 41 regular-season tilts, the Knicks sold an NBA-record 760,226 tickets, including 26 sellouts, several near full-houses, and home attendance that never dipped below 13,000 for any contest. More eye-opening, the Knicks' total home attendance, including the playoffs, would hit 974,776, which topped 11 of Major League Baseball's

21 teams. The Knicks would do it playing just 52 home games, about 60 percent fewer than MLB teams. The latest data offered irrefutable evidence that pro basketball, played in large modern venues and under the right promotional conditions, could compete financially with the other major pro sports.

The proof had been a long time coming. The pro game had dribbled forth in the 1890s as a novel, hand-to-mouth winter pastime. It featured low-budget regional competition, plus a short menu of provocative barnstorming teams that roared into town like Cossacks through the 1940s to match set shots with a local "name" quintet. All these cage matches, for lack of large indoor venues in most cities, were often staged in dingy dancehalls and community centers with seating in the hundreds or low thousands. For promoters used to shilling strapping All-American quarterbacks and Ruthian home-run sluggers in 30- to 50,000-seat outdoor stadiums, pro basketball's nickel-and-dime profit margins were laughable. In fact, to profit off this mostly working-class sport, basketball promoters concocted championship tournaments, value-added doubleheaders, and extended best-of series among popular rival teams (the latter, a tradition the NBA adopted in its playoff format) that strung together a few sellouts in a row. Even then, the profits were nothing compared to the windfalls seen in baseball and football.

Until now, that is. The Knicks were the first NBA team during a regular season to sell over 1 million tickets, home and away. The word "million" proved to Madison Avenue that America, not just New York, loved the Knicks and their City Game mystique. "When everyone started talking about the Knicks and how they were winning," said Roone Arledge, president of ABC Sports, "advertisers said, 'We've got to get that'" for $25,000 per advertising minute on the NBA Game of the Week.[5]

Arledge, like the Garden, could boost his advertising rates during the playoffs, especially if the Knicks and Lakers were destined for a seven-game championship showdown for the ages. East meets West. Gotham versus Tinseltown. Wilt versus Willis, Dream Team versus Dream Team. The NBA Finals, like the World Series and the Super Bowl, was about to enter the realm of American sports spectacle. For how long? Arledge didn't know, and the NBA front office, understaffed and underpowered, had nothing brilliant up its sleeve to brand, baby, brand.

Of course, the New York-L.A. talk remained premature. The Knicks would first need to slay the rising, seven-foot dragon named (for now) Lew Alcindor and his "New NBA" Milwaukee Bucks to claim the Eastern Division championship. Easier said than done. The Lakers? Their "Dream Team" led by the Old NBA lineup of Wilt, Jerry West, and Elgin Baylor would need to master the Atlanta Hawks. Easier said than done. The Hawks, the regular-season Western Division champion, were a locked-in veteran ballclub that gave everybody fits and entered the series holding the all-important home-court advantage.

The Lakers, despite Hawkins' kind assessment, had nearly imploded while working Wilt back into the lineup for the Phoenix series. Without Wilt during most of the regular season, the Lakers ran all game to free West in the open court for easy looks in transition. With Wilt back in uniform, the offense downshifted into a half-court trot that started with lobbing the ball inside to him to shoot or find the open man. Too many tentative cutters zigged instead of zagged off Wilt, and the Lakers fumbled away three of the first four games against Phoenix. Facing elimination, the Dream Teamers summoned their collective basketball superpowers to swish and swat their way to the next round. Now, the Dream Teamers would need to be super again—or super lucky.

Atlanta, April 12, 1970—Some ice, please. Wilt Chamberlain sat in the Lakers' dressing room massaging his rehabbed right knee waiting for an ice pack. The knee appeared swollen after pounding the hardwood for four quarters, but Wilt waved off any sympathy. A shout out to his pride was the better locker-room lubricant. The Lakers, after all, had just upset the formidable Atlanta Hawks, 119-115, in game one of their best-of-seven series. "It's not bad," Wilt evaluated the puffiness, "it's not bad at all."[6]

Neither were his numbers: 16 points, 17 rebounds, eight assists, and just two personal fouls. What had people buzzing, though, were his 10 free-throw attempts on top of Elgin Baylor's 18 charity tosses and the 21 granted to Jerry West. In all, the Lakers shot 60 free throws to Atlanta's 32. Such a lopsided difference favoring the visitors was, to put it mildly, highly unusual.

Drill down deeper, and it gets weirder. Midway through the third quarter, Atlanta was up by 13 points and rolling. From then until the final buzzer, the Lakers shot 32 free throws to Atlanta's nine. With the dead-eye West taking most of the freebies, the Lakers made 27 of 32 foul shots, including 12 down the stretch, to overtake the Hawks for the win. At the final buzzer, the sellout crowd booed, raining down ice cubes and paper cups, while the curious minds at press row wondered what just happened.

"They're always reaching in for the ball," Lakers' coach Joe Mullaney explained the disparity in foul calls.[7] Baylor blamed the grabs. "When we pass the ball to Wilt, everybody starts breaking. There's an inclination for the opposing team to momentarily look back. Then, when we take off, they've been caught in that split second, and the natural inclination of the man guarding you is to slow you down without getting caught by the officials."[8]

The Atlanta locker room, which naturally viewed the outcome differently, mostly muttered no comment until coach Richie Guerin, grumpy from a restless night, reappeared the next afternoon and summoned the press. "I couldn't stay quiet any longer," he declared, then proceeded to rebut the reach-and-grab analysis and rip the officiating in two.[9] There was no point in Guerin pleading his case with Walter Kennedy. The Commish had seen it all from his deck chair in the Alexander Memorial Coliseum, capacity 6,996, the Hawks' admittedly makeshift home while their modern showpiece arena was under construction. In fact, Guerin had reason to believe that Kennedy wasn't displeased at all by the outcome. He and a few of his players overheard him complaining to lead referee Mendy Rudolph before the game. "Look at this place, it only holds a few thousand people," Kennedy reportedly winced, having spent seven long years trying to erase the popular perception that the NBA is a bush league. "We can't show this on national TV."[10]

Guerin, his testosterone pumping, didn't mention his eavesdropping. But he did allude to some possible "spilling of blood" in game two. He said if the refs kept sending Baylor and West to the free-throw line, the Hawks might deliberately take them out of action. Breaking news. Just one game into the Western Division championship, it had come to this: a bush-league mosh pit, two threats of bodily harm, and millions of whispers that the fix was in for a New York-Los Angeles championship series.

By game two, now half-seriously dubbed the Battle of Alexander Memorial Coliseum, the leather lungs in the cheap seats came to see blood. They jeered each Laker starter who answered his pregame introduction like personifications of the five worst of the seven deadly sins then went woozy welcoming their high-topped heroes. (Interestingly, all the Hawks' starters were Black in these racially charged times in the Old South.)

There would be no Confederate battle for respect, though, or letting of Laker blood. The Big Three of Wilt, West, and Baylor, plus rookie sidekick Dick Garrett, "showed up," as they say in basketball vernacular. Wilt dominated the backboards, killing the Hawks' bread-and-butter fastbreak and forcing the action into slower 24-second increments more to the Lakers' liking. The Lakers' perimeter defenders bumped and guided ballhandlers into the paint, where Wilt scowled in wait. Discretion dictated kicking the ball back outside to the usually reliable mid-range marksman, Lou Hudson, one of the NBA's finest. But Hudson, in the midst of a playoff shooting slump, connected on just five of 20 high-archers.

Despite Hudson's around-the-rim-and-outs, the Hawks stayed close into the third quarter. That's when the Laker offense finally found its second-half rhythm, in a one, two, three of jump shots and an away-we-go of dunks. All the leather lungs could do is suffer in near silence. Neither could they blame the scoreboard on the refs this time. A replacement crew had rotated in tonight with special instructions: no harm, no foul. Whistles were fewer and farther in between, and the crew took pains to call fouls right down the middle (Lakers 22, Hawks 21).

Wilt, after playing all 48 minutes on his bum knee, summed up the 105-94 Laker victory: "We just had everything going right tonight, and, when that happens, we're tough, mister, tough."[11] And tough it would be, mister, for the Hawks to rebound from their 0-2 deficit with the next two games to be played in sunny L.A., where the Lakers could conceivably close out the series. The Hawks were ailing, having lost their playmaker Walt Hazzard to a fractured wrist late in game two. For Guerin, the team's rusty, 38-year-old player-coach who would replace Hazzard in the lineup, it didn't look good for the Hawks, which made the memory of the series opener sting even more.

Was game one fixed? Who knows. One weirdly officiated game can be chalked up to a bad night. Nevertheless, this bad night in the midst of the playoffs would help perpetuate a theme that would stalk the NBA for decades to come: The NBA has its big-market favorites that get the calls and the VIP treatment in the playoffs. Just remember that weird game in Atlanta back in 1970.

Denver, April 15, 1970—Denver's sensational rookie forward Spencer Haywood had a bad habit on offense. He liked to hold the ball. He'd stand 15 feet from the bucket surveying the floor while the shot clock ticked, ticked, ticked. The extra seconds let defenses trap Haywood and also collapse into the paint to prevent him from driving. Haywood, the best athlete on the floor, often had to settle for contested jump shots. "I need to take the ball to the hoop more," he explained, signaling the next stage of his basketball evolution.[12] Catch and go.

Tonight, it was all catch and go for Haywood against the Los Angeles Stars in the final game of the ABA's marathon regular season. Haywood caught the tri-colored ball, whirled, and went to put his finishing touches on a rookie season for the record books. Haywood needed 40 points to join Wilt Chamberlain as the only rookie in pro basketball history to score 2,500 points in a single season. He got there in the third quarter, followed by a raucous, arm-waving, God-bless-you standing ovation. The next God bless you came when Haywood eclipsed the team's single-game scoring record of 51, followed by another thunderclap when Haywood broke Connie Hawkins' ABA single-game scoring record of 57. The Rockets, leading by a landslide, finally pulled Haywood with two minutes to go, and the Mile-High partisans rose once more to hail the former Olympic hero's 59-point, 25-rebound masterpiece.

Haywood ended the regular season with league-record averages of 29.9 points and 19.6 rebounds per game. In Denver, "Spencer" was the talk of the town. Attendance was up 47 percent from last season, topping off at an average of 6,561 per outing, second best in the ABA behind Indiana (7,690). The mayor, revved up by the Rockets' season-ending 19-game win streak at home, now supported the construction of a fancy new arena. The House that Spencer Built.

"I've seen or played against them all," Stars coach Bill Sharman mused after the loss, "and I certainly rate [Haywood] over Alcindor."[13] Quite a compliment coming from a former NBA All Pro, but Sharman was in quite a gracious mood. Who wouldn't be? His Stars, after being left for dead by owner Jim Kirst last January, had survived to complete the regular-season marathon. And now, Sharman's Lucky Stars (43-41), the miraculous winners of 17 of their last 21 games, were headed to the playoffs.

The miracle-maker was Sharman. Lacking an established superstar around which to build his team, Sharman molded an excellent fast-breaking, defensive-minded ballclub out of a mish-mash of journeymen and overlooked young prospects. Not one of Sharman's mish-mash could have made an NBA roster to start off the season. Now? Some probably could. George Mikan used to say that the ABA didn't need to sign every big-name All-American to survive. It had time to develop the less-heralded names, hone their skills, and allow them to strut their pro basketball stuff. Sharman had proved the point.

The Lucky Stars would depart in the morning for Dallas to begin their ABA championship quest. Make no mistake about it. Sharman intended to hoist the ABA championship trophy and whoop, holler, and spray champagne afterwards in celebration. Just like he'd whooped, hollered, and sprayed tiny bubbles in Boston with Bill Russell and Bob Cousy. Heck, the Stars probably could afford French champagne. They had a fancy new owner named Bill Daniels, a Denver-based cable TV pioneer and risk-taking entrepreneur wowed by Haywood and the rise of the ABA, at least in the Mile High City.

Daniels bought the Stars for a discounted $300,000 plus two big favors.[14] First, Daniels assumed Kirst's personal services contract with Zelmo Beaty, including the troublesome pension.

For Daniels, it was a cost of doing business. For Kirst, it was a sigh of relief. Second, Daniels agreed to relocate the Stars next season far away from big-market Los Angeles and Jack Kent Cooke, who claimed the ABA had trespassed on his exclusive NBA territory. The ABA, though in need of big markets like L.A., needed Cooke's influential pro-merger vote even more.

Back in the Stars' dressing room, Sharman huddled with his players and spoke with urgency about the playoffs. Winning wouldn't be easy. But with a little luck and a lot of Sharman, the Stars might advance past Dallas to the next round and get another crack at Haywood and the Rockets for the Western Division crown.

Bill Daniels to the ABA's rescue today, Haven Industries, Inc. to the ABA's rescue tomorrow? Haven, a New York-based conglomerate, was on the proverbial fence about purchasing the Pittsburgh Pipers. Shilling pro basketball wasn't in Haven's corporate wheelhouse; but the acquisition might help to expand its footprint into American popular entertainment. Last year, Haven took a tentative step in that direction by purchasing the broadcast rights to the Broadway smash "Cabaret."

Of course, two tickets to a sleepy Pipers' game were hardly like a cabaret, old chum. But over the phone, Pipers general manager Mark Binstein could belt out a breathtaking song-and-dance about future sellouts and ABA championship banners. Binstein roared about the coming transformation of Pittsburgh from an industrial to a financial center. He celebrated its lush Monongahela beauty, its rich basketball tradition, its slow rise as an ABA town, and the inevitability of the NBA-ABA merger. The Haven officials came for a visit, attended a game, then told Binstein that they'd sleep on it.

But before the Haven executives got away, like six other unimpressed investment groups, Binstein said he was willing to improvise. Given the new set of circumstances, that is. Binstein explained that the NBA recently added the Pipers to a list of ABA franchises that were "unacceptable" for the merger. Making the list, like receiving a death sentence, suggested the Pipers were down to months, not years, of ABA basketball. Binstein insisted the death sentence was a mistake, and the NBA would grant a pardon once Haven and its $22 million in hard assets entered the picture. In fact, Binstein could point to the Los Angeles Stars. They made the death list, too. Then came the wealthy Bill Daniels, and they were off it.

Now, about that sweetened offer, Binstein said Haven could have the team for no money down and one huge favor. Binstein, thinking like a stockbroker, said he knew of a New York brokerage house that Haven could work with to offer enough of its own stock as payment for the team and buy out Gabe Rubin, the team's absentee majority owner. That would get Rubin off Binstein's back about selling the team, and Haven would get a nice short-term bump in its stock price. In the meantime, Binstein would continue to own a slice of the franchise and stay on as the team's general manager. That would buy him time to work his NBA connections, solve the merger problem, and save the franchise for the third time in 18 months. However, in the off chance that he didn't solve the merger problem, the ABA would buy out Haven for their asking price. Either way, Haven would come out ahead.

Well, life is like a cabaret, old chum, and the Haven executives accepted Binstein's sweeter offer in close consultation with Rubin's lawyer. On April 20, the deal was officially announced in New York and in Pittsburgh, where Haven praised the fiery Rubin for his civic "contribution" to Pittsburgh and awarded him with about $1 million worth of stock in Airport Services, Inc., a profitable Haven subsidiary familiar to frequent fliers. The dollar amount was significant since Rubin claimed about $1 million in losses during his three ABA seasons. It meant that with one stroke of his pen, Rubin became the lone ABA founder to walk away financially whole from the league. He also would likely pocket a little extra in future dividends.

Haven, however, made no mention of Binstein. Neither did Haven give him a seat on the podium at a later follow-up press conference at a swishy Pittsburgh hotel. But if you looked hard enough, Binstein could be seen nursing a beer at the hotel hidden off in the periphery. Not only had Haven refused to partner with Binstein as a co-owner, they abruptly fired him as the team's general manager. They wanted their own hire leading the charge.

"For 18 months, I worked—slaved—to take over the operations of this club," Binstein rued. "Now, I'm out."[15]

As ABA pioneers Binstein and Rubin exited the league stage right, that left one true original on an ABA payroll: Dennis Murphy in Miami. For how long? Good question. On April 1, the league secretly took control of the floundering Floridians. Bob Howard, Miami's majority owner, had discreetly notified Commissioner Jack Dolph the day before that he'd decided to relinquish his 82 percent ownership in the franchise immediately. Howard couldn't secure the needed city approvals to build his Miami sports palace, so he no longer needed a basketball team to play there. Then there was the NBA death list. Miami also made the list, and Howard wouldn't put more good money after bad to sustain his moribund asset.

Howard's exit leaked across Miami Beach, forcing Dolph to issue a short, nothing-to-see-here statement. It explained that the franchise "is currently undergoing a reorganization of its financial and ownership structure" that "will be completed next week."[16] Both were fibs. In truth, Howard's snap departure wasn't necessarily bad news at all. If the merger came to pass, the ABA could fold the franchise on the cheap, without a buyout or having to fight Howard in court. If not, Dolph could double back to Miami, cobble together new ownership over the summer, and keep Murphy and the Floridians going for another season.

Murphy, usually upbeat, admitted that things had turned "intolerable" in Miami. Intolerable and too zany for comfort. Playing in a makeshift auditorium chilled by ocean breezes, moving into a front office serviced by a pay phone, hiring a new coach sight-unseen over the phone like ordering a pizza, trying to sell the public on a player nicknamed "Instant Hoodlum." And that just scratched the surface. The Floridians finished the season with the worst record in pro basketball, and attendance got so bad that Murphy quit announcing the figure at games and in the newspapers.

But Murphy, unlike Binstein, would stay on in Miami as general manager. Dolph asked him, on behalf of the league, to watch over the Floridians. Just in case. Murphy remained "optimistic" about the team's future in the NBA or the ABA. Everything always worked out. That is, until it didn't. Just ask Binstein.

New York, April 20, 1970—Everybody's a critic in New York, and some of the Madison Square Garden faithful had their gripes with Eddie Layton, the genial house organist at Knicks games. Don't get them wrong. Layton had chops. He was one of the finest melody makers in the business. But with his back to the court like the Phantom of the Opera, Layton couldn't interact directly with the crowd and let his fingers vicariously do their talking to the players and those rotten referees.

Layton's nimble fingers, though, were unusually chatty tonight during the Knicks' close-out of the Milwaukee Bucks for the Eastern Division championship. The Knicks, rising to the occasion, were up by 16 after the first quarter, then 24 at the half, and now into the 30s in the third period. Layton, clearly in the moment, took the liberty of launching into a light-hearted chorus of "California Here We Come." It was melodic reference to the Los Angeles Lakers. The Lakers, after sweeping Atlanta yesterday for the Western Conference crown, would meet the Knicks next for all the NBA marbles.

Layton's California dreaming came with about 15 minutes still left in the game. In coach-speak, that's an eternity. But the Knicks, playing some of their best ball of the season, showed no signs of letting up, and Milwaukee coach Larry Costello soon threw in the towel on a fourth quarter miracle. He pulled his star Lew Alcindor as a sign of surrender, and the slender seven-footer loped to the bench wearing a mask-like indifference. No smile, no anger, no mean mugging. Just an empty stare that the weisenheimers in the mezzanine decided to mock with a salty a cappella reworking of the old ditty "Good Night Ladies." It went like this: "Goodbye, Lewie, goodbye, Lewie/We hate to see you go!"

Others briefly joined in the sing-songy, mass Bronx cheer, while several Knicks cringed at the poor taste and the payback that was sure to come from Alcindor next season. Knicks coach Red Holzman followed Costello's lead and pulled his regulars for the night one by one, starting with Willis Reed, then Dick Barnett, Dave DeBusschere, Bill Bradley, and Walt Frazier. Five straight standing ovations, followed by chants of "Holzman, Holzman," hailing the team's 49-year-old commander in chief. The euphoria bubbled over as the game clock ticked down the seconds. That's when Eddie Layton one-more-timed "California Here We Come," and 19,500 whooped in the affirmative. Bring on Wilt, West, and Baylor. Bring on the Lakers!

New York, April 24, 1970—The Knicks took game one, 124-112. Both teams started sluggishly, drained from their previous series. But the chess match was obvious. The Knicks wanted to run the ball up the floor and score in transition; the Lakers wanted to walk it up and score on slow-developing isolations of Wilt, West, and Baylor. The Knicks also wanted to turn Chamberlain's fee-fi-fo-fum on defense against the Lakers. All five Knicks spread out along the perimeter, including center Willis Reed, daring Wilt to come out and play. "If Reed shoots 20- and 25-footers, and if we get beat by them, I'll still let him have them," Wilt had shrugged beforehand, unwilling to abandon his defensive post around the basket. Reed (37 points) made Wilt eat those words, but it was the Knicks' Cazzie Russell who chewed up the Lakers' defense in the second half with his line-drive jump shots to secure the win.

By the final buzzer, New Yorkers couldn't get a grip. They were three wins away in their best-of-seven series from a ticker-tape parade. The next morning, newspapers ran bold five-inch headlines of just the final score, like the epic results of a Presidential election. Deliverymen swapped stories of random Knicks sightings around town, real and imagined. They were like special-intelligence reports to guide bets and fan worries, mainly about the physically ailing Reed. No Reed, no championship. The Lakers were spotted out and about, too. Jerry West, hoping to calm his anxious mind, spent Sunday afternoon at the Broadway play, "Promises, Promises." When the star of the show Jerry Orbach, a closet Lakers' fan, heard the "guess who's in the house," he insisted on adding a phantom line for the performance that mentioned West by name and shouted out his league-leading 31.2 per game scoring average.

For the first time, NBA basketball owned a New York moment. For the first time, the NBA's World Series seemed, well, world-class. ABC's Roone Arledge had been brainstorming with his fellow network suits about how many games to shoehorn into prime time. Game two was a firm no in deference to Sunday night's traditional family programming. But Arledge had a firm yes for prime-time coverage of the deciding game seven, if needed. Games six and now four were also thumbs up, marking a major prime-time breakthrough for the NBA.

What ABC didn't broadcast, the local stations claimed or punted to the new pop-up cable providers. In New York, the brand-new Manhattan Cable Television, 22,000 subscribers strong (including many corner taverns), aired Knicks' games with the familiar sports voice of Marty Glickman on the call. But for most New Yorkers, game time still meant switching on their radios and riding the clever vocal inflections of the young Marv Albert and his signature "Yes!" after made baskets.

In Los Angeles, it was roughly the same story. There were now a few cable companies to sop up any extra games. But radio was still king, mainly because true Laker fans revered the velvet voice of Chick Hearn over KABC on the AM dial. Hearn was like a trusted member of the family, the Lakers family. His voice was resonant and NBA authoritative, and his witty turns of phrase were endearing. This evening, perched inconveniently in the press box located five stories above the Garden floor, The Voice would turn phrases on a local radio-TV simulcast. On the television side, tonight's broadcast on KTLA (Channel 5) would be the station's second-highest-rated sports broadcast ever.

Hello Los Angeles, welcome to game three of the 1970 NBA finals.[17] Chick Hearn shared beforehand the Lakers' adjustments in game two. The changes mostly involved their man in the middle. Wilt, bad knee and all, would defend more along the perimeter. He also had to shoot more. Willis Reed, though a bear of a man, couldn't consistently move the larger Wilt away from the basket to stop him spinning off his finger rolls five feet from the basket. While both sides lined up for the game-opening center jump, Chick also shared an overlooked statistical nugget: "The Lakers didn't win a single tip in the first game. That's just the same as four turnovers. It hurts. The Lakers GET the tip. They GET it. Maybe that's a portent of better things to come."

Chick's portent held into the fourth quarter. With four minutes left in a tight ball game, Hearn exhaled into his microphone, "It's nervous time at the Garden," The tension, like the gathering cloud of tobacco smoke obscuring Chick's view of the court, was overwhelming.

1:39: Chick oh-my'ed: "The Lakers are totally disoriented defensively. The time and score are of the essence."

0:50: Willis Reed lost the ball, and it popped right into the hands of Walt Frazier for an open five-footer. "GARBAGE play by Frazier," Chick snapped. "He was just standing there straightening his moustache." Lakers 103, Knicks 103.

0:39: Jerry West got fouled on a drive to the basket and stepped to "the charity stripe," a favorite Chickism. No surprise. West made both. Lakers 105, Knicks 103.

0:22: The Knicks worked the ball to Reed, but Wilt blocked his shot. A scramble ensued for the ball that Chick described like a photo finish at the Kentucky Derby. Wilt slapped down twice at the ball; it squirted loose to Knicks' forward Dave Stallworth standing inside the lane. Stallworth's look-what-I-found was followed by the most untimely call of the century: a three-second violation on Stallworth. Lakers' ball, still up by two.

0:16: Rookie Dick Garrett maneuvered into the frontcourt, hoping to dribble down the clock, get fouled, and clinch the game at the charity stripe. Instead, to Chick's on-air agony, Garrett got trapped in a corner just over half court with two Knicks bellying him like stevedores. Garrett, starting to teeter out of bounds, heaved a desperation cross-court pass.

0:07: The Knicks intercepted Garrett's Hail Mary. Reed found Barnett streaking up-court. He raced two dribbles ahead, set his feet, and fired an open 18-footer for the tie. It glanced off the rim.

0:00: "THE LAKERS WIN, THE LAKERS WIN," Chick shouted hysterically into his microphone. "We go home with a split." Then he mocked, "Listen to this mob."

The Garden mob had turned deathly silent. No "California Here We Come" from an energized Eddie Layton, no hip Beach Boys' "Do It Again" anthem. Just an empty parting realization that New York's weal and woe would wend to Tinseltown next for unforgettable games three and four.

Inglewood, Calif., April 29, 1970—For New Yorkers, the championship series was a celebration of the game. Their City Game. Their gritty, chain-link-and-asphalt pastime and its macho *mano y mano* core values of winning, holding court, and denying all comers.

In L.A., the championship series was a carnival of mass-marketed fun. Fine food, strong drink, toe-tapping music, smiling celebrities, VIP luxury, shopping, pretty usherettes arrayed in a Roman-themed fantasy. Need to make a bathroom run? No problem. Chick Hearn's velvet play-by-play was piped into the lobby and over the bathroom sinks. All these embellishments, compliments of the team's marketing-mad owner Jack Kent Cooke, were meant to enhance the basketball experience. For most New Yorkers who settled into a cushioned seat in Cooke's Fabulous Forum, the embellishments distracted. They were a dead giveaway that L.A. wasn't really a basketball town. "For them," protested New York author Phil Berger, "the game was just another spectacle in a smorgasbord city."[18]

Though Berger had a point, he was missing the larger one. Basketball, like pizza, didn't come in just one style. It came in many homespun variations, all with their own customized pièce de resistance, whether thin-crusted in New York, deep-dished in Chicago, or la-la in L.A. In fact, Cooke's spectacle would be just as influential in guiding the NBA's mass-marketed future as New York's City Game. Of course,

Philadelphia, San Francisco, and other NBA towns had also tinkered with rolling out the VIP treatment. But Cooke had mastered it. The proof was in the numbers. In 1961, before Cooke entered the picture, the Lakers drew 151,000 during the regular season. By 1966, before Cooke opened the Fabulous Forum, attendance jumped to about 400,000. During the past regular season, it rose to 536,558, third best in NBA history.

Now add 17,500 more for game three. Another sell-out, another tale of two halves. The Lakers dominated quarters one and two, but the Knicks found their groove in quarters three and four. In this NBA era without the three-point-shot, the Lakers still held an eight-point lead with about five minutes left in the game. Or, in modern parlance, it was a four-possession game. But the Knicks turned up the defense to get some quick buckets and evened the score at 96 with 1:18 left. Both teams fought to the finish, culminating with New York's Dave DeBusschere's partially blocked game-winner somehow wobbling through the net to put the Knicks ahead by two points with three seconds and no Laker timeouts left. Chamberlain grabbed DeBusschere's make out of the net and, without fully stepping out of bounds (a rule violation, though not called), inbounded the ball and started his slow, grumbling agony of defeat to the locker room. West, though, wouldn't concede. Where there's a will, there's a West. He took three hard dribbles as his running start and fired from almost three-quarters court, an improbable 61 feet. Yes! Game three was going to overtime.

The NBA's most classic championship series ever now had its first unforgettable moment. West's miraculous shot that sent game three into overtime would be replayed for a generation of NBA fans, especially in Los Angeles, where it ran like an NBA film classic. Play it again, Mr. Clutch.

Rarely mentioned, Mr. Clutch went ice-cold in overtime (he had a badly jammed left thumb), and the Knicks won game three easily in overtime. But Mr. Clutch was clutch again in game four. He notched a team-leading 37 points and 18 assists, despite his ailing thumb, to lead the Lakers to an overtime win. West's miraculous Friday night to remember, broadcast live in prime time over ABC, was the stuff from which legends are made as marketing fodder for Cooke and the NBA in the months ahead. But first, West's performance—and the inspired play of his teammates—sent the championship series back to New York tied at two.

New York, May 3, 1970—Knicks coach Red Holzman scheduled a team practice the day before fateful game five. Not that he expected his players to do much running. Neither could they. Dave DeBusschere was too fatigued, and Willis Reed was a no show. Reed was splayed on the trainer's table back at the Garden for his daily physical therapy and something or other cortisone-related to numb his aches all over. Before the cortisone kicked in, Reed gimped around like he'd been in a head-on collision. It was called colliding with the NBA playoffs.

Holzman finally called what passed for a practice to an early end. But the low-key Holzman, not much of a motivational speaker, gathered his players to make a point that needed to be made: "These are the most important games any of us have ever been in. And I know how tired you all are. You're going to have to ask your bodies for something extra. Maybe it's there. Maybe it's not. But you're going to have to push yourselves harder than you've ever pushed in your lives."[19]

New York, May 4, 1970—Willis Reed didn't need Holzman's take-it-to-the-limit speech. Two minutes into game five, Reed was already bounding up the court with the guards, setting screens, rolling to the hoop, and colliding every now and then with Chamberlain. It was mind—and cortisone—over matter.

With 3:56 left in the first quarter, Reed got the ball near the free-throw line, looked right, then took one hard dribble and a gigantic stride left. As three Lakers converged, Reed slipped and felt a jab of pain near his right hip that shot down his leg. He skidded chest first to the floor, grabbing at the pain.

Reed eventually rolled over then grimaced to his feet, taking a step toward the Knicks bench with his head down. Another grimace. He couldn't do it. Neither could the Knicks without him on the floor. "I could see the championship going down the drain, man, down the drain," Walt Frazier summarized the despair of his teammates and the hushed Madison Square Garden as Reed was assisted to the locker room for further examination.[20]

Holzman crossed his fingers and sent in Reed's lanky backup Nate Bowman. Wilt destroyed him inside, and the Lakers stretched their lead to 13 points early in the second quarter. Holzman quickly benched Bowman on what amounted to a hunch. Wilt, favoring his bad knee, was only so mobile. Maybe a swifter, shorter, player could be more of a nuisance and buy time for help defenders to double- or triple-team the seven-footer when he got the ball. It worked, especially with the 6-foot-6 veteran Dave DeBusschere on Chamberlain. The ball went into Wilt, and he passed back out to avoid the collapsing defense. Twenty-foot jump shots were lower percentage than five-foot finger rolls and dunks.

At halftime, Holzman hurried into the Knicks locker room and asked his team doctor, pointing to Reed sprawled on a training table, "Can he play?" The doctor shook his head no. After two pain-killing injections to numb the pulled muscle, no luck.

Holzman grumbled onward to his next problem: the Lakers' 13-point lead. He monotoned through some second-half strategy, and Bill Bradley interjected a first-half observation. "They're sort of playing a zone with Wilt in the middle," he said. "Why don't we play a zone offense?"[21] Bradley suggested running a 1-3-1 set. Frazier, the first one, would handle the ball out front. Bradley would man the high post around the foul line, with Dick Barnett to his left and Cazzie Russell to his right as the three in the set. DeBusschere, a reliable jump shooter from 15 feet, would roam the baseline and force Wilt to cover him outside the paint. That would leave the inside open for drives to the basket from Bradley, Barnett, Russell, and later Dave Stallworth.

The alignment also would put five mid-sized guards and forwards on the floor to press the Lakers full-court on defense. Or in more modern jargon, the Knicks would play "small ball" in the second half. Holzman thought it was worth a try. Reconfiguring their lineup midway through game five of the NBA finals would take discipline, courage, selflessness, resilience, and imagination. Then again, that was Knicks basketball at its core.

The reconfigured Knicks went for broke to start the second half, and their small-ball hustle surprised the Lakers. Spooked might be the better word. The Lakers fumbled several offensive possessions, and the Knicks cut the lead to seven just four minutes into the third quarter. "Maybe I should have called more timeouts, maybe I should have done a lot of things," Lakers coach Joe Mullaney described the moment. "Who knows? But suddenly they were forcing the tempo of the game, and we had to play their game."[22]

The crowd, delivered from its first-half gloom and doom and positively giddy at the hustling, go-for-broke comeback, began chanting: *DEE-fense, DEE-fense.* The roof raised with each Knicks' score and sank with each Lakers' answer. The play was as frantic as it was utterly surreal. Chamberlain, the NBA's greatest all-time scorer, had at least seven inches and 50 pounds on DeBusschere and was shooting 60 percent from the field in the series. But Wilt rarely saw the ball on offense. The same with Jerry West, the league's Mr. Clutch, and Elgin Baylor. "We couldn't even call a time out the proper way," West despaired.

The Lakers' zombie offense was back from the start of the Phoenix series. Or, as the *LA Times* captured the moment. "It was like a drug-imposed bad trip,".[23]

With 7:37 to go, Bradley fittingly knocked down the jumper that knotted the score at 87-all. Off came the roof. Bradley made another one to put the Knicks up for good. Down came the house. When the final buzzer sounded, the scoreboard read, Knicks 107, Lakers 100, and immediately flashed "THE GIANT KILLERS." Fans rushed onto the court, and the cops didn't know whether to stop them or toss their hats into the air to join in the revelry.

"We gambled, and we got away with it," Holzman shrugged. But what a run of luck it was. As one onlooker marveled, "It was like tossing 10 straight sevens on the dice table. Or pulling consecutive royal flushes. Or winning all nine races on the day's card. The Knicks gambled . . . and the Lakers always lost."[24]

The NBA could celebrate many classic games over its 23 seasons. Game five of the 1970 Lakers-Knicks series would instantly become one of them. Unfortunately for the NBA, ABC wasn't there to showcase it to the nation. Fortunately for the NBA, New York wouldn't forget this Monday night miracle and, with 1970s America still a heavily print-oriented society, Americans would read all about it in the days, weeks, and months ahead.

The win put the Knicks ahead 3-2 in the series, or one victory from hoisting the championship trophy and lifting New Yorkers to king of the hill, top of the basketball heap. The Knicks would have game six and, if necessary, game seven to get that victory, though the smart money now said it couldn't be done. Not without Reed to contain Wilt. "I'm not sure the Knicks could do that again," Jerry West quipped afterwards.[25] Holzman agreed. He didn't believe small ball could succeed a second time, not for a full game and not with ample time for the Lakers to gameplan for it. Holzman planned to switch back to a more traditional, makeshift lineup while Reed likely remained on the mend and on the shelf.

Anaheim, Calif., May 4, 1970—While the Knicks went for broke in Madison Square Garden, basketball fans went mostly for free into Anaheim Convention Center. Remember the ABA playoffs? The Los Angeles Stars, opening-round upset winners over Dallas, were ready for game three of the Western Division championship series. Their opponent: the Denver Rockets led by the now-league-MVP Spencer Haywood. Remember Haywood's 59-point gem to end the regular season? Well, Sharman had devised a collapsing defense that forced Haywood to hold the ball again. The maneuver earned them a 1-1 split in Denver, shifting the home-court advantage to the Stars for the series' five remaining games.

That assumed the Stars still had a home court. They didn't. The Los Angeles Sports Arena, the Stars' home the past two seasons, had committed to the Ice Capades in early May. Sharing the Lakers' Fabulous Forum was out of the question, and so last week new owner Bill Daniels coyly announced that his team next season would possibly relocate back to Orange County or Long Beach. In truth, neither zip code had a prayer of landing the franchise. The Lakers' Jack Kent Cooke wanted the Stars out of Southern California, not relocated to the suburbs.

But politicians in both zip codes unwittingly took the bait, inviting the Stars to book as many playoff games as needed in their large municipal arenas. They would serve as their auditions for next season. Tonight, Orange County officials promised to pack the Anaheim Convention Center, capacity 8,000, and create a raucous playoff atmosphere. They got exactly 4,468 willing souls, bribing them with cheap or free tickets and color televisions mounted throughout the lobby so that nobody would miss the Lakers game while they were out.

While the Lakers bombed in the lobby, the Stars glittered on the court. Brightest of all was big Craig Raymond, last year the third-string center for the NBA's Philadelphia 76ers. Raymond, slow and cursed with poor stamina, was no match for Wilt Chamberlain or any top NBA center. But Raymond was clever and, in Sharman's nurturing hands, was big and functional defending the basket in the ABA. In the third quarter, Raymond went on a shot-blocking tear, even swatting a few of Haywood's attempts, to turn the momentum in favor of the Stars. From there, his talented teammates did the rest. Their names sounded like a playground ensemble—George Stone, Mack "The Knife" Calvin, Trooper Washington, Wondrous Willie Wise, Bobby Warren (who had a weird sideways spin on his shots), and Merv "The Magician" Jackson (who seemed to float down the basketball court). But like true pros, each did their jobs and finished off the Rockets, 119-113.

The next night, the Stars dazzled in Long Beach before a crowd of 3,422 to take a commanding 3-to-1 advantage in the series. Who needed Jack Kent Cooke's Dream Team? The ABA Stars, for now, were living the dream, even if they were homeless.

L os Angeles, May 6, 1970—It was a new thing, NBA players hosting their own radio programs. Jerry West was the first in Laker-land to talk shop directly to fans with a five-minute weekly broadcast over KABC. In his latest offering, West welcomed special guest Red Holzman. "If you were the Lakers," he asked the Knicks' skipper, "how would you play the Knicks in the upcoming game?" Holzman chuckled. He wasn't about to help West and the Lakers.

Then again, with Willis Reed out of action, the answer was obvious: Slow down the pace, get the ball inside. In game six, West and his teammates walked the ball up-court, spaced the floor better, and lobbed everything into Wilt. Guarding him was the spindly, 6-foot-10 Nate Bowman. For the Lakers, it was a matchup made in heaven: the game's greatest scorer of all-time isolated on a mostly untested third-year backup. It wasn't a fair fight. Wilt and the Lakers built a big early lead that the Knicks couldn't crack, Bowman or later no Bowman. The final: Lakers 135, Knicks 113.

Afterwards, Holzman gave all hail to Wilt, the miracle man who should have been lounging on the beach right now. Few expected him to return this season from his knee injury. And yet, Wilt corralled 27 rebounds and scored 45 points, making 20 of 27 shot attempts. If not for his bad night at the free-throw line, Wilt would have easily topped 50. Holzman let his mind race, and it circled back to the same set of facts. The series, tied at 3-3, returned to New York for its game seven finale. Holzman needed Willis Reed, his captain, in the lineup to knock Wilt's domination down a notch. Without Reed, God help the Knicks in game seven.

New York, May 8, 1970—And so it all came down to the rectus femoris. That was the badly strained muscle preventing Willis Reed from lifting his right leg to run, jump, and even walk normally. That was the muscle that, if mended, would put the Knicks' captain back on the court for the biggest game of the year and probably, up to this point, NBA history.

Well-meaning fans called the Knicks' front office today offering home remedies. The local news broke for live, up-to-the-minute reports from the Garden and aired anxious commentaries about the big one. "This is the night you gotta do it for us. C'mon Knicks," pleaded one talking head, speaking on behalf of the greatest fans in the world. Some newspapers were more lyrical. One wrote: "Like the cavalry thundering over the hilltop at the moment the beleaguered frontier fort is about to fall. Or like Superman exploding from a telephone booth when Lois Lane is face to face with villainy of the worst order, Willis Reed (in the fantasies of thousands of fans of the New York Knickerbockers) will bound onto the court of

Madison Square Garden tonight and save his team from worse than death."[26]

About two hours before game-time, and after every possible rub, tug, and physical test of a rectus femoris, Clark Kent, a.k.a. Willis Reed, was back in his phone booth of sorts— the Knicks' locker room. "I'm gonna play," he steeled himself. "It still hurts, but I'm gonna play."[27] His decision set the stage for another immortal NBA moment, this one even greater than Jerry West's 61-foot heave. Reed's dramatic entry onto the basketball court to join his teammates for pregame warm-ups was captured live by the ABC cameras, optimally positioned by producer Chet Forte and broadcast from coast to coast.

"I think we see Willis coming out, Chet," broadcaster Jack Twyman famously interrupted his on-air pregame commentary, and Forte cut to the dark gangway leading from the Knicks' locker room to the Garden floor. There was Reed emerging from the gangway like Superman in full uniform, minus the mask and cape. But a glowering superhero just the same. The southpaw swished a practice shot, and the greatest fans in the world rejoiced. Reed's rectus femoris wasn't healed, just comfortably numbed from an injection of the local anesthetic Carbocaine.

When Reed swished the game's first shot 19 seconds in, a high-arching thing of beauty tossed from the free-throw circle, the Garden literally roared. It roared again 64 seconds later when Reed swished another one. Across the country, millions adjusted the volume on their TV sets to experience the raw, unfiltered roar of this New York moment, this epic profile in courage later summarized adroitly by the Bronx-born sports scribe Murray Janoff, who thought he'd seen it all during his 35 years on the basketball beat. "You had to be there. You had to be one of the lucky, fanatic, screaming 19,500 fans packed into the Garden to see it . . . To see a man named Willis Reed ignite them to levels unsurpassed."[28]

Between Reed's makes, the astute Twyman shared with his viewers some déjà vu. "The Lakers, as they were Monday night in that upset win by New York, are standing around trying to get the ball in to Chamberlain, so he can try Willis Reed." Over the next several Laker possessions, millions at home watched the one-legged marvel hold his ground against the NBA's Goliath. Reed did it on sheer will, sheer determination, and with a deep, nagging throb pulsing down his right leg. The Carbocaine wasn't working. "I was dragging the leg," Reed described jostling for position and inching Wilt away from the basket. "I hated to pick it up, but I had to keep forcing him out by pushing him before he got the ball. If he got it in close, I couldn't jump."[29]

Jump ahead to the second quarter, and Wilt looked nothing like the dominant Goliath of game six. Pushed two steps further away from the basket with Reed holding his ground, Wilt dribbled-bumped, dribble-bumped to back into his sweet spot closer to the basket. All this dribble-bump was an open invitation for Walt Frazier, Dick Barnett, and the Knicks' ball-hawking defense to swoop in from the side and disrupt Wilt and the Lakers' offensive flow. Frazier in particular kept stealing the ball and hurrying the other way, where he and his teammates sank nearly every shot, near and far. "And you notice," Twyman entertained more déjà vu about the near shots in the Knicks' set offense. "Wilt Chamberlain has to come out on Willis Reed, and it opens up the inside."

With three minutes left in the first half, Reed was whistled for his third foul, and better safe than picking up a fourth personal, limped to the bench with four points and five rebounds. Hardly awe-inspiring numbers, but Reed's one-legged willingness to do the dirty work for his teammates equaled the lopsided numbers on the scoreboard: Knicks 61, Lakers 37. At halftime, Reed braced for a six-inch needle and two more jaw-clenching jabs of Carbocaine, just in case the Lakers' rallied in the second half.

Reed made a few leg-dragging cameo appearances early in the second half, but his services weren't needed. The Lakers, built for power not for speed in the playoffs, couldn't catch up to the runaway, adrenaline-fueled Knicks. "The remaining 24 minutes were as uninteresting as they were unnecessary," sniffed one NBA scribe. As the game reached its waning seconds, the sell-out crowd rose as one, and like New Year's Eve in Times Square, counted down to ecstasy. Organist Eddie Layton serenaded the final buzzer, followed by the mob's crowning chant of "We're number one!" Gotham had its world championship, and the mob could rest easily tonight that New York reigned again over the basketball universe.

In the months ahead, Gotham would rub its reign into America's collective consciousness. A whole new basketball genre and ode to New York hoops would roll hot off the presses that mixed lowbrow jock commentary with highbrow sociology and sports psychology.

The NBA, too, had plenty to celebrate. Officially, league-wide attendance had increased 11 percent from last season and, for the first time, surpassed 5 million (5,146,858). Knicks mania explained some of the uptick, but so did the increase of television cameras to mass-distribute the NBA product and lionize its cavalcade of stars, from Alcindor to West. "Our growth over the last five years, during which we have doubled our attendance . . . was directly related to the telecasting of NBA games by ABC," said Walter Kennedy.[30] The commissioner's admission, of course, hadn't gone unnoticed by the rival ABA.

Denver, May 9, 1970—While the NBA drew the curtain on an epic season to remember, the drama of the ABA playoffs prepared for its final act. Today, the Los Angeles Stars, behind the abracadabra and last-minute swish of Merv "The Magician" Jackson, finished off the Denver Rockets for the Western Division championship. The Stars, once abandoned, still overlooked, and forever resilient, now advanced to the championship round to face the Eastern finalist Indiana Pacers for all the ABA glory. "This is the greatest thrill of my career," beamed Stars' coach Bill Sharman.[31] Again, consider the source and his celebrated NBA past.

Also in a state of thrill was ABA Commissioner Jack Dolph over the large, boxy television cameras that today rolled along the endlines of Denver's Auditorium Arena. They belonged to CBS Sports, which aired today's game marking the first ABA contest (not all-star exhibition) broadcast to the nation. Two more CBS showcases were scheduled for the Stars-Pacers championship series.

But Dolph would lose his thrill over the coming weeks as the ABA's pending contract with CBS, the one he'd promised to deliver, went bust.[32] Talk about rotten luck. Last February, Dolph, still popular and influential with his former CBS colleagues, secured a verbal commitment from the network to air a few playoff games this year, followed by the promise of a contract offer for next season and beyond. The offer assumed any final agreement would be grandfathered into the NBA-ABA merger. No merger, no problem. CBS was committed, at least in the short term, to be the network home of the ABA Though the dollar figures remained to be finalized, the ABA's Saturday afternoon time slot was settled. It would replace the NHL Game of the Week, whose multiyear contract would end this week with the conclusion of the Stanley Cup. The network wanted out of ice hockey, now considered too fast for TV and unprofitable. Last season, CBS lost a reported $750,000 on the NHL.

There was one hurdle, though. The NHL contract, which Dolph okayed while running CBS Sports, granted the hockey moguls the right of first refusal to extend the agreement. To avoid getting sued, CBS recently bid below their agreed-upon $1 million minimum, a lowball slap in the face meant to insult the hockey moguls into packing up their pucks and going elsewhere. No luck. The moguls would accept CBS' lowball offer in principle, presumably to ensure that the NHL remained on national TV at any price.

Though Dolph couldn't prove it, the NBA likely had a hand in the ABA's rotten luck. Some NBA owners had NHL interests, too, including the influential Jack Kent Cooke, Madison Square Garden, Inc., and Arthur Wirtz, who operated Chicago Stadium, home of the Bulls and was a *de facto* NBA insider. All would have heard the ABA's plans to pop corks over its network breakthrough. All would have been inclined to sabotage the agreement. Winning the pro basketball war—or gaining the upper hand in the merger negotiation—caused hearts to race in the NBA board room.

Neither would Sharman and the Stars pop corks to celebrate an ABA championship. They fell 4-2 in the finals to the scrappy Pacers, led by the amazing Roger Brown, who scored 53, 39, and 45 points in successive games. "Gee, you son of a gun," Sharman told Brown afterwards, "you were sensational. That was as good as any playoff performance by a forward I've ever seen, and that takes in about 20 years."[33] According to Sharman, Brown, at age 28, was the "closest thing" in either league to the high-scoring, gravity-defying Elgin Baylor in his prime.

Why wasn't Brown defying gravity in the NBA? Brown, like his childhood buddy Connie Hawkins, had been banned for life from the NBA for allegedly consorting with known gamblers during their high school years.

Hawkins, with the help of his two dedicated lawyers, had cleared his name and entry into the NBA. Brown hoped to do the same. But his case had stalled, and that was a good thing for the NBA's busy legal team. It had multiple court cases to litigate, including a new filing that rose to the top of the stack. It involved Larry Fleisher and the NBA Players Association. They'd been very active during the playoffs.

Endnotes

[1] Mal Florence, "Lakers' Old Pros Demolish Suns, 129-94," *Los Angeles Times*, April 10, 1970.

[2] Doug Ives, "Wilt Triggers Series Clincher," *Long Beach Independent*, April 10, 1970.

[3] Phil Pepe, "Knicks-Bullets THE Ticket," *New York Daily News*, March 27, 1970.

[4] Mike Schatzkin, *The View From Section 111*, 1970 p. 156-157. Others back then agreed with Schatzkin's observation, but they note that the "deefense" chant originated at NFL Giants games.

[5] No Byline, "Knicks Now Making NBA Rich," *New York Daily News*, March 1, 1970.

[6] Priit Vesilind, "With Chamberlain, Los Angeles 'Has a Chance,'" *Atlanta Journal*, April 13, 1970.

[7] Mal Florence, "Lakers Lay It on the Line, 119-115," *Los Angeles Times*, April 13, 1970.

[8] George Cunningham, "LA, West Lasso Hawks, 119-115," *Atlanta Constitution*, April 13, 1970.

[9] Frank Hyland, "Hot Guerin Cries 'Foul,'" *Atlanta Journal*, April 13, 1970.

[10] Joe Caldwell, Interview with author, February 2024.

[11] Hal Hayes, "An Angry Wilt Blasts Hazzard," *Atlanta Constitution*, April 15, 1970.

[12] Ralph Moore, "Spencer Haywood: Mister ABA," *Sports All Stars/1971 Pro Basketball*.

[13] Ibid.

[14] From Minutes, ABA Meeting, April 13, 1970: "Daniels to pay Kirst $100,000 at closing, $100,000 over a four-year period, and $100,000 out of future profits. Daniels assumes all obligations, past and future, of the Stars; these include approx. $105,000 of accounts payable."

[15] Phil Musick, "The Outsider," *Pittsburgh Press*, April 30, 1970.

[16] Gary Long, "ABA Handling Floridians' Finances," *Miami Herald*, April 7, 1970.

[17] This section is builds off of: John Hall, "Chick Addict," *Los Angeles Times*, April 29, 1970

[18] Phil Berger, *Miracle on 33rd Street*, 1970, p. 239-240

[19] Dave DeBusschere, *The Open Man*, 1970, p. 247

[20] Jeffrey Denberg, "Knicks Win It for Willis, But What of Tomorrow?" *Newsday*, May 5, 1970

[21] Ibid, p. 249

[22] Bernard Kirsch, "Reed-less Tempo Disrupts Lakers," *Newsday*, May 5, 1970

[23] Mal Florence, "Lakers Take a Bad Trip—and Collapse, 107-100," *Los Angeles Times*, May 5, 1970

[24] Kirsch, *Newsday*, May 5, 1970

[25] Kirsch, *Newsday*, May 5, 1970

[26] Berger, *Miracle on 33rd Street*, p. 249-250

[27] DeBusschere, *The Open Man*, p. 258

[28] Murray Janoff, "Miracle of Madison Sq. Garden!," *Jersey Journal*, May 9, 1970

[29] Milton Gross, "How Willis Did It," *New York Post*, May 10, 1970

[30] NEA, "Walter Has Another NBA Challenge," *Noblesville (Ind.) Ledger*, January 5, 1970

[31] No Byline, "Win Sharman's 'Greatest Thrill,'" *Los Angeles Times*, May 10, 1970

[32] Lee Meade, Interview with author, June 2010

[33] Dick Denny, Basketball's All-Pro Annual 1971

18

While the pro basketball playoffs dazzled the nation in the spring of 1970, Larry Fleisher dismayed many pro basketball owners. On April 16, the 40-year-old attorney for the NBA Players Association stood at a podium in New York's Time-Life Building and read a long late-morning statement to the press. Behind him in a show of celebrity and union solidarity were NBA stars Bill Bradley, Willis Reed, Kevin Loughery, and Oscar Robertson.

Fleisher already had explained to those present that at 9:15 this morning in New York's Southern District Federal Court, he had filed an antitrust suit on behalf of the NBA's Players Association. The suit, soon to be known as the Oscar Robertson case after its lead plaintiff and union president, sought among its many complaints a temporary restraining order that would bar the NBA Board of Governors from voting on the ABA's merger counterproposal next week. The restraining order would be ruled on tomorrow in the court of Judge Lloyd F. McMahon, famous for presiding over the high-profile trials of New York's leading Mafia dons.

"According to the players, the NBA has used the reserve clause and the college draft to compel them to negotiate with only one NBA team," Fleisher read from his prepared statement. "The appearance of the ABA provided an escape route for the players—providing at least one other group to compete for their services. The merger would be the final step of a concerted plan by the NBA to bind the players involuntarily to one team for their entire playing careers."[1]

A reporter asked Fleisher if the Robertson case was pro basketball's equivalent of the Curt Flood case, then the talk of the baseball world. Flood, a talented center fielder, had taken major league baseball to court to challenge its restrictive reserve clause. "A well-paid slave" Flood famously called himself.

Fleisher answer no, which wasn't exactly true. The Robertson suit, among other things, challenged the NBA reserve clause. But for now, the suit's immediate focus was to block the merger and ensure, as Fleisher worried, that the NBA and ABA owners couldn't sneak an amendment onto an omnibus bill in the United States Congress for an antitrust exemption, similar to the recent legislation that allowed the pro football merger.

The next day, Fleisher scored one of his most decisive victories over the NBA owners. Judge McMahon granted the temporary restraining order, pending a $25,000 good-faith bond from the player's association, stating "there is no question but that professional basketball is subject to [American] antitrust laws" and offering legal justification that didn't augur well for the owners:

> Some of the players who are members of the class plaintiffs purport to represent have already signed contracts to play in the rival league in future seasons. Thus, players who are now free to negotiate for future contracts with either of the rivals would instantly lose that competitive advantage if one of the rivals is eliminated by merger or other combination. When we consider that youth passes away and consequently basketball players have limited professional careers, the threat of immediate and irreparable injury to the plaintiff seems clear enough.

McMahon reached for a pen and signed the temporary injunction. It blocked the leagues from discussing the merger until a May 1 hearing to grant a longer-term preliminary injunction while the Robertson case awaited trail. If granted, Fleisher would be one trial away from killing the merger.[2]

Later that day, an ABA official exited the league's office with a slip of paper and pressed for the elevator on the 42nd floor in the brand-new 1700 Broadway Building in Midtown Manhattan. The official exited onto Broadway at West 53rd Street, entered the nearest Western Union office, and sent the following telegram in all caps:

> TO ALL ABA OWNERS: A FEDERAL DISTRICT JUDGE HAS ENTERED AN ORDER WHICH PROHIBITS UNTIL MAY 1, 1970 THE ABA OR ANY MEMBER FRANCHISE FROM TAKING STEPS IN FURTHERANCE OF AN ATTEMPT TO AFFECTUATE A MERGER OR CONSOLIDATION OF THE TWO LEAGUES. BECAUSE OF THIS ORDER AND THE PENDANCY OF THE LITIGATION BETWEEN THE NBA PLAYERS ASSOCIATION AND THE TWO LEAGUES YOU SHOULD NOT DISCUSS SUCH A MERGER OR CONSOLIDATION WITH ANYONE OUTSIDE YOUR OWN ORGANIZATION. IT IS PARTICULARLY IMPORTANT THAT NO STATEMENTS ON THIS SUBJECT BE GIVEN TO MEMBERS OF THE PRESS IF YOU HAVE ANY QUESTIONS OR COMMENTS PLEASE CONTACT ONLY ME JACK DOLPH COMMISSIONER.

On Friday May 1, Fleisher got the preliminary injunction extended until the Robertson case went to trial. But Judge Charles Tenney threw Fleisher a bit of a curveball. He recessed the hearing for the weekend before formally delivering his decision to give all parties, including Fleisher, a chance to compose the draft language of the injunction. The NBA and ABA lawyers insisted in their weekend write-up that the owners should be free during the injunction period to plan for obtaining a Congressional exemption to federal antitrust law.

Tenney read the draft language on the following Monday and agreed.

"We now have a shelter under which we can work and not be afraid of someone putting up a lawsuit while we're talking to Congress," explained Earl Foreman. "We are at the point we wanted to be."[3]

Tenney's shelter provided the owners with two immediate options. One, reach a compromise with Fleisher, get him to drop the Robertson case, and move ahead with the merger, with or without the antitrust exemption. Two, take their chances on Capitol Hill, where the climate had turned stone cold against professional sports.

The merger committees decided to give both a whirl.

The airplanes descended to the ground every few minutes in an ear-splitting, tree-ruffling, two-wheeled screech and taxied along the runway one after the other. Outside the terminals, small buses shuttled men in business suits from the Chicago airport to the O'Hare Inn, its large, oval fountain in full splash outside the front door. Among today's scheduled events was an initial exploratory session between Larry Fleisher and the NBA and ABA merger committees. If common ground could be reached, their next meetings would be fast-tracked to hammer out a larger plan for approval by the respective league owners.

The roundtable started cordially and remained so until the discussion meandered into the reserve clause. Fleisher said that whatever the final agreement may be, it had to declare the reserve clause null and void. Ned Irish sat poker-faced, but his mind raced. He had been in pro basketball since the dog days of the 1940s when "the crowds were just guys waiting for the pool rooms to open."[4] He had watched too many teams come and go to recount. Irish thought, more than anyone at the table, he knew the pro basketball business from top to bottom. To suggest that the NBA could survive unfettered player movement was, in his mind, just plain wrong. Free agency equaled chaos.

Without saying a word, Irish rose from his seat, gathered his papers, and strode toward the door. Tinkham remembered asking Sam Schulman, "Where's Ned going?"

"New York will never give in on the reserve clause," he answered.

Tinkham, growing concerned, finally went to look for Irish. No sign of him. Irish had boarded the airport shuttle and bumped along back to O'Hare for the next flight back to New York. With him went any hope of the owners and players reaching a compromise.[5]

For the owners, the only remaining option was to seek an antitrust exemption from the U.S. Congress. As a first step down that path, the leagues needed to approve the joint statement crafted in Palm Springs that laid out their plan of attack. The statement called for the NBA and ABA to take the major step of "merging in principle," like a couple getting engaged, before going to Washington to ask for permission—and an antitrust exemption—to formally tie the knot.

That's when Schulman struck again. He advised the members of the ABA merger committee to encourage the league to hold its next Board of Trustees meeting at the Regency Hyatt House in Atlanta on June 17 and 18. The dates and Atlanta location matched the next NBA Board of Governors meeting.

When the ABA announced the change in locations, rumors swirled that the leagues would announce their formal engagement in Atlanta. Walter Kennedy dutifully denied the rumors, reminding everyone that the leagues were under a court order not to discuss the merger. Unmentioned, some NBA governors were getting cold feet about partnering with the ABA, thanks to a little help from the naysaying Franklin Mieuli. He claimed to have lined up seven "no" votes, three more than needed to defeat the merger in principle.[6]

A week later, the wiser NBA heads prevailed. They nixed the dual Atlanta meetings, and the ABA re-scheduled its league meeting for Denver. All agreed that the locations of their meetings were irrelevant to the larger issue. Schulman, with the help of Ned Irish and reportedly now Jack Kent Cooke, just needed to rein in the pesky Mieuli, reclaim three votes, and approve the merger in principle.

But first, an ABA team would have to make an ill-timed confession.

Ralph Simpson had no desire to turn pro after his sophomore season at Michigan State University. The Spartans were on the rise, and so was his reputation as a future All-American. The 6-foot-5 Simpson averaged 29 points per game as a super soph, 10th best in the country, and, as *Sports Illustrated* declared in January, "earned more rave reviews than a Neil Simon play."[7]

But all was not well with Simpson's family in inner-city Detroit. His parents had divorced, and money was tight. "The house we're in now is in bad shape," he explained. "The porch has even collapsed, and it looks terrible for anyone that goes by."

"We always had difficulties," he continued. "But it got to the point where our family was almost ready to split up because of the difficulties."[8]

As the eldest of eight children, Simpson felt morally obligated to keep his family together and afloat financially. He had two options. One, Simpson could drop out of college, hopefully land a factory job, and kiss his basketball career goodbye for a union card and steady paycheck. Two, he could walk in the footsteps of Spencer Haywood, his former teammate at Detroit's Pershing High School, and become the ABA's second hardship case. Simpson leaned toward the latter and contacted Will Robinson, his mild-mannered basketball coach at Pershing who had helped Haywood go hardship. He asked Robinson to make some telephone calls on his behalf and test the ABA waters.

By early March, Robinson had called at least four ABA teams. The Kentucky Colonels, under new ownership and flush with cash, were the first to bite. Simpson recalled springing the pending ABA offer on his father, and Ralph Sr. looking perplexed.

"I want to stay in school," Ralph Jr. said. "But I'll do whatever is needed for us to make it,"

"Well, if they want to give you a little bonus money, we'll take it. Go ahead and turn pro,"replied his father, who would barely survive a heart attack in the weeks ahead and plunge the family into a deeper financial crisis.[9]

Before Simpson could take it, Jack Dolph reportedly intervened. He disliked the hardship rule, knew its disruptive effect on the merger, and fired off the following telegram of warning in all caps:

> TO ALL ABA OWNERS: ALL CONTRACTS AND APPROACHES TO BASKETBALL PLAYERS WHOSE COLLEGE ELIGIBILITY H7AS NOT ENDED MUST CEASE AND DESIST IMMEDIATELY. ANY ARRANGEMENT WITH SUCH PLAYERS WILL NOT BE APPROVED BY THE COMMISSIONER'S OFFICE.[10]

In Denver, Don Ringsby, the president and general manager of the ABA Rockets, ignored the warning. Haywood, his hardship case-turned-20-year-old superstar, was acting out again, demanding the Rockets sweeten his contract a second time in five months. Ringsby had started crunching a new set of numbers and entertaining a second plea from his star. Haywood wanted the Rockets to sign Simpson, who was like a brother to him.

Ringsby knew the name from Robinson's latest phone call. Robinson had joked about his Pershing High team, "People would come to see Spencer, and they'd leave talking about

Ralph." Ringsby decided that he had nothing to lose. Simpson might help to root the restless Haywood in Denver, and maybe Rockets fans would start talking about Ralph, too.

"We needed players," Ringsby recalled the decision to sign Simpson without consulting the ABA's front office. "Everybody in the ABA needed players."[11]

By late March—shortly after Dolph assured the nation's ranking college basketball coaches that the ABA would never sign another underclassman—Simpson and Robinson sat in Ringsby's office. On the table sat an unsigned standard ABA player contract offering a three-year deal worth a $30,000 annual base salary, a $25,000 cash bonus, and a $700,000 Dolgoff Plan (which the Rockets bought him out of the following year for $30,000).

Simpson signed on the spot, and Ringsby handed him a $25,000 bonus check. "Mr. Ringsby told me not even to worry," Simpson recalled, referring to the likely hue and cry to follow over his early signing. "He said, 'You can spend your bonus money if you want to. It's [playing in Denver] going to happen. We'll go to court, if need be. But it's going to happen.'"[12]

Ringsby kept quiet about Denver's latest hardship case. He had until August and the start of training camp to make the announcement. No need to stir the pot while the merger simmered. But the 20-year-old Simpson predictably spent his bonus money to buy a car for his father, a house for his mother, and a pink El Dorado Cadillac for himself. Folks around Detroit and East Lansing quickly put two and two together and started to talk.

On the eve of the ABA's June meeting in Denver, the *Detroit Free Press* contacted Ringsby for a comment on a story that the newspaper would break in the morning. The reporter said multiple sources in Detroit had confirmed that Ringsby three months ago secretly signed Simpson to a "million-dollar" pro contract. Ringsby demurred, terminated the conversation, and immediately announced Simpson's signing in the Denver press.

By morning, the ABA's name was mud. "We supply them with a free farm system," griped Jack Gardner, the head coach at the University of Utah. "Then they go out and raid our ranks and don't pay the colleges a cent. This is certainly hitting below the belt."[13]

"The signing of Ralph Simpson by the Denver team of the American Basketball Association indicates that the ABA has no regard for the welfare of college basketball," began the NCAA's statement.[14] The NCAA called for a boycott of the ABA on the nation's college campuses. The boycott, totally unenforceable, went nowhere. But the NCAA's larger point lingered to shape popular opinion: The ABA was an enemy of Mom, apple pie, and Adolph Rupp.

In Denver, a drumbeat of reporters sought out Dolph for answers. The assumption being, the buck stopped with the commissioner. It didn't. Dolph worked for the owners, and his war-ready superiors mostly high-fived Ringsby behind closed doors for sticking it to the NBA. Yes, the ABA needed players.

Dolph, unprepared for the latest crisis, talked diplomatically out of both sides of his mouth to the reporters, declaring the hardship rule valid, invalid, and then valid again. "If what I have heard today is true, then Ralph Simpson is a definite hardship case," he explained. "However, I must first talk with the boy, his father, and the Rockets before making a decision."[15]

In Atlanta, the NBA, too, issued a statement. The senior league reiterated its commitment to the four-year rule and its college basketball farm system. Missing was a call for blood from its proposed future business partner. Nevertheless, the blood pressure of several NBA governors had spiked after the Simpson story broke. "If merger between the two leagues ever reached bottom, it reached it today," a nameless NBA official muttered.

"It's just another breach of good faith," said an owner, nameless as well. "I once favored merger, but now I feel the ABA can't be trusted."

Some wanted the merger vote removed from the meeting agenda altogether, and Kennedy marched off to call Dolph and ABA lawyer Martin Heller. Kennedy compromised. He postponed today's planned vote. If the ABA put its foot down and disallowed the Simpson contract, a vote on the merger would proceed tomorrow.

Taking in the day's events with glee was Franklin Mieuli. He now chuckled, "All I have to do is keep my seven little men together," and the present merger plan would be dead on principle. [16]

The next day, at around 11 a.m. Eastern time, ABA officials phoned Walter Kennedy with the latest. The ABA trustees had voted eight to nothing to reject the Simpson contract. Jack Dolph would make a statement to the press later in the day.

Kennedy hung up the phone and tottled back into the Board of Governors meeting. The six-page joint statement laying out their plan of attack with Congress was back on the agenda for discussion. The first two pages summarized the benefits of the merger:

> For the fans the plan will mean: (1) establishment of basketball as the most truly nation-wide professional sport; (2) better major league basketball in more cities more quickly, rather than a decrease in the number of teams; (3) more evenly balanced teams and hence more real competition on the court; (4) a chance to see all players, including the stars of both present leagues; (5) the development of healthy sectional and regional rivalries among teams; (6) an undisputed champion of professional basketball.

For the players the plan will mean: substantial benefits, including (1) increase rather than decrease in the number of jobs; (2) a significant increase in minimum salary; (3) more equitable allotment of available payroll funds among veterans and untried rookies; (4) salary ranges for all teams more comparable to those of the wealthier teams; (5) improved pension benefits; (6) the chance to compete in a truly national league before fans in every area of the nation.

For the franchise cities and team owners the plan will mean: reversal of the rich-get-richer-while-the-poor-get-poorer trend which will force some teams out of business and eliminate professional basketball from several cities. Basketball competition on the court, rather than ability to withstand financial losses, will become the dominant element of the game.

For the colleges the plan will mean: alleviation of concern over premature recruiting of college players by professional clubs.

Pages three and four laid out for the first time the crisis narrative that the leagues would send forth to Congress:

Since the inception of the ABA in 1967, every ABA club has incurred substantial losses in every year of operation. Likewise, in each of these same years, more than half of the NBA clubs have lost substantial sums. There is serious doubt whether nearly half of the ABA clubs can continue next season. If they collapse, the number of remaining clubs will be insufficient to form a viable league. The league will itself collapse unless franchise buyers can be found in new or old locations in order to keep a reasonable number of teams in the league. This musical-chair process may possibly work in the short run, but it cannot continue indefinitely. Unless legislation permitting formation of a single league is enacted, disintegration of the ABA is only a matter of time.

Their argument hinged on the idea that "suicidal competition" was inherently bad for fan and country:

Basketball is in the same position as football was a few years ago. Then, suicidal competition between the two football leagues threatened either a complete failure of one league or failure of the weaker franchises in both leagues. Now, basketball fans, players, and franchise cities face the same prospect.

Major league baseball, hockey, and football have all, in one form or another, achieved the stability necessary for orderly expansion and more balanced competition on the field which the fans undoubtedly want. Basketball has not and, without a unified league, cannot.

The joint statement, which included all of the previous stipulations (entry fees, Foreman out of Washington, etc.) discussed in Palm Springs and Chicago, concluded with the following summary:

The single league is a planning objective only. No plan for such a league will be implemented unless and until enabling legislation, comparable to that which permitted a single football league, is enacted. The NBA and ABA clubs will immediately seek passage of such legislation. In so doing, they will ask only that the clubs be permitted to form a single league. They will not seek legislation which would affect other subjects, such as the reserve clause. In other words, the unified league would be subject to the antitrust laws to the same extent as the separate leagues now are.[17]

A motion was introduced to approve the statement, and Kennedy called it to a vote. All in favor? Thirteen hands rose. All opposed? Mieuli raised his hand joined by the representatives of Philadelphia, Boston, and Milwaukee.[18] Three of Mieuli's little men had defected, and the motion passed, 13 to four. In Denver, the ABA owners were unanimous in approving the plan. And thus, the leagues were engaged, or merged in principle.

According to Kennedy, the two leagues would submit the agreement in short measure to the same Congressional committee that oversaw the pro football merger. "We have no sponsors for the proposed legislation at the moment," said Kennedy. "I really don't know when we'll file it, but certainly within the next few weeks."[19]

"Who do they think they are kidding?" Oscar Robertson fired back on behalf of the NBA Players Association soon after the vote in Atlanta. "This merger would benefit only one party: the owners. And all the sweet talk is not going to sway one player in the NBA. We are unanimously against it.

"Anyway, it is an atrocity for them to say what they are going to do when they merge when, to begin with, it is illegal," he continued. "If they [ABA] are going to collapse, then why should the NBA want them? How about all of these stories that I have been reading about how certain ABA teams are such a success drawing nine, ten, and eleven thousand a game. Now it sounds as if they are talking out of both sides of their mouths."[20]

In Denver, Dolph emerged by early evening from the Bonanza Room in the Cosmopolitan Hotel to hold the day's final press conference. He confirmed the merger in principle was a done deal and officially put the kibosh on Simpson joining the Rockets.

"Concerning yesterday's announcement in the press that Ralph Simpson has signed a contract with the Denver Rockets," Dolph began. "If such a contract does in fact exist and is submitted to the commissioner, the contract will be rejected by the commissioner because it violates the provisions of the American Basketball Association bylaws and that the trustees [owners] have authorized the commissioner to assess a fine of $10,000 against the Denver franchise."[21]

Dolph's statement was more act than fact. The hardship rule was indeed written into the ABA's bylaws. Neither was Simpson the only early signee. In January, the college basketball season in full swing, league agent Steve Arnold had signed prematurely three seniors to league contracts. Dolph made sure to say nothing about them.

Simpson and his lawyer promptly filed a $1 million lawsuit against the ABA. In September, Simpson took his case to U.S. District Court in Detroit to seek a temporary restraining order against the ABA that would allow him to join the Rockets. That's when Dolph threw in his losing hand. "On the advice of four legal firms we have decided to settle the Ralph Simpson case out of court effective immediately."[22] The ABA allowed Simpson to join the Rockets but stripped the team of its first-round draft pick next season and fined Denver $10,000 for insubordination.

Don Ringsby pled his innocence once more to reporters but predicted the ABA's hardship rule soon would be abolished. "The opinion of the trustees is very definitely against signing any player with remaining eligibility," he said.[23]

Before the trustees could take scissors and tape to the ABA bylaws, the issues of hardship and remaining college eligibility would rear their controversial heads in the NBA. They would make the 1970-1971 season one of the true historical flashpoints in building the modern NBA. We'll take it up and chronicle the rest of the pro basketball war in volume two of *Balls of Confusion*. Look for it in the months ahead.

Endnotes

[1] Jeffrey Denberg, "NBA Players Suing to Block Merger," *Newsday*, April 17, 1970.

[2] United Press International and Associated Press, "NBA Players Stall Cage Merger Talks," *San Francisco Chronicle*, April 18, 1970.

[3] Mark Asher, "NBA, ABA Told to Ask Congress for Merger Law," *Washington Post*, May 5, 1970.

[4] Jim Murray, "A Tribute to Cousy," *Los Angeles Times*, April 13, 1962.

[5] Dick Tinkham, Interview with author, October 2011.

[6] Wayne Thompson, "NBA To Thwart Merger," *Oregonian*, June 18, 1970.

[7] Joe Jares , "An ex-Doughboy Who Can Shoot With the Best," *Sports Illustrated*, January 19, 1970.

[8] Curt Sylvester, "'I Signed to Help My Family—Simpson," *Detroit Free Press*, June 20, 1970.

[9] Ralph Simpson, Interview with author, April 2013.

[10] No Byline, "Dolph Forestalls Early Signings," *Indianapolis Star*, March 22, 1970.

[11] Don Ringsby, Interview with author, April 2013.

[12] Simpson, April 2013.

[13] Frank Brady, "Professional Goof $1 Million Paper Loss," *Philadelphia Evening Bulletin*, June 18, 1970.

[14] No Byline, "NCAA Statement on Ralph Simpson Case," *Philadelphia Inquirer*, June 18, 1970.

[15] Dave Nelson, "Rockets Sign Spartan Soph Ace Simpson," *Rocky Mountain News*, June 17, 1970.

[16] Thompson, *Oregonian*, June 18, 1970.

[17] Joint Statement, National and American Basketball Association Clubs, April 1970.

[18] Alan Goldstein, "Bullet Injury Status 'Mixed,'" *Baltimore Sun*, July 18, 1970.

[19] Bill Nichols, "NBA, ABA Merge," *Cleveland Plain Dealer*, June 19, 1970.

[20] George Cunningham, "Angry Oscar Robertson Rips Proposed Merger Plans," *Atlanta Constitution*, June 19, 1970.

[21] Dick Connor, "Dolph Threatens to Fine Rockets $10,000," *Denver Post*, June 17, 1970.

[22] Ralph Moore, "Simpson's Rocket Contract Okayed by ABA," *Denver Post*, October 8, 1970.

[23] Ibid.